THE CHALLENGE FOR GROUP PSYCHOTHERAPY

Present and Future

THE CHALLENGE FOR GROUP PSYCHOTHERAPY

Present and Future

with contributions by

R. Battegay, S. de Schill, H. E. Durkin,
A. Friedemann, J. Krasner, D. LaHullier,
S. Lebovici, S. R. Slavson, J. Spanjaard,
J. Wilder, A. Wolf

edited by

STEFAN DESCHILL
Director, American Mental Health Foundation

INTERNATIONAL UNIVERSITIES PRESS, INC.

New York

This work has appeared in German under the title *Psychoanalytische Therapie in Gruppen* (Ernst Klett Verlag, Stuttgart, 1971) and in French under the title *La Psychothérapie de Groupe* (Presses Universitaires de France, Paris, 1973). A Spanish edition will be published by Editorial Alpuerto, Madrid. An Italian edition will be published by Feltrinelli in Milan.

Library of Congress Cataloging in Publication Data

de Schill, Stefan.

The challenge for group psychotherapy: present and future.
German ed. published in 1971 under title: Psychoanalitische Therapie in Gruppen.
Includes bibliographical references.
1. Group psychotherapy. 2. Psychoanalysis. I. Title.
[DNLM: 1. Psychotherapy, Group. WM43 D446p 1974]
RC488.D4413 616.8'915 73-19952
ISBN 0-8236-4447-2

Manufactured in the United States of America

CONTENTS

Foreword

The importance of the continued development of group methods as an effective psychotherapeutic tool is made more pressing by an ever-increasing awareness of the extent of emotional illness. The point that a greater number of patients can be treated through group methods is sound. However, a far more relevant argument speaks in favor of group psychotherapy: even if an adequate number of competent psychotherapists should become available for all those needing professional help — an assumption that forever will remain utopian — treatment by individual therapists or analysts could hardly provide a solution within the financial reach of the majority of patients. Most people can afford no more than the cost of one individual session per week, which is insufficient for effective treatment in most cases. The only hope, therefore, is to develop forms of intensive group psychotherapy — perhaps combined with occasional individual sessions — which will be so effective that the average patient might obtain valid psychotherapy at a cost within his means.

Independent of these considerations, it must be stressed that from a purely theoretical point of view group therapy has gained a place of considerable importance by deepening, widening, and, in some areas, changing our understanding of psychological mechanisms and therapeutic processes, thereby allowing the formulation of better hypotheses regarding psychoanalytic theory and technique. No therapist — regardless how gifted and accomplished — can rightfully claim complete professional competence in this field until he has studied and practiced the art of group psychotherapy over a prolonged period. Neither will he fully comprehend his patient until he has seen him interact as a member of a therapy group. For it is in this setting that the therapist will be provided important additional clues, a broader view of behavior and personality traits, some of which may be surprising.

Our desire, therefore, has been to present herein not a unified system but the diverse and challenging thinking of some of the world's outstanding exponents of different approaches to analytic group psychotherapy. After carefully studying the publications of approximately 400 group therapists in Europe and the United States, thirty two of them were invited to describe their specific methods and points of view. The selection of manuscripts for this volume was influenced by the desire to present methods that will provide a basis for future exploration and improvement. With the exception of the "Introduction to Psychoanalytic Group Therapy," all papers were written specifically for this volume. Each author was encouraged to structure his chapter freely and to express his individual views, regardless of the difference in his orientation from that of the editor or the other contributors. An effort was made to choose only one authoritative spokesman for each orientation, form, or special application of group psychotherapy.

On the whole, these papers provide a broad view of the various methods and uses of group treatment in depth. The clinical research described is ample proof that group psychotherapy sometimes combined with occasional or regular individual sessions, can be an effective method for helping the emotionally disturbed. It is hoped that the theories and techniques presented will encourage therapists engaged only in individual treatment to enter the field of group psychotherapy as well as expand the knowledge of the experienced group practitioner. Published at a time when there is a proliferation of group methods, this volume will help to focus and clarify the essential components of group psychotherapy.

The growth of group therapy in the United States, as in the case of psychoanalysis and psychoanalytically oriented psychotherapy, has been more rapid than in most European countries. For example, in New York City, an estimated forty percent of persons receiving psychotherapy are being treated in group settings.

But while more persons are being treated in group therapy, they do not necessarily receive better professional help. Conscientious and effective treatment of patients in groups is far more demanding and complex than in individual analysis. It must be stressed that group psychotherapy should be practiced *only* by well-trained, skilled, and gifted psychotherapists who have received the necessary additional education in this field. Unfortunately, the expansion of group psychotherapeutic practice has not been accompanied by improved standards in the quality of professional training nor by a significant increase in suitable training facilities.

For many years psychoanalysts tended to be too intellectual in their therapeutic work. In contrast, today, many group forms elicit mere expression of emotions and acting out with a concomitant neglect of psychotherapeutic working through of feelings which have been evoked. This reflects resistance on the part of the therapist toward treatment in depth. Thus, many current group procedures fall short of the required therapeutic effectiveness and some cannot even be considered therapy.

The same problem exists for individual therapy but because of the aforementioned added exigencies of group therapy, we are facing here a truly critical situation. This is caused by an unsuitable system in the selection of students and by the inadequate education and training in the mental health professions. These practices prove to be self-perpetuating and are detrimental to the public welfare, a condition that appears to have taken a turn for the worse in recent years. To counteract this trend, the development of methods for more effective selection and training of group psychotherapists is a prime need. These studies and methods will better enable us to determine the type of personality most suited for such professional work, teach us how to select such persons, and ultimately provide optimal educational and training procedures.

Preface

The Publications Committee of the International Institute for Mental Health Research wishes to express its thanks to the editor of this volume, Dr. Stefan de Schill. The search for and investigation of new ideas and different approaches has led Dr. de Schill to undertake the work necessary to assemble the papers of this book, hoping that mental health professionals all over the world will be stimulated to fresh thinking and more effective service to the emotionally ill.

It was my privilege to witness the brilliant, always carefully thought-out ways in which Dr. de Schill, in his capacity as Director of Research of the American Mental Health Foundation, explored and experimented with the innumerable facets of individual and group psychotherapy, constantly seeking better theoretical formulations and techniques.

Many of these findings have been incorporated into the intensive, low-cost treatment method developed by the Foundation. Thus, in the course of almost a century, psychoanalytic therapy has traveled a full circle, or—perhaps more accurately—an upward spiral. From the six hours per week individual analysis of Freud, severely limited to a small number of sufferers from emotional illness, we have come now to the six hours per week of psychoanalytic group therapy — divided into two sessions — that form the basis of the Foundation method. This treatment form — also described in the volume — offers intensive and effective help to a wide spectrum of emotionally disturbed people at a fraction of the usual cost of psychoanalytic treatment. Thus, an important step has been achieved by the pioneers of group methods, quite a number of whom have contributed to this volume.

Dr. David Gerst, Chairman
Publications Committee
International Institute for Mental Health Research

Introduction to Psychoanalytic Group Psychotherapy

STEFAN DE SCHILL

The theoretical assumptions and techniques employed by therapists engaged in psychoanalytically oriented group therapy have greatly changed over the last three decades. It would be impossible within the limits of this volume—and unnecessary—even to outline the gradual evolution as well as the manifold ramifications. Just as there are numerous forms of individual psychotherapy, there now exist many types of group psychotherapy.

This chapter describes some essentials of psychoanalytic group therapy based on twenty years of intensive research undertaken by the American Mental Health Foundation. Further work and experimentation may bring changes and improvements of the theoretical assumptions and techniques presented here. The points of view of the authors in this volume offer avenues for such future explorations. The description in this chapter of the functioning of psychoanalytically oriented groups will be of help to readers who have not practiced group therapy at all or may have engaged in forms of group therapy that have not included some of the practices reported here.

In the following pages, some of the techniques and procedures that Foundation research has proved to be the most helpful are described. However, it should be stressed that the intention of this chapter is to present a number of basic approaches that are useful for *all* forms of psychoanalytically oriented group therapy. In a later chapter a *specific* intensive group-therapy method developed by the Foundation is described.

Dr. de Schill is Director of Research, American Mental Health Foundation; Vice President, International Institute for Mental Health Research, Zurich.

The results of the Foundation's research on psychoanalytic group therapy have been continually communicated to the professions by means of lectures, conferences, seminars and workshops, participation in national and international conferences, but most of all through publications. The most successful of these publications, *Introduction to Psychoanalytic Group Therapy,* was especially written to communicate the Foundation's findings to the mental health professions, thereby helping therapists to learn, clarify, and improve their own understanding of group techniques. Secondary aims of the text were to enlighten interested persons regarding this work and the value of psychoanalytic group therapy, as well as to put into the hands of psychotherapists engaged in psychoanalytic group therapy an informative booklet they could give to prospective patients. To fulfill these aims simultaneously a special format and style were necessary. As the clinical studies and experimental work of the Foundation progressed, revised editions had to be published. The findings could easily have filled a large volume. The disadvantages of condensing the material to booklet form were outweighed by the benefit of being able to reach a large number of readers. Within a short period this booklet became the most widely used text in the field of group therapy in the United States. Approximately 80,000 copies have been purchased by medical schools, clinics, and mental health professionals.

It should be remembered that this text was initially written almost twenty years ago, when group psychotherapy was attacked and denounced by the vast majority of professionals. The change in attitudes over this period has been remarkable, and group psychotherapy is now accepted as a valid and valuable treatment procedure. The printing of the French edition of this book under the auspices of the Library of the Psychoanalytic Institute in Paris is just one example of the growing recognition of group therapy procedures.

Prior to 1956, it was observed that about two-thirds of the people to whom the Foundation recommended group therapy either disliked the idea or rejected it outright, requesting individual therapy. Furthermore, about fifteen percent of those who did enter a group dropped out in the first five weeks. In this connection, it is important to note that most of the people who were referred to some form of group therapy had not had any previous psychotherapeutic experience.

However, in the period during which the booklets have been given to patients about to enter group therapy, both figures — those who rejected group therapy and those who dropped out — were reduced by more than half. Similar results have been reported by other users of the booklets.

Whether or not a patient selected for group psychotherapy shows initial resistance to the idea of group work, his preparation for it by the therapist is a necessary, but often burdensome task. One patient after another will ask the same questions concerning the principles and practices of group psychotherapy. If the therapists conducts the intake interviews of an organization or clinic, these repetitive questions may cause him to be less patient and explicit than is necessary to sufficiently diminish the patient's initial anxiety. The same problem is experienced by therapists in private practice who work with groups.

Experience in individual treatment will not necessarily reduce a patient's questions about the group therapeutic procedure he is about to share. Often the contrary is true: anxiety over being placed in an entirely new clinical situation and resentment against sharing the therapist's attention with other patients frequently induce strong resistance against group work, which is manifested by the expression of innumerable questions and objections.

Inasmuch as a great number of the applicants for referral through the Foundation were found suitable for group therapy, considerable experience has been gained as to the nature and scope of the questions typically posed by prospective patients.

Eventually it was felt that much unnecessary work could be eliminated for a therapist, whether he sees patients in a clinical or in a private setting, if his patients could be given literature providing basic explanations about psychoanalytic group therapy. Since patients frequently forget some of the verbal information given them and tend to repeat questions, such literature would be doubly useful.

The "Introduction" is divided into two sections. Part I is to be given to patients to whom group therapy is being recommended. Part

II is for those patients who, after reading the first part, and possibly after further therapeutic assistance by their analysts, are willing to enter group therapy. For the convenience of these readers, the text has been arranged in question-and-answer form.

Part I

1. *How do I know that I need professional help with my emotional problems?*

Everyone, no matter how stable and emotionally mature, can benefit from adequate professional help. Yet attention must first be given to the many persons who are prevented from leading useful and satisfactory lives by their emotional difficulties.

People with emotional disturbances often misunderstand or even ignore their manifestations and symptoms and fail to take the proper steps for their elimination. Some people hesitate to admit to themselves, much less to others, that they cannot cope adequately with their own emotional reactions. They may not realize that the inability to overcome emotional problems by oneself is by no means a sign of weakness or of lack of intelligence. Direct application of will power for such purpose tends to be useless. This is true even for those who know a great deal about psychology and psychotherapy.

The following are some of the problems that indicate a need for professional help:

Difficulties in interpersonal relations, marriage, and parenthood; loneliness and withdrawal; feelings of losing touch with reality; feelings of failure; general dissatisfaction with yourself or your life; inability to do things which you feel you should be able to do, such as concentrate, study, or work; feeling compelled to do things which you do not want to do; frequent feelings of unhappiness; expectations that something bad will happen; continued worries and anxieties of all sorts; nightmares; depressed moods and sadness; persistent feelings of being persecuted, blamed, or taken advantage of; pervasive feelings of hate or contempt; feelings of being inferior, of being disliked and rejected by others, of disliking yourself; feelings of great tension, irritability, or excitability; persistent feelings of restlessness.

Because the human mind is intimately connected with the body, one may have physical complaints for which the physician is unable to find an organic cause. These symptoms are often of psychological origin and, in such cases, indicate the need for psychotherapeutic help. Examples are sleeplessness, headaches, sexual difficulties and dysfunctions, heart palpitations, excessive perspiration, fatigue, and digestive troubles, such as frequent constipation, diarrhea, and stomach pain.

2. *How do I know what type of help I need?*

Many persons erroneously attempt to select a form of psychotherapy merely on the basis of personal prejudice, hearsay, or pressure from others. A better way of finding just which type of psychotherapy is most suitable for you is to consult an experienced, well-qualified diagnostician who is fully acquainted with the wide range of existing psychotherapeutic techniques. Such professionals can advise you about the type of help that will be most appropriate for your individual needs. Furthermore, many psychotherapeutic organizations and clinics offer diagnostic interviews for this purpose. In these sessions the applicant is interviewed by a competent professional who is thoroughly equipped to determine his psychotherapeutic requirements.

Remember that any information you may give a psychotherapist about yourself is held in strict confidence. Therefore, allow yourself to be as frank as possible in the diagnostic session to enable the interviewing psychotherapist to make a complete and valid evaluation.

Clinical experience and research have shown that a majority of people in need of professional assistance can benefit greatly from certain forms of group psychotherapy known as "psychoanalytic group therapy," "group psychoanalysis," or "psychoanalysis in groups." This therapy is often combined with regular or occasional individual sessions. In many instances dynamic results have been brought about in emotional disturbances which did not yield even to intensive individual treatment.

3. What is the setting of such a "psychoanalytic group?"

The group consists of five to ten persons. The majority of groups are composed of both males and females, while in other groups membership is limited to the same sex. Meetings last one and a half hours or longer, depending on the analyst's method.

The therapist will always carefully discuss with each new group member the number and nature of the weekly sessions. Many groups meet twice a week, once with the analyst and once without him. Some groups meet for three sessions weekly, two of them with the analyst. In other instances the analyst will suggest that a person participate in two different groups. The specific group, or groups, to which the person is assigned is determined by his particular needs.

"Alternate meetings," those held without the therapist, have extreme value, since a person's feelings and attitudes in the group usually vary considerably depending on the presence or absence of the therapist. This situation brings about more definite clues to self-understanding. Furthermore, alternate sessions help to pave the way to self-assertion and emotional independence. However, some therapists organize their groups in such a way that alternate sessions are not provided.

The analyst will recommend whether regular or only occasional individual sessions will be of the greatest benefit to the particular group member. Individual sessions may be particularly indicated when feelings of reluctance toward psychotherapy or the therapist are very strong. Naturally, such feelings of resistance occur not only in group therapy but in any form of valid psychotherapy.

4. Why is psychoanalytic group therapy so effective?

There are many reasons why this form of psychotherapy is of outstanding value in attaining emotional insight and maturity.

When psychoanalytic group therapy is practiced by a skilled therapist he draws fully on modern psychoanalytic theory and technique. The method utilizes all the psychoanalytic fundamentals such as transference and resistance analysis, free association, and dream analysis. Yet this form of psychotherapy has additional features that are all its own and cannot be duplicated in individual treatment. Among these features, which make the technique so particularly effective, the following are most important:

In a group the members work through their problems in a true-to-life situation of constant personal interaction. They soon become aware of similar emotional difficulties in others. By understanding the feelings of his fellow members, the individual gains quicker insight into his own emotional problems and reactions. His psychotherapeutic progress is continually stimulated by observing, experiencing, and sharing in the achievements made by the other group members.

Constant dynamic relations with the group help the individual to give up overdependency on the psychoanalyst, which would otherwise tend to prolong the process of recovery. Another important element is the relatively low cost of group psychoanalysis, which eases the financial burden often created by other methods of intensive therapy.

An outstanding factor in the beneficial results of psychoanalytic group therapy is the multitude and variety of the interrelationships that take place in such groups. If a person sees the therapist only for individual sessions, he can react merely to a single individual on whom he projects emotional patterns established in childhood (transference). The emergence and understanding of these patterns and reactions are a prime factor in a successful analysis. Therefore, individual therapy alone might be restrictive, since it cannot arouse the whole range of deep emotions buried within the person. In group, however, the different personalities of the male and female members evoke a *multitude* of diversified emotional reactions and provide a number of personalities to whom the person reacts. In doing so he will come to understand his own feelings, behavior patterns, and conflicts.

In the individual session the analyst is limited by the person's subjectively colored reports of incidents and emotional reactions to them. In the group situation, however, the analyst and the group can clearly and objectively detect the manner in which each person's defensive and emotional patterns distort his perception of reality. Thus the group member is helped gradually to achieve insight into his own deviations from objectivity.

People who have undesirable personality traits and behavior

patterns can be better helped to overcome these shortcomings in groups than in individual therapy. After all, the psychotherapist is limited in pointing out such flaws to the patient, since in doing so he might cause offense and harm the therapeutic relationship. However, undesirable characteristics of an individual will often become apparent through group interaction, and group members will more freely point them out. The underlying causes can then be analyzed and worked through.

Because the group situation is more like the outer world we live in as contrasted with the sheltered protection of the private session, any emotion expressed and worked through in a group constitutes a direct step forward. Personality changes thus achieved tend to be more permanent and definite.

5. *Should I join a group even though I feel uneasy about it?*

Many persons initially object to the idea of going into therapy together with other people, either because they feel that they will not be able to speak about their problems or because of an inner dislike or fear of people. But it is necessary to remember that such fears are directly connected with their problems. Therefore it is most advantageous to work through these fears rather than avoid them. Almost invariably they diminish after a few group sessions.

Some people have the erroneous impression that psychoanalysis in groups—because it is less expensive—is more superficial than the usual individal analysis. These persons may want only individual sessions in order to have the entire time and attention of the analyst, or they may state that they do not wish to be bothered with "other people's problems." In therapy, however, what may *seem* to be more gratifying—or less difficult—and what makes for the most effective and intensive method are often two different things. Even though the extended duration of group sessions allows each person ample opportunity to express himself, it must be stressed that the effectiveness of any psychotherapeutic technique is not in direct ratio to the amount of words a person utters. Speaking about the problems of which we are already aware is only of minor significance. A far more important task of therapy is to bring into consciousness the intense emotions which are unknown to the person because of having been repressed in childhood. Being unaware of these blind spots, we cannot directly focus on many of the areas with which analysis has to deal. However, our deeper feelings are inevitably elicited as we react at any given moment to the ever-changing group situation created by the expressions, behavior, and interaction of the members.

The success of therapy greatly depends upon the extent to which repressed emotions are stimulated, brought to awareness, expressed, and worked through. Psychoanalytic group therapy often stimulates feelings more intensively and extensively than do private sessions and may bring into the open important areas of emotional disturbance that might not otherwise have been revealed.

Part II

1. What should I do in the group?

In the group you have an unusual opportunity to express your real thoughts and feelings. There is no necessity to force yourself to behave one way or another. Some people, new in the group, participate actively from the beginning; others may remain silent for a while. Whichever tendency you may have, observe what the others are doing during the course of the session. Become aware of your feelings throughout the meetings. Try also to watch for any anticipatory feelings before the meetings as well as for those reactions which you may experience at any time after the sessions. Sooner or later you will want to express them in the group. If, however, you have difficulty in verbalizing some of your feelings at the time they are experienced, you may be able to do so at subsequent meetings. Should the inability to speak continue, it will be of value to express these feelings in an individual session with the analyst.

The first phase in therapy includes the task of learning to identify and clarify feelings. As strange as it may seem, many people are frequently unclear about their real feelings and confuse them with "opinions," "values," and "intellectual concepts," which are more often than not mere defenses against and rationalizations of their real feelings.

A number of sessions will pass before you can become fully aware of what is really going on in the group. As you participate more and more you will begin to sense what the group and the analyst are working toward. You will gradually grasp the underlying significance of the procedure and become emotionally involved. The situation is like that of watching people dance and then dancing yourself—only as you actively participate do you realize its essence. Consequently, have patience for at least the first four to six weeks.

For a number of people, the initial sessions may be somewhat difficult; they may feel a strong impulse to abandon the group for various reasons, such as resenting or disliking some of the members. No matter how strong these feelings are, it is important not to give in to them but to understand that their full discussion in the group, or in an individual session, will provide valuable material for deeper insight and self-understanding.

You will notice that the group members do a number of things: they speak about past and present experiences, problems, thoughts, and fantasies that are emotionally important to them; they speak about feelings experienced at previous meetings, between meetings and—most of all—during the present meeting; they state their feelings about each other and the analyst. Many of these emotions may appear irrational to you. However, you will soon come to realize that feelings follow their own special logic, and the group's tolerance of any apparent irrationality will help you to discover and express such feelings of your own. The group members also bring up dreams and discuss them, since dreams are a vital factor in understanding a person's emotional problems and his ways of dealing with them.

Some people feel that they want to hide some of their thoughts and actions from the group because they seem shocking, embarrassing, or ridiculous; or they may not want to hurt another member's feelings or incur the dislike of anyone in the group. Be sure to express any such reluctance because the *truthful* expression of your feelings is of primary importance and an absolute necessity for progress. One has to realize that this is not a customary social situation. Here the expression of negative feelings can be most helpful to the other group members as well as to yourself.

If you should repeatedly feel blocked in the group and unable to express yourself, or if your mind becomes blank, your analyst may suggest that you prepare mentally beforehand a list of emotional experiences, dreams, and ideas you previously experienced and which you intended to discuss at the meeting. If you go blank just the same, you might write such items down and use this memorandum in the group. However, spontaneous reaction in the group will usually be of even greater value than prepared material. As you gradually work through your tendency to block and find spontaneous expression easier, you will be able to dispense with these props.

Remember you asked for professional assistance because of your emotional problems and not because you wanted the enjoyment of intellectual discussions. Intellectual understanding alone does not bring about lasting change. Deep emotional understanding and progress will come about only by turning your attention inward in order to become aware of your feelings and reactions which stem from childhood. Therefore, it is most important that you be attentive to your reactions *in any given situation* arising in the group and try to understand the emotional forces at work. This may require some concentration and effort on your part. The continued expression of emotions provides a basis for the necessary therapeutic work which will follow, weakening the unconscious forces that have hidden the deeply repressed feelings and conflicts. As these gradually emerge they become more understandable and manageable.

2. *How about my relationship with the analyst?*

It is of utmost importance that you bring up all your feelings toward the analyst, even though this may be difficult at times. Much of your psychotherapeutic advance will result from understanding the causes for the multitude of frequently changing feelings which are stimulated in your relationship with the analyst and the group members. Even though these feelings may at times appear embarrassing, irrational, or hostile, their frank expression is of great value. If for some reason you are repeatedly unable to verbalize these thoughts in the presence of the other group members, bring up this material in the next individual session. Also, when you express feelings about the analyst in the alternate session, be sure to bring them to his attention in the subsequent regular session.

Many times, seemingly against your will and without your conscious knowledge, inner mechanisms will work against your progress in therapy as painful areas are approached. Frequently such reluctance to delve deeper takes the manifest form of negative feelings against the analyst, the therapy, or both. These feelings may be based on earlier attitudes toward parents and other persons in authority. Your reactions may be so strong that unless the analyst is given a chance to work them through with you they may actually induce you either to forsake professional help completely or, as an escape from the threatening situation, to seek another analyst. It may require a good deal of self-discipline not to give in to such feelings, which at the time may seem quite reasonable.

Doubts may also come up when you feel that you are not making visible progress. It is inherent in all forms of psychotherapy that periods of standstill or even setbacks occur. Most often these periods will be only of limited duration. Old patterns of feeling and behavior are tenacious and the total line of progress includes many ups and downs. Often an old pattern will recur when a hidden wound within your unconscious has been touched upon by therapy, or when the next step forward seems too frightening. Yet these difficult periods are an important part of psychotherapy and provide valuable material for further progress. Such resistance comes up in all types of analysis, including group therapy. To become aware of these blocks, which may take many forms, and to work them through is a most significant factor in your progress.

3. What about my relationship to the other group members?

It is most important that you become aware of and express your feelings toward your fellow group members. Notice also their emotional reactions toward you after you have expressed yourself and see how their reactions affect you. The significance of these reactions may appear in what is said, but sometimes even more in *how* it is said. Often a person's behavior—which is always a most significant clue to his unconscious drives and motivations—will reveal a discrepancy or even be in direct contradiction to his spoken words. This may occur even though the person believes he has expressed himself frankly and honestly.

You might also notice when a person "acts out" an emotion, that is, when his emotion finds expression in action rather than in verbalization. This might be, for instance, turning his back on and ignoring a group member he dislikes, or constantly interrupting him. Acting out also can be verbal. Two simple examples are: a group member may knowingly make false and malicious statements about another group member or the analyst in order to hurt him or may falsely claim affection for someone in group to win his alliance. Understanding the feelings underlying such actions, which are often unconscious, will be greatly facilitated if this behavior is interrupted and brought to the attention of the individual.

Soon you will become aware of the emotional patterns in one or more of the members as they automatically react in an irrational way to certain situations. Your awareness will gradually become enlarged and you will develop such insight into your own behavior as well.

It is customary for group members to call one another by their first names. Everything said in the group by any of its members must be held strictly confidential and any knowledge gained about them, including their identities, may not be divulged to any outsider.

With regard to fees, some analysts charge the same rate to all group members. Others adjust the fee to the income of the member. Thus it is better for group members not to discuss fees, since this may foment unnecessary feelings of jealousy or inferiority. However, once such a situation has arisen, it is desirable to air and discuss fully the feelings aroused.

4. Shall I tell others that I am in group psychoanalysis and what happens in the sessions?

It is entirely up to you whether you want to let others know that you are in analysis. It is wise, however, to use judgment about whom you confide in. Some people still have prejudices against psychotherapy. Others, who may not be well-intentioned toward you, may try to use such knowledge to hurt or annoy you. Well-informed and mature people, however, will respect you for having chosen a path of self-improvement and inner growth.

For a number of reasons, it is always undesirable to speak with outsiders about what happens in analysis—private or group. First of all, you will express to them emotional reactions and evaluations that should be saved for a sessions from which you might derive therapeutic benefit. By expressing such feelings to someone not in the group you will be less inclined to bring them up in your next session, and valuable material may be lost. Furthermore, in the psychotherapeutic setting one is dealing with unconscious processes of all kinds, which will most likely be misunderstood by an outsider.

Another danger exists for those who regularly tell a friend, parent, intimate about the content of their sessions. A time will come when unconsciously they will refrain from bringing up certain material in the session just because they do not wish to repeat it to their habitual confidant. The very process of analysis thus becomes stifled and meaningless.

5. *What else can I do to help my progress?*

Since your emotional structure and behavior patterns have been deeply ingrained since childhood, continued effort over an extended period of time is required to bring about positive and lasting changes. Coming regularly to the sessions is only one of the factors necessary to your progress; your efforts between, as well as during, the sessions are also of major importance.

As you know, the task of the psychoanalyst is far from easy. An important part of his work, upon which much of the success of therapy depends, is to understand your unconscious conflicts and motivations. His efforts in this direction require the *greatest possible honesty* on your part. If necessary material and information are withheld, changed, or embellished, then a serious obstacle to effective analysis has been created.

Many people enjoy being in therapy and the particular group to which they belong. However, for a period of time some may dislike the group meetings. Such people should bear in mind the therapeutic purpose of the sessions. Their discomfort during these limited hours is a relatively small price to pay for emotional gains that will enrich their lives. Furthermore, the very discomfort experienced is a valuable clue to underlying emotional problems.

As you gain more and more insights, it is important that you attempt to make them meaningful in your life, applying them constructively in your day-by-day battle against the old patterns. If you merely content yourself with an intellectual understanding of how it came about you will have gained little except, perhaps, a good excuse for being neurotic.

You will observe that some insights gained during the sessions will slip away quickly, sometimes only seconds later. If this occurs, it is important that it be brought to the attention of the group, so that the causes of such forgetting will be discovered. In addition, try to make a conscious effort to remember any insights you gain. Some therapists advocate writing them down after sessions, if necessary.

Aside from following as closely as possible the various points mentioned so far, there is an additional way to help your progress. As you know, dreams and fantasies are of great value in psychotherapy. Therefore try to remember your fantasies, daydreams, and particularly your dreams, and discuss them in the group sessions. Dreams are motion pictures of the forces moving in your unconscious; psychoanalysis is needed to decipher their real meaning. You will do best, when you wake up, to lie still and attempt to recapture the dreams you have had. Do not open your eyes until after you have recapitulated them. Some people will find that they tend to forget dreams, in whole or in part, even though they have recalled them upon awakening. If your therapist agrees to this procedure, write them down before inner forces that work against deeper awareness erase them from your memory.

In the period just before falling asleep the mind is in a more suggestible state and the unconscious tends to continue working with the impressions it receives. Therefore, if you have difficulty remembering dreams after awakening, try the following technique: at night, just when you are falling asleep, tell yourself in an effortless way that you are going to have dreams and that you will recall them as you awaken. You may not achieve results the first few times, but chances are that shortly you will.

6. How will I know when my therapy is finished?

Many times during therapy people may experience a period of well-being such as they have never known before, or lose painful symptoms that they have had for some time. In response to these improvements they may consider themselves cured and decide to abandon therapy. Actually, permanent and sufficiently deep structural changes may not yet have occurred in all areas where improvements are necessary. In many cases resistive forces will be the underlying cause for this feeling of well-being and, more often than not, unconscious resistance to anticipated anxiety — and not the obvious satisfaction over improvement achieved — will be the real cause for the decision to leave. The discontinuance of analysis then makes it possible to avoid previously hidden painful feelings that are now ready to emerge.

All this points to the fact that no one can be the judge as to when his own therapy should terminate. Your analyst will decide with you when this time has come. Whenever you wish to leave, discuss your intention frankly with your analyst and the group. They will be able to work with you to determine whether it is a result of resistance to further necessary change or a justified decision based on the solid ground of mental health achieved.

REFERENCE

de Schill, S. (1958), *Introduction to Psychoanalytic Group Therapy.* New York: American Mental Health Foundation, 1969, 6th rev. ed.

1

Theoretical Foundations of Group Psychotherapy—I

HELEN E. DURKIN

Any theory of psychotherapy must be contingent upon a theory of personality and the etiology of emotional illness. Analytic group psychotherapy subscribes to the psychoanalytic view that the psychoneuroses, in the broad sense, originate in the early years and

---

Dr. Durkin is Senior Supervising Psychologist and Training Analyst, Postgraduate Center for Mental Health, New York City.

The groups in which my hypotheses have been tested and my theoretical conclusions worked out have met once weekly for sessions lasting one and a half to two hours. They were open groups. Starting in 1937, there were children's groups, mothers' groups, and adolescent groups.

From about 1945 on, they were largely heterosexual groups of adults. With experience, I constituted the groups as heterogeneously as possible within the range of patients who apply for private treatment or for treatment in small guidance clinics, where limited possibilities for selection exist. I tried for a mixture of age, educational level, socioeconomic status, religious background, and vocational experience, but avoided deviations wide enough to make communication too difficult. Once the resistance attached to these differences was analyzed, they proved to be stimulating to therapeutic movement. I soon discovered that heterogeneity as to basic character was of great importance. Defenses typical of any one level of development (e.g., anal obsessive defenses) tend to produce general blind spots so that resistance is reinforced. All diagnostic categories were represented except frank psychosis and psychopathy, but the majority of the patients were neurotic or had character problems.

As a result of experience I also began to put into one group patients who were in combined treatment with me or with someone else, and those who were in group treatment only. Exceptions to these general rules were made strictly on the basis of clinical judgment. Nor did I hesitate to put into one group, patients who paid different rates. Experience showed that all these differences were grist for the mill of analysis.

even months of life[1] as a result of conflict between the instinctual drives and the limitation imposed upon their gratification by the outside world as represented by upbringers. The initial purely physiological frustrations help to bring about a dawning awareness of self, and then, as the ego functions gradually mature, true psychological conflict begins. Conflict between the infant's libidinal strivings for love and his aggressive drive for autonomy soon complicates the struggle. These conflicts culminate in a relatively adaptive or maladaptive resolution by the end of the oedipal period.

Meanwhile, part of the personality aligns itself with the forces of repression. In a series of projections and introjections which occur before the ego functions of perception and comprehension have matured, the infant identifies with what he experiences as the forbidding parental attitudes. A gradient in the ego is formed (Freud, 1921), which initiates the rudiments of a superego.

As the ego develops, its most common way of coping with the unacceptable drives is to relegate them to unawareness together with their attendant anxiety and primitive fantasies. Split off from the rest of the ego in this way, they maintain their archaic character and cannot mature with the rest of the personality. For the same reason they are exempt from correction by simple experience (Fenichel, 1941).

But the infantile drives do not disappear. They continue to produce inner tensions at each level of psychosexual development. These remain unconscious but bring about renewed strivings for satisfaction and release. The still-infantile ego must continue to keep them out of awareness by finding new coping mechanisms (defenses).

Furthermore, the compromises of the infantile ego are seldom adequate, so that new defenses must be added from time to time. As the child grows older, the original defenses are reformulated in terms of his developing ego functions and of the changing circumstances of his environment. As this happens, the unconscious fantasies are also

[1] There has been increasing recognition in recent years of the fact that the trouble begins for neurotics and character problems as well as for psychotics when stimuli from the outside world first impinge upon the infant's primary narcissism (Glatzer, 1962). My own experience in group therapy confirms this view.

modified. For example, the early oral fears of annihilation may become, during the anal period, the fear of being controlled, and later, in the phallic phase, of castration. If these early problems are poorly resolved, those of the oedipal period will be difficult indeed to overcome. From then on, a great deal of energy is required to maintain whatever precarious neurotic balance the individual has achieved. He comes for help when that balance is severely threatened.

Basic Psychoanalytic Concepts that Apply to Group Behavior

Thirty years of experience have established the theoretical foundations for employing the conceptual framework of psychoanalysis and, consequently, its basic therapeutic principles in group psychotherapy. Freud's statement that "individual and group psychology are one and the same" (1921) is amply confirmed by patients in therapy groups. The same cardinal features of personality can be demonstrated in the group behavior of every member. In the group the patients strive to satisfy their needs, including their anachronistic and conflictual tendencies, through their relationships with the other members as well as with the therapist. The several members provide a variety of targets and also actively stimulate a great many dormant needs. In the unfolding interaction, the infantile conflicts of all are repeated rather than remembered. Transference resistance abounds and the group becomes a highly potent therapeutic milieu. Like a theater in the round, it provides a dramatic presentation of the insistent and insidious way in which the past intrudes itself into the present. The therapist must help the members gradually to translate these transferences into terms of the past (Freud, 1914), in order that they may become free to respond realistically to others in the present. The group gives him the advantage of a wealth of audiovisual and experiential evidence to facilitate this task.

At first glance it might seem that the enormous complexities of the interconnecting transference processes together with the requirements of the group setting itself would seriously interfere with the very personal and rigorous psychoanalytic process. Nevertheless, experience has proved otherwise. The members can and do profitably share in one another's analytic experience. The reason is simple—all the members share the same basic drives and the same mental structure, albeit in different proportions. They have lived through the same epigenetic phases and experienced analogous conflicts at each level of development. The fact that each member has resolved his conflicts in terms of his particular capacities and the special circumstances of his personal experience merely serves to enrich their communication and to provide opportunity for acquiring wider horizons while arriving at more complete personal differentiation.

Certain group-determined variations of behavior were recognized by Freud (1921). Since then social science research has more fully illuminated the nature of groups and group behavior. The present-day group therapist is provided with a profound understanding of the milieu in which he works. Awareness of the therapeutic or antitherapeutic potential of the ongoing group dynamics broadens his perspective; comprehension of the group as a dynamic entity puts a new dimension of force at his disposal. But, in my judgement group dynamics are complementary to the analytic process. They neither conflict with it, vitiate it, nor replace it. The major therapeutic thrust remains the analysis of transference and resistance in their new group costumes.

The therapeutic task is, therefore, the same in group therapy as it is in individual psychoanalysis. It consists in an attempt to reunite the excluded tendencies of each member with his total personality to the end that a redistribution of energy will occur which will bring about basic structural change.[2] In the group the principal technique for reaching this goal remains the analysis of transference and resistance. The task is feasible because the infantile tendencies continue unconsciously to motivate the patients so that the neurotic conflicts reappear, as they began, in relationships with other people—in this case, the group members. These constitute the transferences.

[2] This goal is not always reached but it is always the aim. The same is, of course, equally true of individual psychoanalysis.

Because of their inappropriateness, they are identifiable in the group in spite of the fact that the member-to-member interaction is largely subjective. The therapist, on the other hand, adheres strictly to the analytic attitude of concerned neutrality because it helps transference come into clearest focus. He, therefore, analyzes but does not respond to the patients' communications. Because the cognitive shift which his "translations" bring about are meaningful only in an emotional context, he makes them at moments of intense impact. The group is a superb provider of such occasions. The fact that he cannot be completely anonymous in the face-to-face situation with a number of patients does not interfere with the analytic process; the compulsion to repeat the original conflict is too strong to give way so easily.

The intragroup transferences convey the patients' resistance to uncovering the infantile drives. Analyzing the resistance is, of course, the first order of business. In his task of bringing what was repressed back into awareness, the group therapist uses the usual clues (preconscious derivatives), which appear in quantity among the intragroup relationships. The uncovering process is sometimes even more frightening to the patients than it is in individual treatment, and at such times they tighten up their defenses accordingly. That is how the defenses become the resistance in the treatment situation. Their fear of exposing themselves to the group must always be dealt with sooner or later. The sensitive group therapist takes into consideration the patients' need to keep their self-esteem with their fellow members. He may do this by the way he words his comments but he must be firm and persistent in combatting the resistance, nevertheless. More often than not, the group members contribute substantially to carrying out this function. It is much easier for them to perceive transference and resistance in others than in themselves and they call attention to it. Having done so, they are better prepared to gain insight into their own neurotic behavior.

As in individual psychoanalysis, established security measures are not easy to give up no matter how costly they have become. Sometimes, changed behavior follows directly upon insight, but it is likely to be temporary. Working through is therefore as necessary as it is in individual treatment. In stubborn cases the patients' identity may be completely caught up in their neurotic behavior; often their neurotic suffering itself is grounded in masochistic gratification; and most patients cherish an unconscious hope that by paying the neurotic price they will regain paradise lost (i.e., the state of primary narcissism) by finding the perfect relationship and will fulfill their omnipotent fantasies to boot. These deeply rooted causes of resistance to real change become exacerbated when the goal seems within reach. They must be thoroughly analyzed before basic character change can be achieved.

Factors in Group Therapy that Require Modifications in Psychoanalytic Method

The inclusion of the members in the treatment situation does not change the basic principle of analyzing transference and resistance, but it does require some modifications of the techniques which implement it. Moreover, the structure of the group setting itself necessitates certain changes in procedure for the purpose of providing the best conditions for the therapeutic task (Fenichel, 1945).

There are at least two major consequences of working therapeutically with several patients at the same time. The more obvious of these differences is the preclusion of free association; the more significant concerns the development and handling of the transference.

The technique that was designed to gain rapid access to primary process is manifestly impracticable in the group. The question has been raised as to whether any method which does not use this valuable tool can be considered psychoanalysis (Kubie, 1958). But group psychotherapists have long since reached a consensus that "the group produces its own equivalent of free association in the spontaneous flow of communications among its members" (Foulkes, 1964). So many preconscious derivatives appear in the interaction that if the sensitive therapist listens for what his patients, individually or as a group, are struggling to communicate, he will learn much more about their latent feelings and motivation than he can handle in any one session. Moreover, the rapid shifting of defenses tends to put the members off guard to a certain degree so that they unwittingly permit more preconscious derivatives to filter into their conversations. There are also many points during the sessions at which true free associations may be elicited, as for example when a contradiction or an inappropriate or disproportional emotion is recognized.

In order to facilitate the group associative process, the therapist sets up a suitable group analytic situation. He opens by asking the members to speak as freely as possible about whatever they are experiencing. They usually find it difficult to comply fully, so that the therapist must continue to encourage the fullest and most spontaneous interaction possible. He tries to get them to talk with one another instead of directing mo,t of their comments to him. He avoids answering questions and giving advice. He remains neutral but constant in his concern for what they are trying to express. His choice of interventions makes them increasingly aware of the importance of their latent feelings. In other words, he watches carefully over the group atmosphere in order to facilitate the forward movement of the therapeutic process. In doing so he must maintain a delicate balance between his necessarily more active approach and his willingness to let them take over the interaction insofar as they are able. Most important, he keeps analyzing their resistance to exposing their inner thoughts and feelings. In this way he establishes the best possible situation for carrying out the analytic process in a group.

Differences in the Development of the Transference

Transference behavior is ubiquitous in the interaction. But the architecture of the group gives rise to marked differences in its development which require definite changes in its technical management. The individual psychoanalytic situation was set up to minimize the intrusions of reality and to diminish the patient's ego functioning. The quiet, undisturbed atmosphere of the analytic chamber, the couch, and the complete anonymity of the therapist all contribute to the heightening of transference to such a point that all the patient's infantile conflicts are eventually relived through the person of the analyst. This procedure generates powerful tension in the patient-therapist relationship, which is converted into therapeutic leverage. Consequently, transference in individual analysis tends to be thought of as a single entity, an artificial neurosis. It is called the transference neurosis and is usually considered the *sine qua non* of psychoanalytic treatment.

Manifestly, the conditions of group therapy cannot support such all-consuming one-to-one relationships. The therapist, whose responsibility requires him to keep all the group relationships in his ken, simply cannot handle them. Nor does the situation permit their development. There are too many interruptions. Reality cannot be sufficiently subdued. Members who possess characteristics closer than the therapist's to the patients' parental images attract transference reactions to themselves. They also find it easier to displace to their less awesome peers the love or hate meant for the therapist. Moreover, the members react subjectively to one another, so that transference illusions cannot be maintained very long. Instead, frequent changes of transference objects tend to occur, and only one aspect is reenacted with one person at a time, though several may be going on simultaneously. Thus, the manifestations of transference are less concentrated but they are *not* less intense than those of individual psychoanalysis.

Transference in the group, then, consists of concurrent series of inappropriate reactions toward a variety of persons with whom past attitudes and feelings and behavior are repeated. To view these transference processes as a dividing up of "The Transference" is, it seems to me, a consequence of adhering too strictly to the findings of individual psychoanalysis. Actually, a monolithic transference of this kind has never developed in the therapy group.

Transference processes develop in a unique way in the group. From the beginning, the members turn to one another as well as to the therapist in their unconscious search for infantile gratifications. For this purpose they form a number of neurotic alliances of varying duration and intensity. Those who have complementary needs in any one area will tend to engage in a transferential transaction for mutual satisfaction. Those whose needs are similar may identify with one another. Both forms of relationship will carry resistance. Since any one individual's transference reactions may be stimulated, headed off, or ignored by other members in accordance with the most urgent immediate concerns of the majority, transference phenomena will necessarily be less continuous than they are in individual psychoanalysis. The individual members bend, in this respect, to the movement of the group as a whole; but in the long run *all* of their individual conflicts will make themselves felt and become available for analysis. As treatment progresses, the interconnecting transference processes will create a continually shifting network (compare Ezriel, 1950).

A second change in the form of the transference arises from the fact that reality cannot be drastically reduced and free association is restricted in the group. Defensive aspects of the transference tend to remain in the forefront of the interaction. The emphasis is on the ego rather than on the infantile libidinal and aggressive drives. Under these circumstances, each patient's ego development will become apparent and will, of course, reflect the transformation through which his libidinal and aggressive drives have passed (A. Freud, 1936). Unavoidably, therefore, the defensive aspects of the patients' transferences will become the major target of analysis.

On this subject, Ackerman (1954) wrote, "In principle, the structure of the therapy group is less conducive to the unchecked assertion of irrational and egocentrically oriented behavior in the individual than in psychoanalysis." What he fails to note is that the defenses themselves contain the irrational regressive elements. Though they are intended to ward off the original drives, they regularly betray their presence.

Because of the emphasis on the ego, also, a great many of the transference phenomena in the therapy group consist of character defenses. They may be classed as transference because the behavior represents the solution of infantile conflicts and thus bring the past into the present; but they are habitual modes of behavior and tend to be fixed rather than responsive to a particular object (Fenichel, 1945). Because they bind the anxiety so well they are not usually experienced as ego alien. For this reason they are difficult to deal with in individual analysis (A. Freud, 1936) but respond very well to group treatment. The members quickly react to their stereotyped quality. Although patients whose character resistance is being explored in the group also put up a fight, they yield much more readily to the interpretations of their peers who are less threatening than the therapist. Furthermore, they are forced to come to grips with the group's consensus which is generally anchored in reality.

The group is also more effective than individual psychoanalysis in dealing with impulsive characters whose transferences become so intensified that the "ego behaves wholly as an infantile ego" (A. Freud, 1936), for the group members provide what the individual analyst cannot. They exert pressure which eventually succeeds in giving impulsive patients pause to think before they plunge into action. This wedge forces them to become aware of the intense anxiety which heretofore they had done away with by acting out. Once they experience anxiety, the other group members provide the emotional support which helps them to endure it. Inner change becomes possible.

Modification in the Management of Transference in Group Therapy

If transference is to be employed as the principal therapeutic instrument, then each manifestation of it must be analyzed separately, for that is how it presents itself in the group. In other words, the group therapist must be responsive to what is actually happening instead of relying on a preconceived concept from another setting. As he observes the many intragroup transference processes shifting rapidly in ever-changing configurations, he must be alert in order to interpret those that bear resistance. He cannot wait, as in individual analysis, for a slow buildup of single structures — the timing of his interventions must be geared to the empirical situation. Secondly, he must learn to select the transference reaction or transaction which is, at the moment, most pertinent both to the group and to the individual engaged in it. Sometimes this requires that he make an interpretation to an individual who at that point seems to epitomize the major group preoccupation, or whose own need is so strong that he must be allowed to determine the group focus. Since any individual's need is usually responsive to what has been happening in the group, the others are apt to be ready for his contribution. In exceptional cases where the individual is for some reason removed from the group's orbit, he or they may be in resistance. The therapist must assess the situation and act according to his clinical judgment. At other times the therapist may make his comments to two or more members as a unit or to the group as a whole: Whichever he chooses to do, he will follow through by trying to draw everyone into the discussion. Although the other members may not be openly involved in the particular transaction being explored, they will probably be responding to it inwardly. Eliciting these reactions helps them work it through.

The group therapist also shares his interpretive function with the members. He permits the patients to engage in it freely and often finds them extremely insightful. (It takes one to know one!) But because patients frequently use interpretations to express their own unconscious motivation, and because the therapist alone understands the total picture and is skilled in timing, he must reserve for himself the ultimate management of the interpretive function.

The therapist's task then is to spot the crucial transference behavior and to analyze it. In doing so he follows the basic principles of psychoanalytic method but adapts them to meet the changed conditions. He finds that in the group the therapeutic process moves in a horizontal rather than a vertical plane. It resembles a plane trip in contrast to the voyage by rail of individual analysis (Fried, 1954). Moreover, because so many transferences occur in rapid succession and tend to overlap, the group therapist will, *ipso facto,* be more active in dealing with resistance. The pace of the therapeutic process will be faster; its rhythm, more staccato.

The Systematic Analysis of Transference in Group Psychotherapy

The question remains as to whether analysis of transference and resistance may be carried out *systematically* enough in the group setting to bring about the resolution of those infantile conflicts of the members which brought them into treatment in the first place. At first glance the very intricacy of the multitudinous and interconnecting transferences would seem to raise an impossible obstacle to an orderly group analysis. Indeed, reasonable objections have been raised by traditional psychoanalysts on the grounds that such attempts would produce a fruitless "wild analysis," end in confusion, and in all likelihood, leave untouched large portions of any single member's problems (Kubie, 1958).

Experience has disproved this concern. The complexities of the group communications can be reduced to manageable proportions. As the therapist concentrates on the continually reintegrating group relationships, a new kind of patterning becomes apparent to him. Each member's engagement in the interaction process soon begins to reveal a characteristic structure which indicates the nature of his ego development. His major defense system becomes clearly discernible in his repeatedly stimulated transference reactions. In every session there will be a plethora of clues which indicate the state of his id, ego, and superego balance. And there will be others that point to that phase of his development which was most decisive in determining his character defenses. These patterns provide a guideline for a coherent and systematic analysis. As the character of each individual's ego is thus illumined in the total network of the intragroup transferences, it stands out like a figure on a ground, enabling the therapist to streamline his interpretations and to follow them through systematically. They will be directed to the basic conflicts, and the temptation to do a lot of analytic wandering around is avoided. Examination of the protocols over an extensive period of years shows that the major aspects of each member's transference repertoire come to light in the course of the group process; they are explored and given ample opportunity to be worked through. Moreover, the protocols regularly show changes in dreams, attitudes, and behavior, which are expectable in terms of the insights achieved; and they are followed by the appearance of new preconscious material in the communications (Durkin, 1964).

Since systematic analysis and working through go hand in hand, it must be noted that working through, too, has its distinctive features in group therapy. The therapist must pay attention to the "ground" as well as to the "figure." From the standpoint of the individual, therefore, it follows a zigzag course. His neurotic patterns of behavior are explored in all their variations in ever-changing contexts as they occur in relation to other members. Experience has warranted the assumption that the conflict which is being repeated by any one member at a given moment will reactivate unresolved aspects of the same conflict in the other members. Therefore, once a transference has been identified, the therapist follows through by eliciting the associations, reactions, and memories of the entire membership instead of exploring its ramifications only with the individual immediately involved. During this process of group elaboration, transference is consistently checked against reality, and the total process is sharpened to a fine point because of the combined effect of the therapist's neutrality and the members' subjective reactions.

Working through together in this way enhances the group spirit. The members keep motivating one another to find out how their outmoded and now troublesome ways of relating came into being to meet childhood exigencies that no longer exist except in fantasy.

Sometimes, when a patient talks about a relationship with which he is having difficulty on the outside, the members try to be helpful but fail because he is unwittingly trying to ward off its infantile implications. After a while they get discouraged and join him in resistance. But this is usually dissolved very quickly as soon as it can be demonstrated that the pertinent conflict is simultaneously being reenacted in one or another of his group relationships. The discovery of the connection between the there and the here, the then and the now, brings with it surprise and excitement to all group members. There usually follows a renewed spontaneous and lively interchange among the members, who become progressively involved with one another as they pursue their search and share their experiences. The historical vector becomes extremely meaningful in this way and is kept in close relation to the current situation with excellent therapeutic effect.

But there is more. The nature of the group process itself provides a means of unifying the overall group analytic work. The continuous dynamic restructuring within the total network of communication provides clues to the changing emotional preoccupation of the group as a whole. Dealing with it as such may cut through many individual interpretations.[3] Moreover a formidable source of emotional power is created by the convergence of so many physiological and psychological drives in constant interaction (Ezriel, 1950). It is as if they form a matrix (Foulkes, 1964) out of which a new dimension of the group analytic process is born. Its impact on the membership is strong. The therapeutic leverage of such dynamic group interaction is at least comparable to that of the transference neurosis as it functions in individual psychoanalysis.

Regression in Analytic Group Psychotherapy

Although the emphasis is on the defenses, the group therapist by no means avoids the expression of profound irrational infantile feelings. Quite to the contrary, he actively interprets resistance for the very purpose of releasing them. The group members help him accomplish this goal. For although as individuals they tend to become defensive when they are approaching the warded-off feelings, as a group they become irritated with defensiveness in others and pressure one another to be more open and direct in expressing them. When a member does break through his defenses, the group becomes warmly supportive. Moreover, there is no psychosexual level to which their feelings cannot revert. Groups can be exceptionally stimulating to the recreation of preoedipal as well as oedipal feelings. A number of authors, including Grotjahn, Fried, Glatzer, and myself, have made a special study of the fate of preoedipal conflicts in group psychotherapy. For example, Glatzer (1962) reported that in her experience the group is extremely helpful in penetrating the tenacious primitive defenses which characterize orally regressed patients. She feels that both the therapist and the patients are more active in

[3] For example when all are angry at the therapist for going on holiday, or when oral greed motivates everyone to accuse him of depriving them.

making interpretations than is the individual therapist and that this is essential for such basically passive individuals. My own experience unquestionably confirms these findings. Once the resistance has been dealt with, the infantile libidinal or aggressive feelings that have been pent up flow out freely and everyone participates to some degree and in his own way in a common regression. For the individual it may become very intense.

The group, therefore, is punctuated by periods of profound emotion, but, on the whole, such periods do not last long. One or another member interrupts them either because he cannot tolerate too much primitive emotion or because he has been stimulated to express his own needs. In analytic group psychotherapy, such intense though brief periods of regression can be shown to bring about changes in the mental structure, provided they are skillfully interpreted and assiduously worked through. Small quantities of increasingly strong emotion are released in the repeated encounters with various group members. Their intensity seems to be cumulative, and it is magnified by the total group's involvement. They become therapeutically very powerful.

As the analysis of transference and resistance continues, interaction and insight go hand in hand. The members continue to explore their current behavior in the light of early familial experience until the vestiges of the past no longer so flagrantly intrude into contemporary relationships. Realistic relationships with members of the group and the therapist, and also with relatives, friends, and colleagues in the outside world, gradually come to predominate over transference.

Transference Neurosis in Group Psychotherapy

The much-debated question now arises, "Does transference neurosis develop in group therapy?" It is an important question, for, since Freud's recommendation (1914) that all transference be drawn into the treatment situation (where it forms an artificial neurosis), the transference neurosis has come to be generally regarded as the *sine qua non* of psychoanalysis. Rangell (1954) incorporated the concept into the very definition of psychoanalysis. He wrote: "Psychoanalysis is a method whereby conditions are brought about favorable to the development of transference neurosis in which the past is restored in the present in order that, through the systematic attack on the resistances which oppose it, there occurs a resolution of that neurosis to the end of bringing about structural changes in the mental apparatus of the patient."

There has been considerable debate about this subject. A number of group therapists whose major experience has been in individual analysis are very doubtful. Berne (1960) denied the possibility outright. He argued that the occurrence of transference processes does not constitute a transference neurosis. Spanjaard (1959) has a similar opinion. Having linked therapeutic change with depth of regression, he goes on to say that groups do not provide good conditions for regression. In his opinion, limited regression may be acted out in group — as, for instance, adolescent rebellion — but its roots in the preoedipal conflicts can never be analyzed in that situation. Moreover, he considers that most group therapists' interventions are more educative than therapeutic.[4] (Compare Glatzer's views, 1962.)

Both Slavson and Foulkes were originally of the opinion that the group situation was not well suited to working through transference neurosis, but both have come to the conclusion that it can be done. Slavson feels that the resolution of transference neurosis is of secondary importance as a therapeutic instrument in group psychotherapy. Foulkes (1964) writes that after twenty years of experience he has come to the conclusion that individual transference neurosis can be recognized in the group and therefore analyzed; but he adds that it does not develop in pure form and cannot be worked through in the same detail. Schwartz and Wolf (1962) are convinced that it can be done very successfully if the therapist uses his interventions to encourage it and to deal with it. Dreams, they point out, are very useful in this respect. Hulse, in a private communication, voiced the opinion that if the therapist views the

[4] In my opinion, his conclusion is a product of his attitude rather than of the situation.

member-to-member transferences as being displacements from those to the therapist, then the transference neuroses of the individual members can be perceived and analyzed.

Our question is also baffling because the concept has been ambiguous enough to invite a variety of interpretations. Two requirements of transference neurosis are unequivocal. The past must be restored in the treatment situation and the patient must experience his distortions as "real and actual" (Freud, 1914). But ambiguity arises from the lack of specificity as to the degree and duration of the regressive experience. Consequently, some authors who continue to be influenced by the early psychoanalytic focus on the id and have confidence in the therapeutic value of the catharsis put a premium on prolonged "deep" regression. Those who have moved toward the more modern view that only the ego can be influenced therapeutically (Fenichel,1941), and who therefore tend to stress the analysis of the ego defenses, take a different stand. For them the past must indeed be restored; but pervasive and prolonged regression, though welcome if needed, is not indispensable.

Analytic group psychotherapy, as I see it, adheres to the latter point of view; from that standpoint it may be argued that transference neurosis does take place and may be analyzed in the group situation. All transference behavior *is* drawn into the treatment situation and *is* experienced by the group members as "real and actual" (Freud, 1914). Moreover, the regressive experiences are "deep" both in the sense that they are intense and in the sense that they reach back into every epigenetic level.

However, the experience has unique characteristics in therapy groups. The past is lived out not only with the therapist but with the group members, all of whom are to be included in the treatment situation. Secondly, because reality persists, the periods of regression are relatively discontinuous. For instance, one or more of the members may be deeply involved in repeating the past at any given time, but there are usually others who are not as much involved, who recognize the distortions, and who are not loath to point them out. They also support the group therapist in his translation of the transference behavior into the terms of the past. Thus, intermittent periods of regression and insight into reality occur in more rapid succession than in individual psychoanalysis.

Viewing the movement of the group as a whole, one observes that interconnecting and constantly restructured transference processes are always present and are repeatedly being interpreted, until the major aspects of each member's transferences have been systematically experienced and worked through. In this expanded sense, the qualifications of the transference neurosis and its resolution are met. However, because the experience in the group is not identical with that of individual psychoanalysis, it would be more precise to speak of a group equivalent of transference neurosis.

Both the perplexing theoretical problem of the transference neurosis and the broader question of whether analytic group psychotherapy qualifies as a bona fide form of psychoanalytic method can, in my judgment, be resolved if we regard them in the light of the changes that have taken place in the expanding field of psychoanalysis. The cultural schools have come to view the therapist as more of a real person who also plays a more active rolc in treatment (Ackerman, 1954). Social experience beyond that of the family, such as is offered by the group situation, is being given increasing acknowledgement by the interpersonal schools. These ideas have not been accepted by classical analysis, but they have not been without influence upon it. Group psychotherapy, because of its unavoidable tie with reality, is forced to effect these changes.

But of far greater significance for analytic group psychotherapy has been the development of psychoanalytic ego psychology, which put an entirely new complexion upon the role of the ego in the structure of the personality. From having been considered "a baby riding astride an elephant," the ego has come to be recognized as the synthesizer of human experience. It followed that the ego became the major target of analytic interpretation. Anna Freud (1936), spokesman for psychoanalytic ego psychology, accordingly expanded the definition of transference to include not only the infantile libidinal and aggressive drives but the transference of defense as well. Clearly, one may therefore speak of defensive regression also — for the past is restored indirectly through the defenses as well as directly through the reenactment of the drives upon which they feed but serve to ward off.

These conceptual developments provide theoretical accommodation to the group-determined adaptations of classical analytic method into the framework of psychoanalysis proper. Analytic group psychotherapy thus emerges in principle as a legitimate form of psychoanalytic treatment.

The Effect of Group Therapy on Individual Treatment

Experience with analytic psychotherapy groups has, in general, confirmed for me the tremendous viability of the basic principles of psychoanalysis. Its practice has suggested that certain tactical modifications necessary to the group might be profitably employed in individual treatment as well. This was put to the test in the early experiments with combined group and individual treatment. The indications were positive. For example, neither the therapist's greater exposure of his human frailties nor the piecemeal analysis of the patients' transferences in the group interfered with the development of the transference neurosis in his individual sessions or in its analysis (Sager, 1960; 1964).

Moreover, the less-guarded attitude which had increased the group therapist's spontaneity seemed also to give the individual analyst more leeway for creative therapeutic activity. Since then we have been using these techniques in individual analysis except where contraindicated. It must of course be kept in mind that this somewhat increased freedom does not relieve the therapist from the task of keeping his spontaneity within the bounds of his analytic neutrality. His personal emotions, experiences, and fantasies have no place in either group or individual psychoanalysis. Under the changed conditions, the therapist becomes more acutely aware of his countertransferences and is less likely to avoid or repress them. Nevertheless, he must continue to wrestle with them himself and avoid burdening the patient with them. (Who needs it?) His emergence as a real person concerns only his "way of being." Otherwise, it is reserved for special situations, such as responding in a human way to illness or death in the patient's family or his own. From my own reading of

Freud, Fenichel, Glover, and others, I judge these attitudes to be in the spirit of the original psychoanalytic technique, though not always according to the letter of present-day teaching.

The same less rigid attitude seems to give the patient a better opportunity to develop that "real relationship" with the analyst (Greenson, 1967), which reduces the patient's sense of isolation and brings his analytic sessions into closer connection with his life outside. These are valuable contributions.

There are salutary effects, too, when the therapist applies his now more active approach with his individual patients. He decreases his chances of waiting too long for the patient, who is after all warding them off, to become aware of his infantile wishes on his own. The therapist becomes more acutely attuned to resistance and he is quicker to take the first step in directing the patient's attention to what is going on in their relationship. His habit of paying strict attention to what the patient is "doing with" his communications stands him in good stead. The shift of emphasis toward process from content seems to bring about a closer relationship between insight and change of behavior. Furthermore, increased emphasis on character resistance helps to dig down into the roots of the mental structure and facilitates change in it.

Finally, I believe a good deal of time is saved by avoiding, wherever it is not strictly indicated for a particular patient, long periods of deep regression. For instance, it is no longer necessary for the patient to endure the endless torture of frustration in reliving his infantile libidinal wishes. (This is especially true of preoedipal regression.) Quicker intervention in this process means taking the first step in bringing the patient to an awareness of what is going on in the relationship. (This does not mean throwing the book at the patient in an intellectual fashion.) The increased activity cuts down the time the patient spends wallowing in his suffering. The hidden masochistic gratification, which is frequently veiled by this agony, conveys resistance and should not be mistaken for genuine reenactment. Reliving is of course essential, but it can be misused by the patient and does not in itself make for progress. It is the effective translation of actually experienced infantile feelings into the terms of the past that is the mutative factor in treatment. The sensitive therapist will of course remain flexible enough to permit his patient the degree and duration of regression optimal for him, and he will sedulously avoid the kind of intellectual interpretation which makes for an arid "game of psychiatry."

The Future of Analytic Group Psychotherapy

In my experience, analytic group psychotherapy has proved to be a sound and reasonably effective method of treating neurotic, character problems, and many borderline patients. As our knowledge and experience increase, it should become a progressively effective form of psychotherapy, provided we are not hesitant about adapting its basic principles to the needs of the patient population. Psychoanalytic method is more flexible than has yet been realized.[5]

For the present, analytic group therapy seems to have fallen heir to the current disenchantment with psychoanalysts. The hope that psychoanalysis would be a panacea is gone. Those who unconsciously expected too much of it have been disappointed. Like disappointed children, they became angry with the parent whose human limitations have been discovered. Many of these critics turned away altogether from psychoanalysis and sacrificed its productive concepts and techniques, as well as those that need to be changed or discarded.

There are also more realistic reasons for the disenchantment. Many gaps in our knowledge need to be filled and many hypotheses must still be tested, revised, or rejected. Certainly, these limitations are not insuperable. The fact that psychoanalysis as a body of knowledge is very difficult to learn accounts for some defections. As a method of treatment it demands much from its practitioners, not the least of which is the ability to work in a harmonious balance of emotion and reason, activity and inactivity.

[5] For example, I believe that it can be adapted to hospitalized patients who are not on the whole amenable to classical psychoanalysis. Glatzer and I have both had the opportunity to supervise and consult for such patients and have found that if one begins with groups in which only the relationships among patients and with the therapist are brought into the open and *small* quantities of feeling are expressed until the patients come into close contact with themselves, group patients respond very well. Later, these feelings and their patterns of behavior may be examined and finally their origins may be traced in terms of transference.

Moreover, like most great contributions to the world's thought (Christianity and Marxism are examples), psychoanalysis has become somewhat self-alienated at the very hands of those who sought to perfect it. Some zealous practitioners became so engrossed with the letter of the law that they lost sight of its spirit. They became ever more knowledgeable, but also ever more rigid. Analysis of content became increasingly exact, often at the expense of the all-important human element. The relationship between therapist and patient, within which alone the therapeutic process becomes effective, was neglected. Interpretations tended to become intellectual and mechanical in the hands of such analysts. Yet with others they tend to become loose to the point of meaninglessness. Many of its present critics blame the conceptual system and its method for these shortcomings instead of aiming their disapproval at its *misuses.*

A quotation from Fenichel (1941) may serve to recall the spirit in which psychoanalytic treatment — and, therefore, analytic group therapy — is intended to be undertaken:

> We know from the psychology of compulsion neurosis that there can be a flight from the vividness of the world of instinct into the shadow world of words and concepts. . . . We are familiar, too, with a flight in the opposite direction—away from unpleasant knowledge into the dark twilight of vague intuition alien to intellect. . . . In a therapeutic method based on science, both these types of flight have no place. . . . There are experienced analysts who are subject to the same mistakes. . . . A constant and important task of the analyst is to steer a course between the Scylla of talking instead of experiencing, and the Charybdis of unsystematic free floating that corresponds to the acting out of the patient [pp. 4-6].

Continual reciprocal interaction between emotion and intellect, between insight and experiencing (interaction in a group), is pejorative.

But the discontent with psychoanalysis has also had definite constructive results. New approaches have been suggested and tried out which should be studied with an open but critical mind. It is not necessary to be so devoted to psychoanalysis that we rule out innovations categorically, nor so enthusiastic about innovations that we throw out the proved principle and practices it has provided. There is every reason to try to integrate them into analytic group psychotherapy or to utilize them in combination with it whenever indicated.

Most of the recent innovations have been concerned with breaking away from an intellectual approach and reaching through to more primitive feelings. This is partly due to a tendency to confuse the desirable application of intelligence with the defense of intellectualization. But there is also a *need* to find a way of breaking through very rigid defenses in outpatients. Intensive "workshops," marathons, retreats, and the like have this goal in mind. The same is true of the gestalt techniques for achieving greater inner awareness, especially body awareness. Followers of Wilhelm Reich are attempting the same thing by a combination of body manipulation and analysis.

These methods are effective up to a point. The repressed primitive emotions do break through, but we must point out some caveats. The current fervor for experiencing has an air of mysticism about it that suggests Fenichel's "dark twilight of intuition." The experiences provide excitement and they are invigorating, but unless the emotional "freedom" and insight gained are *worked through* in terms of the patients' infantile conflicts, there can be no lasting effect — no basic change in the mental apparatus. For this reason, patients who have these experiences should participate in analytic groups or individual treatment concurrently in order to work through their learnings. Another caveat: There is a close connection between the new freedom and "acting out," which is often consequent upon intensive group experience. The acting out provides blessed relief from anxiety but it prevents these individuals from working out their infantile conflicts. Therefore the neurotic behavior is in danger of being preserved. A third pitfall lies in the fact that these intense experiences stir in patients the hope of achieving that perfect union for which they have longed (the restoration of primary narcissism) and of having their fantasies of omnipotence come true. It is a false hope; only too often it perpetuates the neuroses, for patients tend to be willing to pay the price of neurotic suffering in the hope of regaining paradise lost. This subtle form of resistance must be analyzed. If these pitfalls are avoided, the innovations provide us with additional ways of reaching those infantile instinctual forces that patients so assiduously ward off.

A quite different modern approach is that of social and community psychiatry, which attempts to bring help into areas that have long been neglected. Hospital patients are now being reached *en masse* as they have never been before. However, before we hurry hospital patients back into the community we first must prepare them with adequate therapy. Group therapy is the keystone, and it is used successfully in an increasing number of hospitals. Once analytic group therapists are willing to adapt their basic principles to the needs of the patients, they should be able to make a significant contribution to this movement.

Similarly, work with the disadvantaged is at last being provided by community psychiatry. Emergency treatment, storefront clinics, attempts to meet reality needs and build ego strength go a long way to relieve their condition. But only too often, emotional needs are not met because the all-important factor of sustained relationships are for one reason or another not offered. Analytic group psychotherapy could bridge the gap if the therapist came out of his protected situation and learned to adapt his method *liberally* to the situation.

The future of analytic group therapy, therefore, is, in my opinion, open for tremendous expansion. Surely it will become progressively effective with that increasing number of middle-class neurotic and character problems who come to us for treatment, and it will help to actualize more fully the creative and leadership potential of this half-forgotten sector. Once the flexibility of the method is recognized, it will contribute substantially to hospital and disadvantaged populations. "I have a dream," too, that if we devoted our attention to applying certain of our techniques with the relatively healthy, we could bring about the improvement in communication that is so much needed in our society. All walks of life cry out for change in this area, from family life to international relations. This could be accomplished through broad-scope programs in the schools and by the simple technique of interpreting only the here and now in interpersonal relationships, avoiding any attempts to trace transferences to their point of origin. Analytic group psychotherapy could become the key for this whole wide range of programs. Hopefully there will always be competing innovations, too; for out of such conflict is progress effected.

REFERENCES

Ackerman, N. (1954), Some structural problems in the relations of psychoanalysis and group psychotherapy. *Internat. J. Group Psychother.*, 4:4-131.

Berne, E. (1960), Psychoanalytic versus dynamic group therapy. *Internat. J. Group Psychother.*, 10:98-103.

Durkin, H. (1964), *The Group in Depth.* New York: International Universities Press.

Ezriel, H. (1950), A psychoanalytic approach to group treatment. *Brit. J. Med. Psychol.*, 23:59-74.

Fenichel, O. (1941), *Problems of Psychoanalytic Technique.* New York: The Psychoanalytic Quarterly.

———(1945), *The Psychoanalytic Theory of Neurosis.* New York: Norton.

Foulkes, S. (1964), *Therapeutic Group Analysis.* New York: International Universities Press, 1965.

Freud, A. (1936), *The Ego and the Mechanisms of Defense.* New York: International Universities Press, rev. ed. 1966.

Freud, S. (1914), Remembering, repeating and working-through (Further recommendations on the technique of psychoanalysis, II). *Standard Edition*, 12:145-156. London: Hogarth Press, 1958.

——— (1921), Group psychology and the analysis of the ego. *Standard Edition*, 18:67-143. London: Hogarth Press, 1955.

Fried, E. (1954), Effect of combined therapy on the productivity of patients. *Internat. J. Group Psychother.*, 4:42-55.

Glatzer, H. (1962), Handling narcissistic problems in group psychotherapy. *Internat. J. Group Psychother.*, 12:438-455.

Greenson, R. (1967), *The Technique and Practice of Psychoanalysis.* New York: International Universities Press.

Kubie, L. (1958), Some theoretical concepts underlying the relationship between individual and group psychotherapies. *Internat. J. Group Psychother.*, 8:3-19.

Rangell, L. (1954), Psychoanalysis and dynamic psychotherapy. *J. Amer. Psychoanal. Assn.*, 2:152-166.

Sager, C. (1960), Concurrent individual and group psychotherapy. *Amer. J. Orthopsychiat.*, 33:225-241.

——— (1964), Interaction and insight in combined therapy. Symposium. *Internat. J. Group Psychother.*, 14:403-412.

Schwartz, E. and Wolf, A. (1962), *The Psychoanalysis of Groups.* New York: Grune & Stratton.

Spanjaard, J. (1959), Transference neurosis and psychoanalytic group psychotherapy. *Internat. J. Group Psychother.*, 9:31-42.

2

Theoretical Foundations of Group Psychotherapy—II

ADOLF FRIEDEMANN

This is an attempt to compare our more than forty years of experience with groups of emotionally disturbed individuals with group experiences among medical and paramedical personnel. These experiences were gained in the training of group psychotherapists, as well as with self-study groups of students and physicians. They were compared with data gleaned in group supervisions by social workers and physicians who themselves are engaged in therapeutic work. We shall not attempt here to set down in detail the specific experiences of a lifetime, which, to a large extent, were recorded by means of shorthand or tape; instead, we shall attempt to condense from these experiences a theoretical basis for group psychotherapy.

Let us first give recognition to those authors in whose works we have found important substantiation of our theories. In first place, quite naturally, is Sigmund Freud, in addition to which our thanks are due especially to the two Balints, Federn, Ferenczi, Anna Freud, Meng, Pfister, Schilder and Zulliger. In the area of actual group therapy, many thoughts similar to ours could be traced in the works of Battegay, Foulkes, Levin, Moreno, Preuss, Slavson, Lattke, Henckley, Hermann, Raoul and Walter Schindler, to name only a few.

Dr. Friedemann is Professor, University of Freibürg; Director, Institut fur Psychohygiene, Biel.

Translated from the German by H.F. Broch de Rothermann.

Development and Definition of a Group

Groups form wherever living beings meet. In the specifically human sense, a group exists wherever people congregate to set themselves off spiritually, emotionally, or physically to form a community or society. Every man, be he conscious of it or not, is a whole entity as an individual and, at the same time, a member of a group. Significantly, the Latin word *communis*, from which our concepts of commune and community derive, refers to a community which originally lived within city walls to protect itself *cum munibus* — by means of these walls.

The psychotherapeutic effectiveness of a group consists in the congregation of several individuals with differing degrees of ego development. Each experiences himself as a whole while sharing to a certain extent the responsibilities and achievements of the group. In the group, the individual becomes part of a new whole whose characteristics are determined by the character traits of all participants. Each ego in the group gives to and takes from all the other participating egos. Thus, there exists in the group a constant interchange of human expressions which range from simple nonverbal and emotional reactions all the way to highly intellectualized verbal exchanges. These interchanges express drives and attitudes which are being integrated within the framework of the group as a result of every ego yielding a part of itself. From this system of interrelationships a group personally emerges — a group ego capable of considerable development if group dynamics are kept in flow.

The Ego

In the philosophical sense the ego is the "essence" in us, that which is capable of thought and is endowed with consciousness, somewhat analagous to Descartes' classical concept of *cogito ergo sum*. In other words, the ego is largely identical with being and existing.

Analytically, my ego differentiates me from all others. Freud taught us that this ego and its drives develop only gradually from the purely instinctual structure of the id. The infant comes into the world as an instinctual being. His ego develops in the third year of his life. Significantly, the human capacity for group interaction is found only when the ego already has assumed relative independence. In any case, the participation of the ego in a group only then becomes effective once an ego consciousness can form within the group. Indeed, ego development allows me to experience with increasing consciousness my own personal qualities and my own capabilities. More and more, "I" am able to avail myself of the possibility to assimilate rationally impressions and experiences, thus empowering the "self" to perform rationally. Contrary to essentially authoritarian group rearing and group pedagogy directed by the superego, an increasing number of attitudes, expressions, and experiences will thus fall under the control of the ego and can thus be confronted with rational consciousness. Within the group, each member assesses the possibilities and the consequences of each ego expression of all the other group members. Thus, it is the group ego that also establishes the rules which become binding for each member.

The ego development within the group, to a large extent, is closely related, therefore, to the discovery, the conscious realization, and the further development of the ego within the individual. While the pedagogic group pursues an educational goal serving the ego formation, the vocational group merely strives for a goal consonant with professional adjustment.

The psychotherapeutic group, however, aims at a level of mental health compatible with the group ideal. The major insights into this ego development are due to Sigmund and Anna Freud, as well as to Federn; and these insights are as valid for the ego of the group as for that of the individual. Corresponding to the original concept of the development of the ego aspirations, the ego, together with a whole series of instinctual drives, is governed by this instinct for self-preservation, while the actual fulfillment of these drives is then largely impelled by corollary drives that eventually organize themselves to form the sexual behavior pattern of the individual. According to Freud, the ego on every level and at all times strives to "fit into and adapt itself in concordance with the original sexual behaviour pattern," and he states further that a break in this close concordance between ego and libido in the various phases of their development "may well evolve into a pathogenic factor." This important relationship between the libido theory and the theory of narcissism, as developed foremost by Ferenczi, cannot be discussed here more fully. It is significant, however, that the defense mechanisms, as compiled in particular by Anna Freud, are evident as such within the group; in the interactions of its members, any trained analyst can detect readily the appearance and the working through of these basic types of defense mechanisms: inhibition, regression, reaction formation, undoing, projection, introjection, autoaggression, reversal, and, finally, sublimation or displacement of instinctual goals.

The Experience of Ego Boundaries

The understanding of the development of the group-ego has been helped significantly by the theory of ego psychology evolved by Federn, according to which the development of the ego parallels the ego's own awakening in the dream, a development which Federn terms "orthriogenesis" — "orthria" meaning dawn and morning, in other words, the dawning of the day. Thus, orthriogenesis means for Federn the rapid, daily reiterated ego awakening from deep sleep to the dreaming state and from that preconscious twilight phase to full consciousness, therein allowing the awakening person to reexperience each day all of the stages of his ego development until he reaches complete conscious wakefulness. The dream ego, then, is only partially awake and the ego boundary corresponds to the respective dream boundary. Therefore, what we experience in our dreams is "the ego between yesterday and today," awakening in that phase only to the consciousness level of "an early stage in our life": in our dreams we regain our childhood. According to Federn, the ego *is* "the constant or continuously restored psychic continuity of body and psyche in relation to space, time, and causality."

Phenomenologically speaking, the ego is *being* preserved by the individual, both sensorially and rationally, as an entity since it is felt as a constant and continuously reiterated relation of the physical and psychic experience in terms of space, time, and causality.

In metapsychological terms the ego *rests* on the simultaneous and interrelated psychic cathexis of functions and contents which, physically and psychically, are continuously interdependent upon each other.

Therein, the ego is both the carrier of consciousness (myself) and the object of that same consciousness (as in the above-quoted *cogito ergo sum*). Moreover, there are patent connections to the preconscious state in the degree of cathexis which actually forms the ego, since the ego only gains actuality in so far as the functions and contents proper to the ego are fully cathected. The actual ego becomes conscious upon awakening, while "the balance of the ego is made available for the coordinated functioning, it is being precathected in its self-like capacity."

If we now consider the development of a group, we may well speak, within the meaning postulated by Federn, of an "orthriogenesis" of the group ego, for in the formation of groups one can recognize readily all kinds of symbol transferences and more or less censored expressions, exactly like those that are familiar from the work done on dreams and their interpretations. In its relation with the outside world, the group, provided it is in sound functioning order, behaves exactly like the individual ego, in elaboration. To quote Federn (1956):

> The extent of cathexis constituting the ego is of a changing nature; its specific boundary is the ego-boundary and as such it is being consciously perceived. When an ego-boundary is felt as strongly libidinal (that is, infused with the instinctual drives of love and hate) and is not being perceived intellectually in its contents, a feeling of ecstasy ensues while, inversely, this experience becomes alienated if the boundary is only recognized intellectually but not felt.
>
> We differentiate subjectively between a physical and an emotional ego-experience and, consequently, we also differentiate between emotional and physical ego-boundaries. Whatever confronts an emotional and physical ego-boundary

from outside is endowed with full reality. This reality is empirically self-evident and, as such, not subject to further critical reassessment. A corroboration of this reality only becomes possible because new ego-boundaries have been formed empirically which are then no longer affected by the same outside impressions. However, in both psychosis and in the dream, the later acquired ego-boundaries have either lost or have not been reinvested with their original cathexis. As a result, the reality corroboration either becomes defective or is totally lacking. Whatever confronts from the outside an ego-boundary that in only emotional, is endowed with emotional reality (revelation). Whatever confronts only a physical or an emotional ego-boundary is felt as fear-inspiring if, instead and on the strength of past experience, the simultaneous confrontation with several ego-boundaries was to be expected.

If libidinally cathected ego-boundaries are confronted not by objects but, instead, by other libidinally cathected ego-boundaries, affect reactions either result or are being triggered which, in their quality, are being determied by the nature of the libidinal cathexis of these causal ego-boundaries.

The normal person experiences considerable difficulty in becoming aware of the ego boundaries. He requires special training under appropriate guidance and a concentrated effort at self-control, or — to use Federn's term — an effort to achieve "an introspection into the egotized data." This means nothing less than to record one's own experiences when falling asleep, when under the impact of emotional stress, or, quite generally, when on the threshhold of consciousness, in contrast to the sphere of the nonego and also in contrast to the extraspection of the outside world. It is quite conceivable that in exactly the same manner the group ego not only may be taught by extraspection to perceive rationally the outside reality but could, by suitable guidance in introspection, also be brought to the realization of its inner psychic workings and of the boundaries circumscribing its own group ego.

Cathexis

Another problem raised by the expansion of the ego-boundaries may be described as being epitomized generally by the phenomenon, discovered by Federn, of the so-called ego-cathexis (*cathekein:* get to or reach a certain place), i.e., the specific channeling of the object libido within the sphere of the ego. It is here that the anxiety experience as well as the attempt at overcoming this anxiety manifest themselves most clearly, both in individual analysis and in group therapy, primarily through the awakening to the "I am" of the conscious perception "I feel anxiety" — a process in which, at first and within the group, the real fear of group treason is being camouflaged. This instinctual anxiety remains active as a floating, nondirected anxiety for as long as the group has not been channeled towards a common task and a unifying goal.

As is well known, group anxiety can manifest itself in diverse ways. If the group is left to its own devices and is disappointed in its natural expectation that the group leader is to set it a unifying task, this anxiety is expressed in projections of the inner dissatisfaction directed at the outside world, most frequently at the group leader himself, who will have to bear the brunt of more-or-less overtly aggressive manifestations by the group. According to the degree of overriding censorship, such aggressions take on more or less humorous, playful, ironical, or outraged forms. The group leader, seen as the group father, is expected to assume archfather functions; but were he to do so, he would merely "infantilize" the group.

In the interplay of normal society, the meeting of free groups has developed conventions through which anxiety defenses can manifest themselves in inconsequential conversational gambits, designed to elicit information from the partners, which later may be used in competitive confrontations. This can place the unwary or the overly trusting individual in unpleasant situations: for even at the inception of group formation the stage is set for a confrontation which, according to the personality of the participants and depending on the group atmosphere, repeats episodes of friendly or hostile encounters that had already been collected in such earlier experiences. Thus, group confrontations even in their earlier stages mirror experiences which allow us, precisely as in individual analysis, to recognize time and again the incisive role of the family background and the development of the ego in its "cathectic" meaning and in its various transformations — a fact clearly seen and enunciated by Freud himself.

These confrontations, these "power struggles," may manifest themselves as lust for power, as jealousy, and as a compulsion to subjugate others; or, in their more refined and socially more acceptable forms, they may be expressed as competitive spirit, as ambition, or finally — once insights have been gained into the underlying meaning of these confrontations — as acceptance of the group structure, as self-discipline, and as the voluntary shouldering of responsibilities which can help the group as a whole in its process of maturation. Within the framework of the group, these confrontations are always dominated by the instinctual drives, such as the search for love, for comfort, and for security — drives that must come to terms with the superego of the group and, beyond that, with the egocentric tendencies of the group ego. A conventional frame is being provided for the association and the togetherness of individuals who do not "know" each other as yet. Each participant has a need to achieve "contact" with other human beings, to get to know them. Likewise, each has learned from his own experience that these others will not be willing readily to subordinate their own claims to those of others in the group. The experience is the same as that of the infant when it realizes the unfulfillability of its excessive desires — an experience that is repeated in the early life of every person through the failure of infantile attempts, within the respective family, at gaining satisfaction for expectations that simply exceed the reality potential.

All such claims are bound to elicit from the outside world antagonistic reactions of various degrees of severity, from the merely partial and inadequate satisfaction of such instinctual claims to their total denial and, finally, to the confrontation of even stronger counterclaims which lead ultimately to outright aggressions.

Thus, each participant in the group has at his command a store of earlier experiences that are more than sufficient grounds for his initial vacillation between a desire for contact and anticipatory fear. This unique experience of initial anxiety creates within the emerging group — very much as in the awakening from sleep — a strange twilight condition in which the group-ego very gradually takes shape. This condition also reveals itself clearly when group communications between participants have "fallen asleep" for some time and are then reactivated in their subsequent meetings, thus affording a convincing example of the actuality of Federn's orthriogenesis. In fact, Federn's ego psychology provides a theoretical elucidation not only of the ego function in the individual but, at the same time, of the development of the group's ego and consciousness.

On the basis of these thoughts, we also may gain an insight into the phenomenon which Freud, in individual analysis, has termed "the meeting within the subconscious," a phenomenon which, in group therapy, is expressed in the remarkable fact that problems are brought to the surface without having been mentioned by those persons who are most intimately affected by them.

The Interdependence within the Group

At an early stage of the formation of the group, a mutual and reciprocal interdependence between all the group members, both as a whole and individually, is established on all levels of interpersonal relationships. This interdependence is even stronger if the group leader refrains from assuming the leadership functions urged upon him by the participants and instead confines himself to the role of expert adviser, a role to be described more fully later. In this manner, a definite interaction of budding relationships comes to play within the group all of which find their meeting point unmistakably in the subconscious. Moreno calls this phenomenon a "tele," a concept which he termed, in analogy to empathy, a "dy-empathy" (*Einfühlung* ↔ *Zei-fühlung*). The various egos of the participants meet within the group in their emotions and their urges. It is within this network that the ego can enter the contestations and can achieve the conscious control of the individual's potential and the working through of its instinctual drives. The instinctuality of the group as a whole is to be worked through in the course of the group therapy in exactly the same way and to the same extent as the instinctuality of each of the group members, for Freud's postulate that the id is to be transformed into the ego indeed holds true just as much for the group as for its individual members.

It is within this meaning that the formation of relationships with the byproducts of transference, countertransference, and resistance is experienced within the group. The acquisition of conscious perception leads to catharsis, to the cleansing and elimination of affect impulses, to control by means of reality testing of the whole world of living and dead things, the control of all objects, in the widest sense, with which man has to deal consciously. This recognition fosters the growth of self-awareness — the realization of our true potential and of our actionable fulfillment. Possibilities are thereby discovered of how to work together towards common goals and, thus, to assist each other, helping each other in the perception of the object world and, by the same token, in the reality testing through which a constant check of the ego development becomes possible.

Sociogram and Actogram. It is held that the experienced group leader recognizes all these interconnections without difficulty. Nevertheless, it is advisable to check on the progress of the group functionings by means of control devices. To this end, the tape recorder could be considered ideal if it did not require human mediation and thus did not also become subject to human frailties, such as errors in understanding and in typing. Nor does the tape recorder have eyes with which to record visually events that may well be of crucial importance. Because of these detriments, we have formed the habit of recording the events taking place within the group, wherever possible, by means of "actograms" and "sociograms."

The actogram records in intervals of five minutes (or more frequently, if so desired) the manner in which the various participants in a group react to each other and what subgroups are being formed. The sociogram records the sequence of the group conversations, which is subsequently supplemented by the use of a tape recorder and appropriate transcripts.

For these recordings we have devised a simple graphic coding system. At the beginning of the group session, we establish a numbered seating list, for example:

1. White; 2. Bloom; 3. Smith; etc., which means that 1 sits next to 2, 2 next to 3, etc. Since by preference we seat our participants in a circle, even a spontaneous selection of seats results not only in neighbors but also in persons facing each other across the circle. If at all possible, we wait until one of the participants speaks up. The tape recorder then records the voices and all the background noises while we merely note the sequence of the speakers: 1, 3, 9, 2, 9, 2, 9, 4. 1 starts the conversation, 3 replies to 1, 9 continues the conversation, and so on, and the tape later reveals what is being said by each one. Moreover, we encode the attitudes of the participants according to the following categories: proposals; opinions; assent; disagreement; messages; instructions; friendly approach; hostile approach; neutral approach; ambivalent approach; tension; detente; distraction; solidarity; aggressivity; question, skepticism, doubt.

These symbols are necessary since communication often takes place without verbalization and merely by attitude, gestures and facial expressions. Verbal communications can be recorded by noting key words and, in addition, are recorded on tape.

Even when dealing with highly active or play acting groups, or with psychodramas, actograms recorded at intervals of five minutes are usually quite satisfactory.

Technique and Practical Examples[1]. In the technique of group psychotherapy it is always useful to use two or three assistants, of which one or two can serve as "auxiliary participants" who are to remain silent at the beginning of the sessions but are sufficiently in harmony with the group so as to be able, if necessary, to act as "auxiliary egos." In addition, each group should have a non-participating recording secretary. Indeed, the scrutiny and analysis of the recordings of the group sessions over a period of weeks and months will show very clearly the development of the individual group members. It also will allow for the determination of prognoses and will yield important therapeutic clues.

[1] Abstracted from Friedemann (1959).

Following a suggestion of Moreno, we establish an actogram as a graphic representation of the actions taking place during a given group therapy. This actogram facilitates the sociographic and dynamic control of the group and also shows up all radically disturbing influences. The three actograms reproduced here as examples illustrate three stages in the development of a group of difficult, institutionalized adolescents engaged in psychodrama (Figures 1, 2, 3). These show how the participants react to each other in space motility at intervals of five minutes. Ludwig shows up as a withdrawn member within the group; he is underendowed but physically relatively well developed. He is sensitive but shields himself well. Thus, he selects instinctively for himself roles in the psychodrama that are dehumanized or inanimate — ones confined to uncomplicated actions and not calling for subtle verbalizations or sophisticated acting, such as the roles of dog, horse, ship, or water.

In the first actogram we can see that the whole group is relatively well integrated and engaged in harmonious interplay. Ludwig markedly holds back but nevertheless participates in the group activities. In the second actogram he has relinquished all his reserve and is very active within the group while, in the third actogram, he suddenly withdraws completely. What has happened? Ludwig meanwhile had been granted two weeks home leave with his parents, who, dazzled by the good emotional development of their boy, had tried — without our knowledge — to enroll poor Ludwig, during that time and on a trial basis, in a school of higher learning. There, the boy found himself suddenly in competition with boys of his own age who, however, were intellectually much better endowed than he, and where he soon became the scapegoat of the class, a typical situation of poorly endowed children who find themselves in normal school situations. Ludwig remained in the role of the scapegoat even in the following group sessions, where he became the wallflower; and it took him some time to reintegrate himself into the group in which, previously, he had already felt quite at home.

This case illustrates not only the value of the actogram but also the responsibility incumbent on the group psychotherapist who has to

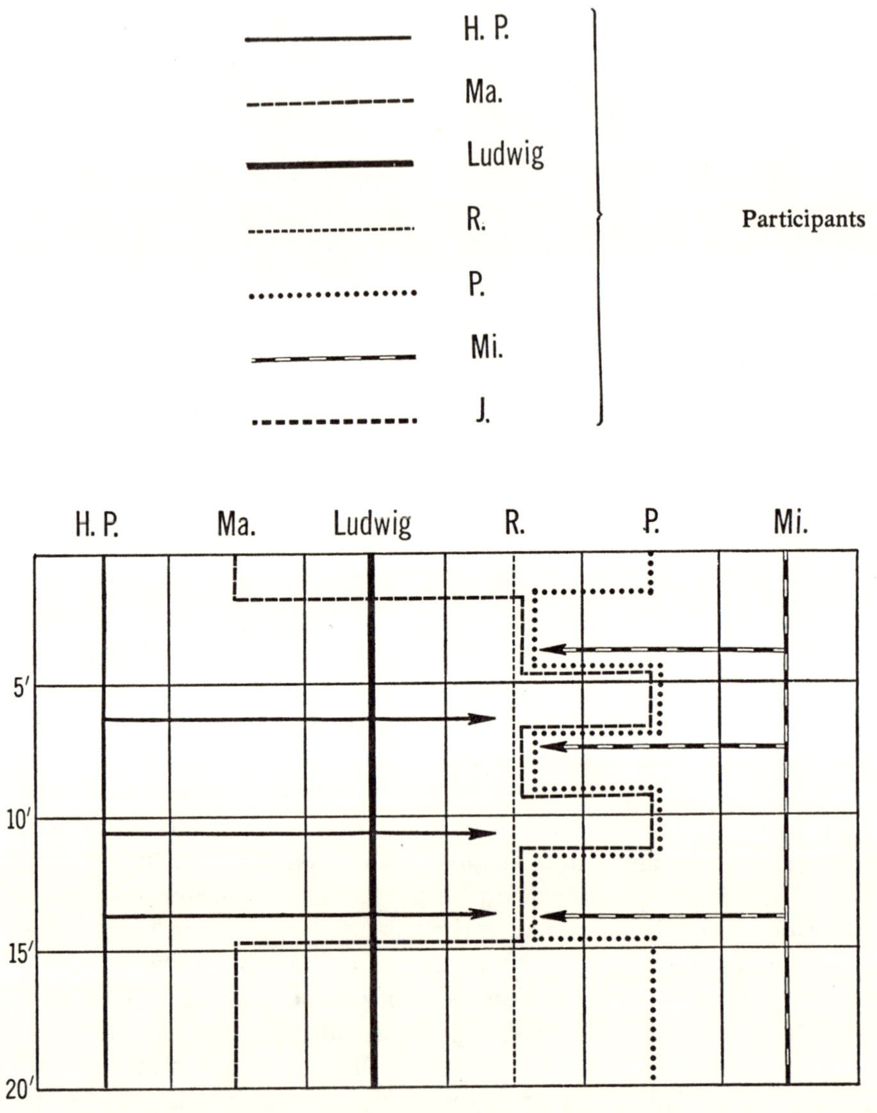

Figure 1. Ludwig stays quietly in his seat but communications, both visual and verbal, are established with Mi. and H.P.

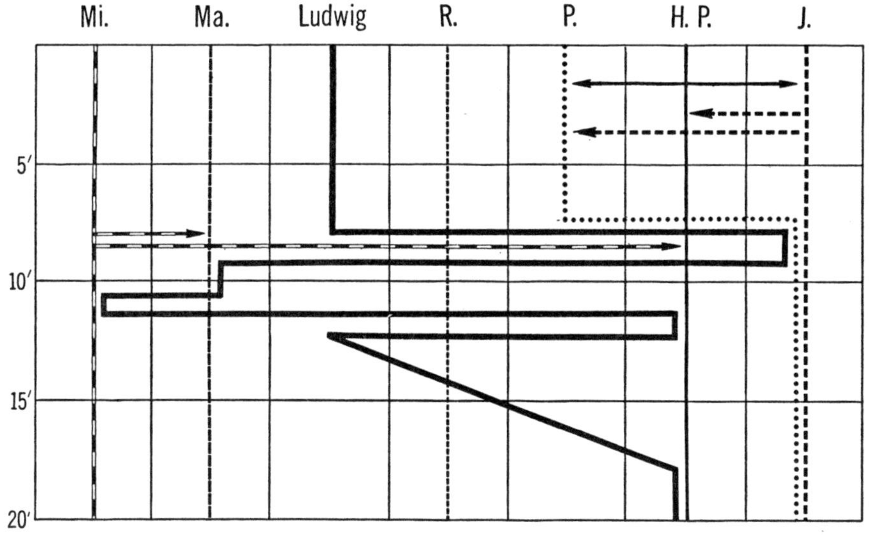

Figure 2. Ludwig actively participates in the group psychodrama, runs from one to the other and engages in animated exchanges with all the other participants in the group.

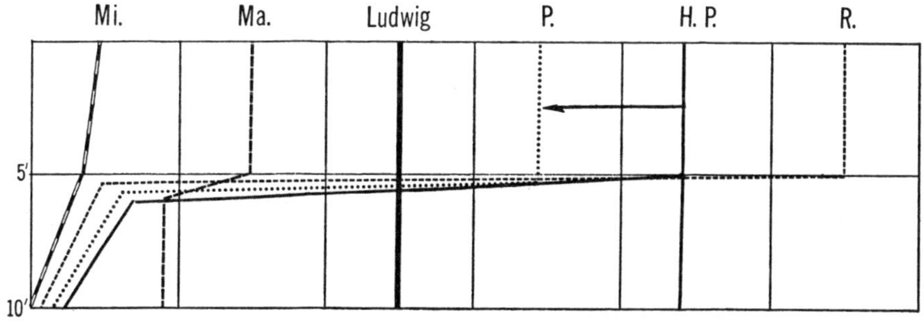

Figure 3. Mi. has now become the key figure in the group. His leading role was already suggested in Fig. 1. Ludwig remains presently completely passive. With the exception of a single verbal approach towards H.P. at the beginning of the session, he stays outside the group.

be familiar with the special case of each participant, must be able to follow their day-by-day development, and needs to grasp fully their individual traits so as to recognize when a patient has to be switched from group treatment to individual therapy and what specific form of therapy is then best indicated. As we have already stressed, group psychotherapy, as a matter of basic principle, never must exclude the possibility of individual treatment and, conversely, there is no reason why one should not consider an individual patient for inclusion in a therapy group. In this way it will be possible to reach true psychic depths even in group work, always provided that the therapist is not only qualified to engage in individual therapy but also has sufficient time to do so.

Any clinical treatment, by its very nature, has as its ultimate goal the cure and the release of the patient. In group therapy, this leads to certain bonds and transferences which call for a number of different solutions in accordance with the nature of the institution. Generally speaking, we always try to assemble our group patients from a single ward, sincc this facilitates the manipulation of the "visitors' group." There are some, however, who prefer to select their group participants from various departments; in this respect, it will always be best to follow local usage.

Where the changeover is sufficiently great, those patients ready to be released can be removed all the more easily from the initial therapy group.

With chronic cases, it was found advisable to transfer patients occasionally from their original therapy group to a new mixed group composed of clinical and policlinical patients and supervised, until the dissolution of the group, by a physician familiar with the cases in the respective wards but not exclusively assigned to them.

The best follow-up results were obtained with patients who could be regarded as socially readjusted and who were able to dissociate themselves completely from the clinical community.

If policlinical or social supervision was still required, it was found preferable to form a new group exclusively composed of outpatients, an indication confirmed especially by the experiences made with groups of alcoholics, such as those maintained by welfare organizations for alcoholics and by Alcoholics Anonymous.

We have also had some experiences in dividing individual and group therapies among several therapists, but such a working method is only feasible if the therapists themselves function well as a group in which perfectly equitable human and professional relations are safeguarded and in which expressions of aggressivity, touchiness, neurotic complexes, narcissistic urges, and professional jealousy are under control.

Last but not least, the therapist must be able at all times to control analytically not only the actogram but also the sociogram of the group. Thus, the actogram alone may often reveal to the experienced therapist the moment when it may become advisable to shift within the group the key figure, the performer, the wallflower, with their respective counterparts, their followers, or their acolytes.

Often the need arises in a therapy group to dissolve certain pathological attitudes that have become "patterned" and fossilized. It then becomes the task of the group leader to guide the group situation so that the individual participant may realize his own psychic plasticity to the full extent of his potential and may thus mature into a truly responsible, reality-adapted personality.

The answer to the question as to how a therapeutic group is to be selected in a clinic and how often such a group is to meet, depends on various circumstances. As we have stressed repeatedly, every ward visit should be structured so as to be fruitful from the viewpoint of group psychotherapy. This does not require, according to our own experience, that all these visits be extended over long periods of time, but it is nevertheless important that the therapist be able to devote approximately one half-hour each morning and each afternoon to a group numbering fifteen to twenty patients. Special groups are to be formed according to needs and possibilities. Thus, in the days of insulin treatment, we used to spend the whole morning assisting during the entire length of the insulin therapy — to the extent that this was feasible — in actual cooperation with the patients and nurses. Indeed, the presence of the physician imparts to the insulin group a very special feeling of comfort and security, which results in an analytically highly profitable situation and one in which the therapist is actually about to share with the patient the regressive periods before and after the insulin coma, as well as the death experience of the coma itself. Thus, he comes to represent for the patient a true protector, the comforting mother, as well as a father image.

So that the full benefits of this particular situation may be reaped, the insulin treatment physician optimally should be the therapist. In connection with the group therapy, very significant insights can thus be gained during the patient's sinking into the insulin coma and during his reawakening, which later, in individual analysis, provide a sound basis for the working through of the patient's anxieties and, more particularly, of his isolation in the coma experience. Together with Mumbert, we reported on these findings in 1957.

The detailed scrutiny of our therapeutic records allows us not only to classify the various attitudes according to their contents and their sequence but, in addition, has given us important indices for the elucidation of group dynamics, and it is specifically these that shall now be discussed.

The confrontations of the various individuals with and within the group are as manifold in their nature as the manifestations of human life itself. Nevertheless, a basic underlying principle can be found in this diversity which may now be schematized in the form of a quadrangle illustrating the parallelogram of forces active within a group. Several group theorists, Teirich and principally Schindler among others, have followed therein the findings established in animal psychology: they postulate the alpha-type as the dominant group member to which all the other types, down to the omega-type as the lowest one, are subordinated. But man has at his disposal physical and psychic means of adaptation that are not available to other living organisms. This is not only demonstrated biologically by the fact that man manages to survive in all the zones of the earth, from the poles to the equator; and that he has been able to adapt to such radically different environments as air and water, the depths of the earth, the heights of the atmosphere and even deep space; it is demonstrated also and foremost by the elasticity of his psychic structure, which is adaptable to the most diverse living conditions and the most variegated social requirements.

THE FAMILY AS ARCHGROUP

In establishing our theoretical foundation, we shall seek our basis in the archgroup formed between the mother and the human offspring. Let us formulate the underlying principle in the terms of a slogan: In the beginning, was aggression.

In doing so we need be mindful, however, of the fact that originally aggression is not necessarily synonymous with hostility; essentially, it merely means an approach, a meeting and a getting together. It is only the nature in which this meeting is then resolved by individuals which determines whether it culminates either in the most intense union, a union resulting in new life and companionship, or in destruction, hostility, and hatred. This realization was espoused five centuries before Christ by Empedocles when he postulated that love and hatred are the basic forces of life, a formulation that was taken up by Freud himself in his later years when he identified the two basic and opposing drives in man as the wish to survival and the death wish, the *philia* and the *neikos,* both forevermore locked in destructive struggle.

Biologically speaking, all life is generated by this aggression. It is the aggressiveness of the sperm cell inseminating the egg cell. And it is this inseminated egg cell which, in union with the body of the mother, fashions the new life of the offspring. Therefore, the fundamental significance of the group lies indeed in the creation of this duality, the confrontation in the dyad of that which is being formed with that which exists already. Something new is gaining shape in something that already has shape. The more that which is being shaped achieves individual form, the more it conflicts with that which already has its own form. Thus, the first confrontation in human life takes place between the mother, the already fully formed being, and the child whose form is only beginning to emerge. Birth then brings about the natural solution and dissolution of this confrontation, but the psychic unity between the two remains for the time being in the dyad. The child, at that moment, begins to experience the outside world, hence the group of which the mother is part; but it experiences it only through the mother. Gradually the mother herself becomes part of the outside world, a part of the group surrounding the child who then becomes increasingly independent in its being. A system of interrelations develops which, though more or less stable, cannot remain static. A static condition would not correspond to life, for life means development, which means change. Development is always dynamic and therefore involves the interplay of opposing forces. Within the archgroup of mother and child, this interplay of forces finds its expression in the confrontations imposed by the growth, the development and the adaptation process of the child to the outside world. In this confrontation the mother initially is always aware, without consciously knowing it, of the various needs of her infantile group partner. Within the maternal womb these needs are regulated and satisfied "hormonally." There exists a regulatory balance between the growth and development potential of the embryo and the growth and development needs for which the embryo requires fulfillment from the maternal organism. The more the infantile organism gains in independence and individuality, the stronger will be his claims for the fulfillment of his needs while, at the same time, the ability of the maternal organism to fulfill these will decrease proportionally. There then ensues the ejection of the offspring, the birth of a being which, while helpless at first, is nevertheless endowed with the full life potential of an individual. The dependence of this independent being is still, for the time being, unconsciously taken into full account by the maternal partner. The instinctual group relations continue to function. The child has needs, which are satisfied by the mother as the key figure. The awareness and the fulfillment of these infantile needs by the mother even goes so far that, during that period, the mother largely renounces any contact with other group members in the society in which she lives.

But as the independence of the offspring increases, these infantile needs upon the key person soon begin to exceed the ability of the mother to fulfill them. Increasingly, the mother is compelled to satisfy also the societal claims of her environment (such as those of husband, older siblings, or possibly even new offspring). Insofar as the child can resolve these denial experiences, these will lead it to assert its independence and to establish additional group relations.

The natural group in which mother and child find themselves is the family. As we already know, the development of the family brings about typical group confrontations. The father has to relegate his own claims on the key figure of the mother when a new being takes shape within the maternal organism. The dyad of the young couple is being expanded into a triad and a significant part of the mother is being denied to the father. How the relations between the spouses adapt to these new circumstances will depend largely on the nature of the relationship established between the parental partners. Quite often the paternal counterpart is unable to resolve adequately the disappointment felt at no longer being alone in his claims on the partner in view of the burgeoning new life. The partner has become the key person for the expected child; the ability to fulfill the claims of the husband to the extent that this was possible as long as the mother's womb did not harbor a new being, substantially decreases. This frequently arouses jealous impulses which in the dethroned key partner — the father, who thus has turned into an antagonist — may readily evoke experiences that he himself suffered as a frustrated child or sibling. In other words, reactions are triggered which can deteriorate into hostile feelings and may, in time, impair the matrimonial harmony and, lastly, the very fiber of the family. If, however, both partners are conscious of their common goal, it then becomes possible for both to act as may be expected in a truly mature marriage relationship: both strive to the extent of their own potential to achieve the optimal well-being of the growing family and again join at those points where they can complement each other without detracting through jealous impulses from the harmony of the triad.

When the family is further enlarged — always conforming to the schematic analogy originally suggested — a situation develops in which, at any given moment, the oldest child is displaced by the later born from the focus of immediate attention of the mother. If the paternal partner, at this point, is not capable of asserting his group role as a harmonizing factor, the older children risk being dislodged from their places in the family core and of being relegated, instead, to the role of passive supernumeraries. Seemingly, they no longer voice any claims of their own and assume within the tetrad the role of wallflowers, like those perenially rejected girls who are never asked to dance at a party. Their bonds with the original group become untied, they begin to float, and, if insufficient claims are made upon them by their counterparts in the group, they seek out other partners.

This loosening of original ties, in its psychohygienic consequences, embodies a decisive opportunity for the determination of one's own life. For if we were anchored within the family as immovable parts and counterparts, the very survival of the family would become endangered through fossilization. As psychotherapists we are all too familiar with those severe interpersonal difficulties, at times leading to total unfitness for matrimonial relations on the part of the patients, which occur when the ties to parents and siblings have hardened into an insoluble union in which two partners in a family group become entwined so inextricably that they are no longer receptive to any additional emotional claim. As every expert knows from experience, patients afflicted by such interlocked involvements frequently disrupt the homogeneity of a group and its therapeutic potential — a threat which, if not recognized and checked in due time by the therapist, may well place into jeopardy thc continued functioning of the group.

We have started out with the family as the archgroup. But we discern in the development of this archgroup a dynamic pattern which is repeated in the formation of all human groups. In this pattern, schematically shown below, K represents the key personality.

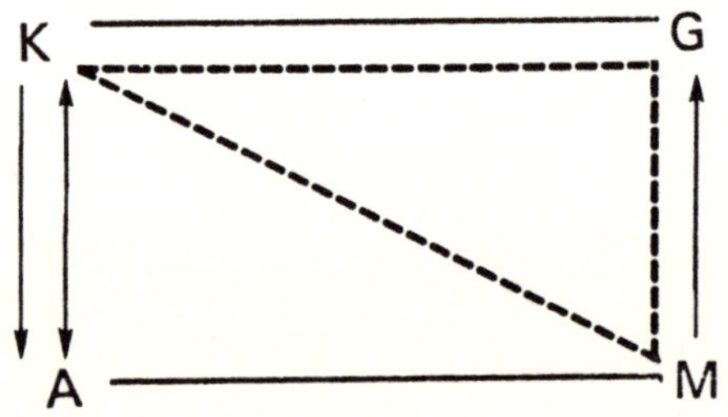

This key personality — who is not in all cases necessarily identical with the mother — collects around it a group of dependents (D). This key personality is unable to fulfill all the claims formulated by these dependents, an inability that leads to frustrations. A number of dependents thus are relegated to the background of the group as mere followers (F). In their disappointment, they either directly approach the counterpart (C), of the key personality (K), who may be able to satisfy their claims more fully, or seek participation sooner or later in other groups. While the emotional potentials of these followers thus become free to combine, if the opportunity arises — either anew with the key personality or with its counterpart, or even with both — they dispose also of the additional alternative of entering new group formations. The opportunities afforded within the potential of this group pattern is of fateful importance to the individual group members: if the key personality is able to establish with its counterpart a fully integrated group relation, the life principle, that is the *eros,* the *philia,* will succeed in holding the group together. The dependents are given the opportunity to fulfill their unsatisfied claims with the counterpart. Inversely, the counterpart is able to liberate those group members who no longer are in need of the group, or he can attend more specifically to those members, who, reduced to the role of wallflowers, no longer dare voice their claims. Key personality and counterpart therein find an opportunity not only to take a helping hand themselves in the development of the group but also to call upon experts, both from within or from outside the group.

What counts in the selection of the expert is his intimate knowledge and his controlled understanding of the prevailing group situations. Therefore, the leader of the psychotherapeutic group not only must be well familiar with the dynamics and the background of the group but also should have achieved full realization of his own self. The same standards apply in this respect as those governing the work qualifications of the psychoanalyst.

For each and every human being it is generally true that group development and group guidance are all the more successful the better the expert is qualified and the more efficient he is in fulfilling his role as group leader. He requires insight, self-discipline, knowledge, and the ability to resolve the phenomena of transference and countertransference, as well as those of the various defense mechanisms. But the superior therapist, in addition, will discharge his functions in the manner recommended to the good analyst by

Meng, namely, with that delicacy which any truly humane relationship requires, with the understanding empathy without which no true human contact is possible, and by always safeguarding that distance which is dictated by the respect for the fellow human being and his personal life history. If we add to this the conscious realization of being, all of us, subject — in the words of Freud — to the constant reiteration of life and death, then the resulting improvement within the group dynamics, in the control of libido and destrudo, of *philia* and *neikos,* of the ups and downs of psychic tides, will surely allow also for a better development of the group.

REFERENCES

Federn, P. (1956), *Ich-Psychologie und die Psychosen.* Bern Stuttgart: Hans Huber.

Friedemann, A. (1959), Gruppenpsychiatrie. In: *Handbuch der Neurosenlehre,* ed. von Frankl, V. Gabsattel, and J. H. Schultz. Munich and Berlin: Verlag Urban & Schwarzenberg, pp. 357-360.

3

Types of Group Psychotherapy and Their Clinical Applications

S. R. SLAVSON

Both theory and practice support the principle that the effectiveness of psychotherapy is conditioned by its suitability to the nosological considerations and to the specific etiological and psychodynamic factors presented by the particular patient. Blanket use of any technique with patients for whom it may not be suitable can only result in failure to them and frustration to the therapist. To illustrate this principle we can classify patients into the three major generic categories — psychoneuroses, character disorders, and psychoses (which can be viewed as a special genre of character or ego disorder). Each requires its own type of therapy.

In his experience, the author has found that in cases of full-blown classical psychoneuroses — where the transference neurosis generated in psychoanalytic treatment is the central armamentarium — are not accessible by groups. Due to the divided or multitransferential phenomenon, only a limited degree of libidinal transference toward the therapist can be achieved in a group, not sufficient to unravel or dissolve the virulent oedipal and incestuous strivings with which such patients come for treatment. In addition, the very dynamics of group interaction militates against it. The therapist's

S. R. Slavson is President Emeritus, American Group Psychotherapy Association; Faculty Member, New York University and Yeshiva University, New York City.

This chapter is adapted from the author's book, *Child-centered Group Guidance of Parents,* New York: International Universities Press, 1958.

unavoidable divided attention and the interruptions of the communications by fellow group members prevent regressive catharsis in any one of them. This blocks the dissolution of the psychoneurotic syndrome. Further, in the process of treatment of a true psychoneurosis, the transferential target (the therapist) must feed the regression by remaining passive and almost nonresponsive. This cannot occur in groups, for even if the therapist does play out this role suitably, other patients and at times the group as a whole react to the communicant. When this occurs, catharsis and regression are interrupted, hindering further the regressive process and frustrating the patient.

All the types of psychotherapies, reports on which appear in this section, are fundamentally based on the foundations of Freudian psychology (not his technique). We accept Freud's formulations of the unconscious, infantile sexuality, the oedipal phenomena, his topological formulations of the id, ego, and superego. But because the type of patient we currently encounter in modern society, especially in the United States with its changed character due to the altered roles of the father and mother and its culture of greater permissiveness to instinctual realization, we were constrained to alter therapeutic procedures. Otherwise, we would have found ourselves ineffective.

The original project in intensive treatment in small groups in what came to be known as "group therapy" and later "group psychotherapy," was initiated in 1934 by the present writer at the Jewish Board of Guardians, a leading community child-guidance clinic. Initially this work was begun with girls and boys in latency years with primary behavior disorders. This modest project soon spread to include patients of all ages and clinical categories. In the more than thirty-six years that followed, we have initiated and tested a number of variations of the original idea with more than 4,000 patients. The need for these variations was pressed upon us by our pragmatic discovery that some patients did not respond to the original technique (activity group therapy). We have, therefore, modified settings and practices, some of which had to be discarded, while others proved effective with *specific* types of patients. These tests and studies have resulted in a number of specific methods that take into account the age of patients, clinical considerations, and the "depth" of the treatment most suitable for each patient.

The list of the *group treatment* techniques evolved are:

For adults and adolescents — counseling, guidance, analytic psychotherapy, para-analytic psychotherapy, psychonursing, child-centered group guidance of parents, coordinated "family therapy," and vita-erg therapy (for hospitalized psychotic patients).

For children — activity group therapy, activity-interview therapy, play therapy, and transitional groups.

Before we describe these various types of group psychotherapy to meet individual needs of patients for age, sex, life-roles, and clinical entities, we must point up the differentials in psychotherapeutic armamentaria employed in contemporary practice.

In order to differentiate the "depth" of the therapeutic effort as indicated by a specific patient's needs, we need to outline three distinct levels commonly used exclusively or at times contemporaneously as the flow of therapeutic content indicates. These three levels we have labeled as *counseling, guidance,* and *psychotherapy.*

Counseling and Guidance

The terms "counseling" and "guidance" are applied to individual or group experiences where the presenting difficulties are those of social adjustment; their solution, therefore, lies in cognitive areas and purposeful effort, as differentiated from intrapsychic problems and conflicts requiring basic resolution and personality reconstruction. In the former only superficial layers of the personality are involved and situational stresses with which an individual may not be able to cope by himself form the focus of attention. In these practices, one deals with people with difficulties who cannot (or need not) work toward radical inner change. Frequently such work is erroneously referred to as psychotherapy, when it is really guidance or counseling.

Counseling. A counsellor may or may not be a trained psychotherapist. He helps the counselee either to arrive at or to accept a solution of the difficulty that worries him. This can be achieved by explanation (as differentiated from insight) or advice. The counselor is an active agent, although he usually follows the rule of all good teaching that the learner (in this case, the counselee) should arrive as far as possible at conclusions by himself.

This process can occur either in a one-to-one or group setting, but the counselor must be aware of the fact that *group* conseling is by far more difficult and sometimes even impossible. This is due to the fact that in counseling problems that concern specific individuals must be discussed, for it would be difficult to find a number of individuals with exactly identical problems, except, of course, in such cases as marital or premarital disharmony, family life, parents of children with special handicaps or illnesses, problems of normal adolescent adjustment, some type of delinquents, etc.

Guidance. In guidance, on the other hand, pragmatic problems and their solutions are considered and, to a limited extent (and perhaps superficially), attitudes and feelings are exposed for consideration. But the underlying unconscious motivations and their sources are not brought to the surface as they are in psychotherapy. What determines the choice between counseling and guidancc is the intensity of the affect involved, the chronicity of the problem, and the elements in the syndrome. Some problems of individuals arise from sources beyond ego functioning; they involve strong feelings that are elaborated in the psyche. Problems with one's landlord, for example, can be resolved by counseling, but counseling can hardly be effective in resolving disharmony between marital partners. The emotional charge in the two relations is vastly different and requires different treatment. It is obvious that guidance is a much longer, as well as a deeper, process than is counseling.

Groups help and accelerate the guidance process, especially where the problems of the members of the group are similar or identical, for during the intellectual and emotional interaction, the group participants activate (catalyze) one another's communications; they also serve as models for each other. Another element is that of universalization, namely, the discovery that others are in the same difficulties, which reduces the stigma of uniqueness and feelings of worthlessness and guilt in each.

A counselor need not be clinically trained, but the involvements inherent in guidance require that the leader be a professionally trained person with experience in psychotherapy. There is an obvious similarity between psychotherapy and guidance, though there is a vast difference in intensity and depth between the two practices.

Psychotherapy

Unlike counseling and guidance, which aim to resolve more-or-less transitory problems that disturb an individual, psychotherapy is committed to resolve inner malformation of the personality from which his maladjustments flow. Its basic aim is to reweight the psychic forces that operate in the individual largely by regression to earlier stages of development thereby bringing to light the traumatic events in the patient's life and by vicariously reliving them in the light of more mature insights and more realistic emotions. The importance of this process is that it releases the bound up anxiety, guilt, and hostility that obsess the individual and impel him to seek treatment in the first place. The repressed feelings and confusions generated by early traumata manifest themselves in a variety of symptoms in later life which psychotherapy aims to eradicate.

The repressed memories and feelings are reawakened by regressive *free association,* which is guardedly prevented in counseling and guidance, since the tensions it generates cannot be *worked through* in those settings. Free association unavoidably awakens the pains and sufferings experienced in the past, and the ego defenses, which are left untouched or little affected in couseling and guidance, are assailed in psychotherapy, which is the chief source of resistances. The task of psychoanalytic psychotherapy in particular is, therefore, the analysis of these resistances with consequent anxiety, guilt, and hostility. Since the real personality of the patient is brought into the open, the psychotherapist encourages their reappearance and employs them as grist in the therapeutic process.

The course of therapy is fraught with much ambivalence and resistance; it oscillates between positive and negative transference feelings, communication and silence, confidence and distrust, frankness, deceit, and avoidance. All these have to be worked through as products of conscious and unconscious needs

> and causes. The patients pass through mood swings between elation and depression, submission, hostility, aggression, expansiveness and diffidence. These need to be observed and their meanings understood. All this takes a very long time, much longer than does guidance and even more so that counseling. Much of the time is consumed in evolving a positive transference, so that patients will grow secure enough to reveal themselves. This relation is strangely tinged with sexual libido. The therapist is invested with strong libidinal significance and may become the patient's sexual object or aim. While the degree of regression to the pre-oedipal and pregenital stages is at its height in true psychoanalysis, the patients' attitudes, in all real psychotherapy, are colored by these irrational, infantile strivings [Slavson, 1964, pp. 108-109].

In the last three decades psychoanalysis has been modified to include a small number of preselected patients who can be treated simultaneously in small groups.[1] Many interpersonal dynamics and personal reactions inherent in all small groups of humans appear also in therapy groups or are modified, while some are unique to therapeutic groups, as shown in the following table.

TABLE 1
THE DYNAMICS OF NONTHERAPY AND THERAPY GROUPS

Nontherapy	*Therapy*
Interaction	Interaction
Interstimulation	Interstimulation
Intensification	Intensification
Induction	Induction
Neutralization	Neutralization
Total compromise	Partial resolution of conflict
Identification	Identification
Assimilation	None
Integration	None or partial
Motivations	Motivations
Collective impulse	Recovery
Cohesion	None
Synergy	Individuation

[1] This development was inaugurated by the present writer in 1934, when he introduced the small-group concept in the treatment of children, and later by him and others for adults.

The differences in the developmental and educational influences of nontherapeutic groups as differentiated from the effect of therapeutic groups appear in Table 2.

TABLE 2
EXPANSIVE AND CONSTRICTIVE INFLUENCES OF NONTHERAPY AND THERAPY GROUPS

Nontherapy Groups		*Therapy Groups*	
Expansive	*Constrictive*	*Expansive*	*Constrictive*
Self-Expression	Group-induced anxiety	Status	Group cohesion
Creative effort	Interindividual threats	Acceptance	Homoeroticism
Social intercourse	Antipathies	Freedom	
Suppression	Rivalries	Security	
Sublimation	Antagonisms	Restitution	
Identification	Restrictive behavior	Knowable character of group	
Allotropism	Ego-functioning of others		
Transition to social participation	Reduction of ego-controls		
Transition from family to ethos	Reduction of superego controls		
Enhancement of self-esteem	Reinforcement of the id		
Development of responsibility	Defense against narcissistic injury		

Differential Characteristics of Groups

The characteristics of groups as differentiated from large assemblies of people are that (1) to insure significant interpersonal interactions they are small in number — a maximum of eight in the case of therapy groups; (2) all groups must have a leader; (3) ordinary groups have a *common* purpose, while members of therapy groups have individual aims though a similar purpose, namely, recovery, but the purpose is not a common one; (4) in all group activities the members are in dynamic interaction; and (5) all groups aid personality growth and affect character development. The special characteristic of *groups* as differentiated from crowds, assemblies, audiences, congregations, mobs, masses of people, is that each member of a group is in some kind of interaction with each of the others as well as with the network of their relations — that is, the individual is aware of and has feelings or reactions to the relations that exist among the members of the group. The simplest example of this is a family (which is a group of maximum intensity), where the father and mother react to each other's *relation* with their children (as well as symbiotically) and the children in turn react to their *relation* as well as to the *relation* of each sibling and to each of the parents.

The difference between therapy groups and other types of groupings in modern society lies in the fact that there is present in the former an element which we have characterized as *commonality of problems.* While the aim of a therapy group is not common, for it is individual recovery from illness that *each* member seeks, ideally the problems which the participants bring to the group should have common elements, nonetheless. This would create a climate of empathy and identification, so that the patients can be of most help to each other in their quest for health. In the absence of this factor, psychotherapy in a group can become individual treatment in the presence of the other members. However, the two common problems that inevitably disturb patients and invariably appear in the group interviews are feelings about parents and siblings and the area of sex.

Perhaps the most important difference between ordinary and psychotherapeutic groups is the element of *synergy.* Synergy is the confluence of energies and effort in a number of persons for the achievement of a common aim or purpose dominant in the cathexis of the participants. It is essential that this phenomenon be prevented, for in synergy the individuality of each participant is to varying degrees submerged in the group. That is, each gives up at least partially the hegemony of his ego and superego, the integrity of which is essential in the therapeutic process and must be maintained. This is fed by each patient's conflicts, values, and hostilities, which are transmuted into positive, negative, and ambivalent transference relations among the patients and toward the therapist. While groups generally are held together by a personal and social homogeneity and common aims, in therapeutic groups the members are held together by anxiety.

Our operational structure of true psychotherapy (as differentiated from counseling and guidance and other means of "helping" people with their difficulties), rests on the specific use of the dynamics of *transference, catharsis. insight, reality testing,* and *sublimation.* This difference is listed in Table 3 below.

TABLE 3
SHOWING THE DIFFERENTIAL DYNAMICS OF COUNSELING, GUIDANCE AND PSYCHOTHERAPY GROUPS

Dynamics	*Counseling*	*Guidance*	*Analytic Psychotherapy*	*Para-analytic Psychotherapy*
Transference	Slight positive	Moderate positive	Intense	Intense
Catharsis	None	Moderate associative	Free association	Associative and free association
Insight	None	Slight	Deep	Moderate
Reality testing	Present	Present	Present	Present
Sublimation	None	Possible	Present	Present

Anonymity. To maintain a therapeutically effective type and level of transferential relations among the patients in an analytic group, it is necessary that the patients refrain from personal and, if possible, also social contact outside the group sessions. Extragroup relations cannot but affect the impact of the personalities involved during the interviews, when there needs to be free-wheeling expression of hostility and resentment and unimpeded discharge of other types of feelings toward each other. Extragroup intimacy gives rise to friendships in some and sibling hostilities in others, which may deter frankness in reactions and criticism. Such friendships will prevent some patients from exposing each other in a negative light thereby vitiating the value of free-associative catharsis. During treatment, patients should maintain emotional distance from one another, except as feelings are engendered in the therapeutic interaction, positive or negative, which are viewed as transferential phenomena and are explored and analyzed. Such feelings most often are the keys to earlier traumatic relationships from which patients' personalities and adjustment difficulties have arisen. As such, they are helpful, in fact essential, in analytic psychotherapy, while relationships acquired or carried on between sessions are prejudicial to sound psychotherapy.

Sexual Acting Out. In heterosexual groups, one of the possible outcomes of extragroup contacts, which frequently occurs among patients, is sexual acting out (which cannot be ruled out in unisexual groups as well), which may present the psychotherapist and the group with an insoluble, and certainly very difficult situation, that may disrupt the group.

It is expected that extragroup homo- or heterosexual acting out with fellow patients (as well as with other persons) is communicated to the group during its interview. However, this frankness occurs in practice only after a considerable period and the revelations prove shocking to some, arousing jealousy and resentment in others, and violent hostility in still others. It opens a Pandora's box of difficulties for the therapist and group.

It is obvious from the aforesaid that anonymity is an important consideration in selection of patients for a group, in grouping them, and in conducting a therapy group.

The "Closed System." Therapy groups operate on the principle of a "closed system," that is, a complex of forces that sustains itself and by its nature allows little or no intrusion of outside forces. Ordinary groups, such as educational, recreational, social, political, or special-interest groups, operate on an "open system" plan. That is, they maintain contact and draw upon outside interests and resources rather than remaining self-contained. This is not the case with therapy groups. The very nature and purpose of a psychotherapy group sets it off from the life-stream around it. The emotional charge, in its intensity, does not permit intrusion from the outside or any diversional influences, interests, and activities that do not proceed from the ongoing therapeutic process of the group.

The closed system principle must be guarded in true therapy groups if successful results are to be achieved.[2] Too-frequent introduction of alien influences that do not arise out of the emotional vortex in the group, both from individuals and their interactions, will decelerate the ongoing process of therapy. They cool off feelings and divert the free-associative process that results from interstimulation and interaction of patients and from the introspective cogitation, which are the chief instrumentalities of psychotherapy. Betlheim suggested the analog of this phenomenon by comparing it to a kettle of boiling water: when cold water is added to a boiling kettle, it at once stops boiling. This principle applies to the interviews of a therapy group, for the patients gain most out of the therapeutic experience when they "boil," as it were, and anything that would lower the emotional temperature should be avoided.

Relative to adding new patients to an ongoing analytic therapy group, it may be said that such additions may not be a serrous handicap in the *earlier stages* of a group's life. However, added patients who are therapeutically on par with a group's members in its advanced stages always presents a shock to the group, but in some

[2] The therapist should seriously examine the advisability of altering the physical setting and of having "visitors," "recorders," "cotherapists," new patients and others whose presence changes the physical and emotional configuration in a group.

instances this handicap can be overcome as the newcomer is therapeutically on par with the group and can be "assimilated" into it.[3]

Para-analytic Group Psychotherapy

Para-analytic group psychotherapy is based on the same assumption and orientation as analytic psychotherapy. Because it was designed more especially, though not entirely, for adolescents, it is of necessity of lesser depth. As is the case with neurotic adults, the problems of some patients stem from the unconscious; but because of the age and the psychic structure of adolescents, the conventional psychoanalytic techniques need to be modified. Free association and the therapist's passivity are still the characteristic of this type of therapy, but it has to be varied to include the reality problems that concern young people, and they must be helped to conceptualize and seek out rational resolutions for them. In addition, the therapist imparts psychologic knowledge to the group members to widen and deepen understanding. This serves to enhance their "psychologic literacy" upon which they can draw in times of dilemma or stress.

This procedure is suitable not only for adolescents but also for adults for whom depth treatment and uncovering unconscious repressed memories and feelings may be too disturbing or would overload their ego reserves. On the other hand, too-superficial discussions of counseling and guidance would be insufficient to unravel their pathognomonic states. These are adult patients who would ordinarily require straight psychoanalytic therapy, but whose egos could not withstand the assailment and stress of a fully uncovering, analytic therapy. Para-analytic psychotherapy, being less stressful, is suitable for them. There are periods and stages even in conventional psychoanalysis and psychoanalytic groups when intellectual clarification and information help engender in patients ego controls over their feelings and behavior.

Para-analytic psychotherapy, though designed mainly, but not

[3] Experience shows that introduction of new members into a group is more disturbing to adult patients than it is in the case of children and adolescents. Because of their self-awareness, adults are more affected when exposed to scrutiny of "strangers."

entirely, for adolescents, is effective in the treatment of latent and borderline schizophrenic patients. Some such patients can tolerate a minimum of uncovering of their motivation and psychic content and the majority of them turn away from any steps in that direction, no matter how lightly they are made. The weak ego reserves drive patients into a state of agitation or delusions and hallucinations.

In the case of adolescents, their state of maturity and life experiences renders them unready for deep introspective probing their unconscious.

> The surface nature of their incestuous and libidinal urges and their transferential antagonism to adults (and, therefore, the therapist) militate against their entering into a relationship and into their own psyche, as required by a true analytic therapy. On the other hand, adolescents whose inner stress brings them to therapy, cannot be helped by counseling or guidance alone. Consequently, another approach is needed—*para-analytic group psychotherapy,* the treatment of choice for most adolescents [Slavson. 1964, pp. 117-118].

Para-analytic group psychotherapy is also suitable for older persons (not the senile) whose decreasing libidinal resources and ascending egotistic preoccupations give rise to an unstable psychic structure. By and large such individuals are unpromising patients and should be involved in frank psychotherapy of any kind only rarely. Evocation of interests and supplying of activities and socializing opportunities that include small group discussions should rather be the rule with the old. However, when therapy is essential there should be a minimum of unraveling the unconscious. Reason and confrontation interspersed with some insight is the indicated regimen, which constitute para-analytic group psychotherapy. In para-analytic group therapy, dreams are employed in the same manner as in analytic groups when indicated, and the unconscious is allowed to be revealed and utilized in the interviews.

If one were to carefully analyze an individual or group analytic interview, one would find that the various maneuvers and strategies above outlined are employed in all types of treatment as they are needed. However, in the depth therapies, they are of transitory or of short duration. In para-analytic psychotherapy, on the other hand, the relation is reversed; that is, in para-analytic therapy the major pattern is as described above, while the periods of deeper exploration are infrequent and short-lived.

The basic rules of para-analytic psychotherapy are:

> The therapist must not press patients for regression to deep levels of the unconscious; the interviews consist predominantly of top realities, dealing with current problems and preoccupations; only a minimal level of anxiety is permissible; rise of the anxiety level has to be prevented, allayed or diverted; introspective or uncovering therapy, if used at all, needs to follow the acquisition of "psychologic literacy" which involves conceptual understanding (as differentiated from emotional insight); free association is not demanded or expected, rather associated thinking is prevalent, that is, horizontal association of ideas, thoughts, feelings and events (as differentiated from vertical, regressive free association); the therapist is much more active than in analytic psychotherapy; and by and large, the therapist addresses himself to behavior of patients and their ego functioning and is less concerned with the libido and superego than he would be in analytic therapy [Slavson, 1964, p. 119].

And the comparative dynamics of para-analytic psychotherapy are:

> Transference is of the same level of intensity as in analytic groups; catharsis is considerably less regressive than in the latter; the same levels of insight cannot be reached in para-analytic as in analytic therapy (though they are much higher than in guidance); and reality testing and sublimations are more or less of the same nature. The greatest difference, and the most telling one, is the activity of the therapist. In para-analytic group psychotherapy, the therapist is much more active in leading and also, at times, directing the interviews. He offers explanations and interpretations, suggests ideas, principles, philosophies,

and guides for conduct and living, and at certain points he may assume the role of a discussion leader. However, as in analytic psychotherapy, he follows the leads and cues from the group and is careful to relate comments and questions to the subjective meanings and unconscious strivings of the patients, although universalizing them more often than personalizing them [Slavson, 1964, p. 118].

It is obvious from the foregoing that para-analytic group psychotherapy draws upon several disciplines: education, counseling, guidance and psychoanalytic psychotherapy. These are fused into one practice and are resorted to at various points as indicated during the process for learning, insight, introspection, and "working through." Some of the values of this technique with adolescents lie in the facts that (1) it engages the eagerness and curiosity of the young, expands intellectual horizons; (2) it clarifies by sound educational means the perplexing and confusing psychologic and heuristic problems characteristic of this phase in the development of the individual; (3) it deepens appreciation of the life process and human relations; (4) it gives direction to life; and (5) it frees the participants from character and neurotic tensions and distress.

To achieve these ends, and more, the therapist needs to go beyond clinical frontiers to the total life-sphere of the young persons in the context of the family, peer and social and community relations, as well as the world of science, art, and literature, which may be touched on during the group interviews as a result of curiosity and the characteristic vitality of the young. Sex enlightenment and dissolution of anxiety and guilt related to it are of special value in establishing mental health at this critical period in life.

Para-analytic psychotherapy is an effective instrument in treating teenagers because by its very nature it diminishes their natural resistance to revealing to the view of adults their doubts, insecurities, and feelings of weakness. They need to maintain a defensive facade of grandiosity, and their rebelliousness against adults and their world and their mores, are threatened by uncovering direct psychotherapy. It therefore must be modified and diluted so as not to activate the defensive armor. This is more achieved by para-analytic psychotherapy. Groups are of particular value in the treatment of adolescents since they serve as protection against the therapist while diluting the transference through the presence of peers. The group provides the adolescent with a culture or climate in which he feels more secure and more esteemed than in the presence of an adult or adults. These characterological issues, some of which are transitory, need to be taken cognizance of in education, in society generally, and especially in psychotherapy.

Para-analytic group psychotherapy originated in residential treatment of court-convicted adolescent boys, fifteen to seventeen years old, conducted under the direction of the writer. It has proven eminently successful and a rather extensive report on it has appeared in a recent publication. Its effectiveness is demonstrated by the results shown in the following table taken from that report (Slavson, 1965b) which show twenty-eight patients improved out of a random sampling of thirty-four.

TABLE 4
SHOWING INCIDENCE OF IMPROVEMENT IN PARA-ANALYTIC GROUPS

Group	*A*	*B*	*C****	*D****	*Totals*
Significant Improvement	6	2	6	4	18
Partial Improvement		5	1	4	10
No Improvement					
Dropped out*	1		3		4
Closed**		1			1
Places late	1				1
Totals	8	8	10	8	34

Reprinted from Slavson (1965b).
*Discharged from village; refused to come to group; one boy ran away.
**Found unsuitable for group therapy.
***Groups still in operation at the time of writing.

The following table sets forth the aims and dynamics of psychotherapy generally and their presence or absence (and the degree of their presence) in the various group techniques discussed in the foregoing pages.

TABLE 5
AIMS AND DYNAMICS IN COUNSELING, GUIDANCE AND PSYCHOTHERAPY

Aims	*Counseling*	*Guidance*	*Analytic Psychotherapy*	*Para-analytic Psychotherapy*
Libido redistribution	None	None	Present	Partial
Regulation of superego demands	None	Slight	Present	Partial
Strengthening of ego	None	Slight	Present	Present
Improvement of self image	None	Slight	Present	Present
Solution of immediate problem	Present	Present	Transitory	Present
Dynamics				
Transference	Slight positive	Moderate positive	Intensive cyclical	Intense
Catharsis	None	Moderate associative	Regressive free associative	Associative and free association
Insight	None	Slight	Deep	Moderate
Reality testing	Present	Present	Present	Present
Sublimation	None	Possible	Present	Present

S. R. Slavson

Psychonursing

In the practice of psychotherapy one cannot escape having patients who by the nature of their clinical problems, their personality structure, or psychologic and constitutional limitations are inaccessible to uncovering psychotherapy or for whom it is clinically counterindicated. Among patients in this category with constitutional deficits are: mental defectives, mentally retarded, intellectually limited, the senile, the dying, and patients with glandular and other debilitating physical defects and imbalances, some of which should receive preliminary medical treatment. Among the clinical counterindications for deeper psychotherapy are some character disorders, especially schizophrenics whose weak ego resources and tenuous defenses would crumble under the impact of analytic introversion and result in ego fragmentation.

Patients with such personality deficits and clinical risks should not be subjected to the stress of analytic therapy (which would be ineffectual anyway) but rather require prolonged guidance or counseling frequently for years or even decades. This is especially true of full-blown schizophrenics, who are in need of ego support and an infantile-type anaclitic relation with someone whose ego is intact and they can draw on, and to a degree even internalize. This is equally true of borderline and latent schizophrenics, for whom a prolonged course of counseling and guidance are the indicated procedures. In most instances this is all that can be offered to such patients, though there are individuals who can sustain with benefit a cautiously applied insight therapy within limited bounds after ego reinforcement through prolonged counseling and guidance.

There may be a tendency to underrate "nursing" in psychotherapy due to its diluted nature and elementary content. This attitude may be justified from a professional frame of reference, but psychonursing is of inestimable value in terms of social benefit. In a great many instances and situations, interpersonal relations are improved through it and community mental health is greatly enhanced by preventing or diminishing conflicts and tensions. Psychonursing can help establish harmony between an individual and his environments where deeper approaches would be resisted or otherwise proved fruitless.

Counseling, guidance, and psychotherapeutic groups meet once a week for a duration of ninety minutes but can be extended to varying periods up to four hours.

Vita-Erg Therapy with Psychotics

This form of therapy with seriously deteriorated chronic psychotic female patients has been tested on two wards of sixty-five patients each. The basic assumptions on which this therapeutic procedure is based are, briefly, that psychosis is a defensive withdrawal from reality and the creation of a world of hallucination and delusions as defenses against incestuous urges, fed by unwise, pathogenic parents, with which the ego of the potentially psychotic patient cannot deal, and against murderous hostility toward parents (especially the father) and all other persons as substitutes of same. The psyche is in the perpetual throes of fear and overwhelming anxiety which make the patient helpless and render him periodically frightened and submissive or enraged and assaultive.

One aim of treatment is to enhance contact and progressive interaction with outer actualities (erroneously characterized as reality) and to improve comprehension of the outer world through expanding exposure to it by realistic needs and graduated demands so as to awaken patients' potentials. The second aim — increasing capacities for relatedness — is in a sense subsumed in the first, since other humans are part of external reality.

To the psychotic, however, people are even a more strenuous actuality than are inanimate things, though the impulsion of these are also threatening to his debilitated, defenseless ego. These inner reactions vis-a-vis the outer processes must be the ever-present and painstaking awareness of the therapist and all other hospital staff. The psychotic has to be helped to break through his defensive incapsulation and isolative existence and his dreamlike state by gradually building bridges between himself and the inanimate and animate world around him. At the same time as these bridges span the chasm between him and the world, the actualities of that world must be expanded in quality and complexity to continuously challenge his gradually strengthening ego and clearer perceptions.

The ward staff must never lose sight of the cardinal fact that the psychotic patient is in perpetual dread, which he perceives as anxiety, and seeks relief in narcotizing drugs, only to fall prey to the same anxieties when their effect has worn off. *It is this basic fear that the staff at all levels needs to be aware of* and must seek to allay by their benign, though firm, attitudes and supportive mien and acts.

The foundations of the roads to reality in the treatment of hospitalized psychotic persons lie in their relations with the staff, especially with the "attendants," who are in the most direct, most intimate, and most extensive and intensive contact with patients, and the ward doctor, whose charismatic powers hold magic promise to the ill. The bridges to reality lay in the feelings of security and support engendered in patients by this most immediate staff, who though firm must be tender and understanding, thereby offering initial comfort and security which form the basis for patients' wider contacts and responsibilities.

Obviously, interpersonal relations are fostered more effectively, and certainly more economically, through group interactions, centered on and flowing from some evocative activities in which more than one person participates. When the necessity for relating and interacting flows from a genuine action interest that engages the individual, it is real and motivates relationships. Hospitalized patients ought to spend as much time in their daily existence in engaging and stimulating activities with others, much of which, however, should be self-initiated. We have, therefore, introduced such a plan.

The plan required a fundamental reevaluating and replanning of the setting and life on the wards where patients spend the major part of their days. Especially the functions of the attendants, who played a passive, nonparticipating role in the past, mostly as servants and overseers, needed revision.

To provide opportunities for intimacy with the objective world and at the same time have opportunities for personal interactions, we have built a modern electrically equipped kitchen, a laundry with electric washer and dryer and ironing boards with electric pressing irons, and a beauty parlor semiprofessionally equipped for personal beauty culture. In the latter, particularly, there was a great deal of mutual help in setting hair, fixing nails, and general social interaction. In addition to the above three rooms, a room for conferences and group meetings was set aside. This room was used to withdraw agitated patients to quiet them down thereby preventing emotional contagion in the other ward residents and the spread of panic.

Privacy for undressing and showering was achieved by minor reconstruction and waterproof curtains. Partitions and hinged, self-closing half-doors around the toilet bowls provided privacy in the formerly open mass lavatory. Restrictions of smoking by patients to specific areas were relaxed and an air of general freedom of movement and choice of interests and activities was encouraged both by the total setting and especially by the altered attitudes and roles of the ward staff.

Instead of retiring small groups of patients to occupational therapy and recreational centers off the wards, these activities were provided in the mornings and some afternoons on the wards themselves. One occupational therapist and one recreation worker had been assigned to each of the two wards. They displayed their wares, as it were, and by example of the "attendants" who worked at these occupations themselves attracted an increasing number of patients to join around the tables where all were busily engaged in sewing, knitting, crocheting, making potholders, working in colored tiles, drawing and painting, playing checkers and dominoes, working on geographic and other puzzles, and reading a variety of material.

Two sewing machines were furnished for each of the wards as well as other more common tools for this activity. Ping-pong tables and large rubber balls for bouncing by groups of patients or patients and a staff member formed, among other things, part of the equipment. Special attention was given to mood music played on radio and phonographs and by regularly scheduled small band concerts which offered possibilities for spontaneous individual and group dancing. (The phonographs were usually operated by some self-appointed patient who managed the change of records.)

The significance of the equipment, of which the above is only a partial list, lay only partially in these objects. Their main therapeutic value derived from the manner in which they were employed. *Vita-erg therapy* relies upon spontaneity, relevance, and the meaning an activity has to the actual life and psychologic needs each patient feels and his readiness to engage in it with profit. That is, it must yield the satisfaction inherent in achievement, have definite utility and a practical value for the patients, and bring recognition to dissipate anxiety, frustration, and failure.

To be therapeutically valid, an activity must have meaning in reality which the patient feels or recognizes. For example, the most meaningful occupations and chores for some patients were the household duties of cleaning dormitories, the ward, shower rooms, and lavatories, preparing and distributing the mid-morning coffee, and baking cookies for the ward community snacks. For others, the most rewarding occupations were individual projects carried on at the group tables, which brought the type of satisfaction that activates the centrifugal flow of life's energies. The sewing of a dress, a slip, or an apron; the knitting of a hat or a sweater; the drawing of a picture that attracted praise; the making of cigarettes for one's own needs and for the ward community were some of the myriad occupations and achievements that helped bring the regressed, mute, hallucinating, encapsulated patients closer to the world of actuality around them, thereby decreasing their isolation, diffidence, and fears.

An interesting observation on the effect of the active ward climate is that there has not been even one instance of frozen catatonia during the years since it was put into effect, while in the past it was not unusual to observe on some days at least one and sometimes two or three patients relapse into that state on each of the wards. Another outcome of the change in the patients' environment and the understanding and *respectful* treatment of patients by the ward staff was the vastly improved comeliness and general appearance of the denizens on the wards.

What gives vita-erg therapy special significance is that activities take place in a *favorable human climate* induced by the ward staff and, more particularly, that the activities have a life meaning and thus increase reality testing. These meanings are engendered from the facts that the activities are *relevant* to the *immediate* life of each patient and flow from an *inner* compulsion rather than being imposed or scheduled by staff. It is a living process rather than programmed participation that robs occupations of the glow that need and reality give them.

To effect the changes indicated, a new orientation and new perception of their part in the lives and recovery of patients was essential in the custodial staff and their supervisors. To achieve these changes, a continuous weekly *practicum seminar* was held with the staff. Emphasis was laid upon the participation of the seminar members in examining the problems they face in their daily work and exploring, as a group, the meaning and significance of developments, possible means for dealing with them, and how to implement the suggested program, which was constantly altered as conditions indicated. Except in the few early sessions, the principle of eschewing purely theoretical presentations was strictly adhered to. Theory grew out of and related to practical problems and actual situations. Practical suggestions for means of carrying out the program were reemphasized and the understanding of the nature and motivations of patients formed the center of the seminar discussions.

Separate luncheon seminars were held for the supervisors, physicians, and nurses, who were responsible for the day-to-day implementing of the program and who were only auditors, not participants, at the attendants' seminars. The advanced seminars followed the discussions with the attendants where the various ideas and problems from the earlier seminars with the custodial personnel were discussed in greater detail. These sessions served as forums of inter-specialist communication and integrated or orchestrated their specialties for the benefit of the patients.

The seminars and meetings yielded many results. Chief of these was the growing awareness in the marginally educated and professionally untrained attendants of patients as "persons" (to use their own formulation) rather than just patients to care for, to train, and to discipline. The focus on patients in the discussions, rather than the staff's habitual preoccupation with ward cleanliness, routines, and "housework" chores engendered a degree of sensitivity toward the patients' plight, suffering, and needs. This was formulated by the attendants themselves as a feeling of "compassion." (They rejected after two intensive sessions the term "love," suggested by the seminar leader.)

As a result of these and other developments, the interest in observing the behavior of patients was greatly sharpened and a curiosity to understand patients' behavior emerged. The attendants had been self-motivated to gather and report for discussion a wealth of significant observations of and information on specific patients and their families who visited them. These observations proved useful in dealing both with the families and the patients and yielded suggestions for therapeutic needs.

A wealth of suggestions came also from the two-hour "supervisory" staff luncheon meetings (which often extended to three hours). The content of these sessions was derived from the attendants' seminars, from the observations and experiences on the wards, and from the reactions and comments by various staff members of the different specialities and levels.

In line with our emphasis on activation of the patients and encouraging active participation, we have introduced the ward meetings, the content of which is predominantly planning activities and enlisting volunteers for committees to carry out specific duties. Among these were committees for preparing and serving the midmorning coffee, baking cookies and cakes, cleaning the ward, bedmaking, decorating the rooms for planned parties, welcoming guests, preparation of refreshments for the parties and cleaning up the room afterwards (since they were held in the largest room on the floor, the dining room).

At first these large ward sessions were disturbed and punctuated by many interruptions from hallucinating and irrational patients who shouted irrelevant and derogatory remarks, obscenities, attacks on the leader, and various demands (mostly to be allowed to go home). Occasional remonstrations and physical fights among pairs of patients frequently arose. However, in time as the patients quieted down and responded to the more humane and respectful treatment by the staff, these tumultuous manifestations greatly abated. As the ward climates grew more tranquil as the result of the patients' diminished hostility and fear, the ward sessions also reflected these changes, as did all other areas of ward life. These were manifested by the appearance of closer friendships and sharing of goods among patients, spontaneous communication among them, which was completely absent before, and equally spontaneous groupings for games (such as card playing) or quiet conversations.

At no time, however, did all the patients on a ward join the circle during discussions. There were always those who preferred sitting by themselves apart from the group. Some were passive, silent participants, and a small number were still too engrossed in their own preoccupations. It was and is our policy not to infringe upon patients' needs for privacy and self-absorption. There were, however, on both wards, a sufficient number of interested, active participants to form an effective core for creating a community feeling.

After about two years, many patients had improved sufficiently to take part constructively in consistent rational discussions and direct person-to-person interchange. At this point small groups of eight to ten selected patients met with two staff members — one male and one female — one of whom was a psychologist. However, here too, the content was directed toward practical matters. This was in keeping with our basic principle of psychotics' need for reality testing. Therefore, subjects were introduced to engage the responsiveness of the group members. Matters such as selecting themes for which some gifted members might write dialogues and poems, writing the plays (mostly of a musical nature involving dialogue, singing, and dancing), and designing costumes, volunteering, and selecting parts in the plays and helping each other in studying the parts and improving their performances.

At times, when relevant, the discussions were planned and directed by the leader, an accomplished musician and one gifted in work with such patients, in examining feelings and attitudes, and in discussing matters pertaining to home visits and relations with parents and siblings. These discussions, however, were conducted carefully and more or less superficially so as not to disturb the patients' inner equanimity beyond their egos' capacities.

These groups, as well as the ward meetings, were held weekly. Their duration was not set in advance and they were terminated as soon as a sign of waning interest appeared or restlessness set in.

It would be a grievous error and detrimental to generations of patients to assume that vita-erg therapy is a cure-all for hospitalized psychotic patients. It was first introduced and experimented with on wards of seriously deteriorated, chronic, and hitherto "hopeless" cases. This was only circumstantial. Few patients of this order can be sufficiently improved by a situational therapy, such as this, to warrant their return to the "normal" community. There has been unmistakable salutary change in patients who presented a more normal facade with much more rational behavior and an increase in relatedness through the program. This was attested to by staff and others. It was commented upon by visiting relatives of the patients and former staff members who dropped in on their former haunts. Many patients had been transferred to other open wards and a number had been discharged. Nevertheless, one would be seriously misled were one to claim that basic structural changes had been wrought in the psyches of most patients by our techniques. The improvements must be considered as *functional* only in response to the more benign environment and better treatment by staff. Most required more direct psychotherapy in groups and individually.

Child-centered Group Guidance of Parents[4] the Family in Mental Health

Even though it is not a completely autonomous institution, the family and the relationships in it are the roots of mental health. The family does reflect and derives its basic character from the larger

[4] Because of the importance of this technique in psychologic and social prophylaxis, it is discussed here in some detail. More detailed elaboration can be found in the author's book (Slavson, 1958).

social climate, but in our culture the earliest perceptions the child develops of himself, of others, and of the world generally — the feelings of being loved and secure — are indelibly stamped upon his personality through the treatment he receives and from the attitude shown toward him by his parents and other members of his immediate family.

Despite the deeper implications of parenthood, men and women have discharged their role as parents with varying degrees of adequacy without having the awareness of any or many of the dynamics that operate in personality development. Men and women who had the good fortune of being themselves nurtured in a comparatively constructive family atmosphere by parents with reasonable tolerance and tact discharge their parental role without creating too many difficulties. There are also men and women who because of external conditions or their subjective states, such as physical health and psychic organization, are able to carry on without excessive strain and negative effects. Parenthood is not an excessive burden to them, and as a result they do not react with glaring anger, irritation, resentment, neglect, or overprotection. This is sometimes described as "readiness for parenthood." While this apt phrase strikes at the core of the situation, it is rather unclear because it does not tell us what constitutes such "readiness." We shall not enter into this complex concept lest we stray too far afield from our central aim, but everyone can recognize interferences with the adequate discharge of parental functions which stem from infantile characteristics, anachronous craving, and other personality deficiencies and problems. While these cannot be always corrected, certainly not in the vast numbers of adults, methods for preparing them for positive parenthood must be evolved so as at least to reduce the strain upon succeeding generations.

The groups consist of eight mothers or fathers who are assigned to separate groups and meet on alternate weeks for ninety minutes or two hours. (Fathers and mothers meet in separate groups.) They are most effective when the children of the parents are of nearly the same age and of the same sex. This is necessary so that the experiences of the participants are as nearly alike as possible. Similar experiences and like situations aid mutual identification, facilitate sharing and mutual help, enhance the significance of communications, and render the discussions more practical and more meaningful. When points of commonality are lacking, the discussions are apt to become theoretical, which is less likely to occur when all concerned are at one in their preoccupations. We shall see presently that discussions and conversations must at all times concern themselves with *actual situations* as they occur in the lives of the parents and *only those that relate to their children.* It is for this reason that the factor of commonality is so important. The report on or presentation of a situation[5] by one parent mirrors in varying degrees those of the other participants. Reactions to and reflections of a situation therefore take, of necessity, a practical turn, since they touch each one in an intimate and realistic fashion. The choice of participants here, as in all types of effective groups — group counseling, group guidance, and group psychotherapy — is the main pivot of success.

From the point of view of mental health, whenever anxiety is aroused, avenues for eliminating it must be provided. The grist of psychotherapy is anxiety. Unless there are clinical indications to the contrary, in psychotherapy anxiety is allowed to run its course, for it is the resultant emotional pressure that propels the patient to continue treatment. This is obviously not the intent in child-centered group guidance of parents. The aim here is (1) to sensitize parents to the nature and needs of children, (2) to alter attitudes and values, and (3) to evolve appropriate ways of dealing with them. This aim determines the selection of group members, the grouping, the role of the *leader*, and the content of the discussions. The parent guidance groups are in every regard different from therapy groups, since the basic conditions and goals are different. To allow anxiety to mount without providing relief or insight would serve to intensify tensions in their families rather than to relieve them.

In the guidance groups with which we are concerned here, the

[5] Note that the terms "problem" or "difficulty" are not used in these groups and are not referred to as such. The terms "situation," "occurrence," "development," and "event" are used instead.

objectives are to evoke empathy with children and a recognition of the fears, anxieties, feelings of weakness, and insecurity inherent in childhood and to eliminate conditions that intensify and magnify them through the climate in the family and other areas of the child's living situations and relationships. This can be conveyed as information by didactic techniques of class and lecture, but information thus acquired has proven ineffective in the vital and dynamic living process requiring responsiveness to the subtle nuances of feelings and emotions.

The techniques of our type of guidance, therefore, seek to give root to thought, deliberation, and reflection by trying them with actual events and experiences. This gives them significance. Parents must come to *realize* that their child's acts, whether annoying or not, are manifestations of his inner necessities and that they are predominantly conditioned by past experiences in which parents played a determining part. Practitioners of this method are always impressed with, and surprised at, discovering the universal trend on the part of adults to blame children for having specific characteristics and behavior patterns as though they were self-created entities and no one had a hand in shaping them. Parents are, by and large, particularly blind to their own influence in these matters.

The reader will recall that a distinct contrast was drawn between psychotherapy and guidance, a contrast that is applicable also to group psychotherapy and group guidance. We have also suggested that in special cases the latter may be therapeutic. This may appear at first glance to be a conflicting statement. However, closer scrutiny will show the statements to be consistent; but before we launch upon the task of harmonizing them, it may be fruitful to bring into focus some of the basic dynamics that operate in child-centered group guidance, which yield the results with carefully selected adults. What follows are some of the dynamics and aims of this practice.

Buttressing Positive Trends. The group discussions are intended to buttress positive trends and constructive elements in the parents' lives. The talks tend to counteract or dissolve hostile and destructive practices as reflected in critical, faultfinding, unreasonably restrictive, and rejecting responses toward themselves and their families. The outcome is clearly an optimistic, hopeful outlook displacing their pervasive hopelessness and sense of defeat. The group members, with the aid of the leader, guide one another toward discovering effective ways of dealing with hitherto frustrating situations, thereby eliminating or reducing their sense of failure and defeat.

The prevalent expectations of failure are diminished and hopes for success and comfort enhanced. In more fundamental terms these groups ally themselves with the life-urge rather than with the negative or destructive impulses. The principle of love and understanding is substituted for hate and irritation. This is partially achieved through the leader's positive, constructive, and helpful attitude and intent, which is inevitably communicated to the members of the group. His attitude reinforces the latent love instinct that had been overwhelmed or subordinated through the overpowering suffering and negative experiences of the past and the hopelessness that these beget.

The mutualistic pattern and clear and honest intent to be helpful and to understand that pervade these groups generate new feeling-responses in the sibling-like setting, alien to the past relations of these men and women. A new awareness of self-other-self-relatedness emerges; new and formerly unknown emotional reactions are activated. Here are people (as exemplified by their leader), who are not propelled to be critical and disapproving; rather they share their difficulties, preoccupations, and problems; they sympathetically seek to help, are interested in each other's welfare, and genuinely aim to be of service. This mutuality and oneness of purpose and their warmth stir new and hitherto unknown and unexperienced constructive feelings that enhance the love impulse with the consequent diminution of hostile, destructive reactions. The newfound feelings give the personality mellowness, tolerance, flexibility, and capacity for empathy and understanding that cannot but overflow to all relations, especially those with mates and children.

Empathy with Children. The groups dissipate rigidities toward children and expectations that they live up to idealized images and adult-approved standards. The interpretation of the child's unavoidable, in fact inherent fears, confusions, and immaturiry predisposes parents to a *willingness* to understand and accept his basic differences from themselves and to respond to children's needs, rather than to demand from them conduct which they are not yet capable of achieving. As a result parents react to their children empathetically and sympathetically rather than demandingly, punitively, and rejectingly.

Self-acceptance. Because the parents in the groups experience for the first time in their lives acceptance, that is, they themselves are not criticized, humiliated, and made guilty, they are able through imitation as well as through newly acquired inner relaxation to accept themselves with less criticism and resentment. Having now had the experience of being accepted, they are on the road to accepting themselves in a more sanguine light; and when this occurs they are also able to accept with greater tolerance limitations and foibles in others. They are rendered more disposed to take a positive view of and to empathize with the struggles a child has in adapting himself to the adult world and to the demands made upon him.

Mirror Reaction. Parents do not ordinarily stop to examine the validity of their ways of dealing with their children; being emotionally involved, they are not aware of the effects of their conduct and of their part in children's difficulties and anomalies. In these groups such matters are mulled over and over until awareness finally emerges. This awareness is greatly accelerated and enhanced through seeing one's self mirrored in the acts of others. While a parent in isolation may succeed through his defensive mechanism and fear of guilt in blocking out and in denying or ignoring his undesirable behavior, this is not as easily accomplished when faced with similar behavior in others. Unless the defenses are too rigid, in which case the parent would not be acceptable for our guidance groups, his identification tendencies lead him to recognize reactions in himself similar to those presented by fellow members. Unless there are present neurotic blocking for it, such mirroring of one's mechanism and acts is one of the important dynamics in loosening up the crustification of convictions, behavior patterns, and defenses and in laying the foundation for emotional detachment, objectivity, and flexibility.

Universalization. Time and again members of child-centered parent guidance groups expressed their relief at finding that others, too, had problems with their children. Reducing the feeling of uniqueness and of being alone with one's guilt and discomfort diminishes tension in these groups as it does also in therapy groups. The discovery that one is not alone in an undesirable trait or in failure allays guilt and bolsters self-esteem. Failure, even if it is not consciously admitted or verbalized, leads to self-devaluation and feelings of unworthiness. On the other hand, the discovery that others, too, are subject to similar inadequacies and errors and are comrades in distress decreases onus and stigma, setting one up in a better light. Universalization is inherent in guidance groups with all the salutary results of relaxing the individual and thus making him accessible to learning and evolving new patterns of behavior.

Mutuality. Due to the fact that all participants have substantially the same difficulties and are preoccupied with similar problems, as well as the fact that a spirit of intimacy, sharing, and mutual helpfulness reigns, there emerges a feeling in groups which we describe as *mutuality.* Our guidance group leaders felt that this was of prime value in enlisting parents for making an effort to deal with their children more appropriately. It was as though they attempted to please the group, gain its approval, and be accepted by it.

It is understandable that when persons with disturbing difficulties are offered a setting in which feelings of isolation are reduced and the sense of failure diminished, they would seek out and enjoy such a setting. The men and women who need such guidance, by and large, have few or no warm or close personal relationships; they feel more isolated and lonely than the average. Being with others in a relation of mutual acceptance and sharing gives them a feeling of inner warmth, pleasure, and security. In fact, friendly relations often extend beyond the group. Members drive each other home in their cars, for example (which is discouraged in therapy groups); they help one another to find parking space for their cars; offer one another discarded children's toys and equipment. They proffer advice to each other not only on matters of dealing with their children, but also as to suitable pets for their offspring of different ages and sexes and ways of caring for them. In one instance a member of a group placed his son in a scout troop led by another.[6]

In large urban communities, where individuals tend to get lost and feel isolated and lonely, a small group such as a guidance group with its atmosphere of friendliness and intimacy fulfills a need for belonging. Another reason for the enjoyment of membership in these groups is that parents of young children have little opportunity to meet with others because they are occupied with their numerous and pressing duties and have to stay home with their children. This limits their circle of social contacts which these groups extend.

It is also possible that the emotional experience of mutual relationships that our groups supply causes the parents to recognize the constructive value of human interdependence, which is a component part of mutuality. This recognition tends to make them more tolerant, more understanding, and more appreciative of the value of their children's dependence on them, which in turn enhances their capacities for empathy and responsiveness. As they accept their normal dependence upon others, they are not as disturbed at the manifestations of these feelings in their children. The leader's attitude toward their foibles in these respects brings home to them the conviction that nonpunitiveness is a more effective and a more constructive way of dealing with situations. The group's mutuality serves to reduce their rivalries and competition outside of the group and is manifested in improved relations with siblings, parents, and mates.

Mutuality, and the security it yields, serves to reduce the defensive aggressiveness in some, and diffidence and withdrawal in others. Just as the frightened and the diffident children in activity therapy groups gain courage to act assertively and with confidence, so do the adults in this confraternity grow in this direction. Many of the fathers and mothers who are characteristically cautious, silent, and fearful gradually become active participants, and some often prove to be the more perceptive and the more thoughtful among their fellow group members. This is one of the number of similarities between activity group therapy for children in latency and guidance groups for parents.

[6] It may be interesting to note in this connection that the man became interested in working with children in his free time as a direct result of his membership in a child-centered guidance group.

Identification with Wholesome Parent Figure. In view of the fact that the leader accepts the members of the group unconditionally, is tolerant and permissive, and respects them and their ideas, he serves as a pattern on which parents model their treatment of children. We have seen how aggressive, intolerant, quarrelsome men and women have curbed themselves. Having been accepted without criticism or castigation, their defensiveness diminished, their attitudes altered, and conduct improved. They grew more tolerant and more accepting as they identified with the good parent figure, the leader. In a real sense these groups are replicas of the family, for in families where parents are tolerant, accepting, and kindly, the siblings are in comparative harmony with one another both because they identify with the parents and because sibling rivalries are at their lowest ebb under such conditions.

By virtue of his position, the leader is a model of identification and of ego functioning whom the members emulate in relation to one another in the group and later toward their mates and children. One woman, for example, stated that through the group she had learned that she could talk matters over not only with her children, but also with her husband. In the past she assumed that her function was to make decisions and everyone in her family had to obey her. Having experienced comforting and gratifying equalitarian relationships and participation in give-and-take discussions, she apparently grew sufficiently relaxed to accept the leader as a model whom in the past she would have rejected and opposed as she did her parents. She then incorporated this new pattern in her family relations.

Acquisition of Knowledge. The positive effects of guidance groups on parents is not solely derived from unconscious and emotional sources. The many protocols of group sessions have revealed that at appropriate times the leader amplifies the discussions by specific information on a subject at hand, giving it body and substance, thereby preventing the spread of unfounded or little corroborated opinions. Parents with little educational background and scanty or no psychological insights frequently go off the "deep end" on subjects of child rearing, child development, human relations, and personality growth. Many of the ideas are antiquated and the information misleading or incorrect. The leader has to be prepared to supply scientifically valid facts and the most reliable and best founded information available. He supplies factual information on matters that may puzzle the group members or when their conclusions are unsound. There is no dearth of information in the field on child nature and development, but care must be taken that the discussions do not degenerate into academic lectures or abstruse peroration. The discussions in these groups must be on a level of empiricism and operational use in dealing with children. Information should be given sparingly and only to butress or clarify points under discussion, and no more.

Reduction of Ego Load. Because of their awareness of failure, of incompetence in dealing with their children, of lack of knowledge of child nature and needs, parents suffer from unavoidable guilt, which imposes a great load upon their egos. It is the ego that is called upon to carry the burden of anxiety, conflict, guilt, and confusion, and control hostile, agressive, and otherwise negative impulses. It is the ego that arrives at compromises, finds solutions, and establishes and operates defenses. When a parent has to carry all these, and many more tensions and burdens, the ego becomes *overloaded,* which often results in impulsive, irrational, and disadvantageous behavior. Tempers overflow, aggressions are acted out in unsuitable punishment, unwholesome relations ensue and the total family atmosphere becomes vitiated and unsuitable both for children and parents.

When this is the situation in the family, reduction of the ego load is indicated. The individual requires help, which in some instances may be forthcoming from his mate, parent, friend, minister, or therapist. Communicating one's burdens and adversities, that is, sharing them with another person, halves the weight of trouble. It is this sharing of ego burdens that persons seek when they talk or seek advice. Talk has been correctly characterized as "unburdening," for bearing pain and tension in loneliness is a great strain, indeed, upon the ego and the total organism.

For this reason "sharing" is so important. It is even more valuable when one unburdens himself to kindred souls, to persons who can understand and empathize because of similarity of difficulties and life situations, which is the case in child-centered guidance groups. "Sharing" in this sense means distributing the load the ego is carrying so that it is freed for other functions and demands. General improvement observed in members of these groups is the result (Slavson, 1952, pp. 145-153). The striking improvement in physical appearance, gleam of the eyes, color of the cheeks, general alertness, mood, and intellectual functions are derived from freeing ego energies hitherto absorbed in holding down or seeking to resolve guilt and conflicts. The energies thus freed are automatically utilized toward personality integration and expansion. Physical improvement of parents in child-centered groups has been commented on by all leaders.

Increased ego reserves for daily function derived from the elimination of intrapsychic tensions that absorbed them before, are employed in more constructive dealing with children. Parents now have more energy available to hold down dissatisfactions, irritation, hostility, and aggression. Their "boiling point" is higher. They can call upon new strengths that have been unavailable before because they were spent in maintaining a constantly tenuous emotional equilibrium. The feeling that one is able to deal with a problem, is not helpless, generates a state of relaxation and detachment, which in turn makes one accessible to reason.

Encouraging Ego Versus Impulse Function. A corollary of the preceding section is the phenomenon of increased ego function (self-control) and a corresponding decrease in id function (impulsiveness). This change in dynamic relation is an inevitable outcome of the shift of ego reserves described. The discussions at the group session enhance this change. Their content is directed toward better treatment of children, which involves also a better understanding of behavior and needs. It is, therefore, inevitable that the parents should become aware of their unreasonableness and impulsive reactions; also of the need for a more controlled, more thoughtful way of responding to, and dealing with, children's conduct. This in itself, aside from the changes already described, tends to strengthen the role of the ego or reality principle as against the id or the pleasure principle.

The trend is amply reflected in the behavior of parents who had been participants in child-centered guidance groups. It is also reflected in some of their verbalizations. For example, one mother stated that: "I find that I have to count till twenty" (before acting). In another group, a father said in discouragement: "Is there any answer to this?" Another answered, "Brother, you'll have to count not till ten but till fifty."

The groups discourage regressive trends and, in a way, expect each to act in an appropriate adult manner toward his children. Members are "pulled up," as it were, by the others when they describe their impulsiveness and uncontrollability (id reactions) by pointing out their ineffectiveness and inadequacy. The group expects them to act with greater appropriateness (ego level). The group in this sense assumes a parental role. When a member seeks approval, protection, and gratification, the group represents (in the unconscious) the mother; when it expects or demands mature behavior, it takes on the role of the father. Here is in a definite sense ego reinforcement that results in a more adequate ego function.

Reduction of Guilt. Since the dominant emotion of parents is guilt, it must become the center of attention of everyone who is attempting to help or reeducate them. The most effective single dynamic involved in this is *universalization.* The others, in order of their importance, are objectification, release through verbalization, and increased knowledge. Parents have repeatedly expressed relief at finding others similarly "afflicted." Not to be alone in failure, or what they consider to be failure, has a salutary effect. In the past the men and women have warded off the depressing and anxiety-evoking recognition of their real and fancied responsibilities for children's ailments, suffering, and maladjustment. Many of these are unavoidable and transitory—part of the growing process—a fact that many parents do not recognize. They feel unjustified guilt because of the painful struggle the child has in adjusting to and mastering the progressive realities incident to maturing. They feel guilty about the necessary exercise of authority on their part in training and inhibiting and applying punishment, as well as for the unconscious hostile wishes they entertain toward their children. They feel uncomfortable and guilty over their envy and jealousy of their offspring and for the increasing difficulties the latter encounter as they grow older.

But in addition to these fancied and inevitable sources of guilt, there are realistic causes for it as well. Parents do overexercise their authority; they frustrate their children and deny them when giving and permissiveness would be more appropriate and more constructive; they do act out their unconscious wishes, which they are unable to inhibit and impede; they act more cruelly than necessary, and they do have little respect for the child's individuality and rights as a person.

In a guidance group parents discover, through their own efforts, that while they have acted inappropriately in the past, much of what they considered to be particular and special in themselves is inherent in human nature and is universal. This discovery serves to relieve a great deal of guilt in addition to the general relaxation as a result of release, ego support, enhanced knowledge, acceptance of the inevitable, and other dynamics already described. Such discoveries, differentiations, and clarity relieve parents of much of their realistic as well as fancied guilts.

Buttressing Parental Instincts and Ideals. The effect of the nature of the discussions in child-centered parents' guidance groups is to strengthen the ever-weakening parental instincts in the modern adult. While biologically this instinct is present and is as intense as ever, unfavorable social conditions and psychologic resistances to it are in contemporary societies on the upgrade. This dichotomy of forces begets conflict and tension. Because the discussions in the groups are centered on children and the members' sole preoccupation is with them, the inevitable effect is strengthening the desire to be good parents and reducing the conflict between the opposing biological and psychological forces that operate in this syndrome.

Support of Cultural Values. The obvious intention of child-centered guidance groups coincides with the communal ideal of parenthood and reinforces it. The groups help parents to acquire status and the ability to live up to the social ideal where they have, for various reasons, failed to do so in the past. It is, therefore, understandable that where no serious intrapersonal conflicts are present, parents readily adopt new ways for dealing with their children, for in addition to other satisfactions and advantages, they enjoy society's approval.

Widening Fields of Operation. As in the case of therapy groups, we have found that child-centered guidance groups for parents also serve to widen interests and encourage social participation. Some parents, especially mothers, are so immersed in the affairs of the family and absorbed and pressed by everyday demands that they exclude most or all other interests. This preoccupation and unilateral interest limits the parents' social participation and is a source of boredom and irritation. We, therefore, have here a situation that in some ways reverses the family process. While parents usually restrain and inhibit children, here, conversely, the children, and the total family setting impede the personality expansion of parents. In some cases children increase this through excessive demands and other devious devices that tie the parents down and force concentrated attention on the child.

Many are overwhelmed by the responsibilities and actual work required to maintain family routines and discharge the numerous and variegated functions in congested living quarters; others, because of personality characteristics, tend to overstress details and thus become overburdened; still others have always been limited in social contacts and, therefore, do not feel the need for outside associations.

Whatever the reason, families and children are negatively affected by such absorption on the part of parents, and the result is impoverished intellectual and emotional development. Children are the gainers when their parents share ideas, activities, and experiences with them and bring to the home fresh points of view and enriched personalities. Without such extrafamiliar stimuli the atmosphere in the home frequently becomes barren; joyfulness, spontaneity, and friendliness are destroyed by monotony and monotonous routines. In such families there are limited educational and cultural opportunities for widening experiences, and there is no urge to seek. The guidance groups, in addition to other advantages, supply to a limited extent variety to lives that are drab and tedious. Though the discussions are confined largely to understanding children and ways of dealing with them, the social contact adds diversity to the parents' lives, and supplies, in some measure, at least, expansive opportunities and experiences. One can also hope that the groups serve as incentives to seek out other associations and are first steps in the direction of expanding intellectual and social interests. During the group conversations, for example, parents mentioned their joining art classes and community, educational, and social pressure groups. One definite development was noted in a father who had become a boy scout leader as a direct result of his membership in a child-centered guidance group. A number of the women had become "den mothers" of junior scout troops.

Supervised Practice in Parenthood. If parenthood is to be considered a skill and not merely a series of instinctive responses (as it is in other animals), then training for it is obviously essential. This fact was made palpable by the questions and discussions in our groups and reproduced in the book, *Child-centered Group Guidance of Parents* (Slavson, 1958). No practice of a craft or a skill can be acquired by theory alone. Skills and the exercise of skills can be acquired only by doing. This is true of all professions and trades. Medical and nursing training includes in-service practice under supervision. Graduation in engineering is considered only a preliminary professional step. Training in architecture is predominantly of a practical nature and the problems the students are asked to solve are in every respect similar to those they will meet in the actual practice of their profession. This is equally applicable to all mechanical skills and trades. Empirical training on the job is the only road to skill.

There is no reason why the same principle cannot apply to the skills of parenthood. Book learning of child psychology and development are helpful but seldom lead to appropriate practices in parenthood. These must be learned by guided action which child-centered parent groups supply.

The content of the discussions in these guidance groups, therefore, is directed almost exclusively toward children's *actual behavior and acts* and the ways in which parents deal with them. The appropriateness or inappropriateness, the effectiveness or ineffectiveness, and the consequences of the parents' reactions and attitudes are examined by the *Socratic method* or in free discussion or in both. Emphasis is laid upon the *reasons* for the child's disturbing, negative, or provoking acts and an effort is made to trace their sources and beginnings in the home. Pure theory is eschewed but is offered to throw light on practice and always follows examinations of an *actual* act or situation in the home. Suggestions for more suitable ways of dealing with a child's *actual conduct* as presented by a parent should first come from the group and be supplemented by the leader only when necessary. The leader has to guard against members' propensity to escape into abstractions and generalizations. Generalizations as to child nature, parental roles, and basic attitudes should be *derived* from the discussions of what had occurred in the home and during the discussions.

Coordinated Family Group "Therapy"[7]

In cases where the malignant treatment of children by parents does not stem from their misconception of the parental role or the lack of knowledge of child development and needs, but is rather an extension of their own personality problems, neurotic or otherwise, some form of therapy is indicated. Treatment may be individual or in groups, according to indications in specific cases. In community mental health centers and child guidance clinics, where both parents and children usually receive therapy, groups are convenient corrective media for those patients where individual treatment is not essential.

"Family therapy" has spread widely in recent years as workers in the mental health field have come to recognize the determining influences of interpersonal family relations and its climate in conditioning personality and in mental health. The most prevalent procedure employed in overcoming the morbid states that generate family conflict and pathology is to treat the family as a unit. The object is to bring into the open conflictual feelings, attitudes, and reactions among family members, which, at various times, involve

[7] More detailed elaboration can be found in the author's paper (Slavson, 1965a).

parents, siblings, grandparents, and other relatives who may be sharing a common abode.

The corrosive possibilities such a procedure entail are quite obvious. The full, undisguised revealing of the hostile, and even virulent, feelings that permeate problem families may irrevocably disrupt its already tenuous existence and lead to its disintegration. To overload the egos of family members by revealing their nakedness is a risk that one should undertake with great caution, if at all.

One serious problem arises as a result of the compresence of members of families. It lies in the fact that the group becomes *reality saturated.*

> Psychotherapy, to be effective, must draw on the fantasy projections and distortions with which the patient operates in life. . . . The presence of excessive reality factors in therapy . . . *reality saturation* should be prevented. . . . This is the case . . . when parents and children or husbands and wives are included in the same groups. In such groups, the resentment and hostilities are brought forth by the same irritants and stimulators as in real life, and . . . are acted out with all their vehemence and rancor. To subject feelings to adequate analysis is both impossible and inadvisable under these circumstances. . . . Psychotherapy deals with *reliving* (hence, fantasies, distortions and projections), and not with living . . . [Slavson, 1964, pp. 138-140].

At best such consanguinal groups can offer counseling or guidance.

Because of the proliferation of "family therapy" in recent years, it is incumbent upon workers in the field of mental health to examine its effectiveness in the light of our understandings as to what constitutes psychotherapy; also whether the results that it sets out to achieve are, in fact, achieved; and whether it is altogether possible to achieve them. We must examine it in light of psychotherapy *as a process* in which reconstruction of personality occurs and more-or-less enduring changes are affected, which is the intent of true psychotherapy. Reconstruction of personality we understand as being a dynamic process in which intrapsychic changes occur through uncovering repressed and unconscious determinants for feelings and conduct as a result of which the functions and dynamic relations of the id, ego, and superego are altered to meet the requirements of mental health.

Compresence of family members presents the risk of irrevocably disrupting the family by overloading the capacity for tolerance in some or all of its members. In view of the intensification of resistances to self-revelation in such a setting, it can be anticipated that therapeutic interviews with entire families may be stormy affairs, may fall flat, or may present many other difficulties in interpersonal relations that may prove destructive or at least therapeutically unproductive. It is illusory to assume that interviews with families in a clinic faithfully reproduce the inherences of the home climate, or that they always favor voluntary revelation of subsurface content stressful to other members of the family group. While some young children may act out and even verbalize feelings, adolescents and adult family members can hardly be expected to reveal noxious and hostile feelings toward their blood relatives or to disclose their vigilantly concealed fantasies, wishes, and transgressions (which is essential in psychotherapy). Whole-family group settings may be fruitfully employed to work through some administrative and management family matters, but roles and procedures, affect-laden and guilt-weighted feelings and intentions are either withheld or, if revealed, often create an intolerable climate in the home that may result in stress and disruption.

Our own experience, supported by many other practitioners, unmistakably reveals that in groups of couples, for example, much less is disclosed than when the marital partners are seen separately. During the absence of her husband in a group of couples, for example, the wife divulged intimate matters of the family which neither had done in each other's presence. She concluded her rather lengthy recital by the statement: "I couldn't say these things when my husband was here." In another group of couples in child-centered guidance, the husband presented himself as an ideal, understanding father to his (latent schizophrenic) son. In session after session he described his sensitive and highly appropriate treatment of the boy. When the group was separated by sexes, the mother reported numerous acts on the part of her husband that gave the lie to his claims. She detailed his impatience, repressive approach, and general authoritarianism, which greatly distressed her son. She withheld this information during her husband's glib recitals obviously to avoid his wrath.

To obviate the resistances and the risks of increasing further the tensions in families, we have experimented in the last four years with a plan of family treatment that can best be described as "coordinated family group therapy," where the referred patients were adolescent boys and girls of junior high school and high school age (fourteen to seventeen). The teenagers were in treatment in para-analytic group psychotherapy in separate groups for boys and girls within an age range of two years.

The fathers and mothers of the patients also met in separate groups, and they were grouped according to the sex and age of their children (Slavson, 1963). Thus, fathers of girls were grouped together, while fathers of boys met in different groups. The same principle was applied in grouping of the mothers. The parents' groups were conducted on the principles of child-centered group guidance, with the seriously disturbed parents receiving individual psychotherapy as patients on their own account. Assignment to the parents' groups was made in accordance with the criteria developed for these groups (Slavson, 1958) and they met fortnightly.

Each of the four groups involved in a family treatment was conducted by a different therapist (for the adolescents) and "leader" (for the parents) and were sexually matched, i.e., girls' and boys' groups were assigned to women and men therapists, respectively. Fathers' groups were led by men while those of mothers were in charge of women. Although the "leaders" of these groups have to be experienced therapists, under this plan no one staff member can be involved with a child and a parent at the same time. That is, a staff member who conducts a therapy group cannot have contact with a parent of any of his patients, either in group guidance or in individual therapy. This separation of function prevents distrust of the therapist and of increasing resistance, and avoids confusion in the transference.

The adjective "coordinated" is derived from the facts that all the leaders and therapists involved in each family were supervised by the same person; all were encouraged to exchange facts and observations of members of families with each other in informal encounters at the clinic during occasional free periods, such as lunch hours and casual interchange at any other time; and formal "integration" (case) conferences were held at regular intervals—or they were called by the supervisor at any time when developments in a family made unitary, coordinated steps necessary or some critical developments were in the making and required attention from all. Included in the regularly scheduled integration conferences were other staff members, such as individual therapists of the child or a parent involved, psychologists who had tested the teenagers, personnel (usually the psychologists) from the referring schools, and at times a staff psychiatrist.

A pivotal element in the coordinating process was the extensive typed protocol reports of each session by each of the three therapists and leaders of the groups. These were carefully read, annotated, and cross-referenced by the supervisor in advance of his weekly sessions with the individual workers, so that the interactions of the individual members of the family group, indeed its total climate, readily and unmistakenly emerged.

Critically conflictual situations, malignant attitudes, and damaging acts never failed to come through in the communications of one or more of the family members.[8] These revelations alerted us to the need for taking therapeutic or guidance steps for correcting or diminishing the family-group or individual pathology as it appeared. Sometimes these steps related to one person only—father, mother or child—and could be dealt with in his or her own group. More often, other members of the family generated the difficulty. In such instances, one or both of the group conductors[9] were apprised of the facts by the supervisor so that, being aware of a situation, they would

[8] Sometimes the number was increased when siblings were also in treatment. In that event the siblings' therapists were also included in all formal conferences and informal sharing of information.

[9] The common term "conductors" is employed here to generically describe both therapists and "leaders."

take the opportunity during the discussions in their groups to elaborate on the problem and its significance without, however, directly relating it to the person involved, unless the latter voluntarily applied it to himself. When the subject would not arise spontaneously, the group conductor was advised to subtly introduce it as it logically related to another topic that was under the group's consideration at some future session.

Depending upon time sequences of group and supervisory sessions, the information gleaned from either member of a family as recorded in the dictated protocols would be communicated to the parallel workers by the supervisor during his supervisory hour or by an interoffice telephone conversation, by the marked typed protocols (left in their mail box with a note), or by a written or verbal suggestion that the two or three workers exchange pertinent information on the family for all to make use of during future group sessions or individual interviews.

An illustration of this simple, though complicated-sounding, process is the oft-recurring subject of money allowances. This subject is unfailingly brought forth in the adolescents' groups, especially where the membership stems from middle-class homes. By virtue of realistic and symbolic meanings, the manner of dealing with allowances is charged with rather strong feelings and is a source of considerable tension and conflict in many homes, a conflict that is carried over to other areas, causing much distress and unhappiness.

In the therapy group of the adolescents, the subject may be approached by exploration of the feelings toward the self, as rebellion against dependency and strivings toward self-reliance and independence; or the subject can be viewed in the context of the reality situation and dealt with accordingly. However, it is obvious that this is not a problem that a teenager can solve by himself, especially when it is charged with strong affect and is only a part of a larger conflictual setting. The parents have to be guided to deal with it with sympathy, flexibility, and understanding. Being apprised of the situation by the therapist of the adolescent group where the subject originates, the leaders of the father's and mother's groups can seize the opportunity or direct the discussion to the topic in their respective groups.

With the subject of allowance as a starting point, opportunities are offered for elaborations that can lead to the parents' awareness of the turmoil in which adolescents live and their struggles within themselves and with their environment, their confusions, their fears, and anxieties—all of which parents have to lighten. The matter of allowance, though it may seem a minor one to some parents, is of utmost significance, especially to boys in the light of their strivings for maturity, responsibility, and self-image. Discussion of such specific problems in child-centered guidance groups usually extends into other related areas in the psychosocial development of personality.

Complaints against, and dissatisfactions with, their children were lodged by the parents just as frequently as the other way around, if not more. The standard complaint was the offsprings' attitude toward, and achievement in, school. The second most frequent concern was related to the children's disobedience and lack of responsibility and cooperation in the home. As could be expected, the third most frequent subject was antagonism among the siblings.

Following the rule of child-centered group guidance of parents, generalities occupied a secondary place in the discussions. Guided by the leaders, the parents were helped by group discussions to identify specific reasons for their children's acting out and to find ways for dealing with them. The leaders carried forward conclusions as to how to understand and manage maturations that activated their children's behavior so that whatever steps were taken proceeded from awareness of needs.

The information on the children's attitudes and conduct supplied us by the fathers and mothers was passed on to the therapists of the adolescent groups (or to the individual therapists, when they were involved), which information they used in the therapeutic grist at appropriate times and context. As a result of inner relaxation and better understanding of each other, there emerged a more harmonious family climate, which made life for all concerned less strenuous and aided in the reconstructive efforts of the children's therapists and lightened the load of teachers in the classrooms.[10]

[10]For details in the improvement in the family climate of patients, see Slavson, 1958, 1963.

The following case illustrates the importance of clarity in conveying ideas to parents and points up the nature and possible pitfalls of coordinated family group therapy.

A sixteen-year-old boy complained in his group that his father was now on a "togetherness binge—everything must be done by the whole family together." At the insistence of the father, the family took auto rides together, went to dinner as a group, and visited the golf course as a unit. This irked the youngster, especially since it exposed him to the continuous presence of a much younger sister.

The leader of the father's group channeled the discussion at the next session toward the need of adolescents for independence and seeking out a life beyond the family. These ideas were discussed and elaborated by the group and the therapist-leader. At the next session of the mother's group, the mother of the boy plaintively described the events of the preceding Sunday. When the family was about to go to a restaurant for dinner, the father peremptorily announced that only the parents and the girl would be going to dinner, the boy was "old enough to find his own company and become independent." The mother was extremely upset by her son's absence and by the father's obvious rejection of him. During the dinner she called home to find out what the boy had eaten and asked him to join the family at the restaurant. He angrily told her that he had already eaten, having found food in the refrigerator, and added, "Anyway, I would not go out with you even if you asked me." He said he had already called up a friend and made an appointment for the following weekend (which may or may not have been true). Obviously the father acted upon an "idea" acquired in the group discussion without having been made aware of the subtle process involved in freeing a boy from ties to his family.

A rather difficult situation was presented by the W. family.

Both parents complained of their sixteen-year-old daughter's neglectfulness, uncooperativeness, and procrastination, especially in her homework. She usually delayed her studies until almost midnight, thus making it difficult to awaken her in the morning and frequently making her late for school. The father reported that he was compelled to go into his daughter's bedroom a number of times during the evening where she lounged in her pajamas and would often find her reading material not related to her school work. He would remonstrate at her lackadaisical attitude and the lateness of the hour.

The parents' bedroom was next to the girl's and during the group discussion it evolved that the father would have the television going every night until after midnight, but, he said, he would "turn it down low." In her group the girl freely talked about her "inability" to get her work done on time and that she could never get to her lessons "till late at night." She volunteered that she would often become interested in works of fiction and nonfiction not related to the teachers' assignments. The mother reported that she and her daughter would frequently get into violent arguments because the girl, arising too late, demanded that the mother drive her to school. Their arguments always ended in the mother's capitulation, since she did not want her daughter to be late.

Some months after the groups began meeting, the father, in puzzlement, reported that in the period intervening between the last and the current group sessions (which were held fortnightly) he and his wife had come home from a vacation trip early one evening to find their daughter fast asleep. Both could not understand it, they said. For years now their daughter had never fallen asleep so early. To us, however, this incident made clear the girl's reluctance to retire and her father's interest in her bedroom occupations. Here were manifestations of a very subtle oedipal incestuous acting out on the part of both: she to provoke his frequent visits to her bedroom and his vicarious enjoyment in doing so. In the light of these dynamics their altercations assumed symbolic sexual meaning. We also considered the father's playing the television late at night as a subtle form of communication with his daugher. This shed light upon the intense conflict between mother and daughter.

In the parents' groups the matter was treated on an administrative basis; namely, it was agreed that the girl should be placed on her own responsibility as to her schoolwork and suffer the consequences of neglect and that the father should turn off the television set early in the evening so the girl would not be "distracted." However, we recognized that the father required individual guidance and perhaps psychotherapy, which was instituted with the leader of the group as the therapist. The daughter and mother were continued in their respective groups.

Coordinated family therapy has two advantages over whole-family guidance or treatment. In the first place, increase in family tensions and possible family disruption are prevented, as already indicated. Another advantage of major proportion is that it obviates blanket application of one therapeutic approach to all the members of the family group, some of whom may best be reached by other procedures such as psychoanalysis, deep individual psychotherapy, conseling or guidance, according to their *specific* needs.

These groups meet for ninety minutes weekly or on alternate weeks, according to indications of the depth of the treatment required.

Group Psychotherapy with Children

One of the important developments in recent years in psychotherapy is the increased recognition of differences in the treatment needs of children and adults. Because of the state of his physical organic maturation and incomplete psychological development, the child presents some needs that exist in adolescents and adults only in a rudimentary state and others that do not exist in them at all. An effort to describe the many contrasts in development would extend our contribution beyond permissible length and, therefore, only a few of the major characteristics will therefore receive mention here.

Basic Characteristics of Children. One of the outstanding differences is the comparatively weak ego organization of the child and his limited ability to deal with inner impulses and external demands. In this he requires support and very careful nurturing and education by persons important and effective in his life. Another, a direct outgrowth of the first, is the basically narcissistic quality of the child's libido organization, his impulsiveness, self-indulgence, and feelings of omnipotence. The third is the surface nature of the child's unconscious. One is impressed with the readiness and almost complete unselfconsciousness with which young children act out and speak about matters that are embarrassing to an older person. This can be attributed to the abscence of repressive forces and sublimation channels that have not been as yet developed. Finally, the child's identifications are still in a fluid and ambivalent state, hence the superego is rudimentary and unformed.

The child is still in the process of emerging, and the struggle between primitive impulses and restraint has not as yet been resolved. He is still working out a pattern for his life, which eventually will lead to some inner balance. Because of his formative state, his emotions are labile and his behavior inconsistent. He is experimenting with himself and with his surroundings. He is transilient; thus his concentration span is brief. Some of these characteristics are the result of organic instability due to growth, others are the outcome of congenital temperament and disposition, still others are expressions of unbridled emotional drives. Generally, the child feels less restricted in his own world than grownups do in theirs, and the child's capacity for change and reintegration is much greater than that of rigidized adults.

Of importance to the psychotherapist is that the child is in the thrall of primitive impulses and, therefore, little able to withstand frustration and, because of his still unregulated drives, given to rages and tantrums. He is intensely concerned with, and has a greater need for, freedom of movement and action and an impelling need for aggression and play. His fantasy life is rich and reality and imagination are reversible, if not identical. This state of flux is derived from rapid organic growth and progressive psychic evolvement, as well as from the resentments and hostilities built up in the course of his brief life.

Education has long recognized the importance of activity for young children. For the child, functioning as he does on primitive levels and with limited ideation, physicial activity is of fundamental importance. The child still has to intellectually discover the realities around him and still has to establish a workable acquaintance with them. Physical activity, however, is very important and has more than educational value; it is also essential for his mental health. His potential energies must find dynamic expression if body-mind equilibrium is to emerge and be maintained. Preventing the discharge of energy produces organic and psychologic tensions, for discharge through the vasomotor system of the body equilibrates emotions (Slavson, 1946a).

Studies have adequately demonstrated that, especially in the early years, inhibiting physical activity in young children as practiced in the schoolroom retards physical growth and psychological development. Many children who might be able to bear up under the deprivations of the average home, become emotionally disturbed and socially maladjusted from the added strains inherent in the ordinary school regime and from the blocking of the spontaneous neuromuscular expression through physical activity.

Because of these considerations and because of the limitations of language as a medium of expression and communication, play and activity therapy for young children was devised. A child is supplied with appropriate materials through which he can convey symbolically his fantasies and preoccupations. Through release in action the young children can overcome traumatic tensions by abreacting in a properly equipped setting with appropriate furnishings and materials. Objects such as toy guns and soldiers, darts, clay, dolls, and water can help the young patients discharge aggressions and reduce urethral, anal, and sexual interests.

Group psychotherapy with children is based on the same assumptions as is individual psychotherapy, namely the ready transmutation of ideas and feelings into motoric expression, the child's impulsivity and transilience, his weak ego organization, his inadequate superego formation, the surface nature of his unconscious, and the nonverbal or *action communication* natural for children. While there are distinct differences in the four types of group treatment employed with children to be described—activity group therapy, play group therapy, activity-interview therapy, and transitional groups—they have some essential characteristics in common. The major of these is that in view of the child's need for motoricity as a form of expression and communication, they all involve physical activity; children's groups are also conspicuous by the absence of "social fixity" as differentiated from "social mobility" (Slavson, 1944). However, free "acting out" is permitted in activity groups, but is limited in play groups of very young children and in transitional groups (Slavson, 1956) of older children.

Activity Group Therapy

General Plan. Activity group therapy is applicable to boys and girls in latency and early puberty. Eight boys or girls (separately) between the ages of eight and twelve years, are grouped by age in accordance with their clinical and behavioral suitability to one another. The first criterion is age. Children within an age range of a year and a half or two years were found to be most suitable, except, of course, where there is great divergence in social, organic, or emotional development. Extreme problems of either a neurotic nature or of behavior disorders, especially of an aggressive type, psychopathic personalities, and psychotics or physically handicapped have been found unsuitable for this type of treatment. Some mild latent schizophrenics with good ego organizations have gained greatly from these groups, however (Nagelberg & Rosenthal, 1955).

Activity groups are supplied with simple arts and crafts materials and tools that they can use freely. At the beginning of the treatment no restrictions of any kind are imposed. This is a *permissive environment.* Limitations, control, and denial arise naturally as members infringe upon the rights and convenience of others, and, at later stages in treatment, from the therapist as well.

All sessions of these groups end with refreshments, usually milk, fruit, and cake. No table manners are imposed. Children can eat with the group or take their share and eat by themselves. They can gulp or chew the food or throw it around if they so wish. By their own suggestion and choice, the members of these groups arrange trips to museums, parks, zoological gardens, industrial establishments, theaters, movies, and other places that may interest them.

The purpose of the setting and activities is to give substitute satisfactions through the free acting out of impulses, gratifying experiences, group status, recognition of achievement, and unconditional love and acceptance from an adult. These help the children overcome basic character malformations, such as emasculation in boys, confused identifications in girls, feelings of impotence, and fear of expressing aggressive and hostile impulses. In such an environment and group relationship, the infantile and overprotected child can become self-reliant and act more maturely; the exploited child becomes a more autonomous and a self-activating entity; and the rejected child, with the broken-down ego and low degree of self-esteem, can be built up.[11]

Image and Function of Therapist. The attitude of the group therapist is permissive. The children who come to these groups must be convinced that he is a kindly, unpunitive, friendly, positive individual. The group therapist is neither domineering nor pampering, nor does he exploit the child for his own emotional needs and gratifications. The children are set free to grow at their own pace through the pressure of the group and to acquire a new orientation toward environment and people, and a new and better self-identity.

While the therapist's role in these groups is predominantly passive, he can succeed only to the degree his patients will allow. Some have an emotional need for him and come to him for help, consultation, and comfort on the slightest or no provocation. Others withdraw and do not communicate with him in any way. The therapist accepts these projections of their feelings on him by each child. This attitude and role we describe as one of *neutrality.* He strives to remain outside the emotional flux of the group, so as to allow maximum interpersonal and intragroup emotional and physical activity. This is essential because patients are chosen for group treatment because they need to acquire facilities to relate to other children as well as to adults.

The above description of the functions and activities of the group therapist is rather deceptive. He only *appears* to be inactive and indifferent. Actually, while he remains physically in the background, he has many duties to perform. He supplies the standard materials, tools, and games to avoid the frustration that their absence might

[11] For greater details of the theory and practice of activity group therapy, see Slavson, 1943.

cause and he prevents the feeling of being neglected by the therapist (a lack of love). The therapist must have a thorough knowledge of the traumatogenic backgrounds of each member of the group and of his therapeutic needs to counteract them, the patterns of each one's ego functioning, and the specific situational and personal response he has to supply as a therapeutic measure.

Thus he might readily help one child with his project and subtly protect him by specific strategies from excessive aggression or humiliation from fellow group members, while in the case of another, the help would not be forthcoming with quite the same readiness and the patient would be allowed to take the full brunt of the interpersonal and group interactions. Recognizing ego weakness and anxiety in one child, the therapist may take up a position or sit near him, while he might remove himself from another whom the therapist recognizes as being potentially capable, though unwilling, to fend for himself or carry his own burdens as a result of an overprotective family background.

While the therapist in an activity group is at first a wholeheartedly "giving" person, as the treatment progresses and the self-image of each member improves, the group is exposed to frustration such as absence of or delay in supplying materials or food. This is done to test controls and the degree of *frustration tolerance* of the recovering patients, which are the acme of maturity and ego strength.

Materials and Tools. All materials and tools supplied to an activity therapy group must be familiar to the young patients so as not to overwhelm them and further extend their feelings of inadequacy and their defective self-image. They must also be so simple that immediate gratifications can be attained through them. The materials must lend themselves to projects that can be completed in the two-hour session of the group or at most in two such sessions. No new types of materials beyond those prescribed for these groups are added throughout their life, which is usually about two years. This rigid rule is observed so that the interest of the patients is not focused on the manual activities. The therapeutic intent is to motivate interpersonal interaction rather than manual or artistic achievement. This transition always occurs. After some months, preoccupation gradually and imperceptably shifts from work with hands to play, fight, struggle, or cooperation among two or three members of the group as a whole. After a year or more, work with hands plays a diminishing role in the interests and activities of the children.

The selection of materials and tools is made on their capacity for *libido-fixating,* i.e., they are intended not to stimulate the patients' unconscious sexual, anal, or urethral phantasies or deep-rooted and intensively charged unconscious feelings and drives. Children who require working through such problems are placed in either individual treatment or in the analytic groups (play or activity interview) to be described presently.

Activity Group Therapy Supplies

Tools

Brace — 10-in. sweep
  set of bits—sizes ½, ¾, 1 in.
3 hammers—11-in. handles—1½, ¾, 1 lb.
1 square with miter handle—6 in.
Hand drill and set of drills
2 block planes
1 7-in. jack plane
3 screwdrivers—assorted sizes to ¼ in.
1 pair plyers, small
1 tin snips — 10 in.
3 coping saws—7-in. blade
  2 dozen coping saw blades
2 chisels—1 in. and ½ in.
1 wooden mallet
2 crosscut saws — 10 teeth per in.
Assorted nails—2 lbs.
Assorted sandpaper, fine to coarse
Glue, wood
(Plastic wood filler)
(1 rip saw)
(2 shoe files)

Arts and Crafts Material
Crayons, all colors
Poster paint and six brushes
Drawing paper, assorted colors
Gimp (plastic, for lanyards) assorted colors
Lanyard hooks
Leather scraps
Leather for wallets, purses, etc.
Leather punch—wheel with assorted sizes
Leather snaps
2 ashtray molds, wood
Pewter for ashtrays and copper
3 wooden mallets for pounding out ashtray
Plasticene clay—1 lb. or 4 small pieces of various colors
Copper
Copper design tracings
3 small scissors

Games
Ping-pong net, paddles, balls
Cards, quoits
Checkers—2 sets
Pick-up-sticks
Tenpins
Carpentry worktable
1 small table
1 large table
1 (round) refreshment table
NOTE: For girls, supplies for making dolls, painting pictures, clay modeling, materials for simple sewing, quiet games, and a phonograph and suitable music would have to be added.

Selection of Patients. Because of the specificity of the therapeutic needs of children, we have compiled, after more than twenty years of experimentation and study, the criteria for acceptance and rejection of patients for activity and other types of group therapy.

TABLE 6[12]
INDICATIONS AND CONTRAINDICATIONS FOR ACTIVITY THERAPY GROUPS FOR CHILDREN IN LATENCY

Indications	*Contraindications**
Clinical	*Clinical*
Oedipal primary behavior disorders	Severe psychoneuroses
Some preoedipal primary behavior disorders	Psychoses
Character disorders	Psychopathy
Mild neuroses	Neurotic characters
Situational anxiety (anxiety hysteria)	Severe anxiety states
Some latent schizophrenics	Latent homosexuality
Some schizoid personalities	Disturbances in libido development
Characterological	*Characterological*
Confused sexual identification	Absence of minimal ego development
Effeminacy (in boys)	Absence of minimal superego development
Masculinity (in girls)	Inadequate capacity for object relationships
Infantilization	Regressive infantilism
Overprotection	Castration anxiety
Nonpathological withdrawal	Excessive generalized aggression
Inadequate ego development	Excessive aggression toward adults
Social hunger	Physical handicaps and deformities
Only children	Stigmatizations
	Mental deficiency

[12] From Slavson, 1955, p. 29.

*Children included in this category of contraindications cannot be placed in groups even when they receive individual treatment. They can be referred to groups only after the basic personality problems have been corrected through individual treatment and may require a period of "socialization," though in some instances, this may encourage regression.

Our observations indicate that considerable levels of spontaneous insight appears through the activities and interactions which proceeds from the patient's awareness of the change within himself and his improved manual skills and facilities to deal with his impulses and the outer world. We frequently hear a child comparing himself as he is now with how he had been in the past. He verbalizes his awareness of his greater powers for dealing with situations, his changed attitudes, and improvement. This is *derivative insight;* namely, insight derived from the patient's own growth rather than from interpretation by other members of the group or the therapist.

Activity therapy groups meet weekly for two hours.

ANALYTIC GROUPS: ACTIVITY-INTERVIEW GROUPS

General Plan. After some years of practice with activity group therapy we discovered that not all children in the latency period (seven to twelve years) for whom group treatment was indicated could be placed in such unrestrained, free acting out groups, such as activity therapy groups are. Some needed groups of lesser *aggression density,* such as very young children and neurotics. Intensely psychoneurotic youngsters in latency become frightened and anxious at excessive manifestation of hostility and aggression; they cannot endure acting it out and become too disturbed and further traumatized. Young people in middle and later adolescence as well do not gain much from arts and crafts in free activity groups. Thus, we found that no one pattern of group therapy can be applied to *all* patients and that other techniques had to be devised for them. We have, therefore, introduced interpretive therapies for the more disturbed children which we term "analytic groups."

Analytic group therapy for children in latency is similar to that of activity therapy groups in the one respect that they, too, utilize free activity or acting out. At the same time, they differ in several important aspects: The materials and toys supplied are aimed at *libido activation* rather than *libido fixation,* as is the case in activity groups. Reflection, explanation, and insight are employed or derived. The therapist's role is different. Unlike in activity groups, both girls and boys are included in the same groups.

Analytic groups for children are divided, according to their ages, into two categories: *activity-interview* and *play groups.*

In activity-interview groups, manual occupations are utilized as a starting point, but they are not the sole treatment, as in activity groups. The child's or the group's behavior is interpreted with regard to the motives of acts. By these means each is helped to understand his problem and a limited degree of insight gradually emerges. Interpretation and insight may come from other members of the group or from the therapist. The more patients help one another in this respect, the better. While we deal predominantly with the sexual libido in analytic groups, in activity groups it is the patient's ego that is more involved, and the nonsexual libido is more prominent. Although both the ego and the libido are involved in both types of group, the difference is in the predominance of one or the other (which is readily understandable in the light of the difference in the quality of the transference relationship), the type of patient, and the nature of the therapeutic process.[13] Activity group therapy, is therefore, predominantly an ego therapy while analytic groups deal with the patient's libidinal fixations and difficulties, as well as with his ego functioning.

In activity-interview group therapy, verbal attacks may be expressed directly against the therapist. Since patients resent him as a parent substitute, they criticize his coming late, question or reject interpretations, openly disagree, and in other ways reinforce one another in their negative feelings toward him. They may even attack him physically. Therapeutically such expression of negative feelings is of great value, for egress of hostility is one of the main requirements for emotional recovery.

Libidinal involvements, the oedipal struggle, and the therapist's interpretations and insight-giving create problems that are not manifested in activity groups; and if they are on very rare occasions, they are of vastly lesser intensity. Jealousies and hostilities are more

[13] The place of libido in group therapy was more fully discussed in Slavson, 1946b.

intense than they are likely to be in activity groups. The analytic group therapist is an object of the patient's libidinal preoccupations to a greater degree. The patient involves him in his oedipal conflict; he therefore becomes the object of ambivalent feelings and genital strivings. This does not occur in activity groups, where the therapist is a *neutral* person, and the members are not neurotic.

Activity-interview groups meet weekly for ninety minutes or less. The therapist may terminate or extend the time according to the need and reactions of the young patients.

Analytic Groups: Play Groups[14]

General Plan. This form of therapy is substantially the same as the preceding technique. The differences are that it is employed with children under six years of age, the *play* materials (which are libido activating) are simpler in their nature, the therapist participates comparatively less, and instead of interpreting the children's behavior he usually "reflects" their feelings and suggests meanings to their acts. Only infrequently would he attempt to "uncover" unconscious implications or background causes. With children of this age, it can be truly said that the "living situation" is in itself therapeutic. The feeling of freedom and love and awareness of the presence of others and interaction with them have a salutary effect.

As already indicated, the materials in play group therapy are libido activating; but because of the level of maturation at this age, they are intended for play rather than construction. Here are to be found building blocks; minitoys with dolls and furniture and trays to arrange different rooms; dolls that can be fed and plastic toy bottles as well as real baby bottles; trays with water; rubber tubing; funnels; small trucks and fire engines with firemen; toy automobiles; toy pistols; plasticene; paper and crayons; small floor mop; sponges; brush and pan; a settee or couch (which is used for putting the dolls to bed); small pieces of blankets to cover the dolls.

[14] In these groups as well, boys and girls are treated together.

As in all other types of therapy, the therapist must be aware of the significance and meaning of play in its many facets. He must recognize that play to a child is what serious, productive work is to an adult. Through play, the child carries out the tasks of his life, and he uses play for many other ends as well. To review the many theories of play — such as experimentation with reality, expression of excess energy, recapitulation of the phylogenetic experience of the race, preparation for adulthood, a form of mastery, an effort to attenuate reality — would take us far afield.

The term *libido-activating* materials as differentiated from *libido-fixating* materials, which we have suggested in relation to work with children, refers to objects and supplies that evoke the deeper feelings of the young patients concerning oral, urethral, anal, and sexual matters that had not been dealt with appropriately by parents and others, or where the child had been traumatized in these areas. The children communicate these problems as a result of specific "activating" materials. Among these are water; finger paints; clay; father, mother, and children dolls (some of which are castration and others are urinating dolls); a doll house and furnishings, especially those of bedrooms and bathrooms; various animals; masks; toy soldiers; and similar objects through which the children can reveal their unconscious preoccupations and sublimate their aggressive feelings.

The manner in which clay, for example, was utilized in such a group, in the play of two nine-year-old boys, demonstrates the nature of libido-activating materials.

Hilton and Mike played with the clay while the girls painted. This evoked a memory in Hilton of a dream in which an octopus had closed its tentacles around him. He demonstrated his reactions with a good deal of affect. He then stated that he talks to himself every night and that he wanted to be a doctor so he could save many people. He then talked about blood tests he had seen at the clinic and dreamed that a nurse stuck a needle too far into his arm and it "became fat." Following this, he returned to playing with clay and built imaginary blood vessels which he pretended to be "studying." Mike made canoes out of clay.

The girls withdrew into the next room, where they played quietly by themselves and the boys fashioned the clay into long round strips. Mike said with a smirk, "Oh, see what he is making." Hilton looked astonished. The therapist asked Mike to give the group a clue. This was given. Hilton took the clue and placed the penis symbol as though it was in action and began to march up and down the room. Mike hastily fashioned small balls of clay and began marching up and down as though defecating while walking. They marched soberly up and down for about ten minutes, completely disregarding the presence of Carl and the therapist.

Hilton remarked that he knows a girl who plays with "her penis and her hiney." Mike knows a boy who likes to expose his penis, especially whenever a woman passed him. Both boys laughed. Mike grabbed Hilton's clay symbol which caused him to cry out, "Give me back my penis! I must have it!" He picked up a piece of clay, modeled it into a long strip to give him a better opportunity to protect it. The therapist asked Mike (who suffered from severe constipation) whether he defecates daily. Mike boastfully replies that he rarely "does it." Hilton said, "I do it every day." The therapist explained elimination to the children, using the furnace as an analogy of what goes on in the human body.

The play revealed a singular freedom from self-consciousness, which was possible because of the therapist's completely noncommittal but friendly attitude. When Mike's mother was seen several weeks later, she informed the therapist that his constipation of long standing had completely disappeared (Gabriel, 1939).

The following taken from the same paper reveals another type of preoccupation, the revelation of which was stimulated by the libido-evoking materials.

As they played, Linda mentioned that she worried over the poor relationship between herself and (her sister) Emma. "It isn't nice to dislike your sister," she said and added that she liked her brothers because "they're cute." (Note: In individual interviews Linda had been revealing fantasies and had repeated dreams, most of which expressed anxiety and curiosity about birth, what happened to the fetus, and also the role the father took in the birth phenomenon.)

During the group play period Linda carried this preoccupation over to the group and narrated a dream. She had been kidnapped, taken to a dark dungeon where the man said he was going to kill her. She screamed. As she related this she commented, wonderingly, that all her dreams formerly were bad but now she has nice dreams, too. She dreamed she was getting married; when she awakened she was eager to find out whether she was really married. The therapist said it was a nice dream and asked whether she thought a lot about marriage and having babies. She admitted this. There was some discussion about difference between boys and girls. She was asked whether she worried because she was not built like a boy. Her response was "No" — she knows boys are different, they have a penis. Her mother had even told her that she would need an operation if she plays with her "pupu." I asked whether she believed this. She said, "Mothers don't lie."

Emma discussed masturbation frankly. Jean, in a carefree manner, laughed. She isn't afraid of operations. At this point Emma and Linda got into an argument, each protesting that she did not wish to impose too much on the other. Linda always procrastinates when she is told to do something and always wants to be waited on. General conversation then led to a discussion about habits of eating and other daily home activities. A significant point which they made was that their aggressive and hostile behavior results from the fact that they are "forced" to eat food they don't want (Gabriel, 1939, pp. 158-159).

Selection of Patients. The children selected for these groups are, by and large, more disturbed than are those who are placed in activity therapy groups. As Table 7 shows, among them are to be found neurotic children with symptomatology, with anxiety states and sexually overstimulated, and the phobic. (The latter may require parallel individual treatment.) Obviously, such children cannot overcome their difficulties by the ego strengthening alone and by improvement of the self-image through group acceptance. They require in addition to "work through" on their own level their memories, feelings, fears, and fancies, through the aid of catharsis that leads to some level of insight (which must be limited at best in children) in an active transference relation to an adult as a parent substitute (as well as to other children).

The assignment of children to these groups — play therapy groups and activity-interview groups — are considerably less rigid than they are for adults or adolescents. Grouping them is, therefore, also less exacting. In play groups the children are either in the preoedipal stage or in the beginnings of the oedipal conflict. Their neuroses, if any at all, are structurally and dynamically different from the postpubertal neuroses (Slavson, 1952). We have found that children under six years of age of various clinical categories, such as reactive (primary) behavior disorders, character disorders, neurotic traits, neurotic reactions, can be placed together. Among the other conditions for which groups are the treatment of choice are only children, children who are more than ordinarily antagonistic and aggressive toward adults, and children who diffuse anxiety and lack minimal impulse control.

Children in latency who are seriously disturbed and the massively anxious require, as do adults, a period of individual psychotherapy before assignment to a group, and most of them benefit from parallel individual and group treatment. More than do adults, children benefit from association and interaction with peers, and group therapy should be used with them extensively.

Here, as well, before a child is placed in a group, his degree of libidinal distortion and sexual attachment for his parents, especially the parent of the opposite sex, should be ascertained. Children whose parents or older siblings had been seductive, sexually provocative, and overstimulating, who slept in the same bed with their parents or in the same room, or who witnessed or overheard the primal scene, require play therapy in an individual transference relation, interpretation, and insight as well as release and cathexis displacement (Slavson, 1952, p. 231).

Even more than in the case of adults, antagonisms toward a sibling may preclude placement of a child in a group. While in most instances sibling hostility can be dissolved by groups, we have found instances where the intensive acting out of these feelings made continuing of the child-patient in a group inadvisable.

Among the children for whom individual therapy is preferred are those who have been subjected to a serious trauma, such as a sudden catastrophe, prolonged exposure to a series of traumatic occurrences, or a total traumatic environment in the family. The anxiety bound up as a result of these exposures has to be released in the security of a positive transference, and treatment has to be focused toward the dissolution of the bound-up anxiety. This can best be done in individual therapy through free play and verbal association and interpretation, which dissolve the child's anxieties. Children in such straits require the security of a relationship with a therapeutically oriented adult with whom they feel comfortable and free. This also removes the burden their still weak and unformed ego has to carry.

We have found that children even with such intense problems gain immeasurably from participation in appropriate therapeutic groups, skillfully conducted. Since the children's ego organization is still in a rudimentary state and because the catharsis in children's analytic groups is both one of activity and verbalization, the skills and vigilance required in conducting such groups are by far more exacting than in directing groups of nonpsychotic adults (Slavson, 1945, 1948, 1950). Because acting out is the rule in these groups it is not suited to children with intense anxiety, particularly if it originates in preverbal and preconceptual stages, that is, children who can be classed as having *neurotic characters.* They do not meet the requirement of minimal ego development for group participation.

Because of the small child's tendency to substitute the therapist for his real parents and attach to (displace on) him the latters' attributes,[15] resistances may be so intense as to block the individual therapist's treatment efforts. It was found that in such instances, a preliminary course of group treatment reduces resistances and defenses and the distrust of the adult. Here as well the communications of fellow group members support and catalize the child so that he can enter into a therapeutic mood. Thus groups can be used as exclusive treatment or to intensify it, to taper it off, or as preparation for individual psychotherapy.

Barring those with very intense libidinal disturbances, ego insufficiencies and psychotics, there are large numbers of maladjusted children for whom analytic group psychotherapy is sufficient in itself.

[15] This mechanism is present also in schizophrenic adult patients.

TABLE 7
INDICATIONS AND CONTRAINDICATIONS
FOR ANALYTIC THERAPY GROUPS FOR CHILDREN

Indications	*Contraindications**
Clinical	*Clinical*
Reactive behavior disorders	Massive psychoneurotic symptomatology
Character disorders	Libido fixations and distortions
Neurotic traits	Neurotic characters
Neurotic reactions	Diffuse fears and anxiety
Anxiety states	Reactions to trauma
	Psychoses
Characterological	*Characterological*
Only children	Intense sibling rivalry
Aggressiveness toward adults	Lack of impulse control
Excessive submissiveness	

*In most of these cases parallel individual and group treatment are indicated.

Functions of the Therapist. In the two types of analytic-activity groups the therapist is more the center of the emotional network and more real as a person than he is in activity therapy groups. He participates in the discussions, reacts to the attitudes of the members, and generally represents the reality with which the patients are familiar, but of a more benign nature than that they had encountered in the past.

In these groups, the major therapeutic tool is the help the therapist gives to each member to understand his reactions and, *within his comprehension,* some of the sources of his psychological stresses and social maladjustments.

As is the case in adult and adolescent analytic group psychotherapy, the degree of insight is limited by each member's capacity to accept and deal with it. The therapist, therefore, needs a thorough knowledge of each group member's problems, his nuclear or central difficulties and his capacity to withstand stress — and he must exercise caution where necessary. Some young patients (as well as adults) may be able to intellectually accept interpretive confrontation by the therapist of a specific problem and yet be injuriously disturbed by it. The therapist must always address himself also to the *lowest denominator* in the group in each situation and in relation to every problem that is brought forth, so as to prevent heightening malignancy in his patients.

The therapist should at all times be aware of where the group is heading. As in the treatment of adults and adolescents, his knowledge of each patient's difficulties and the principles of psychopathology and psychotherapy must at all times be poised for action. Also, as in the case of older patients, a well-timed question can open the sluices of the unconscious and facilitate free association, a process that is aided by the catalytic influence of the therapist and the other group members. Points of fear and resistance that periodically appear in groups must be recognized. At these stages patients must be helped to overcome their differences and fears through appropriate use of the (libidinal) transference relation. The therapist may, as indicated by the situation, analyze the resistance of the group, incite or facilitate expression of hostility to himself, or reassure the group of his acceptance and permissiveness. The line to be taken is usually indicated by the nature of the blocking, the manifest and latent content of the discussions, and the anticipated anxiety sources inherent in the treatment situation.

The therapist's role here is not as permissive as it is in dealing with older children. We have seen that freedom is the primary condition for therapy, especially freedom to express aggression and hostility. But freedom and restraint have to be balanced in education as well as in therapy. The younger the child, the more restraint he may need. Self-restraint in later life flows from the benevolent restraint of adults (discipline) whom he accepts and trusts. The young child emerging from a state of nurture, when all his wants and whims were unconditionally satisfied, needs time, strength, and maturity to incorporate restraints. Discipline and authority *acceptable to him, and graded in intensity,* are necessary for the child's personality integration, but they have to be applied with keen discrimination and great caution.

In therapy, the frightened and withdrawn do not need such control; rather they need release. The overactive and aggressive need restraint. Their diffuse aggressiveness and pugnacious trends have to be impeded. Since the child has not as yet established controls within himself, these must come from the outside, namely, from the adult. It is through a kind, accepting and acceptable, but firm adult that the child will give up his atavistic egoism and narcissism.

Because of the state of their ego controls, very young children naturally tend toward explosive behavior, which may assume violent proportions at times. In a group, they tend to stimulate and reinforce one another and join together for rather extreme hilarity and destructiveness. There is little value, therapeutically speaking, in this behavior. In individual therapy the therapist can treat the manifestations of aggression through release therapy, play therapy, or interpretation, and thus reach the central (nuclear) problem of the child. In groups, aggressiveness initiated by one is taken on through group contagion by the others without its having any beneficial effect on them, except "letting off steam." In groups, therefore, explosive activity that has meaning to the initiator may not be related to the central (nuclear) problem of others, and thus has no particular meaning in terms of therapy. Release through aggression and hostility has value when it is related to a child's problem; when it becomes diffuse, it may have antitherapeutic effect, namely, it may disorganize personality, rather than leading to ego integration.

Play therapy groups meet weekly from forty-five to ninety minutes according to the stage of development of the children.

Transitional Groups

Some boys and girls in later latency years and early puberty (ten to thirteen years of age) who had suffered lesser traumatogenic experiences and, therefore, had ego functioning more socially adaptive than that of patients heretofore discussed, as well as children who had reached this level of development through individual or group therapy, are placed in numerically larger and more reality oriented situations. Sometimes, though infrequently, an activity therapy group as a whole may become ready for expanding social reality and more formal and organized groups.

When such groups of psychically healthier youngsters with social adjustment problems are exposed to the setting of a neighborhood center, they meet with more average community stimuli, such as other groups and activities. These give individual members opportunities to voluntarily join creative occupations or social and special interest clubs. When the transfer is made, as in the case of former therapy groups, they are not provided with arts and crafts materials, food, trips, or any other advantages they had enjoyed in the past. This denial serves as a test of their growing independence and maturity. When some of the children cannot adjust to the new pattern, they are returned to individual or group treatment. Usually, their frustration tolerance is adequate to accept the new regimen. Transitional groups are gradually motivated to set up an organization — with officers, dues, treasurer, secretary, program committee — and they join interclub activities in the center.

We have designated these groups as *transitional* during the early period when they are directed by their group therapist; later they become regular "clubs" under the leadership of a "group work" (not group therapist) staff member. We have found, however, that none of our former therapy groups continued in existence for more than one season as each member finds in the neighborhood center an interest or a club that he joins on his own, abandoning his former fellow patients. Since the element of social or interest homogeneity is absent in therapy groups, the cohesiveness and synergy essential for the existence of ordinary clubs do not arise in therapy groups to hold the members together.

From the standpoint of social prophylaxis, transitional groups are extremely valuable in the ordinary neighborhood or "Y", so that they may stem the flow of the constantly increasing number of problem children and adolescent delinquents. They may be helped to gradually adapt to social living and all that it encompasses. Organized clubs, with definite aims and objectives, proscriptions, rules, laws, and group pressures, present a higher form of group living than many youngsters in the community can accept. They need, rather, a period in an attenuated social climate that would serve as substitutes or correctives. Transitional groups offer these. Their freedom of action and communication, the suitable occupations to meet individual needs, their fluidity and interest variety entice the youngsters in participating in a social enterprise. Transitional groups differ from therapy groups in that the membership need not be so carefully balanced and that the leader, while aware of the difficulties of each member, is more assertive and can function as external authority.

Transitional groups meet weekly for ninety minutes to two hours. Termination of the session is determined by the interest and quality of participation of the members.

REFERENCES

Gabriel, B. (1939), An experiment in group treatment. *Amer. J. Orthopsychiat.*, 9:146-169.

Nagelberg, L. and Rosenthal, L. (1955), Validation of selection of patients for "activity group therapy" through the Rorschach and other tests. *Internat. J. Group Psychother.*, 5:380-391.

Slavson, S.R. (1943), *An Introduction to Group Therapy.* New York: International Universities Press.

——— (1944), Some elements in activity group therapy. *Amer. J. Orthopsychiat.*, 14:578-588.

——— (1945), Differential methods of group therapy in relation to age levels. *Nervous Child*, 4.

——— (1946a), *Recreation and the Total Personality.* New York: Association Press.

——— (1946b), Group psychotherapy today. In: *Current Psychiatric Treatment of Personality Disorders*, B. Glueck, ed. New York: Grune & Stratton.

——— (1948), Play therapy for young children. *Nervous Child*, 7:318-327.

——— (1950), *Analytic Group Psychotherapy.* New York: Columbia University Press. Chapters 8 and 9.

——— (1952), *Child Psychotherapy.* New York: Columbia University Press.

——— (1955), Criteria for selection and rejection of patient for various types of group psychotherapy. *Internat. J. Group Psychother.*, 5:3-30.

——— (1956), The nature and treatment of acting out in group psychotherapy. *Internat. J. Group Psychother.*, 6:3-27.

——— (1958), *Child-centered Group Guidance of Parents.* New York: International Universities Press.

——— (1963), Steps in sensitizing parents (couples) toward schizophrenic children. *Internat. J. Group Psychother.*, 13:175-186.

——— (1964), *A Textbook in Analytic Group Psychotherapy.* New York: International Universities Press.

——— (1965a), Co-ordinated family therapy. *Internat. J. Group Psychother.*, 15:177-186.

——— (1965b), *Reclaiming the Delinquent through Para-Analytic Group Psychotherapy and the Inversion Technique.* New York: Freee Press of Glencoe.

——— (1970), *Because I Live Here.* New York: International Universities Press.

4

Psychoanalysis in Groups

ALEXANDER WOLF

"Tell us how you work in and with the group," the editor said to me when inviting me to contribute to this volume. "A 'how-to' piece would be a welcome contribution."

The request stopped me for a moment. I had been vaguely dissatisfied with the current literature on group psychotherapy, including my own writings. The zest and searching seemed to be gone. Instead of the adventure and excitement of the early years we were now being inundated with evermore parochial and partisan clinical points of view presented as the preferred way to function, or conversely, bitter denunciation because we were not practicing according to one another's prescriptions. It seemed to me a new, overall look at my own life in the work might prove interesting, at least to me. So, the reader is entitled to view this essay as a reappraisal of a field which still commands my zeal and devotion.

A frequent question asked by analysts of their patients is, "How did you happen to choose your life work?" Answering that question for myself, it seems to me, in retrospect, that I had sound manifest reasons for becoming interested in group therapy and for continuing my work in it. And, also in retrospect, I realize today that those reasons were not personal alone, but were also dictated by the larger

Dr. Wolf is Associate Professor of Psychiatry, New York Medical College.

forces in the world of which our craft, or science, or art, or whatever one wishes to call it, is a part.

In 1938, when fairly well along in my own training as a psychoanalyst, I came across some articles by Burrow, Wender, and Schilder. These three therapists, from different points of view and for different reasons, had begun experimenting with the analytic treatment of patients in groups. Burrow stressed the need to challenge the authoritarian position of the individual psychoanalyst. Schilder was concerned with the culture's influence on the individual, with his values and mores, while Wender occupied himself primarily with the disturbed person's need for a community and the responsibility of the community at large to understand and, possibly, fill that need.

I cannot document specifically why these papers caught my attention or commanded my interest at the time. In all likelihood some dissatisfaction with the existing psychoanalytic experience had something to do with it. Whatever the reason, I communicated this new interest immediately and enthusiastically to some colleagues who were in analysis with my own training psychoanalyst and proposed that we form our own group in order to experience for ourselves that advantages and disadvantages of group psychotherapy. My suggestion was met with a thunderous silence. Only my analyst found words to discuss the matter with me. He felt, and not without reason, that my plan was evidence of my own resistance to our analytic relationship; which is what we worked on, while my experimental idea died aborning.

While I was in analytic training, the United States was in the depths of a great economic depression. Fortunately, I had been able to build a private practice in psychotherapy, but after a few years, the numbers of patients who had to be turned away because they could not afford private therapy began to haunt me. Was psychoanalysis going to turn out to be a therapy only for those who could afford it? Undoubtedly so, if no compromise could be found. At the same time, I had begun to feel that even if the process of psychoanalysis could not be shortened, it must somehow become a more immediate, dramatic, and meaningful experience for patient and analyst alike. It was then that the idea of trying to work with groups reoccurred to me. This time I was in the fortunate position of being my own "authority" and could put my idea into operation. Without being too insistent, I began to present the possibility of group therapy to the patients already in analysis with me. To my surprise I found that most of the patients shared my enthusiasm at embarking on a new adventure which had a serious base and held the promise of increased personal fruition.

The original group consisted of ten patients, five men and five women. They met with me three times a week in sessions lasting one and a half hours. Shortly after the group became cohesive, they reported back to me that they were continuing their meetings in a nearby coffee shop and that many different things were being observed during these extracurricular gatherings. I saw no reason to forbid these meetings without me. And so, almost immediately, the "alternate session," which I will discuss in more detail later, was established as an integral part of my plan for the practice of psychoanalysis in groups. This psychoanalytic orientation did not change, and now after thirty years, I still find the precepts of psychoanalysis the broadest, most reasonable base for effective group therapy.

Although this personal beginning was still in the pioneering days of psychoanalytic group psychotherapy, the first actual record of group psychotherapy in the United States was presented by Dr. J. H. Pratt, a Boston physician, in 1906. Dr. Pratt, working with tuberculars who could not afford institutional care, quickly found that his classroom instruction on tubercular home care had beneficial emotional side effects. By 1956 he was referring to his work not as "Home Sanatorium Treatment for Consumptives" (1906) but as "group psychotherapy" (1956). Between these two dates, group psychotherapy came of age. Moreno has written how he worked with groups in Vienna in 1910. Lazell reported on group treatment of psychotics in 1921. Burrow introduced the term group analysis in 1925. Wender reported on his work with psychoanalytically oriented groups in 1929, and Slavson introduced, among other noteworthy innovations, activity group therapy. In 1931, Marsh reported on his twenty years of group psychotherapy utilizing the repressive-inspirational method and the idea of milieu therapy. And in 1934,

Schilder introduced group psychotherapy into Bellevue Hospital in New York, combining social and psychoanalytic points of view in his technique.

By this time the economic depression in the United States had hit bottom. Tensions were further increased by the threat of imminent war, and the combination of these social forces undoubtedly did much to spur the acceptance of group psychotherapy as a recognized method of treatment. It was the Second World War, however, that gave group psychotherapy its greatest impetus. I embarked on my own tour of military service with four years of clinical experience in group psychotherapy behind me. During my term of service I had the rare and invaluable opportunity of working with hundreds of groups of men on a short-term basis and of training younger therapists in a method that had now become one of military necessity. Many devoted practitioners of group psychotherapy were developed during this trying period, and all of us were pleased by official recognition when, in 1944, a War Training Bulletin, issued by the United States Army, stated, "The favorable response of patients to comparatively brief treatment in groups warrants widespread adoption of this method of therapy."

Major Trends

In the postwar period, despite the misgivings of many individual therapists, the number of group psychotherapists continued to grow. Probably the last holdouts among psychotherapists were the psychoanalysts. Nevertheless, today, hardly a psychoanalytic school exists which does not admit the technique of psychoanalytic group psychotherapy to its course of training. In addition, many new schools of psychotherapy have grown up around the practice of group psychotherapy. These are discussed elsewhere in this volume in more detail. For my purposes here, a brief discussion of certain major trends may serve to clarify my own position. For example, there is the "experiential school," which considers the immediate emotional experience of group interaction to be of paramount importance almost to the exclusion of history and working through. Some of these therapists also believe their own feelings, reactions, etc., should be exposed as freely as those of the patient. To many of this school, thinking is the enemy of therapy and rationality only a repressive and destructive influence.

The group dynamicists, currently very much in vogue, are also dedicated to the "here and now" and to the supremacy of the group over the individual's problems. They, however, are not as inclined to include the therapist as a superpatient, as it were, nor even as an authority figure above the authority of the group. Group dynamics, pioneered by Lewin, has proven itself very helpful to community organizers, educators and business organizations. However, because of its nonanalytic stance and its lack of a theory of the cause and cure of mental disorder, I have serious reservations as to its value as a method in treating the mentally and emotionally disturbed. I also find myself out of sympathy with the tendency to look on any sort of group activity as a form of group therapy. Many such activities may have constructive outcomes with no justifiable claim to being regarded as therapeutic techniques. I must confess that the heat generated at discussion of these various points of view, (to which heat I have made my own considerable contribution), on sober reflection, leaves me slightly bewildered. Anyone who has participated in group psychotherapy knows that nonverbal communication, for example, is important, provocative, disturbing, supporting, etc. Why then is it necessary or even desirable to build an academy of nonverbal communication therapy around the concept, or even to denigrate verbal communication? And why should there be any contention against the appropriate use of both? By the same token, any experienced group therapist will learn very soon that every group has a life and character of its own and that group cohesion is necessary in some measure for productive therapeutic work. But is it necessary or wise to put the group above the individual at every instance? Or at any instance? I happen to think that a group worthy of its name can often handle recalcitrance, destructiveness, or acting out on the part of members better than a single authority can. In other words a group can usually set its own limits, can interrupt its own members' acting out. What is less hardy is the status of the individual self. And if there is a choice of emphasis, I prefer to put that emphasis on the side of the preservation of each individual's integrity, without removing him from the group but encouraging him there to achieve effective and successful peer interaction.

General Precepts

To this end, I have found these general precepts to be of immeasurable help. First to provide a reasonably serious, relaxed, purposeful atmosphere so that concentration and freedom to work is encouraged. This requires the setting of some ground rules which each therapist will choose according to his own personality. I prefer to make my ground rules very general for the most part and quite specific in some parts. For the general rules, I ask that each patient try to discuss his associations, reactions, fantasies, and feelings as frankly as possible, about himself, his fellow group members, his family, friends, work associates and his therapist. I ask further that the alternate meeting be considered an integral part of the therapy plan, to be attended as faithfully as the regular meetings and that any interchange which takes place outside the group setting among individual members or subgroup of members, be discussed within the group. These rules are not given as either-or propositions: either obey or get out. Nor is there any intimation of *laissez faire.* The instructions are given with the full knowledge that each member of the group will absorb them according to his own level of understanding, organization, degree of resistance, and attitude toward authority and peers. And the chances are excellent that collectively the group will regulate its own behavior toward constructive work.

Another rule I follow for myself and indirectly impart almost immediately to the patient is that any material which is compulsively emphasized or repeatedly left out of discussion is something to be investigated and analyzed as evidence of resistance. Therefore, if a patient discusses only his family or never his family, always the therapist or never the therapist, always others or never others, always his dreams or never his dreams, only history or never history, it can be assumed that he is hiding something it would be better for him to explore. This eliminates a good deal of endless discussion about which technique is more therapeutic or more effective: here-and-now activity or probing into history, interaction or introspection, verbalization or nonverbalization. They are all important, all at some time used in the interests of self-revelation or resistance, depending on the particular situation of the particular patient at the particular moment of study.

In other words I do not believe that emphasis on any one level or modality of the human being — conscious or unconscious, interpersonal or intrapersonal, interpsychic or intrapsychic, intellectual or emotional — is of any help to therapy if it willfully excludes the other levels. All are important, all must be studied as they emerge in the individual patient, to the end that more and more doors are opened for further insight into his psychodynamics and psychopathology, their effect on the group members and they on him.

It is my further conviction that to practice this way requires intensive training in theory and in actual experience of both individual and group analysis. When I first started training group psychotherapists, the students were members of my heterogeneous groups. Today it is not unusual for the therapist to have his group experience with members of his own profession. I deplore this tendency as violating the true principle of heterogeneity and would very much like to see the student forego the protection of his professional peers and grapple with the problems a cluster of garden variety mortals present. In this way he will learn more about his own unconscious operations, his ability to expose himself appropriately or his need to disclose himself inappropriately, his attitude toward authority, peers and "inferiors." Certainly the more heterogeneous and vivid the group analytic experience, the less rigidity and the more reasonable spontaneity should result. And these qualities are the *sine qua non* of the group analyst who is prepared to deal with the multileveled analytic design with which this essay deals.

Now to some specific details of how this basic design for psychoanalysis in groups might work in actual practice. In my original writings on this subject I found that my own need for structure forced me into a "stages" design, which I feel has not proved itself clinically. Stages of therapy occur at different times with different patients. Some come concurrently, some earlier, some later. If one is conversant with the basic precepts of psychoanalysis, if one can handle one's own transferences and countertransferences, it should not be too difficult to pursue a reasonably disciplined plan of therapy for each individual, always seen against the background of his interaction within the group.

Many images have been used to describe the therapeutic group and group therapist. Some have likened the group to an orchestra with the therapist in the role of conductor. Others think of it more as a theatrical improvisation with the therapist as director. An image which often presents itself in my mind is that of a beach. The sand is always there, but every breath of wind, change of sea or faintest footfall rearranges the sand particles. To try to prearrange the configurations of sand particles according to any rigid pattern, set of patterns or stages would be futile. To maintain that these patterns, stages or even results are constant or absolutely predictable would be untrue. And what holds for the sands holds for the therapeutic group. Is there nothing for them to hold onto but shifting sands? No. Each patient has his characteristic pathology, his characteristic resistances, and a set of transferences, which he repeats over and over again. We come to know and expect these particular responses of his, behavior that typifies him, that give him a stamp, so that we learn: if we behave so, we can predict that he will react thus and so.

I shall try my best to describe the process of psychoanalysis in groups as I have experienced it and as I have practiced it.

Question: How does one establish a comfortable, relaxed atmosphere? The first necessity is to realize that the setting is important as a background for group members' interaction. To use a modern colloquialism: it is the "scene." I myself prefer to hold group sessions in a squarish room, large enough to hold a circle of ten comfortable chairs, clustered around a rather large round coffee table, a setting not large enough to substitute for a living room or small enough to be a den. In one corner is my own leather chair, quite different from the other chairs, but not ostentatiously so. There are two clocks, one in my line of vision so that I don't have to refer to my wrist watch during the session, the other placed so that every group member can be aware of the passage of time if he so wishes. The walls are lined with bookshelves and in the single window there is an air conditioner.

These may sound like petty details, but one soon learns that no details in group can be too petty. My chair, for instance has sparked more transferential hostility, speculation, and acting out than any other single item (except perhaps my "passivity"). Some patient is angry at me. Why? Because I reserve the most comfortable chair for myself (like his father or brother or mother or wherever his transferential button is). I have my own clock. What's the matter? Am I afraid I'll be giving them an extra five minutes and so lose some money, or maybe I'll catch myself giving somebody something for nothing. My walls are rather dark. Is that so they won't show the dirt? What are all those books doing on my shelves? I don't sound as if I ever read any. Are they there just for window dressing? These slightly humorous, critical and half-truthful observations may relieve a great deal of the tension accompanying the expression of hostility and may hopefully open the door to deeper levels. In the same way I have found that a straight sofa may be "separating" in the sense that one of three people on either side may be separated from the sofa subgroup. The circle of independent chairs is part of the atmosphere we want — separate but together as a group — in a room that is not overwhelmingly luxurious nor antiseptically bare.

Forming a Group

Now, with the group room ready, we are able to begin the formation of a group. The first step is to prepare the individual patient for joining a group. Sometimes this is not necessary since some patients with prior individual therapy come specifically for group therapy. Even these may need some time with the therapist alone before entering a group. In the majority of cases, some individual preparation is necessary, in order to overcome fairly common resistances to joining a group. Usually these resistances fall into the following categories: The patients who (1) think group will be a mortifying invasion of their privacy; (2) fear their difficulties will be publicized; (3) want exclusive possession of the therapist;(4) fear the group will reproduce a nightmarish family situation; (5) cannot take even a breath of hostility; (6) cannot give up the illusion that their neurotic defenses are justified and should be strenghtened and encouraged rather than changed; and (7) who cannot see how a bunch of neurotics can be of any possible help to them.

The well-trained therapist can allay these fears in prior individual private sessions which may number as few as one or two or stretch over more than a year. The prospective group patient should be assured that he need not reveal any intimate material until he is ready to do so. He need not even tell his last name. The patient who wants the analyst to be exclusively his can be led gradually to the insight that this is an infantile demand for the possession of the isolated parent as represented by the analyst and that the way to maturity is to learn to undo the tie to the parental figure and make a more appropriate and reasonable relation to people in and out of the group. Often, of course, such understanding is not achieved until the patient has been in group for some time. For those who fear the reincarnation of a nightmarish family, the therapist can promise and deliver a permissive protectiveness for a time, using his skill not to stifle other members of the group but to encourage ventilation of feelings, dreams, fantasies, and biographical material from the overfearful one, from the provocateur, and from the onlookers. So everyone in the group has a chance to be both participant and observer, helper and helped; each patient is encouraged to play a liberating, creative, expansive, and socializing role as he gives up his own repressive, destructive, and antisocial trends.

When the patient is ready to join a group, he may ask for and be given or not (depending on whether or not the therapist believes it to be necessary in his case) brief, general, anonymous descriptions of the other members. The times of regular and alternate meetings and the fee expected are discussed.

A heterogeneous group of eight to ten people is now ready to start therapeutic work. The heterogeneity of the group is a point which cannot be stressed too often, since that heterogeneity provides the structure which by its very nature promises greater reparative possibilities than could be afforded by a homogeneous group. It is worth repeating that the homogeneous group tends to defeat the individual patient, to force him into a conforming collusion which may be able to comfort him for a while, but will, in the end, betray him unless the therapist and patients struggle hard to uncover their latent heterogeneity. Every patient wishes, in some part, to justify and rationalize his neurotic maneuvers. If he is injected into an environment that largely mirrors his own disorder, or which demands identification and conformity, his resistance is fostered, and the goal of strengthening his differentiated resources is retarded.

Conversely, the heterogeneous group provides a structure which by its nature has greater reparative potential because it must stir the patient to change; it must stimulate, provoke, excite, and challenge him. Diversified interaction will elicit and promote multiple transferences and at the same time help break down the rigidity of the transferential reactions, while the variety of personalities to whom he assigns projected roles will more quickly highlight the discrepancy between his distortions and reality.

Despite this emphasis on heterogeneity, certain readily identifiable types are better treated individually or in homogeneous groups and are best excluded from the average heterogeneous group. Among these are: manifestly exploitative psychopaths; severe alcoholics, who cannot come to meetings sober; seriously disabled stutterers, who can exhaust the patience of other members; paranoids, who are apt to include group members in their systematized delusions; intensely masochistic patients, who manage always to seduce others into aggression; the senile, who are too out of contact; the very depressed and suicidal, who are too disturbed to tolerate interaction; the gravely autistic, who cannot become involved; the rigidly obsessive-compulsive, who are too preoccupied with their own rituals; the mental defectives, who can burden a group; and the cardiac patient, for whom the excitement and drama of group interaction might precipitate anginal spasm. The homosexual, who some therapists believe cannot be treated in a heterogeneous group, I have found to benefit enormously when included in a "general world atmosphere" and not limited to a homogeneous (homosexual) environment. And many of the types listed above can eventually be included in heterogeneous groups after individual treatment or after a homogeneous group experience. Only the cardiac patient who experiences anginal pain with affect should be kept out of any group, homogeneous or heterogeneous.

Although the hypothetical group I am describing here is one that is newly formed, it is in no sense a closed group. From now on, to reinforce the principle of heterogeneity, this group will be ongoing and open-ended. If a member leaves, he is replaced by a new member. And by the same token if, for one reason or another, the group in its development becomes homogeneous in character, rigid or overconforming, it can be broken up and its members transferred to several other heterogeneous groups. To give an example of this: a homogeneous group, despite all efforts to establish a serious, working climate, prefers to act out verbally, to use banter as the prevailing tone of verbal interaction and uses the alternate meeting primarily as a social activity. These same members, split up and placed in several other groups where the work of psychoanalysis is considered paramount, quickly adjust to the new level, since consciously at least, they are suffering from their neurotic disturbances and really want therapeutic help.

But to get back to our newly formed group. They are now ready for their first meeting. As far as I am concerned, this is the only group meeting which can be called typical. No matter how well prepared the participants may be, practically everyone (including the therapist) experiences some anxiety at a first group meeting. Adequate preparation has enabled the group to gather, but all the rest of the experience still lies in the realm of the unknown, which is always somewhat anxiety-provoking. The patients usually meet outside in a waiting room and introduce themselves informally. When the therapist arrives, they all enter the meeting room and seat themselves in a circle. Someone may start the meeting going by asking for clarification about the ground rules. But often each member will wait for someone else to begin. It is at this point that the therapist may routinely be expected to "get the interaction going" (one of the most frequently asked question about group psychotherapeutic technique). The therapist does this by asking the one question he can safely assume will be responded to by everyone: "Did anyone experience any anxiety about coming here today?" Someone or another is bound to answer, and the likelihood is that most will be willing and eager to discuss their mutual anxieties. From that point on I, at least, have generally not found it necessary to stimulate interaction, to get it going, to initiate or to lead, or to direct group members. Whatever such qualities or tendencies I may possess, I reserve for the purposes of pursuing analytic interventions. And, as the members become more experienced and sophisticated in understanding latent content, I gradually encourage them to become more and more autonomous, intervening only when I believe it to be necessary and appropriate.

I believe that analytic work can begin in the very first session, usually with the ventilation of anxiety as just described. Once interaction has started, it is not at all unusual for a patient to recount a recent dream, a recurrent dream, or an old nightmare. Failing that, the analyst encourages the telling of daydreams, fantasies, and reveries. He asks members to avoid censorship of fanciful speculation about one another's productions. In this way the different personalities begin to emerge and the first steps are taken in the development of mutual rapport and antagonism. During these early meetings the therapist plays a more active role, contributing his own spirit of warmth and optimism by a sympathetic, permissive attitude toward each patient's ventilating his frustrating problems, dreams, and aspirations.

Gradually, the sparking of interaction will be taken over by the members of the group and the therapist will sit back more and more, letting the interaction develop and the tensions build up. Every well-structured group usually contains one or more catalytic agents ranging from the healthier patients — those who wish to do constructive work and get on with the process of mutual discovery and wholesome interrelatedness — to the more neurotically motivated provocateurs. Among the latter are (1) the exhibitionists, who do not hesitate to boast of their exceptional qualities and accomplishments; (2) the seducers, who are quick to inform about their sexual superiority; (3) the approval seekers, who continually stress their own infallibility or inadequacy and who collapse at the slightest breath of criticism; (4) the chronically anxious, who cannot bear a moment's silence; (5) the attention seekers, who cannot bear to be out of the spotlight for even one minute; (6) the habitually detached, who force themselves into desperate interaction or who remain dolefully silent; (7) the compulsive organizers, who must adhere to the same rigid structure and who cannot tolerate one minute of spontaneity; (8) the compulsive socializers, who must keep the party going. Even patients with slight psychopathic trends may provoke productive group reactions. While such members may try to exploit the group in order to express their irresponsibility, lack of discipline, and moral laxity, such behavior tends to evoke vivid responses and to mobilize feelings in defense against it. Patients who chronically feel misused often carry their triggered fear into meetings, demanding their money's worth out of every session. Hypomanics are obviously a stimulant, while the schizoid are exceptionally facile with unconscious material. In fact, every patient has some provocative tendencies, and the astute analyst will look for opportunities to bring these submerged catalysts to the surface.

If a patient persists in remaining silent, the analyst may leave him alone, refusing to indulge his silent provocation, and let the frustration build until he speaks because he must speak or burst. In other instances the therapist may struggle to analyze a resistive silence or simply encourage the patient to speak. Those patients with weaker egos should be helped toward verbalization. Of these, the analyst may, at first, ask directly for a dream or a fantasy, hopeful that the symbolic nature of the communication will serve as a defense against the anxiety of self-revelation. Failing that, and only as a last resort, the patient will be urged to discuss immediate or current problems of his life outside the group. With notable exceptions, most patients are too prone to compulsively recite and review their current difficulties or case histories, and it is just this form of resistance that successful group therapy tries to discourage.

The recounting of dreams, fantasies, and reveries and free association to these unconscious productions and tentative interpretations are among the first devices used to stimulate group interaction and to establish group rapport. The next step is to encourage free association of members to each other. Until recently I used a technique I called "going around." Here a single member was asked to free associate to each other member of the group. Eventually, as patients became more sophisticated and appreciative of the power this artificially centered position gave them, I noticed that there was never enough time, and before I knew it, each "going around" took up most of the regular session, naturally causing extreme frustration to some other members of the group. Today I use the device only rarely. And when I do, I encourage immediate responses to the member "going around." I feel the same effect can be realized by promoting the free flow if interaction which inevitably gives rise to free association concerning group members and by constantly referring other free associations back to group members and familial antecedents. Let me give an example of how this might work and go hand in hand with other phases of analytic pursuit. Peter complained that he couldn't trust women. He free associated to his mother and sister who were "always ready to jump on him." Kay, a group member asked, "Does anyone here remind you of your mother or sister?" Peter answered, "Yes, Jane. You're like a tight spring," he tells Jane. "I'm afraid you'll suddenly uncoil and snap at me. What are you afraid of? Do you, any time you're approached, feel you're going to be raped?"

Jane resented the association and the interference. She refused to accept any of it as valid for her, insisting that it revealed nothing but Peter's own projection. But that night she had a dream which uncovered her obsessional fear and concomitant wish to erotic contact with the father. At succeeding sessions the deeper intricacies of erotic interest in and fear of the father were elaborated and working through begun through analyzing her interaction with the men in the group. This one example illustrates the use of basic psychoanalytic techniques — free association, the use of dream material, the subsequent uncovering of repressed material, of transference and working through — all brought about by interaction within the group.

Analysis of Resistance and Transference

The analysis of resistance is also greatly facilitated by the group setting and the group process. For example, as patients interact, the person rigidly blocked in erotic, transferential interest in the analyst, is helped to insight by the other members of the group, who are quick to assert their own special investment in the authority figure, while at the same time resenting the lack of attention being given them by the therapist or their peers. The commonly seen resistances or acting out of a missionary spirit, martyrdom, scapegoatism, etc., are among others most easily exposed in the group for the neurotic commitments we know them to be. Another form of resistance, not so easily available for direct study in individual analysis but glaringly obvious in the group situation, is voyeurism in its more socially acceptable form of "living through others." The injustice collector, the consistent diagnoser of other peoples' ills, the judgment dispenser, the hider in historical detail, all these and many other resistive manifestations are clarified in group interaction and are made available as they become familiar and characteristic operations of the individual.

The analysis of transference, closely allied to the analysis of resistance, is one of the most important and productive aspects of psychoanalysis in groups. The projection of parental and sibling images onto other group members are phenomena requiring exhaustive study, and the analysis of this transferential process is the largest single area of concentration of this particular method — except working through. Under the analyst's guidance, patients discover the extent to which they invest one another with early familiar qualities. In the group setting, where a member may not only project a significant historical figure onto the analyst, but may also single out members of the group for the same purpose, the field for transference, in formation and in working through, is appreciably extended.

At first the analyst stresses certain truisms about the transference phenomenon. He explains that all of us carry a heritage out of childhood which impels us to endow the present with old forms, that we see ourselves and others in terms of our own circumscribed experiences, that this attributes to others qualities they may not actually possess and results in the distorted relationships which lead to the pain and self-defeat of all neuroses and that therapeutic help, if not cure, can be measured by the extent to which these distortions can be revised in the patient himself and tolerated when directed toward him by others. Patients are alerted to the general qualities of the transference reaction — such as irrelevance, compulsion, repetition. irrationality, overcompensation, etc., so that they can learn to spot these transferential reactions as they occur in themselves and others.

As I said before, I believe the discovery, analysis, and working through of transference to be the most important work of psychoanalysis in groups, since transference repeatedly interferes with the patient's true estimate of reality and since by its nature it must pervade every area of the patient's life. In the group it is possible to study this phenomenon in all its myriad mutations and to demonstrate over and over again its repetitive and all-pervading qualities. Once the patient has been alerted to these general qualities of transference, he is ready to observe and analyze its manifestations in interaction. Since, as we all know, the transferential response is unconscious, we must expect considerable resistance to its recognition. Here again the group can be of great help. Since there is a great variety of interaction, the endless calling of attention to transference need not become a mechanical bore. So, we are in a position to remind the patient time and again when he is reacting to a mask which exists largely in his mind, when his reactions are illogical, unreasonable, absurd, or at least archaic and when he exhibits affective disturbances or anxiety, extreme irritability, depression, fearfulness, or even panic and terror.

Other qualities of transference are more easily observable in group than in other treatment situations. Here we can see how rigid are the transferential patterns, how excessive, how helpless is the person in their grip, and see how inhibiting they are to projector and object alike. By examples and illustrative material presented at the moment of occurrence, the analyst repeatedly verifies these identifying features of transference, using every opportunity possible to clarify the particular response in terms of the present reality and the possible historical background of the response.

Sometimes transference is so rigidly fixed in the character structure that a patient projects the same distortions on everyone around him, no matter how different the other personalities. These patients are easy enough to diagnose: they are often psychotic. But they are much more difficult to treat. Here again the group can be of immeasurable help, by provoking less threatening versions of the transference in the form of less-menacing peer personalities. Every group will contain some such less-threatening figures and allow the emergence of penumbral variations of response which, later on, may make it possible to reach the core transference problem with the therapist.

For example, a patient rigidly fixed in transference gives a complicated historical picture of a powerful, inimical family of parents and siblings. In individual analysis the patient may project onto the therapist at one time or another all these images. It is not always possible in the individual analytic situation to pursue these multiple, volatile responses. Certainly it is not always possible to differentiate the source of the particular projection. In group, the situation is reversed. "You are my sister, brother, father, mother, aunt, or uncle," the patient may say at one time or another to analyst and group members. Or he may say to each one, "You are my mother; everyone is like my mother." In either case, his response remains the same. And the group is bound to respond compulsively as well as spontaneously to these irrational investments, dealing with them in the less-threatening peer interaction, until the rigidity of response is worked through to more flexible and realistic alternatives. At this point it is easier for the therapist to start to deal with the thematic or central transference, which is usually centered on him. Since this is usually a reproduction of a relationship to a more significant parent or authority figure with whom the patient was most ambivalently and affectively bound, it must also of necessity pose the greatest threat to the defenses of the patient. With the groundwork for this laid beforehand in interaction and analysis of peer relationships, penumbral transferences, etc., the threat is no longer so great. Now, hopefully, the door has been opened to tackling a core problem which would have been too painful to approach earlier or more directly.

In group, when transference is evoked, the patient is asked for both the immediate provocation, so that the validity of his response can be evaluated, and for the possible historical background for the response itself and for his estimate of the quality of that response. Thus the searching for historical data and for the releasing of this data becomes not an obsessional maneuver to evade reality, but rather a search specifically focused on clarification of the transference as an opening door to reality. I believe that the therapist who can concentrate early in treatment on the analysis of transference can shorten the duration of treatment considerably and can more reasonably expect that the benefits gained from treatment will last.

I would like to cite here one example of this process, which highlights the totally different responses exhibited to me by a patient when in individual analysis and when transferred to a group. In thirty preliminary sessions, Joe and I got on famously. Joe was brilliant, serene, and exceptionally friendly; he made rapid progress. There seemed to be no obvious resistances. He interpreted a dream, and I would add some additional points. These Joe would accept and perhaps add some modifications which seemed entirely appropriate to both of us. Suspicious as it might sound, there seemed to be no stumbling blocks. The whole relationship was simply too unneurotic, and I began to wonder why Joe was in therapy at all. I suggested that he join a group, so that we might have a chance to explore certain areas of his personality which individual analysis had not revealed. Joe agreed. I was not able to detect any lack of enthusiasm toward my suggestion. But at the very first group session, Joe exhibited his first sign of negative transference. He was a changed man. Our harmonious relationship, his warm appreciation of what I had done for him, his eager willingness to act reasonably, all vanished. Now, at this very first meeting, he challenged everything I said. He used his fine intellect and keen intuition to analyze all his fellow group members, unconsciously managing to forestall or to belittle any contribution I might dare to make. Whereas in the prior private sessions we had had easy interchanges, in the group he would hardly allow me to open my mouth. He interrupted, he anticipated and predicted — often accurately enough — everything I was about to say. I let this go on for some time. In fact I let it go on until the group began to notice his compulsive behavior and began calling it to his attention. Joe could hardly believe his ears, and finally he turned to me for confirmation. I remarked then on the sharp contrast between Joe's friendliness in our individual sessions and his truculence toward me in the group. This time Joe was surprised and embarrassed. But he could see that what I said was true. And, almost immediately, he could allow repressed memories, which had not seemed appropriate in the individual situation, to come into consciousness. In subsequent sessions, Joe recalled with what pontifical dignity and Victorian strictness his father had held court at the dining room table when Joe was a child; how one had to tiptoe about the house when his father was napping; how he was not allowed to speak unless spoken to in his father's presence. His rage mounted as Joe recalled other indignities reaching back into early childhood as, for example, that his father could visit with his mother while she was taking a bath, while he, Joe was excluded. As time went on, Joe's field of insight widened. He began to realize that he could relate freely and well with one person — so long as that contact was self-limited and circumscribed. He then was able to recall that he could always talk with his mother when he was alone with her but that she was not too often available to him for any extended periods. In a group, however, he felt driven to excel, to be the genius of the living room. In other words he discovered that in every social gathering, he habitually recreated the family milieu and automatically strove to become its guiding intellect. The group suggested and Joe agreed that what he was acting out was his father's role and that probably he had often fantasied as a child that he would one day successfully challenge his father in everything he said and did. Joe was then able to see how consistently he had been acting out this unconscious fantasy in his business and social life, to his own self-defeat; because, though he was relatively successful in both areas, he was far from reaching his full potential, a fact that had brought him into therapy. Now the group had given him the chance to act out the fantasy in a situation where it could really be explored in depth.

It was then made clear that when Joe was in a one-to-one relationship of limited commitment, as he had had with me, he could reproduce the pleasantries of his relationship with his mother. But that when I was in the group, I became his father and the group his family. From this insight we were able to proceed more deeply into his oedipal conflict, his intense attachment to his mother, his repressed rivalry with his father and his compulsive replacement of his father in the regenerated family. Obviously, Joe's transfer to a group revived old family ghosts who would have appeared in individual analysis with difficulty but who had been almost immediately and spontaneously evoked in a group situation. What's more they had been evoked with such undeniable drama and concreteness that insight had to be experienced by anyone not desperately ill. The group setting proved just as concretely helpful in the working through of his transferences. And what held true in Joe's case has been observable in many other cases that heretofore were held to be "unanalyzable." As his father transference to me was worked through with me, I again became the preoedipal mother from whom he was ultimately able to separate himself.

As the foregoing indicates I am still committed to the practice of psychoanalysis in groups with the modifications which necessarily must come with the change in setting. I believe that human behavior is largely determined by original provocation and the formation of early distortions. I do not believe that man functions accidentally, as a consequence of impulsivity or imagination that is totally self-generated and unrelated to causality or etiology. I believe rather, that a patient's behavior, his illness, and his health are also largely consequences of his history and that transference in the present is the repetition compulsion of an earlier relationship, which can be worked through, so that there is a gradual but radical displacement of the negative history in the course of treatment. The group analyst need not avoid or reject spontaneity, inspiration, choice, or accident. But neither does he give up trying to discover, at every turn, the patient's motivation, the original causes of his pathology, the development, and the laws that govern its present operation. While in early treatment, he allows spontaneous interaction to build up. He also consciously and expertly enters into the therapeutic relationship, always with the aim of facilitating freedom from compulsion by dispelling projective illusions. Gradually he helps supplement the technique of spontaneous interaction with an encouragement to strive for conscious, methodical sifting and planning of verbalized responses in the best personal and mutual interests of the members of the group. This is always a process of intense struggle for the patient — struggle with his own transference reactions when they cannot be justified or condoned, when insight without acting on it cannot be tolerated, when character change must replace explaining, and when self and group discipline demands personal reconstruction. This struggle is how I see "working through." And, like all other struggles taking place in psychoanalysis, it runs throughout the course of treatment. When termination is near, however, it takes precedence over the other phases, and in group is a generally rewarding phenomenon. When the other members begin to remark with pleasure on the changes in attitude we know that the patient is on the way to termination.

One test of readiness for discharge is the patient's ability to analyze and dispose of his own transferences by choosing more realistic alternatives and his ability to recognize situations where formerly he might have reacted in transference and instead of acting out verbally his lateral transferences to other patients to respond more appropriately.

The Role of the Therapist

All this calls for considerable skill on the part of the therapist. His role is complicated, much more complicated than that of the individual analyst. And therefore it is also one of the most controversial topics of discussion among group therapists. There are some who see him as the most important patient in the group, participating on every level as the patient participates. Others liken him to the conductor of an orchestra or the director of a play. Others see him as a "leader" or conversely as a silent figure who represents leaderlessness and whose object is to build up the ultimate in frustration among group members.

My view of the group therapist is much more conservative, conventional if you will. I believe the group therapist should be first and foremost a well-trained psychoanalyst. He should be trained in the principles of individual psychoanalysis, and then later specifically for psychoanalysis in groups. He must have self-understanding and a capacity for empathy. These should be enhanced by study so that these endowments are under his conscious control and cease to be a source of wonder to him or to others. But above all I believe he should have the ability to scrutinize and work through his own transferences and countertransferences. This is why he needs a thorough individual analysis and in addition a sustained heterogeneous group analytic experience. I am a firm believer in postgraduate workshops where the young and not-so-young therapists focus their attention on and continue to resolve their transferences and countertransferences to their patients.

I hold this point of view not only to protect the patient, which is our therapeutic responsibility, but also to protect the therapist himself. If he is really doing his job in the group, he must expect constant efforts to manipulate him; he cannot afford to be discouraged or thrown off balance by the intensity of interpersonal feeling which occasionally develops in meetings. He must even encourage the most timid to react to him, and he must support the angry or loving patient who will test him to the utmost. He must be strong enough to lead and to exercise control where control is in the patients' interest. He must be strong enough to acknowledge his errors and secure enough to relinquish the initiative to the group or to a patient as the situation of the moment demands, without feeling that his authority is being threatened. He must be able to control any tendency to play the proselytizing missionary or arbitrary dictator. He must remind himself at all times that the meaning of the interaction within the group is the significant focus of his attention and the jumping-off point for all analysis, and that, therefore, he must regard the patients in his group as partners in the analytic pursuit, while at the same time maintaining the reality position of the guiding expert — a position he can neither relinquish nor misuse if he abides by the reality principle established by the tenets of psychoanalysis.

This is by no means an easy position to maintain at all times and in all situations. Nevertheless a conscious attempt should be made to find ways of doing so. I think there are two ways, among others, for the conscientious therapist to accomplish this. In the first place, it is of paramount importance that he check continually on the possibility of his own countertransferences interfering with his relationship to the patient. He must also look for ways to build the self-confidence and ego strength of his patients, so that the dependency on the authority is steadily decreased, and material which must be repressed or hidden from that authority is released.

The Alternate Session

It was in the service of this last principle that I introduced the formal concept of the alternate session, and my conviction as to its importance, theoretically and practically in any group therapy plan, has grown stronger with the passing years.

The alternate session, as I have indicated, is a scheduled meeting of a therapeutic group without the therapist being present. These sessions alternate with the regular sessions when, of course, the therapist is always present. Usually alternate sessions take place in the homes of various members of the group, with the objective of utilizing a still more informal atmosphere, so that interaction and participation is further stimulated. I have rarely given formal rules as to how these alternate sessions are to be conducted. But experience with hundreds of patients has demonstrated that the alternate session usually becomes an extension of the regular session and tends to preserve the tone, form, and quality of the work done when the group is with the therapist.

The alternate session serves many purposes adjunctive to and helpful to the therapeutic picture in both the horizontal and vertical levels. On the horizontal level it emphasizes the important role interaction with one's peers must play in therapy. Members learn they can disagree with each other and settle their differences without the intervention of the authority. In other words they learn they can stand on their own two feet without running to mama or papa for protection. Many patients feel freer to interact at alternate meetings when transferences to the therapist are less threatening or less repressive. Some report they can experience, see, and define different transferences more easily in these circumstances, and others say that it is largely at the alternate session that they can really feel they are relating to their fellow members. Necessarily, these are also attitudes that need to be worked through. At the alternate meeting the patient has a greater chance to learn how to ask for help from his peers, and conversely he can give help in circumstances he would ordinarily leave to the therapist to handle.

Another important function of the alternate session is that it gives members a chance to compare their behavior in the two climates. Anyone who has had experience in these different settings will tell you this is not a trivial factor in human relatedness. As far as I am concerned, it is one of the reasons I believe tape recordings of analytic sessions or watching through one-way mirrors is unsatisfactory and does not give a true picture of what actually goes on in such meetings. Since, ethically, the patient must be apprised of these mechanical interventions, they are naturally conscious of them, even if they themselves maintain it makes no difference in their behavior. The same contention is almost uniformly expressed by patients in group. Almost to a man they deny there is even the slightest difference in their behavior between one meeting and the other. But continued verbalization usually proves just the opposite. Rarely, the therapist may ask some questions about what happened at an alternate meeting, though I have found that usually this is not necessary and often unwise. The pertinent facts will be disclosed sooner or later. So I find out from one member or another that the patient who praises me to the skies in the regular meeting saves all his complaints about me for the alternate session. The therapist-patient who is a genial colleague at the regular session is an agent provocateur at the alternate, openly inciting the members to revolt against me or to quarreling among themselves. The conventional lady, compulsively conforming, may fantasy all kinds of escapades the mice might indulge in while the cat's away. The habitually silent member who waits for a chance to be able to get something said at a regular meeting, while the others are not busy vying for my attention or to get their money's worth, is allowed to speak only at alternate sessions. As I have said, at sometime or other, the "alternate" material is introduced in regular sessions sooner or later. For example, shortly after the war, there was a therapist-patient in one of my groups who wanted to learn about group therapy as well as resolve his neurotic difficulties. He was an older man, experienced in individual psychoanalysis, with emotional problems of his own. In the group was also a younger man who had suffered the horrors of a Nazi concentration camp in his early adolescence. The therapist member was not Jewish and had displayed latent hostility toward me as a father figure, but no feelings tainted with prejudice. At one regular session the young Jewish man suddenly blurted out, "If anyone calls me 'dirty Jew,' I won't be responsible for what I will do!" Everyone looked rather embarrassed, and he repeated his threat. I did not probe for clarification, because I was not certain how much the accusation had to do with reality and how much was a manifestation of his illness. I was also waiting for more background material. A week later, one of the women was angry with the therapist member and accused him of deliberate taunting. "The way you kept needling Abe at the alternate, always asking him, 'What would you do now if someone called you dirty Jew'?" The occasion gave all members a chance to discuss their reluctance to be tattletales, though all were angry at the "therapist" member. It gave the latter a chance really to get his teeth into his own transferential disturbance and it gave Abe a chance to ventilate his pent-up violent feelings against those he felt had misused him so horrendously. It would have taken a much longer time for this material to have emerged if the group had met only in regular session. And I wonder sometimes if it would have come out at all. There is no doubt in my mind that for a clearer picture of the dynamics of any given patient the alternate session is invaluable. In the analyst's absence members develop a relationship to each other on their own where they can learn to assimilate and tolerate their own contradictory feelings, and this fact alone can often motivate a group to stay together as well as to engage each other. This is one reason why I see the alternate session as ego demanding and therefore ego building.

It would seem then that the alternate session would be an accepted part of all group therapy plans. This, however, is far from the case. Many therapists are still extremely fearful that the members of the group will become negatively involved in a way which would endanger not only their therapy but also the reputation of the therapist. Sexual acting out is usually given as a chief danger; physical violence ranks second among the fears; and emotional damage or disturbance because of inept, premature, and amateur interpretation and wild analysis is third.

I have never seen any figures, statistics, or case histories to substantiate these objections to the alternate session. And I, myself, have never seen anyone seriously hurt because of these sessions. Sexual acting out has occurred on rare occasions during my years of practice, but as far as I know there has been such acting out in the groups of therapists I am acquainted with who do not permit the alternate session in their therapy plan. Physical acting out of an aggressive nature is equally uncommon. So far no one has been seriously hurt. As for the third fear, I have found patients eminently able to defend themselves against premature insights. Either they do not hear what they are not ready to hear, or they remind the attacker of his resistances, that he too is sick, or they ask to see his permit to practice, or they call on the other members for support. If, in spite of these choices, too much anxiety does result, the analyst and the regular session are always available.

With so much positive evidence for the desirability of the alternate session and so little clinical evidence against it, the conclusion seems inescapable that the objecting therapist must find the reasons for his theoretical assumptions within himself and his relationship with his patients. As for myself, I continue to maintain that since the relationship to authority and peers is one of the primary problems in mental disturbance, we are fortunate to have at our disposal a treatment scheme which enables us to deal with the problem practically and clinically. A group therapy plan which does this by reinforcing the individual's interactive relatedness with his peers, instead of encouraging and perpetuating the often neurotic patterns of rebelling or submitting to authority, is, I think, a realistic one for the patient without requiring the therapist to be in absolute surveillance. At the same time the regular session provides a setting in which authority problems can be dealt with.

Having gone this far, I would like to elaborate a bit more on the alternate session, mainly to answer some of the more-frequently-asked questions.

When in the course of treatment does the group start having alternate sessions? As far as I am concerned, the first regular group session can be followed immediately by the first alternate session. If the therapist thinks they patients are "too sick" to gather by themselves, he may wait until he feels more secure. And I believe that if patients are well enough to function outside of a hospital and to be engaged in some sort of life outside of group, there is little reason for exaggerated fear that gathering with fellow patients will lead to some kind of disaster. I think it is worth repeating that therapeutic groups have always in my experience set their own limits and, if left to their own devices, will be able to control their acting out. Of course, if the therapist himself acts out and unconsciously encourages the group to do so, the problem becomes quite different. Irrationality can be infectious. But if the therapist can transmit his conviction that acting out retards therapy and demonstrate its resistive character, the extent to which the group goes along with him will not differ radically between regular and alternate sessions.

Another question which puzzles many is how the therapist can do his job when the patients know so much more about what is going on than he does. The answer is that the therapist knows more than they do, not necessarily every detail, but more of the psychopathology and has more of a conscious plan for working through. Besides, the alternate meeting is part of a continuum. It does not exist in a vacuum, nor is it isolated from the regular session. If anything of moment happens in an alternate session, it is bound to come up at some regular session. But more importantly, the alternate meeting is there to help the patient, to get him to understand the nature of, let us say, the repetition compulsion, the all-pervading quality of transference, to raise questions about how he can resolve his frustration and to bring these problems back to the regular session until he can function more appropriately on his own.

New "facts" as such are not necessary to convince the analyst that they exist. I did not need confirmation, for example, that the provocateur I described earlier had a father problem. What I did need was sufficient repetition of his provocations in varied enough form, so that he and the group could see it. And this the alternate meeting helped us all to get.

Another common question is: Is it necessary to hold alternate meetings in the homes of members? No, of course not. I do, however, think it is desirable. Some of my groups cannot afford the extra time alternate evening meetings take, and so must meet in my office. There is, of course, nothing we can do about these reality matters, if, for example, a member has a night job. But if these concessions are made, the therapist should be fully aware that certain drawbacks will be present. These meetings simply will not be as free, in breadth, depth, or relaxation. If, for one reason or another, they must be held in the analyst's office, I suggest that they be held after and not before the regular session. In the prior session there is a strong tendency for many to withhold until the therapist arrives. I had one such experience with a patient who was generally accepted by the group and myself as being a hard and conscientious worker for his own therapy and that of others. We tended to forgive his temper tantrums when others, in his opinion, talked too much, as being part of his particular problem. This group had switched their alternate meetings from members' houses to prior sessions in my office. I had not noticed that whenever I entered the room for the regular session, this patient (let us call him Max) was always launched on some discussion or other, until one day, one of the women in the group took the bull by the horns and accused him of a plot. She pointed out that he was always very active with the other members of the group, flattering them with his attention and offers of help and sympathy, right up until two minutes to one, when the regular session was scheduled to begin. Then, suddenly, as if a bell had been rung, he switched the subject to himself, and continued on it, as I entered and seated myself.

Max, naturally, denied any such plot, and, since none of the others had noticed this method of operation, he stood more or less group supported, and his accuser was seen as a projector. What happened thereafter, however, was most interesting. It was not too important to check on whether Max continued his maneuver. It was much more important to see that once the modus operandi had been exposed, all the other members thought it such a splendid idea, you couldn't get anyone to discuss anything more personal than the weather before the magic hour of one. Gradually members started drifting in later and later to the presession, so they could start talking later and later. All attempts to analyze this, though interesting, did not solve the reality situation of the waste of the presession. I ended switching the presession to a postsession with a full explanation of the reason for doing so and the expressed hope that meetings soon would be held again in members' homes. That summer, when I was on vacation, the meetings were resumed at the homes of patients, and postsessions in my office were never asked for again by that particular group.

This brings me to my last reason for sponsoring the concept of the alternate session as strongly as I do. It gives a continuity to the group life which most patients have missed in their own lives. During the long summer vacations, the struggle for realistic communication can still proceed. Life does not or need not stop just because the therapist goes away. This is especially necessary for the patient who literally thinks he dies when his analyst is gone. This type of patient will still suffer, but there is a chance of mitigating that pain when it can be discussed with the group in a relationship which already has a base of operation without the therapist. In the same way, the alternate meeting can be an important part of any short-term group therapy plan. In short-term therapy different levels of results can be hoped for or expected, but the idea of continuity and the possibility of holding the group together for a while longer through the alternate meeting plan can be very comforting to people who dread the end of help.

At present I provide regular weekly sessions for one and one-half hours with the analyst, alternate meetings once or twice a week without the therapist for two or three hours at a time, and selected individual sessions for three-quarters of an hour. This program provides for the exploration of peer and vertical vectors and shows the optimal usefulness of each procedural variation in the therapeutic fields of operation.

Combined Therapy

Some might say my stand on the alternate meeting is a far cry from traditional psychoanalysis. They might say the same about my attitude toward combined therapy, that is, the routine treatment of a patient in group and simultaneous individual analysis. My stand on this question is quite simple. I am neither for nor against combined therapy. What I am against is its routine use, except where absolutely necessary. There are certain things one must do "routinely," but I don't think combined therapy is one of them. There are many patients I have treated who did not need individual therapy at all, others have had to have combined therapy throughout their group experience, and still others have not been able to take the group experience at all. Here, once again, a pet theory of the therapist can be a hollow one when placed against the needs of a particular patient. The need of the particular patient at a particular time should determine whether or not combined therapy is indicated. It is as simple as that.

I seldom use regularly scheduled private sessions in addition to the group, except as indicated below.

Some patients need the one-to-one experience with the maternal surrogate in the person of the analyst before they can join and interact with their siblings and peers. Others cannot avail themselves of the dyadic relationship with the therapist until they have had a liberating experience with their peers.

The group therapist who provides regular individual sessions has too little regard for the therapeutic effectiveness of treatment in a group. Individual hours are often promoted not out of the patients' real needs but out of the therapist's countertransference. Individual sessions are frequently rationalized as necessary in order to precipitate a transference neurosis as a step toward working it through, but such a requirement is unusual. For as resistances are analyzed in the group, preoedipal and nonverbal reactions emerge and can be resolved in the group setting.

Some group therapists provide individual hours on the assumption that if a patient is silent in the group or avoids a dyadic relationship with the analyst, he needs individual sessions to resolve one-to-one problems in the vertical vector. But it is a misunderstanding of group therapy to think that dyadic relationships do not exist in group interaction. One-to-one ties and connections develop in the group both in the horizontal and hierarchical vectors.

The regular use of individual hours often leads to an increase in resistance. Often the patient, certain of his routine and private access to the analyst, does not show in the group his responses to other members but saves them for exposure to the therapist alone. This leads to indirection and deviousness rather than a working through to more straightforward responses. It also prevents the members from getting more immediate understanding of their mutually provocative behavior. It blocks reality testing and a detailed on-the-spot and vigorous mutual investigation.

The belief that all patients at all times need combined treatment obscures differences among patients. It obscures the uniqueness of a patient's behavior in one context and another. It confuses the special value to the individual of the regular and the alternate sessions. It muddies the differences of the members. It might be more relevant for the therapist to ask himself with each patient why he wants to offer private sessions just now. Would individual hours facilitate treatment at this point? Can the analyst accomplish the same ends in the group setting? Would individual sessions promote the patient's resistance?

The patient may ask for individual hours in order to avoid participation in the group. Or he may misuse the group in order not to relate to the analyst. Or he may exhibit destructive behavior at group sessions and constructive behavior in individual interviews. Or the reverse may take place. Or he may resist telling the group what has taken place in individual treatment. Or the therapist's fear of the projected dangers of group members' interaction may lead the group to fall apart.

There are certain patients who ask for individual sessions, whose requests have to be denied and analyzed. Among these are regressed psychotics in preoedipal attachment to a prior individual therapist or to the group analyst himself. The same caution needs to be exercised with the borderline psychotics. Others wish to control or seduce the therapist or to isolate him from the rest of the group. Such a maneuver may not be discovered until the analyst has seen the patient individually.

The generalized and nondiscriminative use of individual sessions parallel to group therapy tends to make treatment too leader-centered. The therapist's anxiety over the projected dangers of group interaction and acting out leads him inappropriately to provide too many overprotective individual hours. He invests group members with a helplessness and aggressivity that demand individual attention. As a result patients are infantilized and subverted in their wholesome need to use their own resources in working through to a more maturating giving and taking with one another. Accordingly, I suggest only occasional rather than regular individual hours, when their use is appropriate and realistically necessary. Such sessions should be group-centered, and the patient should be encouraged to tell the group what transpired in the individual meeting.

For many passive dependent patients, unless there is peer interaction, therapy does not take place. This has taught me in conducting individual analysis to promote the patients' interaction with other persons outside the therapeutic situation as well as in the treatment setting. Of course, with patients who are terrified of closeness, such deep anxiety proscribes interaction except in very small doses, built up slowly as treatment proceeds. Even these isolated individuals make no progress until they are drawn into interactional experience. Patients who are very passive, inactive, schizoid, or character-disordered profit enormously from the promotion of peer interaction with other group members.

I treat the patient in the group setting. Where transference involvement with me is intense, individual private sessions may deepen the pathology. There are specific indications for providing adjunctive individual hours in certain circumstances and at certain times in the course of treatment.

Psychoanalysis in groups does not exclude individual sessions where they are indicated. Each patient's treatment begins in individual sessions, and he is free to return to them, if they are in his interest. My concern is that the patient not be forced into an entrenchment of a transference neurosis or psychosis. His dependence on the group operates against such a hazard. I see the dangerous entrenchment of the preoedipal attachment all too often. Most of my patients come to me from overextended transference neurosis or psychosis to one or more individual analysts. One such came to me quite psychotic after eighteen years of individual treatment in the service of the id, not the ego. Group therapy frees the patient from his regressed dependence upon the mother invested in the analyst.

There have been some attempts to be discriminating in the selection or rejection of particular diagnostic categories of patients for combined therapy. However, in the hands of different therapists the varieties of patients include the whole range of diagnostic possibilities. The criteria for selection, it appears, are not explicit. The problem remains unsolved. We need more adequate clinical experience and research.

It is possible, however, to be a bit more specific with regard to those patients who would benefit from associated individual sessions, where there is little danger of entrenching regression. Such patients have fairly intact egos. They are not prepsychotic or psychotic. For them, regression is in the service of the ego. Others who benefit from associated individual sessions are the oldest or nearly the oldest siblings in a large family who in childhood were prematurely forced to assume surrogate parental roles with the birth of each new sibling as the actual parents abdicated their parental responsibilities. Such patients may need individual sessions before they relinquish their compulsive mothering and fathering of group members, individual sessions in which they have the experience of being children in fantasy. Still other patients who may require individual hours are those who are in a sudden panic or severe depression, those who are unable to express their basic problems, silent members, severe sadomasochists, patients who act out, and those who remain too long on a resistive plateau in the group without forward movement.

Orthodoxy versus Unorthodoxy

All of this is a far cry from traditional psychoanalysis. But I believe that Freud himself was farsighted enough to know that certain changes in form and technique would have to be made as society changed. One of the good things about psychoanalysis is that in many instances it has been able to adapt to cultural change so that it could make some contribution in terms of the society in which it operated. Where it has not, where it has remained rigid or flown off into irrationality, psychoanalysis has become the butt of humorists and a scapegoat for the bitter, the skeptical, and the dislusioned.

There are those who behave and write as if Freud were responsible for all the ills of the present world. There are those who take the equally unreasonable position that if one would just psychoanalyze everyone in the world, there would be no problems, no wars, no famines, no disasters — natural or man-made. And there are those diehards who would tell you that to strike out one word of Freudian text or change one iota of original analytic dogma would be tantamount to treason if not heresy.

Although I am not one to run away from a good fight, I believe many of these battles are unworthy of us. To take extreme positions for one form of treatment as against or totally excluding any other, and to hold that extreme position at all costs, does a disservice to patient, therapist, and discipline alike. I am content to be connected with a behavioral field that is flexible enough to meet the challenges presented by our rapidly changing society. This society is moving more and more toward group orientations, which presents a particular dilemma for modern man. His struggle to adjust to complex organizational demands and yet retain some measure of his individuality and his agony as he finds himself enmeshed in increasingly threatening clashes between Goliaths are bound to have their effects on the emotional problems presented in therapy today. And, with such massive group pressures, where the individual feels more an more confused, anxious, helpless, and hopeless, it seems to me only natural that the therapist should propose and the patient accept group therapy as one logical means of dealing with personal problems as placed against the new reality of group demands.

We must remember that Freud and his original followers developed their one-to-one psychoanalytic techniques at a time when the individual still saw himself as the hub and center of the universe.

Today, we in psychoanalysis in groups still consider the individual as the center of treatment, but we also feel that the group is a realistic, pertinent setting for the resolution of those personal problems in the context of our society today.

The conflicts of the human condition — life and death, good and evil, success and failure, love and hate, male and female, work and play, conformity and individuality — are, alas, eternal. But history has proven that the circumstances of each new age highlight one or another of these conflicts, creating distortion in all of them and so affecting the values and behavior of the individual. We live in an age where widely differing ideologies are confronting each other. Their ultimate clash might mean catastrophe for all of us. During the present standoff, the pressures toward conformity have become so overwhelming that the individual has become submerged and, to some extent, dehumanized.

Psychoanalysis in groups is just a drop in the bucket against this trend, but I believe it can be one of the last strongholds where the uniqueness of the individual can be preserved. At least my experience with psychoanalysis in groups has shown me that, in successful treatment, as each individual interacts more constructively with his fellow group members, his fears of individual and group pressures both inside and outside the group are lessened. And, as this constructive process continues, each individual in the group increases his capacity for positive fulfillment, personal responsibility and more humanized and creative adaptations.

Three decades in the practice of psychoanalysis in groups has influenced my views on psychoanalytic theory and practice and brought about modifications of my individual analytic techniques.

The therapeutic group more easily challenges the therapist in a way the individual patient has greater difficulty in doing. The group promotes the expression of free association and affect toward patients and therapist. The individual patient's caution in exposing attitudes and affect directed toward the therapist tends to feed his grandiosity and sense of omnipotence, a dangerous hazard for the individual therapist. The knowledge of the isolated patient's reserve has led me in individual analysis to encourage the patient more strongly to present all his mixed thoughts, associations, fantasies, dreams, and feelings about others in his life and about me.

One of the ways group members develop better egos is derived from their alternating roles of helper and helped. It is almost impossible for the patient in individual analysis to help the therapist. But aware of the value of this experience in psychoanalysis in groups, I have spoken to patients in individual analysis about the value to them of helping in treatment by valuing *their* dreams, *their* associations, *their* interpretations, as a great help to me in facilitating my understanding of them.

Psychoanalysis in groups has made me more aware of my own transferences and countertransferences, largely through listening to patients' perceptions of me, their criticism and corrective suggestions. While a part of their observations was distorted and transferential, another part was always in some degree appropriate. So the practice of group therapy has led me to be more self-examining and self-critical in both group and individual analysis, more attentive and regardful of what each patient has to say of me, not only in terms of his distortions but in terms of his valid estimate of my behavior.

Psychoanalysis in groups with its greater activity has enabled me better to understand ego psychology and given fresh direction to my practice of individual analysis. The observation of patients' social behavior has impressed me with their need for activity, for ego activity, not just ego support. In individual treatment, therefore, I ask the patient to take action, not just to talk, think, or feel but to do. I ask him what he plans to do in reality with this or that insight. The analyst is often a poor example just sitting, thinking, and feeling. He, too, needs to do more, to take appropriate action, make appropriate interventions without acting out.

Psychoanalysis in groups has led me to question the necessity of *total* frustration of the patient's archaic needs. Freud questioned the wisdom of such absolutism without the benefit of experience in group therapy. An analyst, practiced in psychoanalysis in groups, took a patient's hand in the group situation, because not to have done so would have been a traumatic repetition of her father's silence and rejection of her. The therapist could have taken the same action in individual treatment. Here then a gratification of an archaic longing was seen as an immediate therapeutic necessity. But the analyst needs to be discriminating. I would not, for example, take the hand of an asthmatic patient of mine, because her aim in pleading for this was to control me.

The aggressive evaluation and criticism of one another that goes on in group therapy is in part an acting out but also a genuine, relevant estimate of each other that is very insightful. Its critical quality demands of the observed and observer a movement and change toward a more realistic adaptation. It has taught me to be less neutral in my role as analyst. It has made me more challenging than I used to be. I am not neutral with regard to the patients' pathology. I do not accept his resistance, his distortions. I keep questioning his commitment to outmoded ways of thinking, feeling, and acting. I do not accept his rationalizations. I pursue his latent motivations more actively. I am equally assertive in promoting the necessity for him to be as questioning and challenging with regard to everything I say and do.

Group experience has demonstrated to me the value of the presence of peers in the horizontal vector. In the individual analytic setting only the vertical vector is present, and peer relationships are usually not experienced. Accordingly, the patient works through his relationship with authority, the father and mother invested on the therapist in the hierarchical vector. Sibling relationships tend to be neglected. Therefore, in individual treatment I am much more alert to the patient's relationship to his siblings and his peers beyond his dyadic involvement with me. This means that I pay more attention to his contacts with his fellows apart from his oedipal and preoedipal engagement with me. This leads to a working through of his vertical relationship with me and to freedom from overly long regression.

The need to attenuate the hierarchical vector, to remove the patient from his parents and their surrogates in or out of the therapeutic milieu, is facilitated by putting the patient in a therapeutic group of peers. In individual analysis, when the patient has worked through his oedipal and preoedipal transferences, the therapist is experienced more in the horizontal vector as a peer, a dyad in which sibling relationships emerge and are worked through.

Psychoanalysis in groups has led to a more refined understanding of family life, of how the patient invests members of a group with counterparts of mother, father, and siblings, and of how he relates to a stranger to the family in the group member who is not so invested. This experience has led me more and more in individual analysis to explore the patients' relationships not only with his primal and current families but with his professional and work associates, colleagues, friends and enemies alike, as well as strangers.

My group experience has taught me to be less the parent who induces preoedipal regression and more the authority and peer who gives and takes, who will not incorporate or be incorporated, who pursues the security of the patients' primary trust in me to the end that he develop his own autonomy.

Questions of Regression

The recovery of patients in psychoanalysis in groups has led me in individual treatment to demand less regression, to use face-to-face sessions more and the couch less. It has taught me not to frustrate the patient too much. It has taught me to be more discriminating about regression. It is necessary for some patients to regress in order to survive. This is regression in the service of the ego, as with the borderline behavior of adolescents who behave in novel and bizarre ways as a defense against becoming quite psychotic. It is not unlike psychologically determined fainting. Some regression, however, is in the service of the id, or in the service of the id and the ego. For example, a psychotic episode is preferable to certain death. And paranoid grandiosity as a means of survival is not a bad defense in the face of the gas chambers of a concentration camp. Acting out against authority, challenging the father or the analyst is often in the service of the ego. The aggression expressed by group members has led me to be more challengging and provocative of individual patients. Perhaps more patients would be more analyzable if therapists did not insist on such deep regression. My group experience has taught me to be less interested in the depth of regression and more interested in helping the patient to see and accept reality.

This raises the question of the nondiscriminative necessity for regression, for the development of a transference neurosis which may turn out to be a transference psychosis. That is, the trip into the preoedipal experience is not always necessary in therapy. It may, in fact, be contraindicated — as with psychotics and some borderlines, who are already too severely regressed.

For some time analysts have been preoccupied with what harm the parents did the patient. More lately analysts have attended to their own transferential and countertransferential roles in misusing the patient. My group experience has taught me to reconsider this focus. Group members bring out what is done by the neurotic child in the patient, his provocative role. Group interaction clarifies not only what has been done *to* the patient but *by* him as well. We observe, for example, how a female member intrudes whenever another patient and I interact, in order to exclude her sibling and have the mother in me to herself. Behavior is interactive: bilateral, triadic, quadratic, etc. The child psychiatrist tends to view the mother as hurtful to the child. But the mother does this in part because the father rejects her for her involvement with the child. This kind of triangular reenactment in group therapy illustrates the importance of understanding behavior in its multilaterality in individual analysis and recognizing that the behavior of two persons changes with the addition of a third person, a fourth, etc. In individual analysis, therefore, I look for the unseen third or fourth member in the manifest dyad of the patient and therapist. For example, a male patient, who in his transference neurosis experiences me as his mother and tries to escape me as he does all women, would take flight largely because the father is present in absentia, a castrated appendage with whom the patient identifies. It is my dealing in the dyad of the patient and myself with his triadic and quadratic transferences, with the unseen group, as it were, that has enriched my individual analytic treatment.

Patients function differently in the dyad, in the regular group sessions, and at alternate meetings. The individual analyst who has had group therapy experience will explore the patients' fantasies about triadic and quadratic extensions of the therapeutic dyad. My experience that the patient behaves differently in different social contexts than when with me alone leads me in individual treatment to ask him: "And who else was there?" The introduction through fantasy of a meaningful third or fourth person is commonly seen among individuals who conjure up different partners in the act of intercourse or who have, after intercourse, to go off and masturbate with a particular fantasy in mind. Group analytic experience enables the individual analyst to see the complexity of multiple relationships latent in the manifest dyad. There is a multiple psychology in operation, not just the dyadic psychology of mother and child (patient) or father and child. There is in operation the triadic psychology of mother, father, and child, the quadratic psychology of mother, father, sibling, and child.

Looking to the Future

What is the future of psychoanalysis in groups? Some of us, who are concerned about the future of the world, might consider this foolhardy, while others, who are slightly confused about the present state of psychoanalysis, might consider it presumptuous. Both are, in many respects, correct. I have no crystal ball nor the "I predict" conviction of certain television personalities. My prediction is made up of one part hope, one part fantasy, and one part just plain ignorance.

There are some things we all know, however, whatever our professional or personal daily pursuits may be. We know we live in a world where racial, national, economic, and political pressures are increasing daily. We know we are being called upon to adapt at a moment's notice to shifting policies of racial integration, war and peace, taxation, rising living costs, to problems of housing, traffic, juvenile delinquency, and increased criminality on our streets. We are seeing established authority being challenged around the world and the cop on the corner being shot with his own gun. And, most of all, the threat of atomic extinction hovers over us all.

I could suggest a philosophic way out of this bewildering state of affairs. I might suggest that we try to reevaluate our needs, our beliefs, our passions, and our purpose, so that we can find in a new evaluation the firm ground to be flexible without falling over, that we strive to find the courage to discard what is old and no longer usable and the greater courage to receive the new and strange and make it workable.

Or I could take an even easier way out and spin happy fantasies about many gimmicks that might conceivably become part of the practice of psychotherapy in the space age we are entering. Certainly a lot of pills will be concocted which will be useful in inducing any physical or emotional state, from a sleep that is hibernation to the ecstasy of orgasm. But I suspect there will always be some of us who will prefer the old-fashioned methods already known to us to achieve similar results. There will certainly be machines invented to diagnose and possibly treat the mental ills of mankind. But here I also suspect there will be many of us who will feel that their greatest need is for human contact and human interaction, and who will insist on finding ways to get it. This is where I think psychoanalysis in groups will play its greatest role and deliver its greatest service. For the search to understand the thoughts, feelings, and behavior of people will never lose its fascination as long as humanity exists. That fascination will die when humanity dies, and humanity will die if the search for mutual understanding dies.

How can that search be kept alive? By communication, by learning to know what makes us tick, what makes the other fellow tick, and how he affects us and we him. And the more "other fellows" we know and who know us, the more we will communicate and, hopefully, the more we will understand. Group psychoanalysis of the future will try to understand and treat the individual and will direct its efforts to the end that he be able to adapt to the world in which he lives and also to change it, and to the end that he be able to communicate with and respond constructively to others by word and action. The standard for mental health will be in terms of the widening of the boundaries of one's active and interactive life rather than simply the solution of personal problems.

Considering the situation in the world today, in this context alone, psychoanalysis in groups cannot wait. It must become psychoanalysis for today, or there will be no future. Patients must get off their couches between sessions and analysts must get out from behind their couches between sessions and join people everywhere, especially when national and international crises are to be faced. Why, for example, should we all not be doing something, committing ourselves in some way or other, on the question of atomic testing and atomic bombing? If we do not, there will be no life with which to pursue liberty and no happiness to be sought with the help of psychoanalytic means. And those of us who are too persistently dedicated to the couch may, one day before long, find there is a sudden and dreadful peace from which no human being will escape.

It is part of the analyst's credo to be committed to the value of reason and against unreason; to consciousness, not unconsciousness; to reality, not unreality; to sanity, not insanity. How realistic, sane, conscious, and reasonable is he, pursuing the subtleties of repressed conflict in the individual patient over long years, when hovering over him and all of us is the possibility of sudden and total extinction? His dedication to mental health is an illusory pursuit, unless he also does all he can to mobilize himself and others into effective relationships and activity in the world about him with its demands, its problems, and its responsibilities. To pursue mental health, we need first to be certain that we keep our bodies and brains very much alive. Of course, to avert something like atomic catastrophe, analysts and their patients are not enough. Only all of mankind will do. But we must make a start — by coming out from behind our soundproof doors and joining with others, emerging out of bomb shelters, out of hiding, out of the passivity that waits to see what may happen and try to do something about it no matter how small.

Scientists are often too neutral. Atomic physicists have, with some notable exceptions, devoted themselves to the discovery and uses and misuses of atomic energy with an alarming neutrality with regard to its application. Psychoanalysts also suspend judgment in dealing, let us say, with a patient. They do this in order to allow the repressed to emerge during the course of treatment. But this suspension of judgment is sometimes unreasonably applied — just as it is by parents who yield to every whim of their children or make their children yield to every whim of theirs or by people who feel they must yield to the impulses or misjudgments of their leaders.

I do not mean to say that psychoanalysis can solve the problems of the world. I happen to be interested in psychoanalysis in groups as a method of treatment, but I do not join those therapists who would like to bring the blessings of group therapy or of individual or group analysis, to solve mass conflict on a national or international basis. Nor do I agree with those who feel that all government leaders should be analyzed as an answer to the problems we are facing.

Still, the theories of Freud and those psychoanalysts who followed him have affected our society profoundly. Extensions of psychoanalytic thinking are evident everywhere: in the study of psychosomatic medicine, anthropology, sociology, philosophy; in literature, theater, painting, and criticism. Psychoanalysis in groups is a technical extension of those theories, particularly suited to the needs of our times. And it, in turn, will create its own extensions in our professional, creative, and personal lives.

I wish to underline the trend in group therapy away from the concept that the patient can be helped by only one person — God, the father, the mother, the analyst — or by only one kind of analysis. This is especially important for us today, when paternalism on the one hand is being fostered and encouraged by the "organization man" structure and on the other is being violently rebelled against by a large part of the world. Analysis in group directs the patient away from the idea that there is only one source of help, only one omnipotent source for sustenance and development.

Some people have already learned this lesson, whether through experience in groups or not, I do not know; but somewhere, somehow the idea has caught on. Some years ago, a letter written by a psychologist in Stockbridge, Mass., was passed on to me, and I am going to present parts of it here, because it is such a splendid and moving example of how people's getting together in groups can be extended beyond the treatment of mental illness.

The letter begins by describing concern about the world crisis, with its threat to all of us. It describes the personal and long-unexpressed fears of the writer and his feelings of utter helplessness. Then he goes on to say:

> We have discovered the beginnings of hope—a hope born of desperation and of a stubborn belief that it is better to do than not to do — that it is better to face the awesome enormity of our peril than to comfort ourselves by denying that peril and all its implications. We have begun to share our loneliness, our fears, our anguish and our sense of helplessness about the perilous world situation. . . . At first we were afraid to let each other know of the dread we have had locked in our hearts. . . . But then one of us timidly and tentatively let escape a hint of our deeply buried sense of burden and anguish. . . . And then the other of us, somewhat less timidly but still with much discomfort and embarrassment allowed himself to say he, too, had been similarly burdened. And subsequently these two spoke to a third and a fourth and each time the effect was the same. We began to share our deep distress. We began to say so more openly. We began to discover that to talk and to share feelings and concerns that even the sheer act of doing something, even if it was only talking, somehow was helping us.
>
> We began in a clumsy way—awkward in our self-consciousness. None of us knew any answers, least of all to the question—what can we do? Then we began one by one to talk and to ventilate our thoughts and feelings. And as we listened to each in his turn, we saw ourselves. His words may have been different, and perhaps his thoughts and the course of action he advocated also were different — even alien. But in his sense of common peril, he was all of us.

The letter goes on to say that as this small social group continued to meet, they began soon to speak of specific things: some argued for shelters, some against, others wondered how medical supplies and uncontaminated water could be provided let alone distributed. And, to quote the letter again: "A strange thing happened. We started to feel less alone. We began to feel better. She sheer fact of talking to each other, and sharing loneliness with each other was helping us."

I wish I could present the whole letter, but space forces me to summarize. The original group split off into sections, each to form its own groups, oriented to the same purpose, until most of the town was included and every shade of opinion was being aired. Later there was communication on a wider level, through newspapers, radio, and television. So grass-root movements have been started before and so may this become one.

But to get back to our point. This letter describes very well one level of experience in psychoanalysis in groups. It is not easy to describe. Some people are afraid it might smack of Buchmanism, of the public confessional, the revival meeting, but it is not that at all. Psychoanalysis in group or out, past, present, or future, has always tried to get the patient to know himself, to look his true thoughts and feelings in the face and thereby improve his attitude toward himself and his relations with others.

Malraux is reported to have said that portraiture in modern art is practically nonexistent, because mankind has committed so many crimes in our era, it dares not look itself in the face. Group interaction is usually effective in trying to bring that very thing about. It is not easy for analyst or patient. It is only human nature for all of us to resist those who insist we put the mirror up to ourselves. In other interaction we usually employ face-saving devices. To keep social interaction going we are apt, more often than not, to conceal the truth of our judgments and feelings. But for psychoanalysis to work, these face-saving devices need to be exposed and then analyzed. One of the things the analyst tries to show the patient is that it is possible to have a good relationship with him, at least, even if the truth is revealed. And he keeps trying, no matter how the patient resists, ambivalates, projects, and distorts in his struggle against knowing the reality.

In group, this situation is heightened and dramatized, because a member may refuse a relationship with fellow members who challenge him by letting down their face-saving masks. He may even villify the analyst for allowing it. There are some who cannot tolerate the truth about themselves and who insist that others remain bound by the same chains. But there are others who take heart from seeing the struggle to ferret out the real from the illusory and who gain courage thereby to continue their own fight for mental health. I think the letter I just cited proves one thing, at least, that this level of interaction happens, that it is good to have happen, and that it makes the specific analytic treatment of the individual less isolated, less self-absorbed, and more in contact with humanity — and therefore all the more clearly experienced.

The reader may ask why, if groups can take care of so many more patients, if such treatment is less expensive, if there is a shortage of analysts, and if analysis in groups can be so effective, why are so many analysts resistive to it?

I believe one reason is that they have not had the experience of analysis in groups themselves. Another possibility is that analysis in groups can be hard on the analyst, who has been trained to sit with one patient at a time and usually behind the patient, where the analyst's actions and reactions are not under such scrutiny, and where he is in less danger of being challenged for his interpretations and reactions. The analyst in a group is called on by others, if not by himself, to examine his own reactions.

More and more analysts are, however, welcoming this trend toward examining their own reactions, not only because it is in tune with the positive trends of our time, but also because giving up their godlike role spares them much of the iconoclastic malice they are subjected to in the popular press and humor magazines. Not that we do not deserve some of it or that we should not be able to take a little ribbing now and then. But there are enough pitfalls to being an analyst without having people demand that he always be perfectly healthy with a perfectly healthy wife and children, that he be omniscient, all-powerful, and magically able to solve all difficulties.

It is true that some few analysts believe their own publicity and try earnestly to live out their patient's image of them. But most of us understand that these jokes and attacks have a deeper origin in resentment that the analyst does not live up to these demands of perfection, that he does, indeed, have feet of clay.

Well, in a group, the analyst who does understand has a chance to practice what he preaches: to show in his own conduct of the group and his own interaction with its members, that he is not a god or a miracle worker but a human being with certain skills and certain professional training, and human enough to make some mistakes and as capable of learning something new as any other person. What is more, such a situation is healthy, for how else are we to get new insights into human problems and behavior?

I will say more of psychoanalysis in groups, because in the immediate future, at least, psychoanalysis is moving in that direction. Perhaps anlysis may, one day, be incorporated, like Newton's theory, into a much larger and more appropriate theory. Today we have moved from Newtonian to Einsteinian physics, from earth space to outer space science. Perhaps one day, psychoanalysis will move to a larger view of the minds of men, in a grander, more realistic understanding. Perhaps one area of research will be the question of why we are so fearful of knowing ourselves and of being seen and how to deal with our need to hide. The analyst needs to know that himself as well as the patient. There would not be so many schools of psychoanalysis and so much acrimonious debate about different methods if analysts themselves were readier to welcome knowledge from outside their particular spheres and biases.

I am reminded of a symposium of analysts from a certain school we call, for want of a better name, "orthodox." They had invited a lecturer from another school, who spoke fervently of the need to revive, in our professional vocabulary, such words as "faith," "hope," "ideals," etc., as positive facets of an integrated human being.

His audience was polite but, over coffee in the cafeteria later, faintly derisive. What kind of nonsense was he talking, it was asked? Did he really think you could apply those words to science?

Nevertheless, one of them continued to press for some kind of integration, some meeting ground where the guest and they could join and understand each other. And suddenly he had it! "I know," he exclaimed, "you can hope you'll kill your father! You can have faith you'll sleep with your mother!" and so on.

Broader Training Needs

Well, unorthodoxy is like the weather. We all talk about it, but very few of us do anything about it — in the sense of fostering and welcoming it (unorthodoxy, not the weather) What we badly need in analysis is a United Methods Institute, a UM of Psychoanalysis, evolving from the many dissident groups existing today, where unorthodoxy and flexibility will be seen as desirable and as a healthy manifestation of mature minds engaged in a mutual search, rather than as an excuse for flight, splinterings, and introversion. Psychoanalysis needs new ideas. The world needs new ideas. New ideas arise out of conflict — conflict within one's own group, with other groups, and within oneself when old patterns have ceased to function well. New ideas arise also when theories, hypotheses and experiences are communicated and shared in an atmosphere of cooperating and harmony, with the privilege to criticize and disagree. Discord and harmony coexist in nature. They are part of the reality of man. And it is with the complexity of that reality — intrapsychic, interpersonal, and interactive — with which psychoanalysis has chosen to deal as a science and as an art. By its very nature psychoanalysis must deal with the basic themes of human life, love and hate, money and power, birth and death, and sex. This calls on all the resources of the patient and of the analyst, as a human being as well as a scientist.

This is why the training of the future analyst in groups will be much broader in scope than it is today and will include many disciplines only skimmed through in training today. With this background, the group analyst of the future will listen carefully to the experience of his elders but be less fearful himself of trying the new and the different. He will be less apt to stick rigidly to prescribed schools of thought, more tolerant of the right to dissent, less afraid of the danger of taking calculated risks, of examining the skeptical and heretical position. He will, in the future, value more and more his freedom to explore the prescribed, even as his knowledge and experience increase. He will learn with his patients that none of us is absolutely unique, but are, at the same time, homogeneous and heterogeneous. That we do not live alone or apart, a fact which makes it impossible to conceive of a one-person psychology. That not only authorities but peers are important and that help can come from them, that even his patients being together without him in alternate meetings can be reconstructive. In this future time, "socialization" will no longer be a dirty word in analysis whose only mean: is resistance. It will be acknowledged that socialization can be, at times, therapeutic. If it takes two to tango and at least two to tangle, just think of the possibilities that are opened up when there are eight or ten people in a therapeutic group.

This method of expanding boundaries of communication will also call for expanding boundaries of training for the group analyst himself, who will not only be a psychiatrist, a psychologist, or psychiatric social worker. He may also come from other ranks: sociologists, anthropologists, and hymanistic discipline, just so long as he has demonstrated a genuine will to train further along group analytic lines.

It will not be demanded that he be a scholar so much as that he be endowed with horse sense, with reasonableness, a combination of common sense, intuition, training, and wisdom. And he will retain that essence of childhood, so dearly clung to by creative scientists and artists, the sense of wonder, which enables one to see freshly again and again, to question, to accept, and to renew.

The group analyst of the future will have a certain kind of knowledge and a love of that knowledge, not confined to neurology or statistics or research but including as much as possible: history, philosophy, education, anthropology, comparative literature, mythology, the arts and sciences as they pertain to as many facets of human relatedness as possible.

And he will be a doer. He will have demonstrated in his own life that his own creative impulses and powers have areas in which to breathe outside his chosen profession. Can he sculpture, paint, write, garden, or have a family? Each will find his own room and way of expression, but in order to help his patients find theirs, somewhere, somehow, it needs to be part of his own creative experience, so that we and he know he functions as a total person, with a combination of head, hand, and heart. The kind of person he is will rank high in the table of standards for selection, because, above all, we would wish the group analyst of the future to be a humanizing force, and for that he himself needs to be a broad human being who has given up his own isolation even as he strives to bring his patients out of theirs. He lets himself see and be seen outside his office hours. And he finds the community and the outside world eager to meet him, eager to implement and expand their own boundaries on the community level as well as the personal.

This does not mean that we are advocating or recommending analysis in groups for everyone. That would be impractical and unnecessary. There are, however, good grounds for supposing that psychoanalysis in groups will not only be a setting for the treatment of neurotic illness or the training of the well-rounded analyst. One day, surely, group psychotherapy or some version of it will be exploited for its preventive possibilities and will be made available to adolescents in high school and even to children in elementary school. A school psychologist, trained in group therapy techniques, for example, would be in a position to counsel and guide teachers in dealing with less serious problems in day-to-day contact with students. It may be possible to catch some neurotic tendencies in children before they get too firm a foothold in the personality, and we may be able to uncover the secret, positive yearnings of the child and help to encourage them. I hope that more and more teachers and parents will elect to have a subjective experience in a therapeutic group, not only to stabilize themselves in their chosen professional work and in their social lives, but also to enable them to apply preventive mental health hygiene principles in their dealings with students and children.

With these innovations, public interest in group therapy is likely to grow, if only for the opportunity it offers for escape from isolation, the plague of modern man, into a kind of communication that is encouraged to be free and honest. All of us have disturbances and gripes on one level or another, and an opportunity to ventilate them can be beneficial, especially if, at the same time, the other fellow is encouraged to communicate his response. Trade unions, parent-teacher associations, and other professional groups, sharing common interests, may approach (some have already done so) insurance companies with a view to making psychoanalytic group therapy available at a lesser cost. And these companies, finding that analysis in groups is just as effective as individual analysis and less costly besides, may well take the initiative in supporting psychoanalytic treatment in a group.

While I was writing parts of this paper, I happened to hear a rebroadcast of one of John F. Kennedy's press conferences. He said at one point: "We happen to live, because of the ingenuity of science and man's inability to control his relationships one with another, we happen to live in the most dangerous time in the history of the human race." Analysis in groups is one attempt to deal directly with this problem of man's disturbed relationship with his fellow man. In group the patient is asked to give up his isolation in therapy, the analyst is asked to give up his omnipotent position which puts him into a kind of isolation. We hope the increasing ability of the individual to control his relationship one with another and one with the group will spread to the community and from the community to the state, the nation, and the world, though we know that to this end analysis itself can play only a small part.

I am reminded, as I bring this paper to a close, of a sign in the subway some months ago. It read: "PEACE by 1969!" Underneath someone had written: "With or without people?" The answer to that question must, somewhere or other, lie in our individual hands. We have to be the first to realize that analysis, individual or group, is not the be-all and end-all of the problem of human existence. Some people of the world are hungry and medically uncared for and need life first. Some have life and need liberty. Some have life and liberty and need happiness. In some societies children do not have much of a chance to live beyond five. Life, liberty, and the pursuit of happiness are, in that order, as much our concern as anyone else's. What is more, as we have often seen in groups and as we are witnessing in the world today, sometimes all these three are being fought for at one and the same time.

How are we to meet these chaotic emergencies? By remembering that the search is greater than any one given answer and that if an answer is found, it proves itself true by opening the way to a greater search. It is a truism that the revolutionist of today is the arch-conservative of tomorrow. That need not be if we resolve never to abandon the search.

Let us, in the future, find the courage to be pliant, to accept authority without ever relinquishing the right to question and criticize that authority. To think of possible differences without fear of retaliation and then to try the different. We want the courage to be adventurous, to take chances without being foolhardy. Today's spaceman was, according to some psychiatric thought, yesterday's schizophrenic. It took courage to be the first man in space, but it also took careful planning. It is this courage of the consciously aware, objectively prepared, that group psychoanalysis of the future will strive to foster. For that we will need to work together. If we are to meet the future face to face, it is better done hand in hand. From now on let it be said that group psychoanalysis is still dedicated to treating the emotional and mental disturbances of the individual; the future trend will be in the direction of decreasing his separateness and bringing him more and more into contact with his fellow human beings. Perhaps that way we will be able to answer partially the age-old questions propounded by a Talmudic scholar (Rabbi Hillel) "If I am not for myself who will be? If I am not for others, what am I? If not now, when?"

5

Group Psychotherapy as a Method of Treatment in a Psychiatric Hospital

RAYMOND BATTEGAY

Psychiatrists are becoming increasingly aware that the mental illness of individuals implies a corresponding sickness of the group. The very fact that a mentally sick person has to seek the help of a doctor or hospital shows that the (family) group to which he belongs is decompensating and thus can no longer care for the patient from its own resources. The psychiatric patient cannot therefore be regarded as an isolated individual; he must rather be seen as the representative of a family or group connected with him in a variety of ways. If, therefore, we are attempting to treat a mental patient, we must place him in his own social context, and so select the appropriate therapy. Freud (1921) rightly said that the social environment becomes a part of the psychic life of the individual. But we know today that the system of communication in which a person is involved can never be ascertained from whatever image, ideal, or caricature he has formed in his own mind. In order to know someone we must know his (human) environment and his relationships with it. He can only be known for what he is in and with the group or groups, of which he is a part. He can judge himself only by the reactions of his group or groups, and without them his words and actions have no weight. Man's deeds have no real existence except in the memory of the

---

Dr. Battegay is Professor, University of Basel, Switzerland; Chief, Psychiatric University Clinic, Basel.

group. A word merely drops into the void unless there are people there to hear it. And nothing is more unbearable to man than to find himself in a void (Binswanger, 1942; von Gebsattel, 1959). Humans are so closely bound up with their environment that they cannot be considered without it (Lindemann, 1960).

As it became more widely realized that if we are completely to understand a man his social milieu must be taken into account, the group, which had already played an important part in the healing process in past cultures, both advanced and primitive, was rediscovered as a therapeutic agent in the twentieth century. This led to the development of group psychotherapy, through which it became possible to place the mental patient in his own social dimension and treat him accordingly.

A psychiatric hospital, in itself a microcosm, provides an ideal background for the study and therapeutic exploiting of social behavior and interaction, with the help of sociometric tests (Alnaes, 1963, Moreno, 1954, Friedemann, 1959). It is therefore to our advantage to make the hospital wards into therapeutic units. The participants gain by the direct influence of the group on individuals or of individuals on each other; in addition, group psychotherapy also works indirectly on the whole ward by creating an actively therapeutic atmosphere which affects every member. It is scarcely possible to give deep individual psychotherapy to every patient who enters a psychiatric hospital, but treatment in departmental units ensures at least a minimum of medical and psychotherapeutic attention.

It is also desirable in a psychiatric hospital to constitute smaller groups, diagnostically more homogenous, with an average of six to eight patients, in which patients with fairly similar illnesses and problems can work towards a solution of their difficulties through reciprocal influence and support.

In the psychiatric hospital of the University of Basle, in certain departments we considered suitable, we have been holding group psychotherapeutic sessions since 1955 with all patients who wished to take part. Since 1957 we have also been working with small groups of patients, diagnostically more homogeneous. We made no plan as to which types of illness were to be specially considered; we simply grouped together those patients who had been hospitalized in large numbers in our clinic and with whom additional collective treatment gave promise of deeper understanding and a better therapeutic result. We moved only gradually towards group psychotherapeutic work with the most diverse diagnostic categories.

Since mental illnesses are rooted in the patients' human environment, it is reasonable from a therapeutic point of view to include patients' relatives in the groups. It is thus possible to become better acquainted with the family groups, which have left their mark on the patients, and thus with the formative influences on their characters (Toman, 1963). But above all we can influence the patients' environment and give them more emotional scope and freedom within their own milieu.

In our hospital, as in other psychiatric hospitals (Boenheim, 1963), it is also clear that group treatment, like every kind of psychotherapy, becomes more difficult if the nursing staff does not have its part in the program. Nurses often do not instinctively understand the psychological and sociodynamic laws that operate in the wards, and they cannot approach objectively the patients' behavioral tendencies — their transferences, resistances, and regressions. Therefore, in 1957, we began group work in our nursing school. In 1959 the hospital administration (Kielholz) also began to give the various categories of nursing staff the opportunity of a few hours' free discussion in groups in annual refresher courses. In the spring of 1962 we began to organize analytical training groups for hospital doctors, in which they can work through the more-or-less conscious conflicts activated in them by the therapeutic groups and experience first hand the processes that take place in a collective body.

The development of group psychotherapy has been helped in the last few years by the increasing concern of psychiatrists to give the patient himself some responsibility for his cure. Naturally, however, we would not expect an endogenous depressive with corresponding anxiety and psychomotor inhibition or agitation to make the effort to take part; such behavior on the doctor's part would drive a patient suffering from melancholia to desperation or even suicide (Kielholz, 1959, 1961). We are thinking, for example, of neurotic and psychopathic patients, alcoholics and drug addicts, and also of epileptics or schizophrenics, in whom the assumption of at least a certain degree of responsibility provides a stimulus to face up to social reality, to stick to a long-term medication routine, or to conquer an addiction. In this connection we should mention the observations of Napolitani (1961). He gave schizophrenics considerable independence and saw that they were not only more able to cope with reality outside the hospital, but more quickly became capable of overcoming difficulties. This "community therapy" is unique and individual; it should not be thought of in group psychotherapy. Most particularly, the collective psychotherapeutic sessions take on a considerable importance for the functioning of the wards, since the patients help and support each other by working through such difficulties, problems, and tensions as may arise.

Special Methods: General Remarks

Events follow substantially the same pattern in every therapeutic group, regardless of the culture, character, and intelligence of the participants. For instance, an almost identical struggle for hierarchical position occurs more or less openly in every group. Some push their way "upwards" almost compulsively; some, almost equally automatically, take the lower positions. These rules apply more or less independently of the type of individuals forming the group; thus it is hard to understand why different authors use different methods for group psychotherapy. At the same time it is clearly an advantage if the therapist can take into account certain particular features of the participants or local peculiarities. And every therapist will give preference to those techniques in which he is particularly interested.

In our hospital two essentially different methods of group psychotherapy are used: (1) group psychotherapy with diagnostically heterogeneous wards (large groups); (2) group psychotherapy with small groups, diagnostically homogeneous.

In the following sections we shall discuss the special characteristics and the techniques appropriate to each.

Group Psychotherapy with Diagnostically Heterogeneous Wards (Large Groups)

If the treatment in a psychiatric hospital is to be as comprehensive as possible, it is essential to create a therapeutically active atmosphere; we should, therefore, consider the wards as units from the point of view of group therapy. While single patients are treated by somatic methods or individual psychotherapy, group psychotherapy with the patients of a ward leads to the integration of individual treatment methods in a psychotherapeutic plan that includes both individual cases and the ward as a whole. The special aspects of every case are firmly kept in mind, but the patients are centered on the group, and this forms a unifying bond that lifts the different patients out of their self-imposed isolation. Individuals feel less at a disadvantage with regard to fellow patients who are undergoing a different course of treatment and find it easier to tolerate a treatment when others are having it at the same time. Group therapy involving a whole ward results in a psychotherapeutically active atmosphere in which patients feel themselves accepted with all their conflicts and can thus gain confidence.

Although Johnson (1963) describes group work with a whole ward not as "group therapy" but as "group activity," we feel that the size of the group has no bearing on its effectiveness as therapy. It will as a rule be easier, of course, to do psychotherapeutic work with a small group. But the same pattern of events stands out, sometimes in the foreground and sometimes in the background, with every group, whatever its size. We have, therefore, no reason to say that this method of treatment is not group therapy. We also feel that the distinction made by many authors between group *psycho*therapy and group therapy is questionable, since not only the analytical, but also the directive method is accepted psychotherapeutic procedure.

Before going into the characteristics of treatment in and with large groups, we should briefly indicate the technique we use. We carry out this type of group therapy with a women's ward and a mixed private ward, each of which has twenty to twenty-five patients widely differing in psychiatric diagnoses. The sessions, which are held weekly, last one to one and one-half hours. These, naturally, are what are known as open groups, since patients are constantly leaving the ward or being admitted to it.

At first we began by reading aloud a short story, usually a fairy tale lasting a few minutes. We chose stories that presented a problem that especially related to one or more patients. The patients were encouraged to discuss not so much the story itself as the emotions it brought to the surface in them. It was easier for the participants to express themselves, as they did not have to begin by speaking; the story was there to speak for them. We were using for these groups a principle similar to that of Moreno (1959) in his psychodrama, when he brought in the "auxiliary ego" to activate the problem in the patients and induce them to speak. The reading of the short story certainly stimulated the participants, but partly because this method obscured the therapeutic purpose of the sessions, and partly because they set up resistances against a deeper and more fundamental examination of their conflicts, they inevitably failed to penetrate beyond the superficial content of the story. The therapist was in danger of entering upon highly intellectual discussions, which largely left out of account the emotions behind the individual conflicts. Thus the reading of the story sometimes stood in the way of a deeper communal experience and the acquisition of new points of view. We changed, therefore, to letting the patients express themselves spontaneously; we simply told them they could bring up anything about which they felt strongly. We also stressed the fact that the purpose of the meeting was not to have their questions answered by the therapist or to let him lead the discussion; the point of the sessions was rather that the patients should discuss their problems as freely as possible amongst themselves and thus gain fresh insight into certain inner conflicts and tensions. It must be constantly stressed at the beginning of the sessions that every individual member of the group must be able to count on the utmost secrecy.

Since, as we have said, these groups are open, certain difficulties are bound to arise. The principles of group treatment must be constantly brought to the attention of the patients; and even so we cannot be sure that they will be observed. Indeed a good indication of the individual's general attitude is his approach to these rules — whether, for example, he openly resists them or accepts them without question. It is important that the attitudes that come to light should be discussed by the members and constantly referred to.

It goes without saying that these large groups also show the multiple and multidimensional transference patterns (Mullan & Rosenbaum, 1962; Slavson, 1951; Stokvis, 1960, and others) and complex resistances that are characteristic of group dynamics. It is for the therapist to recognize these occurrences and try to sharpen the patient's understanding of them. To begin with, the members of the group usually tend to expect the therapist to answer all their questions while they remain in an infantile passive role. They like to think of the doctor leading the group as a superior being whose words and actions can remove their suffering as though by magic. The feeling that the patients had about their parents in early childhood comes to life again in such a group and gives rise to regressive tendencies in the patients. With the therapist's help they gradually reveal to the group the true background to their attitude, which makes it easier for them to become more independent and self-sufficient. A tendency to reciprocal identification (Slavson, 1964: identification transference) often becomes noticeable at a very early stage.

If a participant expresses satisfaction with the doctors and the hospital as a whole, this circumstance, as a result of reciprocal identification tendencies, often has a very favorable effect on the whole ward by increasing confidence. Naturally, however, the participants can also easily identify with a patient who rebels against the treatment, the doctors, and the nursing staff. These identification tendencies, then, are not always therapeutically helpful; they can also have a negative effect. Especially when a therapist is inexperienced, there is the danger that the complaining type of patient may find a platform beyond his wildest hopes and succeed in manipulating an entire ward into a negative attitude towards the therapist and the hospital as a whole.

In these groups the participants' feelings towards their parents, siblings, or schoolfellows are reanimated. The therapist will soon be able to recognize the origin of their propensities, but those concerned will achieve this only after detailed discussion of their attitudes and behavior in the group.

A single woman of twenty-three suffered from an infantile neurosis. A domineering mother had prevented her development, and her father had shown little interest in her upbringing. She suddenly declared that the therapist was exactly like her mother; he had pointed out to her beforehand in an individual interview that it was no use trying to change her mother and that she would have to alter her own attitude. When the others drew her attention to the fact that her notion that the therapist resembled her mother was absurd and probably an illusion stemming from her earlier experiences, she began to recognize the transference situation in her feelings towards the doctor and also to realize that she had to run her own life and not continue to accuse her mother while remaining as dependent on her as ever. It was perhaps characteristic of the identification tendencies in the group that another neurotic woman of thirty-two, divorced and also extremely infantile, who also had grown up with a tyrannical mother and a father who took little part in her upbringing, now said that she too saw in the doctor a reflection of her overstrict mother. Doubtless the emergence of the memory image led her to see her mother for the present only as hard and cruel. Meanwhile it was a valuable experience for her to come to grips with the image of her mother, in the transference situation possible in a therapeutic group, and to detach herself from it at least to some extent.

Group psychotherapy, even with a large number of patients, not only is quicker to bring out feelings rooted in the past, but often leads to abnormal behavior being recognized as such more quickly than with individual treatment. The criticism of a group of patients is often considerably more caustic than that of an individual therapist. This has the advantage that the patients become aware of their offenses. But it is sometimes traumatic for them to be very sharply attacked.

Before long, relationships of many kinds and on many levels begin to appear in these groups, and the patients begin to influence each other. Even those who are not active, but simply listen in silence, are drawn into the group and can share in the anxieties and worries of the other members. It is often a help to recognize problems similar to their own in other patients. Individuals are drawn into a network of interactions and thus freed from the loneliness and isolation attendant on mental illness, at least as long as the sessions last. Even the fact that group psychotherapy requires the presence of the whole ward brings them out of their isolation and into society. Melancholics and involutional depressives in particular — whose illness brings with it a feeling of exclusion from real life, and who suffer from delusions of guilt, poverty, or disease — often, it is true, do not show any substantial lightening of mood; but they are usually helped and relieved by the sympathy of the other participants. Although they may perhaps be unable to express their relief in words, it is still possible to see that sharing their misery with the others brings considerable alleviation of their sufferings.

These large groups, in which the patients influence each other in so many ways, possess a "reality intensity" which prevents emotional inhibition. At one time schizophrenics deteriorated not only by the natural progress of their disease, but also because of the unreal, uneventful, torpid atmosphere of a hospital. Group therapy makes the mentally sick individual try to communicate instead of retreating into himself. The individual thus becomes aware of his fellow beings and emotional defect is prevented.

As the members of the group become aware of human relationships and show interest in their fellow patients, the wards gain a cohesion, otherwise rarely found, which makes it possible to leave the buildings unlocked. Psychotics and other patients abscond from the hospital much less often than before. The reality of the group obviously exercises a fascination over them, and they are so attracted or absorbed by it that often they can scarcely bear to leave the group and feel very lonely if they have to.

We sometimes find, however, that it is not only the group to which the patient is attached. If, for example, we move patients from a ward in which we have been carrying on group psychotherapy into another, more modern one and give them permission to continue to take part in the sessions, they feel left out nevertheless. Involutional depressives in particular, who in any case have difficulty in adapting to new situations, can feel left out of the group to such an extent that they become suicidal. This shows the close relationship between the group and the locale, which occurs not only with whole wards, but also with small groups. Basically it is nothing more nor less than the "participation mystique," which according to Levy-Bruhl (1927) is typical of the members of a primitive culture. As the primitives feel that the ground on which they live belongs to them and is a part of themselves, so the room in which the group sessions take place is a part of the group itself. Even in the large psychotherapeutic group it is clear that the reactions, behavior patterns, and attitudes of the participants do not all spring from the situation of the moment, the patient's history, or the cultural environment, but from a heritage of age-old patterns of behavior and attitudes common to all mankind. In fact, as Jung (1936) says, they are "the sediment of the lives of our forefathers."

Using the hospital ward for group therapy, we can see what position a patient holds in the group. It soon becomes obvious, without any special sociometric tests, how great a combination of emotional attractions and repulsions the various members represent. Similarly, we can very soon recognize the hierarchy of a group. In a well-constituted group, of course, the structure is constantly being modified. On the whole we can agree with Schindler's division into positions from alpha to omega (1961), although he does not take sufficiently into account the dynamics of a group and the fact that the hierarchic position of individuals is usually not fixed. However, if a patient remains in one position, he runs the risk at least of persisting in a certain attitude, thus decreasing his chances of developing therapeutically effective insights and experiencing changes. Sometimes there is danger to the group as well; prestige-seeking and complaining individuals can easily monopolize the discussion. In this way, especially if the therapist is inexperienced and supports their behavior by his uncertainty, they can attain a leading position from which they cannot be deposed except by excluding them from the group. There is a risk that the group will fall completely under the influence of a monopolist of this type and do only what he wants. The needs of individuals are no longer of any importance, only the demands of one pushing member. The danger is then that from being a well-structured circle, differentiated according to individual needs, and close knit both emotionally and intellectually, the group may become unstructured, its members linked only by feeling and instinct, a "mob in miniature" (Battegay, 1963). In our hospital we have repeatedly seen the group degenerate into a mob, especially where the therapist was still inexperienced. This not only brought the patients no therapeutic gain, but usually caused them positive harm, because their mob behavior, which made them carry out blindly what the monopolist required of them or left them simply bewildered and disorientated, awoke fresh guilt feelings in them.

Such things could naturally happen also in wards in which no group psychotherapy work was done. For that reason the patients in one ward should not be mixed indiscriminately, since, without the control of a doctor experienced in social behavior, "mob characteristics" might appear. Nevertheless, this change to mob behavior occurs extremely rarely in psychiatric teaching hospitals, in which, unfortunately, social processes are still very little studied. It cannot be mere chance that such a situation arose only after group psychotherapy had been carried out with a whole ward for at least a year. The group organization can give the patient in quest of leadership a platform which he would not otherwise have had. Certainly this platform is unrestrictedly open to him only when the therapist fails to take the situation in hand — or even smooths the way for him.

If we now consider the general impression given by a ward to the whole of which group psychotherapy is applied, we realize that with this (additional) method the patients can be diagnosed and treated much more intensively than without it. They feel much more responsible, in the group, for themselves and for the others, so that they do not passively submit themselves to therapy but take a more or less active part in the treatment.

Group Psychotherapy with Small, Diagnostically More Homogeneous Groups

Where patients with a similar mental illness are associated together it is often possible for them to apply to themselves the questions brought forward by the various members of the group, to recognize their problems *mutatis mutandis* as their own, and to make a new approach to the specific subjects troubling them. It is therefore an advantage to place together patients with more or less similar diagnoses in smaller therapeutic groups, so as to give them the opportunity to find mutual support and help in facing and solving the difficulties and mental conflicts which they have in common.

Small groups with an average of six to eight members are naturally easier for the therapist to supervise than the large groups we have mentioned. It is also easier to attract individuals into the discussion than it is in the large groups, some members of which are always able to withdraw into passive silence. In a small group the participants are more continually in the limelight than in a larger one and so find it more difficult to stay outside the activities of the group. If they have agreed to take part in a therapeutic circle of this kind, they usually feel more or less duty bound to contribute something to the success of their treatment and that of the others. Individuals are considerably more responsible for themselves and the others than in large groups, and it is even clearer that the patients can be brought, through group psychotherapy, to take an active part in their treatment (Battegay, 1961).

The emotions of some participants bring out similar latent feelings in the others. Affects are mobilized and set to work. We have therefore spoken of a "reinforcing effect" of the (therapeutic) group (Battegay, 1961). Long-repressed emotions, which would otherwise have remained imperceptible or unclear, come out into the open. In group psychotherapy unconscious emotional conflicts often come to light more quickly. However, it is obvious that the problems that come to the surface can hardly ever be worked through as intensively and thoroughly in a group as in the *tête à tête* of classical psychotherapy. It is true that among the different participants more instances are brought forward than in individual therapy between patient and analyst, but the observations of the other group members are scarcely as well-founded as those of an experienced therapist. In addition there is scarcely enough time for a detailed and profound examination of all the associations which come out in a group. Having said this, we must add that group psychotherapy can bring deep-seated conflicts to light as quickly or even more so, but these conflicts cannot be as thoroughly examined as in the classic psychoanalytical situation with only patient and analyst present.

Transference feelings usually become clear much faster in small groups than in large ones. We find quite often, for example, that a patient may consider a fellow patient as her sister, the therapist as her father, and the whole group as her family and act towards them accordingly. At about the same time similar or different emotional stirrings appear between other members of the group.

Resistances to the analyst's approach are also often seen more quickly in the small group than in the large one. Resistances do perhaps appear early in larger groups, but owing to the greater number of members they are often masked. In small groups the resistance of individuals or the whole group against the therapist or the therapy is naturally of more importance; they are more quickly observed, and both the doctor leading the group and the patients must come to terms with them. Here too, multiple resistances of one participant against another and/or the whole group appear, and at the same time there are similar or dissimilar resistances by other members of the group against others of their fellows.

In small groups the interaction between the different group members, and between individuals and the group as a whole is often deeper and more intensive than in large groups. We must also take into account the fact that in larger groups only a few patients usually play an active part, while the others are passive, keeping out of the evolution of the group to a greater or lesser extent.

If the patients are put together in a small therapeutic group with others suffering from the same illness they are given a chance to escape from loneliness and from the anxieties caused by feeling themselves in a special position. Often they are quicker to gain courage to fight against their illness and to work with the doctor to overcome it. The "togetherness" of the group also allows these patients, who are as a rule very sensitive and easily hurt, to achieve a certain detachment and independence of their environment. They are thus more readily protected from unfavorable outside influences than they would have been if left to themselves.

In order to give a fairly concrete picture of this type of group psychotherapy, we will allude briefly to our experiences with our various treatment groups.

The considerable number of *alcoholics* admitted to our hospital is in itself enough to induce us to deal with them not only individually, but also in therapeutic groups. These patients are eminently suitable for group treatment. Very often they spontaneously seek out a group of "colleagues" in order to drink in company. Alcoholics have a great need for society. Either the group gives them back some of the security which they enjoyed to the full in childhood through an indulgent mother, or, if they were frustrated in childhood by their mother and did not get enough security from their father, it gives them for the first time that comforting feeling of companionship, which they have never had up to now. As we said in an earlier work, these patients find in the group an "affective forum" around which to gather.

Our policy now is to invite alcoholic patients treated in our hospital (Battegay, 1958) to join our "internal" group. We offer them nonalcoholic drinks and *stumpen* (a cheap cigar very popular in Switzerland) as a substitute for the forbidden alcohol, so that they may have at least some satisfaction for their usually heightened oral cravings and to give them a sense of the genial atmosphere associated with the tavern.

Discharged alcoholics are also gathered together in an "external" group to give them an emotionally satisfying milieu in which they can feel at ease without being exposed afresh to alcohol. We hold the sessions for discharged patients in a nonalcoholic restaurant in the town.

The hospital group meets for an hour every week, but the discharged patients' meetings often last longer, up to two hours. The patients in the "external" group are mainly on Antabuse (disulfiram). The hospital group is led by a doctor together with a social worker specially appointed for the care of alcoholics, whereas the outpatients' group is run entirely by social workers. Both groups are open; that is to say, new patients are constantly joining them and the old ones leaving.

Alcoholics usually have a strong desire to become part of a

group, and so as a rule they have no difficulty in fitting into this type of society. At an early stage they begin to show tendencies towards identification. If, for example, one of the participants asserts that the cause of his drinking is to be found in his wife or in her lack of understanding of him, the others too insist that their wives treat them unfairly at home. This often happens even when relations between the couple are good and loving. There is a danger that these patients may be content to blame their wives or other relatives and their environment and not bother about the solution of their own problems. Thus, although the alcoholic patient's identification tendencies can make it easier for him to fight against alcoholism, since in this way he can work in association with others, they have also certain disadvantages, such as the risk that their natural tendency to shift the responsibility for themselves and their drinking to others may be strengthened (Mullan & Sangiuliano, 1961). It is very understandable that these patients should express in group therapy the most acute and varied resentments against their whole environment. On the one hand it is indeed essential that these people, who often feel very frustrated in the outside world — often they cannot cope adequately with external reality — should have the opportunity to be listened to and accepted by an understanding circle and rid themselves of their hostile emotions. But on the other hand it is no less necessary for them to recognize their projection tendencies for what they are.

Many of the emotional relationships between the members of these groups have their origin in childhood experience. An elderly alcoholic, for example, speaks to a young member of the group as though he were his son. Problems and conflicts which occupy the patients in their associations with their relatives and others around them can come to light in this way. The patients learn to recognize the emotions which come to the surface and thus to deal with them. Transferences become obvious, and with their help they find it easier to free themselves from the burden of the past.

Guilt feelings, which weigh heavily upon alcoholics and are harmful rather than therapeutic, leading to fresh bouts of drinking, often come to light in the group sessions, though usually only after much resistance. If the sufferers realize that the group, including the therapist, does not judge them but continues to be friendly towards them, the mistrust which is often present in alcoholics is dispersed.

With group therapy we can give alcoholics the possibility of fighting alcoholism together with fellow-sufferers, in the security of a circle of friends. They support each other mutually, feel stronger and are better able to withstand new temptations to drink. The out-patients' group of former alcoholics does particularly sterling service in this respect. The patients often find in such groups a support that can save them from relapses. A promise of abstinence, given before a group of patients who are all striving to keep away from alcohol, can often be more readily kept than when it is given to a therapist alone. The greater extent of such a circle leads to an increased feeling of responsibility on the part of those concerned, and they will often be better able to keep away from alcohol than they would have been without this extra method of treatment. Besides, the outpatients' group makes it possible for the social workers to keep in touch with those in their care more unobtrusively than by individual visits.

Naturally we collaborate actively with Alcoholics Anonymous. This body consists mainly of former hospital patients who have taken part in the inpatients' group. For this reason, and simply because the work of Alcoholics Anonymous is carried on chiefly by the group system, their successes depend on similar principles to those of group psychotherapy. When these patients give their word to Alcoholics Anonymous, they feel it subjectively as binding upon them, and it is easier for them to give up alcohol than if they were thrown upon their own resources.

For some years we have admitted to our hospital in growing numbers a type of patient that is common in this country: those who abuse "light" analgesics — mostly combinations of phenacetin with caffeine and a hypnotic, which are often taken for headaches with various etiologies — and hypnotics — often preparations without barbiturates, which are available without prescription — (Kielholz, 1964).

Since these patients are often, to a greater or lesser extent, unable to relate to others, the therapeutic group gives them above all the opportunity to communicate with individuals who, having similar difficulties in human relationships, are closer to them than people who can communicate more freely.

We run these groups of drug addicts without any external aids. When we began in 1957 they met for an hour twice a week, but we changed later to meetings every two weeks for just over an hour. When the group was meeting less often, it became possible to include discharged patients. As a rule the participation of former patients has a favorable effect on those still hospitalized, because they can learn from the experiences of the others. It is not easy for drug addicts to form a new group after leaving hospital, and for this reason too it is a good idea to bring them into the hospital group. This group is led by two doctors. A social worker of our hospital, who was leading this circle temporarily, successfully carried out sessions of "autogenous training" alternating with the group discussions (Schultz, 1956). This combination, which naturally presupposes a sound knowledge of this method of relieving tension, was effective in encouraging the participants to express themselves and in deepening the emotional level of group discussion.

The drug addicts' group is kept closed as far as possible, as these patients generally have difficulties in adapting to constant changes of people and situations. We admit a new patient to an old group only occasionally, when the group members have declared themselves willing.

The drug addicts' suspicion of their fellows often shows itself in the psychotherapeutic group.

A thirty-nine-year-old office worker, always very reserved and withdrawn, who lived apart from her schizoid, infantile husband, met only with aggressiveness the attempts of her fellow patients to draw her into group discussion. She remarked, for example, that she did not want to talk about banalities like the others and that she had no intention of saying anything about her problems, although the others were obviously longing for her to do so. She began to knit ostentatiously, with the obvious intention of irritating the other members of the group. This aggressive attitude towards her fellow group members expressed all her mistrust of people in general, which was perhaps at the root of her addiction, and which became more and more marked in the course of time. When at the next meeting the group members tried again to reach her, she suddenly became more approachable; and when a fellow patient said she wanted to roast a goose for Christmas, she asked her, half ironically, but half-seriously too, if she would invite her.

Obviously drug addicts, as Fort (1955) has shown, need their aggressions, even in the narrow circle of the therapeutic group, in order to reach the other members or be reached by them. If the others remain friendly towards them and let them use them as a target, they take this as proof that they really belong. The group becomes for them a place in which they feel more or less comfortable and can talk about their cares and worries, perhaps for the first time. Whereas in the beginning they can enter into an emotional or intellectual relationship only with the therapist, later the whole group and its individual members become their partners with whom they can converse and seek a solution to their problems, some of which are common to all. However, with these patients there is a risk that in group discussions they may avoid tackling their difficulties and try to talk on either banal or highly intellectual themes. The therapist must recognize the underlying emotional problems and bring them into the discussion.

We have already mentioned that drug addicts are usually completely isolated from their environment. This is shown by the fact that all members of the drug addicts' group complain at least occasionally of the lack of understanding shown by their spouses, parents, or children. The social isolation, which had earlier led them to take refuge in drugs, now becomes the motive for the formation of a group, as it stimulates identification between the participants. The therapeutic group becomes the place where patients who were formerly thrown back upon themselves can make contact with similarly lonely people; the sense of community this brings will make it easier for them in the future to renounce the pleasure and self-forgetfulness offered by drugs. The therapeutic group, by gathering drug addicts together and introducing them to each other, performs the essential service of smoothing their path back into society.

Through the contributions of the other participants, group therapy helps the drug addict to achieve a more rapid and comprehensive insight into the conditions and causes of the addiction. It often takes many lapses to convince a patient of the necessity to keep off drugs; but we find that with the help of a group he is much quicker to realize that he really must give them up. Patients who before joining a group could not keep free from drugs find it much easier to avoid lapses afterwards.

A woman born in 1908, of athleto-pyknic type, most of whose childhood had been spent with foster parents who gave her no warmth or loving care, married, in 1944, a man three years younger than herself whose first marriage had ended in divorce. At first the marriage was happy. In 1960 he made the acquaintance of a much younger woman, and the patient found this out in April 1961. In September 1961 the couple was legally separated. After the patient had been deserted by her husband she felt isolated and lonely; since 1940 she had been increasingly hard of hearing and suffered from paroxysmal fits of giddiness with occasional loss of consciousness (according to an electroencephalogram, temporal lobe epilepsy). After the legal separation she had increasing recourse to the hypnotic Noludar (methyprylone), and having been recommended to take a nightcap before going to bed, she also took alcohol in increasing quantities. Finally, on October 24, 1962, she attempted suicide with sleeping pills. Withdrawal treatment in our hospital from October 24 to November 21, 1961, produced no substantial result, and by the end of January 1963 she had begun to take Noludar and alcohol in excess and in ever-increasing quantities. She had therefore to be treated by us for the second time, from September 5 to November 12, 1963. During her second period in hospital we admitted her into the therapeutic group for drug addicts. She developed a tremendous need to express herself, but she was also interested in the other participants' worries. At first she complained over and over again that she could not forget her husband and so was often depressed, but in the course of a year during which she attended the group regularly, she became noticeably more balanced and confident. She began to take an interest in her surroundings again, bought a television set, took a pride in her appearance, and began to enjoy good food as she had formerly. During this time she also took a part-time job in which she has to work on her own, and she is very highly thought of there.

For this woman the group obviously became at least a partial substitute for her lost husband, perhaps also for the other relationships she lacked. She pointed out in many of the sessions how much she looked forward to the group meetings every time and how intimate she felt the atmosphere of the group to be. An essential contributing factor to this affinity to the group was probably the fact that one patient in particular was encouraged by the group discussions to take a lively interest in her outside the group sessions. The patient has now been off drugs for over a year, and thanks to her rediscovered interest in life she is happy. Naturally it is too early to decide finally whether the treatment has been a success. However, we have the impression that group therapy gave the patient a foothold which individual treatment could not give her.

The therapeutic group gives drug addicts the chance to discuss new problems as they arise and to gain comfort, support, and advice from the other members. There is less risk that feelings of unhappiness, which were often at the root of the addiction, can reawaken. When emotions arise in the group members because of unfavorable outside influences they can enter into the general conversation and receive an understanding hearing, whereas previously the drug addicts kept everything to themselves and so built up new resentments against an apparently rejecting environment. These patients are often deeply suspicious of those around them, but the group gives them the new experience of seeing the people they meet as human beings. In their eyes, other people did not understand them or were even downright hostile to them; but now, in their fellow group members they are meeting, perhaps for the first time, people who approach them openly and without reserve. Drug addicts who in their childhood received too little affection (Kielholz & Battegay, 1964) or, on the contrary, were overmothered and spoiled (Schultz, 1953) often receive compensatory treatment from the other members of the group. The other members generally find out very quickly who has suffered frustration and needs emotional support, and who must be made aware, by denial, of how much emotional attention they have a right to expect from their fellow beings.

Although the formation of a group is considerably more difficult with drug addicts than with alcoholics because of the addicts' marked sensitivity and unsociability, we have the impression that therapeutic group work is especially important for them. It not only gives them valuable insight into the nature of their illness; above all it offers them a chance for unprejudiced social contact. We must remember in this connection that it was often this very incapability of adapting themselves to reality which led them to excessive drug taking.

For some years hospitals have been admitting increasing numbers of young delinquents and social misfits; this led us to reconsider the treatment of these patients. On the one hand they cannot adapt to society as it is at present, but on the other hand they tend to form gangs; they are asocial in relation to adult society, but there is no reason to suppose that their attitude to social life is always negative. We decided some years ago, therefore, to treat these young people not only individually, but also by group psychotherapy.

We now take an average of six to eight of these young people twice a week for one hour. Besides the doctor in charge of the group, a woman social worker specially appointed for these patients also takes part. At first we had both sexes working together. Later, however, we restricted group therapy to the delinquent girls, who entered our hospital in greater numbers; with these unbridled young people relations between the sexes had developed which were jeopardizing the success of the therapy.

We observed that these young people were able to shed their reserve or even antagonism towards the therapist more quickly in a group than in individual psychotherapy. If they see that others in the group are beginning to talk about their thoughts and longings and their earlier adventures, they realize that it will not be taken as a betrayal if they too begin to talk about themselves and their experiences. The fact alone that the doctor and the cotherapist are present throughout the conversation and utter no word of condemnation leads to a therapeutic rapport. If this is followed up, transference phenomena are generally quick to follow. The members of the group, for example, speak of the therapists as "Teenager-Mammi" and "Teenager-Pappi," or a girl declares that she wishes that the social worker leading the group were her mother. The image of a friend can also occasionally be projected onto the therapist.

When these transference feelings arise, the therapeutic relationship usually becomes so strong that these girls lose their old suspicion of adults. There is also often a regression to an earlier stage of development. The girls want all the problems confronting them to be solved by the therapist. They crave support and want the doctor and social worker to stay beside them all the time and protect them, if necessary, even against their own parents.

On the one hand it is now important to give them sufficient support so that they can feel that the trust they have placed in the two therapists is absolutely justified. On the other hand we must take care at the right time to let them gradually assume a part of the responsibility for themselves.

We have found the provision of a day center outside the hospital for these young delinquents and misfits to be of great value, particularly with a view to increasing their independence. When these patients begin to show the transference feelings we have mentioned and the relationship with the therapist appears to be holding together reasonably well, we receive them in this center for three days a week. There they have the chance to keep house themselves under the guidance of two youth social workers, to cook, and to create something of their own in occupational therapy. They have already acquired a "togetherness" and family feeling through group psychotherapy in the hospital; but since we extended the group treatment of these girls to the day center we have been even more successful in keeping them, largely as a result of this feeling of cohesion. Although some have absconded since then, the therapeutic group has had a centripetal influence on these young people which stops them from running away. They can also often accept the rules of the group more easily than those of their own family, so that they no longer have to turn away from social reality, which, according to Meyer (1962), is characteristic of young absconders. They can often accept the reality of the youth group when they reject other social institutions. However, we cannot allow everything, unconditionally, in group sessions with these young delinquents and misfits. We must rather take care, as Friedemann (1957) said was also necessary in group psychotherapy with children, that a sense of social proportion is awakened in these patients. They must learn not to seek the immediate gratification of their own desires but to bow to reality, as typified by the group.

If we are to draw a conclusion from the group treatment of these young people, we must say that it allows us to make therapeutic contact with them and lead them back into society better than exclusively individual psychotherapy could. If these girls are put into a therapeutic group it first becomes for them a pattern of society, and their social instincts are awakened; and then they find security by realizing their responsibility to the group for their words and actions.

A patient born in 1943 lost her mother in her fourteenth year. Her father spoiled her on the one hand and made too many demands on her on the other, as she was obliged to take her mother's place in the family. She began to associate increasingly with young hooligans and was obviously becoming delinquent. In July 1962 she was committed to a reformatory, but soon absconded. During her stay in our hospital from July 19, 1962, to August 9, 1963, she not only received individual psychotherapy, but was also included in the group of delinquent girls. Whereas at the beginning she rejected all attempts at therapy and remained defiant, she showed herself in the group to be dependent and in need of support. A secure relationship developed with both the doctor in charge of the group and the social worker. The urge to run away, which the patient had at first and partly put into practice, receded further and further into the background. In contrast to her earlier attitude, she was now ready to begin training (in beauty culture) and did so in the summer of 1963. She has now (February 1965) kept up this improvement for more than a year, still comes every week to the group sessions in our day center, and is on the best of terms with the social workers there. This patient, who after her mother's death had to take on responsibilities that were obviously too heavy for her, could depend on grown-ups again in the psychotherapeutic group, where she found security and support, and also a mother-substitute in the person of the cotherapist.

In the spring of 1964, after having worked analytically for years with groups of doctors (we shall have more to say about this later) we decided to form an analytical group consisting exclusively of neurotics. We were guided in this chiefly by the experiences of Foulkes (1964), Genevard (1961), Grinberg et al. (1960), Kemper (1959), and Wiesenhutter (1961). It is usually not very easy, however, to find patients in a psychiatric hospital who are suitable for inclusion in a group of neurotics. Neurotic patients rarely need hospital treatment, and as a rule they are hospitalized only for a short time, so that we must first find out whether they will be able to continue to take part in group activities after their discharge from hospital.

For the reasons mentioned we included only neurotics with the most difficult social backgrounds; these were the only ones who stayed long in a hospital. We also had to take care that no patient in the group received individual psychotherapy from either of the two therapists. If individual treatment and group therapy were given at the same time by the same therapist, too many varied and complicated transference relationships might arise, which would certainly overtax the patient's capacity for integration. We felt, however, that group work carried on simultaneously with individual psychotherapy was indicated for these patients, since they had had particular difficulty in fitting into a social environment, which was why their hospitalization had become necessary. Initially our neurotics' group was made up of four female patients between the ages of twenty and twenty-five; we have just added a fifth. Only female patients were chosen, since attempts to include male patients in the group failed because they could not always promise to continue once they had left hospital. There were other disturbances when one of the patients stayed away from the group for external reasons, and another patient had to be introduced.

These patients found it very difficult to form relationships, and at first they spoke only to the group leader and expected the solution of their problems to come from him; but gradually a deeper relationship began to form between the group members themselves. There was always the danger, however, that one of the patients, a twenty-one-year-old neurotic with regressive and demonstratively hysterical tendencies, who had grown up partly amid parental discord and partly in uncongenial children's homes, would attempt to monopolize the discussion. The other three were at first not in a position to check the tendencies of this patient, so that during this initial phase the doctor in charge of the group had constantly to intervene. Another of the participants, a twenty-four-year-old neurotic depressive, whose sight had remained poor after operations for double congenital cataract and double secondary glaucoma, developed during this time from a completely withdrawn personality to a remarkably open and receptive one. It was obvious that her concern for the patient with infantile hysterical tendencies, whose deep psychological distress showed clearly beneath her exhibitionism, helped substantially to strengthen her badly damaged self-confidence.

The most varied transferences soon began to appear. The patient with the tendency to hysterical demonstrations acted towards the elder of the two group leaders (Dr. B) as though he were her father. She had been brought up without a father, as her mother had separated from him on account of his alcoholism. Although on the one hand she identified with her mother and rejected her father, she longed, on the other hand, to find a good father and thus an ideal man and the security he might bring her. At group meetings she often made derogatory remarks about men in general, and sometimes indulged in verbal aggression, particularly against the older therapist. However, the fact that the other patients trusted the therapists implicitly made her begin to revise her attitude toward men. Her changed attitude can be recognized in the following dream, although it still contains a certain ambivalence:

"I was on a cliff with other girls, and I kept slipping. I was frightened of falling. So I climbed down from the cliff. On the way down I met Dr. B. He pulled me up again. I slipped and fell down again. Dr. B. pulled me up again." This was repeated several times.

Another patient, who previously could not bring herself to accept any individual therapy, a twenty-five-year-old neurotic depressive nurse, was at first constantly pouring forth self-accusations arising from severe guilt feelings. In the course of group psychotherapy she gradually came out of herself and was clearly becoming better adjusted to the group, though she did not yet show such clear transference indications as the patients we have mentioned. She even began to talk about beginning a psychoanalysis. The fourth member, who has been in the group for the shortest time, was a very infantile twenty-year-old who had never been able to hold down a job and had not enough courage to take part spontaneously in group discussion. The intense neurotic disturbance of the others were manifest in the fact that they scarcely noticed this patient's reserve, and it did not occur to them to draw her into group discussions. It was for the therapists to support this infantile patient, who was quite incapable of holding her own, and to prevent her from being totally ignored.

We cannot yet say much about the neurotics' group, as it has been in action for so short a time. But we have the impression that although three of these patients (and the one who has just joined us) are also receiving individual psychotherapy, and the fourth is soon to begin a psychoanalysis, the group psychotherapy is offering them a social experience they would not have otherwise had. It could not, for instance, have been an accident that the hysterical patient, in the dream we have mentioned, found herself on a cliff with other girls. Her earlier dreams held very little suggestion of community with other people. In this dream we can recognize at least the beginnings of it.

Because group psychotherapy provides an experience of reality through the interaction of the group members, it is sometimes possible to dispel neurotic delusions that persist despite their elucidation in individual psychotherapy. The group members, who, as a result of their psychological conflicts, have focused their attention almost exclusively upon themselves, are beginning to take an interest in each other and in the activities of the group. With the help of individual psychotherapy, complemented by work in the social field, an essential contribution is being made to their resocialization. We are also specially helped in the recognition of neurotic symptoms which obtain in the social sphere and of repressed conflicts which have their roots in a collective situation such as the family group in childhood.

We had observed since 1955 that some of the schizophrenics included in large diagnostically mixed groups had shown themselves to be suitable for group work in various specific ways. In the spring of 1963, therefore, we began to form a small group of seven to nine (at first there were five) twenty-year-old to thirty-year-old female schizophrenic patients. We were encouraged to do this by the experiences of Bour (1961), Brack (1962), Powdermaker & Frank (1953), Schindler (1958), Slavson (1961), etc. The selection of female patients only does not mean that we felt it was not possible in principle for both sexes to take part together. However, the therapist happened to be in charge of the women's ward of the hospital and was naturally more interested in the psychotherapeutic treatment of women; and it was felt from the beginning that to take only one sex would avoid complicating still further a situation which would be difficult enough if the group was composed solely of schizophrenics.

One symptom of the serious breakdown of the schizophrenic's ability to communicate was the fact that during the first session the patients sat along the walls without speaking a word to each other. It took several meetings, at which they spoke only to the two therapists, before they entered into any relationship among themselves. It was a fortunate circumstance that a small room had been chosen for group treatment. It is true that the participants perhaps felt themselves too crowded together in the space allotted to them, but when their original fear of losing their individuality, or, as Benedetti (1964) put it, of being unable to separate themselves from their fellow beings, was diminished, the social distance to be bridged was smaller and presented less of an obstacle in a confined space.

As the group work advanced it was clear that the group situation can often interest patients in external events more readily than the psychotherapeutic *tête-à-tête*. This happened, for example, with a thirty-year-old hebephrenic, whose illness had lasted seventeen years. In the group, she frequently paid no attention to the others' conversation, being fully occupied with the question whether the doctor in charge was God or the Devil. On several occasions when she voiced her insane notions aloud, seeing every action of this therapist as a "proof" of his diabolical nature, the other group members would do their best to show her that her ideas were psychotic and disproportionate. When this happened, the patient often stopped talking and listened to the arguments of the others and even, for the rest of the sessions in question, took a sensible part in the conversation.

The record, kept by one of the two group leaders, of a meeting at which this patient again made these assertions about the therapist, may perhaps make it clear how the patient finally showed an adequate grasp of external reality.

Miss B began with her constant theme: fear of the group leader. She was being grilled, she said he was the Devil, and so on. After the others had at first tried to talk her out of it, they stopped taking her seriously, and laughed at what she said. She at once realized that she was being laughed at, became aggressive and threatened to box their ears. Miss B felt frustrated again, tried to escape, and when prevented from doing so, burst into helpless weeping. Her whole body trembled, she was obviously terrified, and expressed fears like "Dr. B wants to kill me; he wants to take me to Hell; they all want to hit me", and so on. The group was thrown into confusion. Miss S and Miss M tried to help, and talked persuasively to her, but they were too uncertain, and this outburst of emotion left them baffled and somewhat intimidated. After some attempts to change the subject of conversation, interrupted for a long time by terrified outburst and weeping from Miss B, the emotional tension was suddenly relaxed. Miss M succeeded in calming Miss B by her sincere sympathy, and this brought a sudden access of cheerfulness and jollity to the whole group. It is interesting that from this moment on, Miss B herself began to laugh at her unreal ideas, and encouraged the others to do the same. The original tension had given place to complete relaxation. Miss B declared that she now saw the group leader in quite a different way — as a doctor who, as a nurse had explained to her, took care of all of them. She said she was no longer afraid of him.

This patient had been having individual psychotherapy for years and had also been psychopharmacologically treated. Individual treatment had certainly had the effect of making her substantially calmer than previously, and she had, in particular, lost at least some of her mistrust of her fellows. But it was really the group treatment that brought her nearer to social reality. We observed over and over again, with the other patients too, that the therapeutic group has a more intense feeling of reality than the classic psychotherapeutic situation of therapist and patient. The group is sometimes able to convince schizophrenics of the existence of their fellow beings and their relations with them more readily than the more exclusive relationship of doctor and patient. The group's appeal to reality, as the above example shows, has naturally more effect on schizophrenics than on neurotics, since the difference between internal and external worlds is much more marked with psychotics. In a schizophrenics' group, therefore, more spectacular changes in behavior can ensue than with neurotics.

The reciprocal emotional relationships between the schizophrenics in a group and the therapist are often different from those of neurotics, both quantitatively and qualitatively. The patients in the group we have mentioned showed both affection and aversion with great intensity, or wavered between the two opposing affects, so that their emotional attitude became completely ambivalent and their inner confusion clearly visible.

Transferences, too, are often incalculable in schizophrenics' groups. A patient can speak to one of the therapists or a fellow patient as if to her father or sister and then say nothing more about it at the next session. The patients identify with each other very quickly, often because of a similarity accidentally noticed; but these identifications do not last long as a rule. On the other hand we notice that when schizophrenics belonging to this group tend to stereotyped movements and attitudes, the group continually questions their behavior and thus places them in a dynamic situation which at first makes them anxious, but then obliges them to change their attitude.

Group psychotherapy leads to emotional relationships and transferences that are more intense, though more transitory, than those found in individual psychotherapy. Participation in a therapeutic group gives schizophrenics a greater incentive to emerge from their psychotic world into external reality. Psychotics can thus regain, within the group, a sense of their human environment.

Work with the relatives of schizophrenics presented some initial difficulties. This is not to say that the parents or siblings ignored our invitation to a preliminary meeting. However, with the exception of a mother with an overprotective attitude towards her thirty-three-year-old daughter, a hebephrenic of ten years' standing, they failed to attend regularly the weekly group sessions we arranged. We decided.

therefore, to hold a group meeting only once a month, and the participants appeared at these at almost full strength. In all, eight relatives took part, led by two therapists. Schematically speaking, they showed three broad types of attitude and behavior towards their schizophrenic relatives.

1. *Suspicious Paranoid Attitude*

These relatives are deeply mistrustful of medical treatment. They let it be seen that they have no confidence in the therapy and are even of the opinion that it does more harm than good. The father of a twenty-one-year-old schizophrenic, whose mother is in hospital for degenerative schizophrenia of many years' standing, tried, on the occasion of a short paranoid episode on the part of the patient, to convice the group that she, too, would remain chronically sick, and that, all considered, it would have been better if she had never been born. When the therapists gave a relatively good prognosis—as a matter of fact the daughter has in the meantime been out of hospital for a long time, is staying with her former foster parents and earning an independent living—he became suspicious and said the doctors knew very well how serious her illness was and were hiding the truth from him. He could, moreover, be really cruel to the patient and compare her quite openly to her mother. He would not even listen to the arguments of other relatives who backed up what the doctors said. He simply became more suspicious still and later stopped coming to the group sessions.

2. *Overprotective Attitude*

Two mothers of young schizophrenic patients showed an overprotective attitude. One in particular, whom we have already mentioned, the mother of a thirty-three-year-old hebephrenic, was very willing to talk about her sick daughter. She has seven children besides the patient; and in the group sessions she talked constantly about how, in the family and outside it, she had to take responsibility for the patient, protect her at home, give her her chloropromazine tablets, go with her to buy clothes and shoes, etc. Her manner became markedly more lively as she spoke, and we had the impression that since she was constantly dissatisfied with her husband, a railwayman, and her other children had married and left home one after another, she was glad, in a way, to be able to look after and protect her daughter. But on the other hand, it came out in the group that this woman, who identified to a very high degree with the patient, suffered greatly from the condition of her schizophrenic "child." Relatives of this type are not entirely easy to fit into the group, since, with their flow of information about their sick relatives, they often make demands on the others that can sometimes be more than they can bear.

3. *Coldly Objective Attitude*

These mothers, or other near relatives, have an almost terrifying objectivity in describing the symptoms of their relative's illness. They may perhaps insist on their sympathy in words, but there is nothing to show that they are really moved by their daughter's or sister's illness. They are mostly very polite, formal people, who behave correctly in the group in all circumstances. They even listen with great interest when other relatives talk about their worries and their patients' symptoms. In this connection we were particularly impressed by the mother of a twenty-two-year-old patient, whose illness began seven years ago, after she had confessed to incestuous relations with one of her brothers (she has nine siblings). It presented at first the picture of a compulsion neurosis, but then developed definite catatonic features. This woman, who, like the father, tends towards religious fanaticism, showed in the group remarkably little feeling for her daughter but plenty of "understanding" when it came to asking the doctors for explanations of her daughter's illness or helping other relatives over their troubles.

Work with the relatives of schizophrenics made it clear how far the patients' disturbances are the products of their environment. None of the relatives showed an adequate, sufficiently sympathetic, open kind of approach to their fellows. The communications of these near relatives of the patients were always disturbed in one way or another. This group of relatives thus presented a picture which, superficially viewed, was not very different from that of the patients' group; it is all the more essential to try to influence the relatives in this way. To carry out the "treatment" of the relatives in a group not only saves time but helps them to feel less isolated by putting them among others with the same problem.

In collaboration with social workers specially appointed for the welfare of alcoholics, we had a succession of meetings with ten to fifteen wives of alcoholics who were being treated in our hospital. We saw again and again how these women, often of a very maternal type, have suffered from their husbands' alcoholism and in spite of everything are still ready to stand by them and support them. In the group they relate their sufferings, expecting and usually receiving the others' approval of their perseverance. They have a great need to express themselves; each of these women wants to tell the others about her experiences. Contact between the group, like that of the alcoholics themselves, was good from the start. The group for them is above all a place where identification can bring them relief. There are, however, individual women who do not present this picture of the anxious, maternal wife, but appear youthful and distinctly feminine. These latter were usually the ones who found their alcoholic husbands a heavy burden, felt neglected by them, and were hovering on the brink of divorce.

If the husbands of female alcoholics are collected into a group, it is at once obvious that their understanding of their sick spouses is as a rule much less than that of the wives of male alcoholic patients. They often utter very severe criticisms of their wives. In these groups we see very little in the way of loving care; on the contrary, these men are very ready to judge their wives, to "write them off" and turn towards a new future. The husbands of alcoholics show no feeling of "togetherness," either existing from the beginning or gradually appearing; the main reason for this seems to be that the emotional ties between them and their wives have already loosened perceptibly. Nevertheless regular work in groups with these men can perhaps improve the outlook for their marriages. We feel that in view of this, group psychotherapy is indicated for these relatives also.

Analytical Training Groups for Doctors

We agree with Kemper (1964) when he says that we can acquire a fundamental knowledge of group psychotherapy only by personal experience. Realizing this, we began in 1962 to form analytical training groups for hospital psychiatrists. We did so on the basis of our own experience as a participant of the "Lindauer Psychotherapiewoche" (Stolze, 1960) since 1960 and also based on reports from various authors such as Beukenkamp et al. (1958), Ganzarin et al. (1958), Friedemann (1963), Hulse (1958), Stokvis (1960).

Besides forming the doctors into training groups, we also make them cotherapists with patients' groups, let them lead therapeutic groups under supervision, and give them theoretical instruction in lectures, seminars, and discussions, all as part of their training. In the work with training groups (Battegay, 1964) — at the time of writing (February 1965) the third has been in action for more than a year — it was from one point of view an obstacle that a doctor employed in the hospital itself (as a senior physician) acted as leader of the group. The members of the doctors' group could not feel entirely impartial towards a leader whom they met, as colleague or superior, in the everyday work of the hospital. However the arrangement had the advantage that a therapist belonging to the hospital was familiar with the special conditions and was in a better position to integrate the group work as smoothly as possible in the hospital's daily life and in the postgraduate training program.

Six doctors took part in the first group and seven in the other two. It became clear in all the groups that the participants did not regard themselves as therapists so much as human beings with their own more or less unconscious problems of the kind met with in patients.

In this way they learn to recognize what happens to patients in group psychotherapy. A difficulty that arises almost always at first with groups of doctors is that they are led into intellectual debates, distracting them from the actual problems which come to the surface.

Naturally there is no question, in the training group, of creatively discussing and finding solutions for all the problems hinted at or openly brought forward by the participants. It is much more important that the attitudes and behavior of individuals towards each other and of the various members towards the "therapist" should be analyzed. Once insight into their approach to the group is achieved, definitions and possible solutions to their questions will appear of themselves. As we accept colleagues into the group who have not yet had a training analysis, membership of the training group can serve as an incentive to begin an individual psychoanalysis. As we have already said in an earlier chapter, the group therapist should never be the individual analyst of one of the group, since that might lead to transferences that could scarcely be ignored.

One inconvenience of group analysis with the medical personnel of a hospital is that the composition of the group is more or less accidental. Everyone who asks to take part must be accepted into the group. This caused difficulties in the first group, for which some of the doctors who came forward were friends before entering the training group. A "group within the group" was formed, which sometimes impeded free interaction and led to resistances that could be cleared up only with great difficulty.

The doctors' groups meet once a week for a session lasting one to one and a half hours. The end of the training in the first two groups came chiefly because colleagues had to leave. The first ended after eighteen sittings, the second after forty-six. The third group, after forty-nine meetings, is still in progress and will probably end when a colleague goes to another hospital for further training. The departure of one member gave rise to an entirely different group situation, so that the remaining members had to give up the idea of carrying on the same self-analytical work with the same group. We take care that before the group closes the participants should be as clear as possible about the processes and transferences that have taken place, so that they can learn to recognize the therapeutic possibilities and limitations inherent in a group, and also to evaluate their own reactions as reflected in the therapeutic circle.

As with the patients' groups, there is usually a phase in which the members seek the reasons for their difficulties in outward circumstances only. This can lead to really emotional outpourings of long-suppressed resentment or aggression against near relatives, colleagues, or other persons in their environment. But the very fact that they can express feelings they have hitherto revealed to no one often has a liberating effect on the participants. It is then for the therapist to point out to the members that many of their tensions are subjective in origin. As a rule reciprocal transferences come to light, making it clear that their handling of the patients is not always based on objective facts but is also determined by some transference situation. The doctors thus have the opportunity to examine the motives for their treatment of the patients and place it on a more professional basis. In all these groups the various members relived emotions stemming from earlier group experiences in childhood or later periods in life, such as, for example, rivalry with siblings, ambivalent relationships with parents, and so on. It was usually one of the members of the group who drew attention to this fact (Horwitz, 1964). If the group did not see it, it was up to the therapist to offer for discussion the attitude that had come to light, or even to suggest a meaning for it. Frequently in all these groups one of the participants took over the role of therapist spontaneously; during this time he, instead of the group leader, made a substantial contribution to the clarification of unconsciously based attitudes and behavior through his questions and observations. By acting as "assistant therapist" in this way, the future group leaders learn how a therapeutic group should be conducted. But it is essential that the same doctor should not always assume this position or he will take over the group, and its free development will be hindered.

We can see how deeply group work can penetrate in the following transference-based dream of a woman colleague who was taking part in a self-analytical group.

> I was in a room in which there was a table. In the room were Dr. X and a female figure which alternated between Dr. Y [a member of the same group] and an earlier acquaintance, a contractor's daughter, who resembles Dr. Y. The room had to be cleaned. There was a lot of dirt under the table. Dr. X and Dr. Y

> were lying on the floor. I thought—with my innate passion for cleanliness—"there's still some dirt there," and, seeing that my two colleagues looked very relaxed, I wondered whether they were drunk. Besides, Dr. X was lying under the table.

A detail that came to light was that in reality she thought Dr. X very hard-working. But, earlier, her husband had been (unjustly) called lazy by her mother on account of his calm, easy manner. She herself had had to learn gradually how to combine leisure with work. The changing image of the female figure was seen as a thread spun from the present to the past; and the whole group together insisted that their colleague had obviously not yet completely solved the question of relaxation and leisure on the one hand and devotion to duty on the other. The group member Dr. X served within the group for the transference of an obviously still unsolved emotional conflict which had at one time arisen in her marriage. It cannot be an accident that this old conflict came up again within the group. The therapeutic group obviously reactivated the old family image and the demands of her mother, which had meanwhile been taken over by her own superego. Our colleague could thus recognize that she was still measuring new events by old standards, and she found it easier to detach herself further from her severe and intolerant superego.

Above all, the experimental group helps the doctors to recognize which emotions come up in a group and what their origin is. They will not in future be at the mercy of whatever emotions of theirs may come to the surface in a group situation but will be able to trace them to their original motives as they did in the training group. They will also be capable of detecting emotions in the social field that might cause groups to degenerate into unruly mobs and could thus be dangerous.

We consider that the doctor who is engaged in a group analysis should undertake an individual training analysis if he has not begun one already; and we are also of the opinion that individual training analysis not complemented by a training group is incomplete. However, we leave it to the free choice of the doctors whether they want to take a training analysis or not, as we believe on the one hand that their personal freedom should not be compromised, and on the other hand that they will become aware, in the course of their activities, of the need to throw some light on their unconscious motivations.

Group "Therapy" with Nursing Staff

In a psychiatric hospital the nurses are thrown into an environment that requires of them, exactly as it does of the doctors, that their own inclinations should be set aside in the service of the patients. This demand is not always easy to fulfill, especially as life on the wards is of a nature to arouse the nurses' own inner urges. It can, for example, be difficult for the nursing staff to understand why the doctors take such intensive care of a patient with regressive hysterical tendencies. They may well know that such conduct often hides childish helplessness; but their own worries and frustrations, with which they are unable to cope and for which they are, more or less unconsciously, demanding help, prevent them from completely accepting the doctors' treatment of the patient. Occasionally the nurses' own anxieties, ambivalences, and uncertainties can be an obstacle to adequate psychotherapeutic procedure (Boenheim 1963). It is, for instance, not easy for the nurses on a ward to alter, where necessary, their normal permissive attitude to one of refusal. And yet firm refusals are often necessary. It can happen, for example, that one single patient demands all the attention in a ward. Since this would hinder the development of the other patients, the nurse on duty must refuse to satisfy his exclusive demands. Or it can become necessary on occasion for the nurse to relieve a patient who is constantly forced into the position of underdog by sometimes taking on that role herself.

So that the nursing staff can play their part without hindrance in the social and therapeutic life of the hospital, they need appropriate training as well as dedication and courage. The activities of the nursing staff take place in a "miniature society," and each single patient has his place in the network of relationships that go to make a ward. Sociological knowledge are therefore useful. However, theoretical instruction is often too abstract. The best training is social self-analysis in a therapeutically orientated group. For this reason we began in 1957 to work with psychotherapeutic groups composed of classes from our nursing school.

For our group sessions we take a class of ten to fifteen members on an average. We meet every week during their training periods; otherwise we see them when the nurses in question have to be withdrawn from their duties for purposes of instruction. As a rule one of our three sister tutors takes part in the group sessions. At the outset the therapist — who, for obvious reasons, should not be their class teacher — explains why they are summoned to a group session. They are told that the purpose of the group is not so much to discuss outside circumstances as to examine the problems that arise within themselves as a result of their work. In this circle they can bring forward whatever difficulties they have met in the course of their duties, particularly their own inward reaction to their work, the hospital atmosphere, their superiors, their workmates, or any other possible sources of conflict.

When a class comes to one of these sessions for the first time, its members often have some difficulty in realizing the purpose of "group psychotherapy." They think they are to receive instruction from yet another lecturer — as they often mistakenly suppose the therapist to be — and that they have to take it in more or less passively. But towards the end of the first hour, or perhaps not until the second, the participants gradually realize that they have to talk, without any other end in view, about any themes, concerns, or interests that may come out spontaneously. In discussion with the other group members, the sister tutor, and the therapist, they usually come up against their own inner conflicts. Tense situations that have occurred in the course of their duties, with one of the sister tutors or with staff nurses, come to light in the group, often as transference difficulties. An antagonism against her own mother or an older sister, for example, can make a trainee nurse inwardly very reluctant to accept an order from a nurse in authority. Or one of the young nurses may be bitterly disappointed if a staff nurse she identifies with her mother does not conduct herself as she expects of her. The situation of the nurses' group reactivates earlier attitudes and feelings towards the whole family, parents and siblings, and it is essential for these nurses to succeed in recognizing the true nature of emotions that appear in the therapeutic group or in the course of hospital life and are often attributed to outside circumstances.

Through taking part in the group sessions, the nurses are not left alone with their problems, and they gain support in this way. They are, moreover, taught to take a critical view of themselves and not always to look to other people first for the sources of tension. And at the same time they acquire a deeper understanding of the patients they are caring for.

When we first began our group work with the trainees, certain of the qualified nurses were skeptical or even suspicious. This attitude may have stemmed partly from the fear of being talked about during the sessions. When it had been explained to them that the group sessions were not for the purpose of denigrating their colleagues or superiors but of helping individuals to recognize projections from their past, the group activity usually met with approval. We came to a particularly good understanding after 1959, when the medical superintendent of our hospital (Kielholz) began to form the various categories of qualified nurses into groups. We began by inviting the sisters or male charge nurses of the individual wards to sessions at regular intervals with the medical superintendent and the senior psychiatrists. The superintendent or other doctors have thus the opportunity to instruct those present and also to confer with them. Naturally, emotions sometimes come out which had hitherto been held back, and all the participants are thus able to relieve their feelings. If they see that certain highly emotional assertions are met by the others with astonishment, they perhaps realize that the causes of their feelings are to be sought in themselves or in their past. If, on the contrary, they meet with friendly understanding, they will usually give up their unreal notions and be much more ready to carry out their hospital duties without prejudice. The medical superintendent and his doctors can also get to know in these group sessions which of their projects is approved and which rejected, so they can change their plans or learn how better to defend them. This procedure has proved useful in the planning of new wards; the medical superintendent meets the most varying groups of hospital staff so that the project can mature in an atmosphere of discussion and mutual advice.

In 1959 we began withdrawing all qualified nurses by stages from their duties for two days in the year; during this time we gave them refresher courses and taught them more efficient working methods. We then introduced a few group meetings to give the nurses a chance to discuss subjects that interested them, including their own problems. Tensions that come to light often can be clarified in this way. It must be made clear to the participants that these group discussions do not necessarily show practical results in the daily activity of the hospital; their purpose is rather to dispel mutual suspicion, to make each other's acquaintance, and to widen their horizons by seeing each other's point of view. In some of the larger wards we arrange group sessions for the nursing staff every month. There too we discuss not so much professional questions as problems arising in the course of their work. It often becomes clear to all the participants that a nurse's attitude towards a patient or a fellow worker is not based on objective facts but is a result of his or her own projections.

The group discussions have a liberating effect on the whole of hospital life. Long pent-up or repressed emotions come to light, and their emergence frees the atmosphere of the hospital from an undercurrent of resentment. The participants also acquire a wider view of the motivation behind their treatment of the patients and thus are not as completely at the mercy of their unconscious conflicts as they were before. Whereas previously it was not always easy to interest the nursing staff in the patients' psychotherapy, the nurses now feel much more responsible for the psychotherapeutic treatment of particular individuals. They will feel they have a share of responsibility for the patients in their care and for the progress of the hospital to which they belong.

Importance and Value of Group Psychotherapy in a Psychiatric Hospital

1. Group psychotherapy carried on in a psychiatric hospital allows us to treat the patients in a more intensive and comprehensive way than is possible with the exclusive use of individual psychotherapeutic methods. This is obvious in the fact that a large number of patients can be given at least a minimum of

psychotherapeutic treatment. In confirmation of the experiences of other authors (Pinsky et al., 1964), we have observed that the introduction of group psychotherapy into a psychiatric hospital brings with it increased communication between the patients, and also between them and the doctors and nurses. They are drawn into an active social situation that encourages them to seek human relationships and to abandon the kind of behavior that makes contact impossible.

When the patients are assembled for group therapy, some who have previously lived side by side in the ward without forming any relationship have entered into communication. Group psychotherapy, then, can change the vegetable existence of many hospitalized patients into a communicative group life.

2. It is true that in therapeutic groups static tendencies constantly appear; attitudes once taken up, or processes once completed, tend to become institutions. For example, a definite seating order in the group is often maintained. However, in a group led in a therapeutically meaningful way, there is a permanent dynamism which constantly works against this unfortunately strong attachment to stereotypes. In a hospital where group psychotherapy is active, the patients do not run the same risk of moving along rigid predetermined lines. This, in the case of schizophrenics, can help to prevent intellectual deterioration. As Lewin (1963) was able to prove by experiment, the influence of the group is quicker to bring about a change of behavior than any individual influence, even when it is the individual who is affected, as can happen for example at a lecture in the presence of a large number of people who are there at the same time but have no connection with him.

3. Group psychotherapy in the psychiatric clinic allows the patients to be observed in a "social" context and appropriately treated. The behavior of patients in a therapeutic group, as Racamier (1963) very rightly stresses, can give information on the psychodynamic phenomena behind it. For example, the strength or weakness of the ego in a patient can be judged by whether he can stand up to the interactions that take place within the group, or whether he is pushed out of it. The manner and the intensity with which a patient shares in the worries of his fellow group members, or

isolates himself from them, can also show how capable he is of solving his own problems, or how far he is trapped in his own world even when important events are taking place outside. Participation in the emotions of the other group members and a distinct identification with them can, however, exist as a result of an identification transference (Slavson, 1955). If regression phenomena appear and one member of the group is visibly pleased to be fussed over and cared for by the rest, we can conclude that unfulfilled infantile wishes are being brought out by the group activity. Thus observation of the group dynamics can provide far-reaching information about the unconscious psychic motivation behind them.

4. What happens in the therapeutic group is the product of multiple collective experiences stemming from the composition of the group as it is at present, memories of the family group in early childhood, and the primeval consciousness of mankind in general. We notice over and over again that the processes that take place in the "therapeutic" group are very similar for all cultures. Although different therapists and different countries use different methods for group psychotherapy, the laws of group dynamics, as reported from countries no matter how far apart, are largely the same. It follows from this that the behavior of the individual in the group is not only typical of him but also characteristic of the species. If there are different therapeutic groups in one hospital they can be compared, leading to the conclusion that they all proceed in the same manner and in the same sequence: initial expectancy, accompanied by more or less obvious anxiety; catharsis with release of aggression; the appearance of multiple and multidimensional transferences, including resistances; elucidation of the transference or resistance; insight and transformation of the participants. The hospital offers an opportunity, through comparative study of psychotherapeutic groups, to become acquainted with laws of group dynamics that are common to all mankind.

5. As the emotions of the different members of the group call forth a response in the others, a "reinforcing effect" (Battegay, 1961) on the emotions occurs. The strenghtening of the emotions can indeed lead to otherwise imperceptible feelings becoming manifest and thus

capable of being worked upon. But occasionally, if the composition of the group is unfavorable, this very effect of reinforcement causes the emotions aroused to become dominant in all the members at once; this happens especially in large groups. Even previously well-structured groups are in danger of degenrating into an undisciplined mob, the various members of which either follow blindly or else behave in a completely inadequate and confused manner (Staehelin, 1947). On several occasions we have seen large therapeutic groups degenerate into a "mobs in miniature"; but this only happened when the therapist, through lack of experience, did not realize the possibility of such a development and did not exclude in time the attention-seeking and monopolizing, querulous, manic, or hyperthymic patients who were causing it. But if the group searches for the causes of the emotional conflict that was thus cathartically released, this exercises a mitigating effect on the emotions of the participants. This happens most frequently in groups of nurses or doctors. These therapeutically orientated groups have, therefore, a cleansing and relaxing influence on the whole hospital.

6. Knowledge of group dynamics makes it easier to judge the progress of therapeutic groups and also to understand the way groups are spontaneously formed in the hospital. Unfavorable grouping of patients in the wards can be altered when necessary, and in this way obstructive influences can be averted and therapeutic stimuli set up.

7. The cohesion that takes place in therapeutic groups, and the intensity of the group activity, act on the participants as a centripetal force, counteracting possible impulses to escape. Feelings of responsibility and duty towards the other members help the patients to make their own group discipline. Not least in importance is the fact that it is often easier for the patients to tolerate restrictions and denials imposed on them by their fellow patients than doctors' orders. For that reason, too, running away is rarer in a group-centered hospital than in one which is not divided into these small collectives. The group structure of a psychiatric hospital takes the place of confining walls. Our hospital is in any case divided into separate blocks and thus into (large) groups, and a few years ago we took down all the enclosing walls and found that there were even fewer attempts

to escape than before, since the attraction of climbing a forbidden wall was gone.

The patients, the majority of whom came to us voluntarily, and who, as we have said, enjoy considerable freedom, take a much more intensive part in therapeutic activities than if they were compelled to do so. Therapeutically, they share the responsibility for themselves. But the staff too learns to realize that the demands of personal responsibility — and that does not mean excessive demands — are better for the patients than keeping them completely dependent behind walls. Since 1929, for example, all patients in our hospital who are not dangerous to themselves or others have been granted weekend leave, and only a few occasionally stay out. In general the patients are very glad to come back to their familiar hospital. Occasionally their affinity to the group and the group-centered hospital may be such that they are unwilling to leave it or, after discharge, soon want to come back into the protection of the group. We found a suitable solution: discharged patients who are thus attached to the hospital but do not attend any outpatients' groups are invited once a week to a social evening on the wards. In this way they do not feel completely divorced from the group and have something to hold on to. If they carry on with the therapeutic group or remain in touch with hospital life — which is after all simply a large group — their prognosis also improves.

The increasing group structure of the hospital has made it possible to speed up the opening of previously closed wards and of the hospital in general. This, as Harris et al. (1960) also observed, is improving the contact between the hospital and the outside world. Relatives are no longer afraid to visit; they are interested in the patients, and now we see streams of friends and relations coming into the hospital at visiting hours, whereas previously only a few near relatives found their way to the patients.

8. Group psychotherapy is not usually the only method of treatment used in the psychiatric hospital. But it complements psychiatric and pharmacological methods in the social field and gives the patients the chance to collect experiences of reality. If a whole ward is organized as a large therapeutic group, the collective therapy

becomes a unifying bond between all the patients. The additional group treatment keeps a balance between individuals, and the patients can then be variously handled according to their separate needs, without the risk of conflicts and rivalries.

9. If the doctors know, from personal experience, the natural course of events in a therapeutic group, they will have a deeper understanding of the dynamic processes that develop spontaneously in a hospital ward. They will also be better able to grasp what happens in the actual therapeutic groups. If at the same time group psychotherapeutic work is done with the nursing staff, they too will become an active part of the whole. A team will be created capable of sharing the psychiatric treatment with the doctors. Group work with doctors and nurses has still more to contribute; it brings to the hospital a therapeutically active atmosphere.

Simultaneous group treatment of the relatives of patients allows better contact with the family. Any possible abnormalities in the patients' family environment come to light much earlier, so that the therapists can come to grips with them.

Since as a rule we appoint two therapists to lead a group, so that they may check and complement each other, it is also possible to appoint as cotherapists beginners in group psychotherapy or those requiring further training. This possibility, combined with the creation of training groups and the appropriate courses, means that the hospital is able to offer training to new group psychotherapists.

Group psychotherapy with large, nosologically varying groups; with small diagnostically homogeneous groups; and with groups of doctors, nurses, and relatives results in a more active therapeutic atmosphere and, above all, permits the mentally sick to be diagnosed and treated in their proper social context. If we use it simultaneously with other methods, treatment is directed not only at the individual but also at his social involvement. We can measure, by the patient's attitudes and reactions within the group, to what influences he was exposed in his early childhood and later or is still exposed to today and also what environmental factors have had, or are having, a pathogenic effect upon him.

It might be assumed, from our comments up to this point, that we recommend unrestricted group psychotherapy. In this context we must remember that collective treatment runs, for example, the risk of forming mobs or gangs. And group psychotherapy can scarcely do as much for the individual as the deeper penetration of his own problems. In certain circumstances, moreover, group therapy can have an unfavorable effect on some patients: for example, agitated depressives, manic patients, schizophrenics with very weak egos, hyperthymics, hysterical and attention-seeking or querulous personalities. The group and its dynamics suffer through the participation of such patients, so that they have to be excluded from collective treatment.

However, all these disadvantages and contraindications cannot hide the fact that the introduction of group psychotherapy into clinical psychiatry is a further step towards comprehensive treatment of the mentally sick. But all the same we shall have to continue to seek out methods that permit an even better and more flexible approach to mental illness.

Group Psychotherapy versus Individual Psychotherapy

Group psychotherapy should not be considered a more superficial method than individual treatment. On the contrary, the reinforcing effect of the group on the emotions often helps the participants to reach depths of experience that could scarcely be expected in so short a time or at all from individual psychotherapy. Qualitatively, the group achieves different psychological effects from those arising from the dual psychotherapeutic situation. The group is particularly fitted to reactivating in the participants' imagination past or present collective situations, whereas individual psychotherapy brings out relationships with individual persons in the past and present. In the (therapeutic) group, too, the "Great Mother" comes to life much earlier than in individual psychotherapy. Group psychotherapy is thus not only quantitatively but also qualitatively different from individual treatment. It is not merely a method of seeing more individuals at the same time. On the one hand, it is true, we are not of the opinion of Preuss (1966), who states that group psychotherapy does not allow more patients to be treated in the same period of time as with individual therapy. But on the other hand we agree with him that group psychotherapy is not purely a way of saving the doctor's time. Group psychotherapy has its specific effects and thus, in exactly the same way as individual psychotherapy, it is indicated in specific cases.

The fact that the patients are not only dealt with by a therapist but also surrounded by fellow sufferers means that the therapy is in the hands of a collective, not a single person. With the help of the group, the therapist has an easier time than if he were working alone. Often a member of the group will give an interpretation that will save the therapist from having to intervene. But on the other hand the therapist's task can also be more difficult in the group. Not only does he have to steer his way through a many-sided transference situation on many different levels, but the fact that untrained persons are taking part in the group activity makes his therapeutic work difficult. It is true that an interpretation made through the group often makes more impression on the patients than if the work were done by the therapist exclusively. But we can never expect from a group the subtle approach that we can from a trained analyst. The individual relationships in a group are never as intensive as they are when only two persons are concerned; but the total intensity of the individual relationships in a group is usually greater than the emotions that come up in individual therapy. The confrontation of two individuals in the group is never so intensive as in the dual psychotherapeutic situation. The individual in the group can always avoid an argument with another member, while in the classic psychotherapeutic situation the confrontation must take place. For that reason individual psychotherapy is much more suited to working through a conflict situation than is the therapeutic group. In the intimate relationship between doctor and patient in psychoanalysis it is very difficult to avoid a confrontation; but in the collective situation a patient's resistance can more easily and unobtrusively find a way to sabotage the therapist's efforts. Although all the members, and the group as a whole, can consciously or unconsciously help to discover and dispel resistances, the very intensity of interaction in a group can cover the resistances — skilfully camouflaged — of individuals. For that reason we look upon individual psychotherapy as a more thorough method than collective treatment. As a rule it gives better scope than the group method for making a thorough examination of whatever conflicts emerge. Greater thoroughness, however, is not to be confused with greater depth. As we have said, group psychotherapy — often in a very short time — can reach emotional depths that we scarcely ever see in individual treatment. However, simply because several individuals are taking part at the same time, the group cannot consider questions that arise in such detail as in individual therapy. Group psychotherapy, as we said in the last chapter, makes it possible much sooner than in the dual psychotherapeutic situation to recognize typical attitudes of the individual and of the whole group. Especially because so much interaction is going on in the group, individuals are constantly led to take up new positions or to react in the accustomed way to new situations. Whereas individual psychotherapy permits an analysis of "content," a psychotherapeutic group gives a special opportunity for analysis of "attitude." To take an extreme case, we may say that a patient in individual analysis can gain a comprehensive insight into his basic problem but has not necessarily the opportunity to learn new, healthy standards of behavior.

The intense emphasis of the group on reality means that the patient may perhaps have little time for acquiring insight but much more chance to learn new attitudes and to change his character and outlook. Balint (1962) was probably thinking along these lines when he wrote:

> Everyone who has experience of both fields [group psychotherapy and individual psychotherapy] will agree that the therapeutic results are quite different, although it is hard to say exactly in what the difference consists. Let us nevertheless try to give a definition, sketchy and badly documented, which will at least show the direction in which this difference is to be sought. We could perhaps say that after successful psychoanalytical treatment the patient is *distinctly less neurotic* (or psychotic) *but*

perhaps not absolutely mature; after successful treatment with group methods the patient is *not necessarily less neurotic, but distinctly more mature.*

These concise definitions are not meant to be taken literally but simply as an attempt to fix the special essence of the two psychotherapeutic methods. The very fact of the multiple and multidimensional transferences that take place in the group must lead to a working out of neurotic conflicts. Similarly, the dual psychotherapeutic situation also offers an opportunity to recognize and dispel abnormal attitudes. In individual therapy those in analysis report their (social) experiences in the interval between the sessions; so in individual therapy too there is a constant process of *deconditioning* and *reconditioning.* We cannot say, therefore, that individual therapy does not permit experience of reality. Nevertheless, the therapeutic group, with its close-knit interaction and its intense reality, is usually in a better position to show the patient the external composition, the principles, and the coordination of society. In group psychotherapy the participants are drawn into analytical work and a *social learning process* at one and the same time, while individual psychotherapy separates analytical explanation and social learning. From this spring the advantages and disadvantages of both group and individual therapy. The fact that group psychotherapy aims simultaneously at analysis and social experience makes it a timesaving method, since two therapeutic processes move parallel to each other. However, as we have already said, there is the danger that it may not be thorough enough and perhaps may try too hard to conform with reality. Individual psychoanalysis, on the other hand, has the possible disadvantage that social data are not sufficiently taken into account in the therapeutic work.

An essential difference between individual and collective psychotherapy is that group treatment makes it possible for individuals to gain in self-knowledge. Speaking in front of an interested group is often enough in itself to give them greater self-confidence. On the other hand an adequately constituted group does not allow an individual to monopolize the conversation. It is scarcely ever possible for a member of the group to focus the attention of the others upon himself for any length of time; and nor can any member keep his own attention upon himself for long. The group has a wide variety of interactions, and its different members expect and demand a variety of different things. It will not allow libido to be more or less completely withdrawn from objects and directed upon anyone's personal ego. We have repeatedly observed that patients in individual analysis who belong to a psychotherapeutic group obviously have not sufficiently dissipated their (secondary) narcissism (Freud, 1917), in the dual psychotherapeutic situation. If they were then attacked somewhat harshly by the group, they might at first react in a very sensitive way. There was even the risk that they might leave the group. But if they carried on with the therapeutic group, they generally succeeded in becoming conscious of their narcissistic tendencies and gradually to work through them with the group.

A member of a doctors' group stressed that he had a very friendly relationship with another member of the group who worked with him. Another member, however, burst out with the assertion that she had come across this doctor in the course of her work and remembered him vividly. He had, she said, called her in to discuss a patient whom she had referred to him, and he had kept her listening for about two hours to a discussion between himself and the patient, without giving her the chance to speak. She had perceived that she had been made to play a secondary part. From that moment she remembered him most distinctly as a domineering type. The colleague addressed grew red, was obviously hurt and indignant, and tried to shift the blame for the difficulties between his colleague and himself onto the patient, who had very serious problems. But she persisted in her assertion that he had struck her as very authoritarian. Although his self-love had obviously received a blow, he appeared gradually to be considering what she had said. It was apparently becoming clear to him that he could not maintain in the group his narcissistic fiction of being an important, inaccessible person. We saw in this way that the narcissism of a group member who had already gone through an individual psychoanalysis could be successfully called in question by another member in front of the group. The presence of the group was by no means unimportant. In fact another member twice commented on the behavior of the doctor who had been so harshly attacked, saying that he behaved oddly and spoke almost unintelligibly; he added loudly that he was sitting on his high horse quite unjustifiably.

In a dual therapeutic relationship in which the psychoanalyst is occupied exclusively with one patient, the subject of narcissism can, it is true, often be brought up in exactly the same way by the therapist. But the fact that the analyst is concentrating all his attention on the patient for a considerable time may even strengthen his narcissistic tendencies. For this reason it is desirable that every individually trained therapist should also join an analytical training group. This would not only give him the chance to discover his own unconscious motivations of the kind that come up in a collective situation, and to understand his patient in his social environment; it would also help him to recognize and dispel his narcissistic tendencies, which can only cloud his vision and hinder his approach to the patient.

If, however, a group member is too hard pressed by the intensive reality of the group, there is the danger of his libido being thrown back upon the ego. When schizophrenics take part in a psychotherapeutic group, the libido which they had centered upon themselves may often be directed more towards the others; but the reverse can also take place, and their narcissistic tendencies become still more marked. The group reality has demanded too much from them, so that they now withdraw themselves from it completely. This is to say that the intense degree of reality of the therapeutic collective can not only help to mitigate every kind of egocentricity, even autism, but occasionally it can lead to an even more persistent withdrawal from external reality. Group psychotherapy brings outward reality much nearer to the individual than does individual psychotherapy. However, the outside world can press upon an individual so strongly that if the ego is weak there is a complete withdrawal from the world. Schizophrenics with weak egos do not as a rule find any menace in individual psychotherapy, though they occasionally do in group psychotherapy. The "we consciousness" of the group is more likely than anything in individual psychotherapy to bring confidence and a feeling of support. It may happen, however, than an individual who is shut up in his own narrow world, such as, for example, a depressive or a paranoid schizophrenic, can no longer shut his eyes to the many-sided processes of the group operating on many different levels; the therapy can then lead to serious suspicions much earlier than with individual treatment. A patient in classic psychotherapy will scarcely ever doubt or even despair of his fellow men to the extreme degree that we have seen in collective psychotherapy.

It can perhaps be said that individual psychotherapy is more intimate than group treatment. But this does not mean that intimate problems come out only in *tête-à-tête*. On the contrary, the reinforcing influence of the group means that the participants often divulge their deepest concerns, expectations, and impulses at a very early stage — usually more quickly, in fact, than would have been the case in individual psychotherapy. But they are induced to do this by the other members of the group, and their confessions are often made too soon, so that they later regret having said anything. Then as a rule they feel deserted and imperfectly understood.

But usually the therapeutic group absolutely guarantees the intimacy that is indispensable for the formation of transferences. Naturally the transference relationships in a group are considerably more complicated than when only two people are involved. In the group situation one member can form the most diverse transferences simultaneously to the other participants and to the group as a whole. At the same time transference impulses go out from other members, into which a member is not necessarily drawn. So, as we have already said, the transferences in a group are multiple and multidimensional; from the point of view of a member they are many-sided, and from the point of view of the whole group they are many-layered, that is to say that different transference processes can go on side by side. Rivalries with other group members and authority images of the therapist may, for example, be built up simultaneously by a participant (multiple transferences). In addition, while, for example, one participant is involved with another in sibling rivalry, others, on a different level, may be engaged in conflict with the therapist as an authority figure (multidimensional transferences).

Our experiences show that in therapeutic groups the problem of authority often appears more readily than in the dual psychotherapeutic situation. A therapist working in a group as its leader clearly brings out original authority images in the life history of individuals earlier than in the dual therapeutic situation. Sibling rivalries too often come to light in the group very early and very distinctly.

A member of a doctors' group betrayed his more or less unconscious intention of raising himself above the others by asking probing questions of one member after another. He did not stop until a member protested vigorously against his behavior. In the discussion that followed it became clear that this doctor — probably unconsciously for the most part — was laying claim to leadership, because in this way he would gain the upper hand over his colleagues, whom he saw, in transference, as brothers and rivals.

It is true that similar anachronistic fantasies of rivalry and authority are relived also in the dual situation of classic psychotherapy. But the intimacy of the dual situation causes problems of power and rivalry to come up, or at least to become clear, more slowly. The mirror effect of the group often leads to the members becoming aware of their authoritarian and competitive behavior earlier than those treated individually.

Resistances, like transferences, are more complex in group psychotherapy than in the dual situation. They too are multiple and multidimensional, and for that reason are often more difficult to disentangle than in the classic analytical situation.

The task of "leading" a therapeutic group is more difficult for a therapist than the function of an individual psychoanalyst. The group analyst not only needs training in social psychology besides his knowledge of depth psychology; the fact that he is caught in a crossfire of transferences and resistances and that at the same time emotional processes are taking place in the group by which he is not directly affected, makes his work extremely difficult. There is no objective basis for the common assumption that the task of leading a therapeutic group can be simply allotted to a doctor, without any further consideration. I had enough experience, at the beginning of my group work, of what it means to cope, unprepared, with the "leadership" of psychotherapeutic groups. In individual psychotherapy, ignorance of the laws of depth psychology can do harm to one single person, but in the group, damage can be caused to several individuals at once. In group psychotherapy complications are possible directly, through the unfavorable psychological influence of the leader on the participants or of the participants on each other and also indirectly, if social processes develop that result in an unfavorable psychological effect on the members of the group. For instance, a group can degenerate, especially if unsuitably directed, into a "mob in miniature," in which individuals no longer fulfill distinct functions but simply follow blindly, without any responsibility of their own. But it can also turn into a "rabble in miniature." Although the participants are still sitting side by side, they no longer have any emotional rapport with each other. They have "mentally emigrated" (Muchow, 1959) and have no real relationship with anyone else present. Such a degeneration can be seen when reciprocal influences are too closely interwoven and people fear the loss of individuality and independence, and so withdraw into themselves. We need no further demonstration of why both the degeneration to a "mob in miniature" and the change to a "rabble in miniature" have an unfavorable effect on individuals.

The many and various interactions in the therapeutic group give it a strong sense of reality; this feeling of "here and now" is of much greater importance than in classical psychotherapy. It is perhaps largely due to the effect of group treatment on individual psychotherapy that we have learned to pay more attention, even in the psychoanalytical dual situation, to the actual evidence of the patients' words and behavior towards the therapist. It is true that we have, since Freud, seen that the transference neurosis is essential in psychoanalysis. But we have also learned through our experience in group psychotherapy that it is not only a matter of helping the patient to acquire insight; we must also be continually questioning deviant behavior in the present relationship of the patient to the doctor to "decondition" it and make it possible for the patient to practice new attitudes and conduct.

If we compare group psychotherapy and individual psychotherapy in this way, we shall realize that the two methods are by no means mutually exclusive. We would rather say that they complement each other. To summarize:

1. Group psychotherapy goes deeper under certain circumstances than individual treatment, but individual therapy is more thorough.

2. Treatment through the group shows more impressive results, but the dual psychotherapeutic situation permits a more subtle approach.

3. In the therapeutic group consisting of several members it is easier for patients to opt out of the effort of participation than in individual treatment.

4. Resistances and transferences in the group are many-sided and operate at many different levels. They are therefore usually harder to keep a check on than in the classic psychotherapeutic dual situation, in which, at least up to a certain point in time, transferences and resistances are more clearly defined.

5. In the group, with its greater intensity of interaction and reality, the therapeutic purpose is an analysis of attitude — which of course is always accomplished at the level of basic conflicts — rather than of content.

In psychoanalysis, on the other hand, with its more intimate relationship between theraipst and patient, greater weight can be placed on the analysis of the stuff of which conflicts are made. We can, like Balint (1962), put it in a grossly exaggerated form and say that group psychotherapy leads to a maturing process but no cure for neuroses, and psychoanalysis cures neuroses but does not mature. More moderately expressed, we mean that in group analysis the processes of deconditioning, reconditioning, and social learning play a more obvious part than in individual psychotherapy, while in individual psychotherapy more stress is laid on insight and on the working through of problems.

6. The group, with its more intensive interaction, allows secondary narcissism to be dispelled better than does the dual situation of psychoanalysis.

7. In group psychotherapy the problem of authority often ap-

pears earlier than in individual psychotherapy. As a rule the intimacy of the psychotherapeutic *tête-à-tête* is slower to allow problems of power and rivalry to emerge. It is therefore possible to recognize and deal with the conflicts connected with them more quickly in collective psychotherapy.

8. Group psychotherapy, for its part, has influenced individual therapy in the sense that it has led to greater attention being paid to the situation as it is at present.

REFERENCES

Alnaes, R. (1963), Soziometrie und Gruppenanalyse. *Acta Psychiatr. Scand.*, 39, Suppl., 169.

Balint M. and Balint, E. (1962), *Psychotherapeutic Techniques in Medicine.* Springfield, Ill.: Charles C Thomas.

Battegay, R. (1958), Group therapy with alcoholics and analgesic addicts. *Internat. J. Group Psychother.*, 8:428-434.

——— (1961), Die Verstarkerwirkung der therapeutischen Gruppe. *Praxis der Psychotherapie,* 6:9.

——— (1963), *Gruppenpsychotherapie und klinische Psychiatrie.* New York/Basel: Karger.

——— (1964), Zur Ausbildung von Gruppenpsychotherapeuten. Arbeit mit analytischen Selbsterfahrungsgruppen. *Schweiz. Archiv Neurol. Neurochir. Psychiatr.*, 93:346-361.

Benedetti, G. (1964), *Der psychisch Leidende und seine Welt.* Stuttgart: Hippokrates.

Beukenkamp, C., Mullan, H. and Berger, M.M. (1958), Training in group psychotherapy: Symposium. *Amer. J. Psychother.*, 12(3).

Binswanger, L. (1942), *Grundformen und Erkenntnis menschlichen Daseins.* Zurich: Max Niehans.

Boenheim, C. (1963), About the expansion of group psychotherapy in mental hospitals. International Congress of Group Psychoterapy. Mailand, July 18-21, 1963.

Bour, P. (1961), Psychothérapie de groupe et psychodrame a l'hôpital psychiatrique. *Ann. Med. Psych.*, 119:849.

Brack, E. (1962), Bifokale Gruppentherapie von Schizophrenen. *Z. Psychosomat. Med.*, 8:133-141.

Fort, J.P. (1955), Psychodynamics of Drug Addiction and Group Psychotherapy. *Internat. J. Group Psychother.*, 5:150-156.

Foulkes, S. H. (1964), *Therapeutic Group Analysis.* London: Allen and Unwin.

Freud, S. (1917), The libido theory and narcissism. *Standard Edition,* 16:412-430. London: Hogarth Press, 1963.

——— (1921), Group psychology and the analysis of the ego. *Standard Edition,* 18:69-143, London: Hogarth Press, 1955.

Friedemann, A. (1957), Gruppentherapie und Gruppendiagnostik an Kindern. *Z. Diagnost. Psychol. Pers. Forsch.*, 5:295-304.

——— (1959), Gruppenpsychotherapie. In: *Handbuch der Neurosenlehre und Psychotherapie,* bd. 4. Munich/Berlin: Urban and Schwarzenberg.

——— (1963), Gruppenpsychotherapie in Zusammenarbeit mit Arzten. International Congress of Group Psychotherapy, Mailand, July 18-21, 1963.

Ganzarin, R., Davanzo, H. and Cizaletti, J. (1958), Group psychotherapy in the psychiatric training of medical students. *Internat. J. Group Psychother.,* 8:137-153.

von Gebsattel, V. E. (1959), Die phobische Fehlhaltung. In: *Handbuch der Neurosenlehre und Psychotherapie,* bd. 2. Munich/Berlin: Urban and Schwarzenberg, pp. 125-142.

Genevard, G. (1961), La psychotherapie analytique de groupe. *Med. & Hyg.,* 19:375.

Grinberg, C. Langer, M. and Rodrigue, E. (1960), *Psychoanalytische Gruppentherapie.* Stuttgart: Ernst Klett.

Harris, C. E., Brown, L. E. and Cawte, J. E. (1960), Problems of developing a group-centered mental hospital. *Internat. J. Group Psychother.,* 10:408-418.

Horwitz, L. (1964), Transference in training groups and therapy groups. *Internat. J. Group Psychother.,* 14:202-213.

Hulse, W. C. (1958), Training for group psychotherapy in the U.S.A. and abroad. *Internat. J. Group Psychother.,* 8:257-264.

Johnson, J. A. (1963), *Group Therapy.* New York: McGraw-Hill.

Joray, R. (1961), Bandenbildung und Bandendelikte. *Psychologische Praxis,* hft. 28. Basel New York: Karger.

Jung, C. G. (1936), The unconscious in the normal and pathological mind. In: *Two Essays on Analytical Psychology. The Collected Works of C. G. Jung,* Vol. 7. New York: Pantheon, 1953.

Kemper, W. (1959), Psychoanalyse und Gruppen-Psychotherapie. *Z. Psychother.,* 9:125-133.

——— (1964), Zum Problem der Ausbildung von Gruppenpsychotherapeuten. *Z. Psychosomat., Med.,* 10:191.

Kielholz, P. (1959), Klink, Differentialdiagnostik und Therapie der depressiven Zustandsbilder, Documenta Geigy. *Acta Psychosomatica,* 2, Basel.

——— (1961), The present state of out-patient treatment of depressive states. *Psychosomatica,* 2(1).

———(1964), Erfahrungen in der Schweiz. In: Laubenthal, Sucht and Missbrauch. Stuttgart: Georg Thieme.

——— and Battegay, R. (1964), Aktuelle Probleme der Medikamentensucht in der Schweiz. Praxis, 53:447.

Lévy-Bruhl, L. (1927), *The "Soul" of the Primitive.* New York: Macmillan, 1928.

Lewin, K. (1963), Feldtheorie in den Sozialwissenschaften. In: *Deutsche übertragen,* ed. A. Lang and W. Lohr. Bern/Stuttgart: Huber.

Lindemann, E. (1960), Die soziale Organisation der Lebewesen. Cited by R. Battegay in: *Munch. Med. Wochenschr.,* 102:1566.

Meyer, J. E. (1962), Katamnestische Untersuchungen an jugendlichen Fortläufern. *Z. Psychother.,* 12:49.

Moreno, J. L. (1954), *Die Grundlagen der Soziometrie.* Köln-Oplaten: Westdeutscher Verlag.

——— (1959), *Gruppenpsychotherapie und Psychodrama.* Stuttgart: Georg Thieme.

Muchow, H. H. (1959), *Sexualreife und Sozialstruktur der Jugend.* Reinbek bei Hamburg: Rowohlt.

Mullan, H. and Rosenbaum, M. (1962), *Group Psychotherapy.* New York: The Free Press of Glencoe.

——— and Sangiuliano, R. (1961), Group Psychotherapy and Alcoholics, the Phenomenology of Early Group Interaction. International Congress of Group Psychotherapy, Wien, August 21-26, 1961.

Napolitani, F. (1961), Report on a Psychiatric-therapeutic Community Self-administered by Patients. In: The Third World Congress of Psychiatry, June 4-10, 1961, 107. McGill, Montreal: University of Toronto Press.

Pinsky, S. Glasgow, D. and Louvier, A. (1964), Differential Use of groups in Development of Milieutherapy Programme. International Congress of Group Psychotherapy, London, August 24-29, 1964.

Powdermaker, F. B. and Frank, Y. X. (1953), *Group Psychotherapy.* Cambridge, Mass.: Harvard University Press.

Preuss, H. G. (1966), Wirkungs- und Indikationsbereich der analytischen Gruppenpsychotherapie (Gruppentherapie versus Einzeltherapie). In: *Analytische Gruppenpsychotherapie,* ed. H. G. Preuss. Munich/Berlin/Wien: Urban and Schwarzenberg.

Racamier, P.C. (1963), Indication du psychodrame analytique et des actions sociothérapiques dans les psychoses. In: *Pratique de la Psychothérapie de Groupe.* Florence: Editrice Universitaria.

Schindler, R. (1958), Ergebnisse und Erfolge der Gruppenpsychotherapie mit Schizophrenen nach den Methoden der Wiener Klinik. *Wien. Z. Nervenheilkunde und deren Grenzgebiete,* 15:250.

——— (1961), Der Gruppentherapeut und seine Position in der Gruppe. *Praxis der Psychotherapie,* 6:1-8.

Schultz, J.H. (1953), Grundsatzliches zur Suchtfrage. *Z. Psychother.,* 3:97.

——— (1956), Das autogene Training, 9. Aufl. Stuttgart: Georg Thieme.

Slavson, S. R. (1951), *Analytic Group Psychotherapy.* New York: Columbia University Press.

——— (1955), Group psychotherapies. In: *Six Approaches to Psychotherapy,* ed. J.L. McCary. New York: Dryden Press, pp. 129-178.

——— (1961), Group psychotherapy and the nature of schizophrenia. *Internat. J. Group Psychother.,* 11:3-32.

——— (1964), *A Textbook in Analytic Group Psychotherapy. New York:* International Universities Press.

Stahelin, J. E. (1947), Massenpsychologie und klinische Psychiatrie. *Schweizer Archiv. Neurol. Psychiat.,* 60:269-278.

Stokvis, B. (1960), Grundlagen und derzeitige Situation der Gruppenpsychotherapie. *Z. Psychother.,* 10:129.

Stolze, H. (1960), 10. Lindaüer Psychotherapiewoch, May 2-7, 1960. Cited by R. Battegay in: *Munch. Med. Wschr.,* 102:166.

Toman, E. (1963), Die pragenden Wirkungen der Geschwisterkonstellation auf den Charakter. *Z. Psychother.,* 13:113.

Wiesenhütter, E. (1961), Gruppenbestrebungen im Licht der Sozialanthropologie. *Praxis der Psychotherapie,* 6:13.

6

Group Therapy in a Psychoanalytic Institute

A Study of the Development of the Transference Neurosis in Psychoanalytic Group Therapy

JACOB SPANJAARD

One would expect the department of group psychotherapy at a psychoanalytic institute to be a team of several therapists who meet regularly to discuss their experiences. Unfortunately this is not necessarily the case. At this writing, group therapy has been on the program of our Dutch Institute for thirteen years, but it has been conducted by only one therapist, who worked in relative isolation. Therefore, there has been no opportunity for intracommunication, criticism, control, or indeed any comparison with the methods of other psychoanalysts. Only recently has this situation changed, since the inauguration of an enlarged group therapy department.

Under these circumstances, one might question any justification for the title of this chapter. The special climate of a psychoanalytic institute, however, does make research possible. A considerable number of patients of many clinical categories can be thoroughly examined, carefully diagnosed, and made available for study. Working alone, I tried to create a manageable research situation by setting up groups that manifested comparable dynamics. For a period of five years each, I treated two groups composed of male students of good intelligence who were well educated, unmarried, had as yet no real place in society, and who all experienced serious difficulties at

---

Dr. Spanjaard is Staff Member, Psychoanalytic Institute, Amsterdam.

work. In order to be able to evaluate the influence of group therapy, individual contact was avoided following their preliminary examination, and the attempt was made to obtain all results in the group sessions themselves. There were no alternate meetings, visitors, or observers. My reports, therefore, are rather subjective. I dictated them immediately after each session, attempting to make them brief and always adhering to the same kinds of observations. The conditions of the sessions were as similar as possible: in the same room, at the same time, twice a week, and lasting one hour. Each group was kept closed until one had been reduced to five persons and the other to four — more a little family than a real group. Breaking the policy of a closed group and adding new members furnished important new experiences.

Selection of a group is time consuming, considering the necessity of combining people with some similarity in their ways of living, levels of verbal development, and possibilities of communication. Often, after the therapist believes he has assembled a circle of men who are not too disparate, the peculiar dynamics of grouping reveal their laws, and he is soon faced with his mistakes. My thesis is that the selection and composition of the group is the crux of this therapy and that the indications on data drawn from the initial individual interviews can often be misleading in this respect.

It might almost seem unnecessary to mention special interest in the development of the transference neurosis in the context of group therapy research in a psychoanalytic institute, since, after all, transference is the keystone of psychoanalytic therapy. Yet, in the context of group therapy, the transference presents special problems. The therapist can discern transferences only by remaining uninvolved in the ongoing emotional processes. For the group members, involvement and not detachment must be central to their therapeutic experience. As they become involved with one another, the transference manifestations between them ought to disappear. The therapist must assume behavior appropriate for the development of a good, visible transference. He will therefore concentrate on the development of transference by influencing group processes in order to favor the relationship between each group member and himself.

The therapist should try to sever each member's ties with the other members insofar as these ties allow easy and superficial communication on the safe ground of a "tacit agreement" accepted by all. This "tacit agreement' or "code of behavior" is a typical resistance in group psychotherapy whereby each member hides individual traits and feelings that seem shameful or dangerous behind a generally acceptable facade. The therapist's disruptive technique has nothing to do with the passivity of the so-called "mirror." It derives from the point of view of the individual psychoanalyst, who creates his own style and his own typical experiences. It is an active interference, a structuring of the situation with an outspoken alertness to all resistances. The similarity to individual therapy is striking in that the investigator remains on well-known territory with the great advantage of being able to compare each experience with others common to him.

Methodologically, there are many possible objections to this investigation. It is of a typically clinical nature, founded on subjective impressions, referring only to scarce data regarding the patient's illness that were not systematically collected. Also open to criticism is the technique of hindering the spontaneous interaction of the group, the very process that is always regarded as the great therapeutic force of this setting. It is hoped, however, that this investigator will be forgiven his inclination to direct communications in specific directions, since his aims were to create therapeutic situations for investigation wherein there would be the possibility of working with a well-developed skill and of making comparisons with past experiences in individual analysis.

In group therapy, naturally, one has to deal with forceful processes and events never encountered in individual therapy. An unpredictable interaction can bring about relations that, when fully developed, may produce circumstances that paralyze the influence of the therapist. For example, the dominance of one resistant member can be an insurmountable hindrance. Here one sees an important difference from individual therapy, where this kind of resistance is seldom untreatable. In a group, the therapist takes on the aspect of a dictator if he directly opposes and criticizes the obstructing member. One may interpret the behavior of such a member, but he is unlikely to discontinue it as long as the other members are submissive to his actions. For the therapist to seem critical rather than interpretive would make the obstructing member too anxious. Therefore, the therapist becomes largely dependent on the relations of the forces between the members who, as peers of the obstructing member, are in a better position to criticize his negative behavior.

Naturally, the therapist can subtly attack the "tacit agreement" resulting from the resistance of the dominating member. For instance, when the dominating member suggests that cooperation with the therapist would constitute dull and feminine behavior, and the other members show their compliance, the most obvious reaction of the therapist — to directly discredit the idea — would be a mistake. His only course is to bring into the open the meaning of the "tacit agreement," to make the group members conscious of it and of their fear of abandoning it. Such an examination of the "tacit agreement" will be crucial to the dominating member, who is generally the most anxious and therefore imposes his opinion with the greatest power. His anxiety is often sensed by the other members, who in turn are compelled by their own anxieties not to undermine his defense. The therapist may have to wait until a member spontaneously attacks the "tacit agreement," but in the meantime he can focus on their mutual relations and anxieties toward one another. Sometimes the situation will not change, and the only solution is to expel the dominating member. I once had to do this.

Forces within the group may become manifest in other rather unpredictable forms, such as the isolation of one of the members, the formation of subgroups, or extremely long silences. I am convinced that these resistances in a group can only be treated by a broad, general approach. Interpretations must concern every member in order to be effective. When a member cannot be reached because he is under submission to another member, or for any reason whatsoever, therapy may be seriously handicapped.

We have seen how the necessity for depending on the forces of relations between members can hinder treatment in ways not encountered in individual treatment. However, there are also advantageous aspects in the tensions and "tacit agreement" that develop within a group setting. First, the great influence of the common opinion of the group members is not always in the service of resistance. It can be entirely comparable with the "therapeutic alliance," the "therapeutic transference," the *tragfähige Uebertragung*. Throughout the group therapy, one can see this adaptational force working. People gradually experience the possibility of communicating very intimate matters, of revealing weaknesses and aggression hidden in their daily lives. Guided primarily by the therapist and the most courageous member, such a therapeutic climate develops continuously. Another advantage is the increased opportunity to convince a patient of his unconscious behavior. In his view, the therapist may be but one other human being who can make a mistake in judgment. In a group, on the other hand, the patient is faced with a small community whose collective observations about his behavior may be more forceful and inescapable. The majority of members may seem to him to know the truth, and one man is not capable of fighting alone against a settled opinion. To realize the potential power and value of such encounters among peers in the group, one needs only to recall the difficulties met in analyzing the aggressive, provocative behavior of moral masochists in order to show them how they bring about defensive and self-punitive situations.

After this short introduction, we may now examine various phases that develop in the course of group therapy. There is, of course, no clear-cut manifestation of these phases in the course of time; they are of an ever-varying character, overlapping, alternating and useful only in order to make certain distinctions. In the discussion of these phases, we must not forget that the development of transference neurosis is the constant center of our investigation and technique.

Every group contact begins with an orientational phase, in which members investigate each other. The attitude toward the therapist during this period is mainly a passive-dependent one. He is seen as the undeniable leader, and the member may seek refuge with him from the others or may unite with them against an unknown imminence. He is the oracle, the sorcerer who can ameliorate all sufferings, and the members usually feel they must be as docile as possible. It is a challenge for the leader not to continue this flattering situation, or be narcissistically seduced by it. The therapist who fails to distrust this positive group transference, in spite of all warnings in the literature, nourishes the development of a typical group structure of common resistance. In such a situation, the general approach on the part of the therapist is necessary, and interpretation of similar behavior by group members must be formulated. First, one must turn all questions back onto the members themselves, a kind of Socratic technique. One must exploit every difference between ideas in order to present new problems and to scrutinize how ties between members may represent resistance. This technique will always lead the members into exposing new information to each other, which will increase tolerance within the group. The patient's responses during this stage may take the form of acting out. The group members begin to love each other and find solace in their communal suffering. "We are glad to be neurotics together, and we need not be ashamed of our complaints and anxieties." This is clearly a defense against their feeling of being inadequate to face the outside world. The unanimity of this typical group resistance is a kind of perversion of the "therapeutic alliance" mentioned previously. What an escape from the threatening world around them in daily life! However, this "tacit agreement" often requires, in addition, a behavior accepted by all, which is primarily established by the dominating member. In a group composed of males, the attempt to save some masculinity in the midst of such passive behavior will become obvious in their communications about women. I was also struck by the number of sexual affairs, betrothals, and marriages that took place at this stage of therapy. Although I did not feel it was a desirable consequence for the members to take such steps, I did not attempt to dissuade them in light of my uncertainty about the results of this form of treatment.

Submissive behavior in therapy is especially remarkable on the part of new members. They are immediately seduced into an exposition of their characters, their complaints, and the settling of their tension with the others. They must find their unanimity with the prevailing code. Here the therapeutic factor is determined by group dynamics and by coping with all interactions; an equilibrium is automatically sought. It is a very lively experience, characterized less by silences than by long soliloquies.

For the development of the second phase, the stage of the transference neurosis, the integration on a group level should be undermined by the therapist. He should resist the group's inclination to stereotyped communication in a brotherly democracy and encourage the individual responses of every member. Here one may naturally point out that there are other ways of conducting a therapeutic group. But the leader, by his relatively unrevealing behavior, will become the center of the transference formation, thereby furthering for every patient the regression that is indispensable for psychotherapy. I believe that in group psychotherapy two forms of regression predominate. One is that of the "grouping," which is mainly post-oedipal and especially a dynamic of adolescence. This post-oedipal situation is an ever-present refuge for every member in group psychotherapy (as in the mother-child relation of a very regressive kind, the primary transference in individual psychoanalysis). The other form of regression, the dyad and triad, is expressed in the oedipal and pre-oedipal transferences and their derivatives in the post-oedipal period. Naturally, it is the transference toward the therapist or toward one member (a matter intentionally omitted in this paper). But I believe, with others, that on this primitive level the group itself also has the significance of a person and especially a mother. We see, therefore, that with the therapist and group, triad relationships are possible as well. However, because the situation in which we work in group therapy is in fact post-oedipal, a regression to oedipal and pre-oedipal levels is possible only from time to time.

One must not forget, however, that grouping means restricting one's individuality to some extent and becoming subordinate to a common principle, which includes the transferences to all present, and not only the transference between two persons as in individual analysis. When the latter sort of transference is reached with the therapist, the interrelationships of the members show a preponderance of competition, a kind of sibling rivalry for the attention of the therapist.

It is my opinion that at this stage of the treatment the opportunity exists to do real structural psychotherapy. The therapeutic factor becomes mainly limited to the relationship with the therapist, the only person present who is able to react and communicate without acting out in terms of a countertransference. Naturally, at this stage, interaction among the members will continue to promote adaptation, but an adaptation determined by the needs of the group and its equilibrium rather than by the needs of individual members. It is in oscillation between these two types of relation and transference that group therapy now occurs. Set forth below are two case histories chosen to demonstrate the influence of the general tension and its transition into the little drama of the individually directed transference neurosis. It is here that one may see the interplay between the two forms of regression mentioned above.

Case A: At the beginning of group therapy, Pat was about twenty-seven years old. He had stopped his study because of severe work disturbances of a compulsive character. Born in the tropics, he settled in Holland when he was eight years old. At that time his parents were already separated, and in about two years a divorce was arranged. Pat's compulsion neurosis, described further on, started in adolescence, and intensified greatly after he left his maternal home to become a student living alone in a great university town. His puberty was characterized by quarreling with his mother, a very domineering and authoritarian woman with a psychopathic style of living. His efforts to become independent were met with punishments of concentration camp severity. At the same time, the mother was seductive, sought all kinds of intimacy, and disturbed Pat by her ambivalent intentions. In Army service he became paralyzed by his compulsions and further deteriorated.

Upon commencing therapy, Pat was a totally isolated young man with no real contacts. He lived alone, avoiding meetings with his mother, since they invariably ended in severe conflict. He occasionally visited other members of his family but showed only superficial warmth and half-hearted interest in them. He was apparently afraid of everyone and has withdrawn into an attitude of cynical superiority. Since he did not share with others, no one understood the queer symptoms he revealed with great difficulty and with the vagueness characteristic of the compulsive neurotic. Although he attended sessions regularly, his protest became increasingly clear. He tried to cope with questions put to him by returning them, and shrugged his shoulders when this behavior was pointed out to him. Theoretically, one must place this conduct under the heading of the orientational stage. It was a defense against the new orientation that threatened to remove him from the isolation of his everyday life. This conduct continued rather unchanged for nearly a year. By this time, the constancy of the situation, the experience of contact with others who would not be disturbed by his attitudes, began to make him more courageous, induced his "therapeutic alliance," and some sharing began to take place. He obviously began to feel at home in this little "family" and exhibited more of his emotions, his lofty ideals, and his sensibility toward music. Positive transference toward the group was developing, which meant that everyone had become involved in some sense with his compulsion neurosis. He made endless narratives, since he felt compelled to impart information in this way. None of the members dared to object to this behavior, knowing — intuitively, it seemed — how deeply affected Pat would be. An interruption would have brought total withdrawal, and everyone was afraid of the consequence this might bring to a man so isolated and disturbed.

In the second year of treatment, his protesting attitude toward the therapist changed to one of trust and admiration for the "head of the family." The transference now became more defined as a personal relationship with the therapist rather than a part of his relation to the group as a whole. Signs of the repetitions of childhood situations now became clearer, and feelings toward the father began to emerge. In the context of a long tale of misery, the group learned more about his symptoms. He told how, prior to therapy, he had fallen increasingly in the grip of unavoidable compulsions centered, for the most part, around his toilet activities. He had gone so far as to make a check list to assure that no part of the ritual would be omitted. It was forbidden to interrupt these ritual actions in any way. Any interruption or omission made it necessary for him to repeat the entire ritual from the beginning, and doubt compelled him to endless repetitions. Consequently, he needed hours to take a bath and put on clean clothes.

His reading and learning habits were also affected. He had to feel certain of knowing every word on a page before progressing to the following one. Naturally, he had not been able to produce much work in his years at the university. Fortunately, his employers were acquainted with his illness and supported his efforts to obtain therapy. Studying, however, had become entirely impossible, and he had suspended all effort in that direction.

After more than a year in treatment, he told the group of having made omissions in his ritual and even of having forgotten to shave himself before going to work. Simultaneously, there appeared in his dreams, as well as in his information, other symptoms of a tendency to exhibit. He spontaneously revealed that an elderly woman, one of his superiors at his place of work, showed great interest in him, which evidently he had provoked by an irresistible inclination to reveal very intimate matters to her. It seemed that she responded greedily to these revelations because of her interest in Jungian psychology and her need to meddle in his life. He told her his dreams, which we also discussed in group, creating thereby a collision of psychological conceptions, since she became irritated with "the shortsightedness of this Freudian analyst" and could not agree with the interpretations of the therapist. Obviously he had begun acting out and had sought another transference object outside the therapeutic situation. He seemed to have an inclination to seek intimacy with this woman, to bare himself emotionally and ask for care. In light of her great interest in psychology, he seemed also to have chosen a person comparable to the therapist and created an opportunity to play them against each other. This fact seems to be of greatest importance in the context of the transference neurosis. The patient was shocked to find that his woman friend considered the therapist's ideas superficial and irritating. He told several dreams, apparently produced for this "other therapist," that were of a typically exhibiting character, showing that he wished to be undressed for her but to remain concealed in the presence of men and the group. In one of these dreams he allowed a woman to sever his contact with a male teacher. The significance of these dreams became clearer with a knowledge of his life history. His parents lived in continuous conflict, and his position between them was most precarious. His swinging to and fro between them was repeated in the transference neurosis, as will be further described below.

The group's failure to understand Pat's actions was remarkable, and in order to shelter him I had to demonstrate clearly my unshocked attitude. Their irritation was most obvious when he told of complaints to his friend of therapy's failure to ameliorate his symptoms and her reaction of heaping grim criticism upon the therapist. He gradually developed insight into emotions that drove him to betray his therapist by sharing in the criticism of his friend. This insight was accompanied by important infantile recollections, such as his mother's aggressiveness, her expressed pity that he had not been a beautiful girl, and her teasing threats to give him away, especially when he displeased her. She also threatened to trade him to natives for a hen, an idea that was particularly frightening to him, since he was well acquainted with the cruel way chickens were slaughtered. More important was his recollection of a flight toward his father. When his mother became enraged, he ran for miles to his father, who received him kindly and allowed him to stay with him at his work. These experiences were in contrast to those of the other group members, who always sought the mother's protection against the father's aggression.

The separation of his parents was a very real fact for Pat, made more disturbing by his idea that he was not the child of this father, since he had learned during his latency period of extramarital experiences his mother had had before his birth. In the situation with his "second therapist," it was evident that he was acting out in an opposite direction, fleeing from his father to his mother. He must, therefore, also have been very frightened by a positive tie toward a father figure. Pat himself became aware of a possible connection between his symptoms and homosexual inclinations. His bed-wetting seemed to play a special role in this conflict. When he was a child, the threat of trading him to the natives for a hen was made because of his enuresis. One may suspect, therefore, that he subsequently used this symptom with the hope of thereby being thrown among men. This idea seems supported by the fact that the enuresis reappeared when his father was again living with his mother, shortly before he disappeared forever. When Pat discussed this history with his "Jungian therapist," he ended by having a migraine attack, a symptom he had never shown and that seemed in this situation to repeat his fear of the overactive, interfering mother.

Pat then began to feel that his behavior in the group was in outstanding contrast to his behavior under other circumstances. In the group he was less tense and felt freer, but he perceived nothing of this in his daily life. A few weeks after this realization he informed us that there had come a crack in his "neurotic facade." This crack was his discovery that he had forgotten to perform some of his meticulous measures of checking and that these omissions caused him no anxiety. Thereafter, his actions became much quicker and smoother. Especially noteworthy was his improved performance at his office. Pat was very disappointed that the group did not react with what he could consider appropriate enthusiasm to these revelations. His disappointment was particularly outspoken toward the therapist at the point when he also revealed his break with his "substitute therapist." Naturally this was a great gain, in that he was able to stop his acting out and openly express his need for love.

After a short vacation, Pat reported a dream that was an obvious expression of his positive transference toward the analyst. Thus ended the little drama within the transference neurosis, which had lasted only a few months but involved strong and complex emotions. He apparently acted out the conflict with his parents, a longing for a father to love and to protect him against the aggressive mother. He found this father in the group therapist, a father who did not leave him and who was able to protect him from the aggressive transference figure who took the place of his mother. The beginning of his neurosis was in prepuberty, when his father disappeared forever and he was left unprotected against the aggressive and erotic capriciousness of his psychopathic mother. His brothers and sisters were many years older than he and no longer living at home.

Because of his fear of homosexuality, too intimate a relationship with the father threatened Pat, and he soon submerged himself into the group as much as possible. Nevertheless, through the "reliving" experience of the transference neurosis and the analysis of it, he was able to give up some of the most serious symptoms. He estimated that his work capacity had increased about five times.

Shortly afterward, there was an occurrence that confirmed our idea about Pat's fears of homosexuality. When a man whose homosexual tendencies were known to him came to work in his office, Pat was disturbed by his presence and entertained thoughts of giving up his job. He remained at work, however, and his anxiety toward the homosexual lessened and in turn he lost more of his compulsive symptoms. During this time, Pat recalled his fear of other homosexual men during the period of living alone at the university, and he saw a possible connection between these fears and the increase of his manifest compulsion neurosis. Simultaneously, he remembered a very disturbing conflict with his father when he was about three years old. His father punished his disobedience by breaking some of his most beloved gramaphone records, whereupon Pat sought protection on the lap of his mother. This was a disturbing incident to a boy who loved records above all things. Clearly, Pat never felt entirely safe in his youth and could not trust his parents, since both behaved toward him in a castrating manner. The nucleus of his neurosis is his running back and forth between them for protection, a pattern repeated twice during therapy, first in his flight to the Jungian woman friend, and secondly when he felt threatened by the homosexual man at his office.

Following the loss of symptoms discussed above, Pat remained in group therapy for several years with relatively little further gain. He continued to be less tense and worked very well, but he continued to live alone and without friends. It seeed impossible for him to make contact. All his attempts to find a girl friend failed. His only hobby and source of "companionship" was a cherished record collection. His increased work capacity made it possible for him to become a technical specialist, even though he had given up his university studies. He developed into an excellent research man, competent in following studies in his profession without difficulty. Nothing more was achieved in the four years following the developments described above. Pat merged into the group, since he found it the only trustworthy contact he had, and he remained a somewhat paranoid member, gossiping about events in his life and showing a typically paranoid fear of being suggestible. In reality, he was not suggestible at all. Although he himself remarked upon his lack of improvement, he continued to come to group meetings, since he knew how lonely he would be without these contacts. Nevertheless, he experienced group communication as an empty, annoying routine. It seemed clear that this feeling masked his severe aggression against the others, especially with regard to his jealousy and competitiveness; but it was impossible to bring him into contact with these emotions. Therefore, Pat left therapy with his compulsion neurosis limited to those symptoms in his private life, which concerned his toilet activities. It seemed unlikely that there would be much later change in this syndrome, which remained static following the analysis of the short transference neurosis. Data obtained after two and a half years confirmed this prediction. He works well and with pleasure, but lives without contacts.

Case B: Frank was a physics student for ten years without any appreciable accomplishment despite his superior intellectual gifts. When he came for treatment on account of study difficulties, he was totally unaware of his neurosis but soon became very much interested in therapy. He appeared to possess deep introspective capacities. His life was chaotic, and he was always in debt. He had worked his way through college but now "floated" from job to job. Behind a forced gregarious behavior, shown mainly by his ready wit and bon mots that enabled him to compete with everybody, there was a deep-lying depression and depersonalization with strong homosexual tendencies. Frank gained insight into these aspects of himself as a direct consequence of his contact with other group members from whom he received an unprejudiced view of his neurosis and its symptoms. Naturally, the therapist played a definitely meaningful role in Frank's acquisition of these initial insights. Ultimately it is always the therapist who determines the depth and quality of communication by interpretation of the resistances to the revelation of the deeper layers of an individuality.

After a time, Frank began to stand out in the group, since he was well provided with gifts for verbal expression, and his personal relationship with the therapist came into the foreground. Through this relationship he developed a passive transference to the therapist, acting out his feeling of being doomed to failure. He had a good reason for these feelings, since his family life had shipwrecked when he was twelve and his father committed suicide in a very dramatic way. In relation to this event, the fantasy that he acted out with the therapist soon came to light: if things go very badly, father will come back to the rescue; if they go successfully, father will never come back. In group, therefore, the relation to the therapist was very involved because it meant being with father again, receiving power and strength. Homoerotic masturbation fantasies, previously vague, were now recognized by him as being of a definitely feminine nature. Indications of oral fixations occurred again and again. He became aware of greediness and a longing for fellatio, but it was impossible to bring to the surface the roots of this relation with the mother, of which only a slight indication appeared in the transference.

Working through of the internalized traumata in the transference took only a relatively short period. It came about in a way entirely comparable with common psychoanalytic experience, and Frank showed a definite change. After two years of treatment he ceased being hypomanic, became more stable, and began to adapt well socially. He gave up his studies and devoted himself to the commercial career for which he was well suited and became successful in it. His condition remained the same after the period of working through his transference neurosis, with very little new material brought forward during the last three years of treatment. There remained remnants of serious neurotic complaints, such as ejaculation praecox, pruritis ani and other symptoms, which pointed to the fact that his relations with women were still unstable and disturbed. After breaking contact with his pauperized family and his psychopathic elder brother, he married a foreign woman.

In Frank's case, too, it is very striking how the little drama accompanying the development of the transference neurosis forms the kernel of therapy. Before it and after it, with the exception of insights mentioned above, little of any real importance can be said to have happened. Following the transference drama, Frank also ceased concentrating on his relation to the therapist and merged with the group. At this point he talked about his pregenital inclinations and became clearly involved with the mother figure, but was unable to relive the situation because of the presence of too many "siblings" with whom he had to share the attention of the therapist.

Therefore, with sibling rivalry predominating, the transference became loosened, and it was possible to terminate the therapeutic relationship with the knowledge that an analysis might go further and ameliorate the pregenital disturbances as well. Those ideas about Frank were confirmed when I met him by chance a few years later. He was very thankful indeed; his life had changed thoroughly. He had a very good job and social adjustment but complained about his relationship with his wife, which was unsatisfactory. He expressed an uncontrollable urge for sexual relations with other women, for whom he felt no love. Moreover, this urge toward them was marked by a "queer kind of aggression," to use his own words.

In the second stage of therapy, which has received most attention in the data of these examples, a few remarkable factors may be discerned. First is the concentration on the relationship with the therapist, with all the implications of the development of a transference neurosis and its influence upon the relations of the group members toward each other. It is evident that the therapy chooses its own terms at this point and that all energy is absorbed by adjustment to the ensuing tensions.

A second striking feature is the fact that all transferences in the group setting show, especially, aspects of relationships that originated at puberty or shortly before. Perhaps this throws light on the origins of transference in group therapy. The general opinion is that transference always has to originate from relationships of the period which is lost in infantile amnesia. I believe one can say transference always has an unconscious source, but I received the impression that in a group the transference neurosis turns on a repeated relationship stemming from traumatic experiences shortly before or during puberty. Simultaneously, however, I also saw experiences from preoedipal and oedipal sources of which the pubertal relationship is a "second edition." In any case, the repetition in a transference neurosis of the vicisssitudes of these rather recent relationships was striking to me. My experience with groups of men struggling to begin adult adaptation might show a unique accent on these problems which arise in communication with peers who feel the same conflicts. The relations with each other are filled with authority conflicts and frictions brought about by styles of living and community codes. Parental images seem to take two forms. In the development of a dyad transference relationship, the therapist represents an individual person with aspects of the early father or mother. However, when the patient interacts with the other group members, the therapist becomes the parent or parent substitute of adolescence, the leader, the representative of morals, style, and code, or the figure against whom one rebels. These images are of an outspoken post-oedipal character, originating in the stage when the child loosens its dependent, anaclytic ties to the parent and grows toward the group or the gang and its leader.

It is evident that the problems spoken about in the foregoing examples are of a prepubertal nature. In case A, the symptoms were initiated by the divorce of the parents and developed afterward during puberty and adolescence with the mother. The conflicts appeared again in the transference neurosis, with a clear reference to analogous conflicts in the pre-oedipal and oedipal periods. However, the accent remained on the post-oedipal period, and therapy would not advance beyond this point; the group setting seems to be insufficient for the development of intimacy on a true oedipal or pre-oedipal level.

In case B, material from the pre-oedipal period was undoubtedly presented, but was not really part of the transference neurosis. Indications of original conflicts from the oedipal stage were also evident and could be partially analyzed. However, the most important experiences in the therapy originated from the severe trauma in prepuberty, the father's suicide and its consequences.

Thirdly, it is obvious how dependent this therapy is on the tensions that arise within the situation. Here lies the importance of the composition of the group. The leader is relatively powerless to do much with a poorly selected group in which the deeper needs of the members are too similar. But he is also paralyzed by a too-disparate group.

If, for instance, a member who is cognizant of group processes dominates from the beginning to such an extent that others cannot develop their own vision, there is little the therapist can do. The therapist is dependent on relations within the group itself and may be effective only by using the shock of opinions to split subgroups. Tension between members is very important, but so is the possibility of eliminating tension when necessary. Naturally, it is the therapist who defines the nature of this communication and gives shape to the contrast between the contents of the individual superegos and the general code. He cannot, however, influence these matters without a sufficient amount of divergence and support among group members.

To summarize, it is sufficient for my purposes in this paper to discern three stages in the course of group therapy in which one centers on transference neurosis toward the therapist.

First, a stage in which the new environment and its therapeutic goal defines the tension and contrast whereby orientation and subsequent adaptation will take place. I hope it has been made clear from both case reports how this adaptation furthered the communication of defended feelings and the development of the transference neurosis, which leads to the second stage wherein the dyad relationship with the therapist develops. The author supposes that this development is more outspoken in groups of less than six members.

The third period is one in which the tension lessens. Members lose interest in the group and do not experience from it what they did at an earlier stage. Regression stops; the transference neurosis, in the limited form it can develop in the group setting, has been analyzed and worked through. The group becomes more rigid, governed by its "tacit agreement," its "code," and only a change in its composition or the breaking of existing resistances, frequently unsuccessful, brings progress. Therefore, it is evident how dependent the therapist is on the existing situation in the group. However, he is also continuously the focal point of the situation because of his constant leadership and authority, which induces identification in the members. Especially with relatively young members, he will be the center of a pedagogical influence. Such influence is less with older people of more settled opinions. It was my experience with both these groups that the first, which started with younger men, was more molding in terms of the therapist's model than was the second, which started with older men.

In this connection it is important to discern two predominating influences exerted by group therapy. (Spanjaard, 1959). First the pedagogical influence that molds the content of the superego and the ego-ideals through identification with the therapist and with the "tacit agreement" or "code" of the group, which is the common denominator of all inducing forces. This factor is effective throughout all phases of group psychotherapy. In the first stage weakening the resistances, in the second furthering urges and feelings of a very intimate nature, and in the third, especially, inducing adaptation to reality and growing to the termination of the therapy.

The second influence results from a working through of the transference neurosis in its structural sequences, the problem to which I have given emphasis in this paper, since I consider it the more important of the two. I was constantly aware of my own structuring of the situation in an attempt to influence common themes and to break resistances and loosen ties between the members. Every structure in the group was considered as a hindrance; only an involvement with the therapist may give true analytic therapy, even if one cannot work without the factor of the group as a whole. The latter factor is continuously appearing in the "tacit agreement," in which one finds expressed all the directing forces of personality, psychoanalytically defined as superego and ego-ideal. Its determining influence in favor of, as well as against, the course of therapy, is discussed above.

In conclusion one may say that grouping remains the predominating dynamism in this therapy. A good group composition is difficult, but a prerequisite. The grouping relationships between the members and the "tacit agreement" determine the influence of the therapist as well as that of the members upon each other. The group remains throughout the vicissitudes of the therapy something to fall back upon as a regressive situation, a source of dependency and protection perhaps comparable to a mother. But, certainly in little groups as described here, every member will emerge from it into the dyad relationship with the therapist and find there the tensions of transference neurosis, the working through of which may bring him real structural improvement.

Analyzing my own function in this process, I considered my main task as group therapist to be the undermining of individual and general resistances, thereby furthering the exposition of repressed material and the development of the transference neurosis.

These points of view do not differ from the common theoretical and technical basis of psychoanalysis proper. However, the possible danger of a mere suggestive influence by identification rather than a real working through of the transferences probably is a greater pitfall in group therapy than in individual psychotherapy.

However, the psychoanalyst who uses group psychotherapy will meet some facts new to him. He will get an increasing interest in post-oedipal experiences and traumata of puberty and adolescence. Perhaps his idea about the origins of transference will become less certain. Must transference always be a repetition of relations and feelings from the period of infantile amnesia? Perhaps much later events play a role, at least when they are warded off and unconscious.

There exists another problem that has to be solved by group psychotherapy: Are there traumata that could be called "group traumata," such as with children badly prepared to begin school or adolescents suddenly exposed to much more adult mates? Naturally, their unprepared disposition originated in their families, especially their parents. Does the group therapy situation exert a beneficial influence on these patients? In individual analysis, too, I believe every therapist who is acquainted with group psychotherapy recognizes instances that make him wonder if there are "group traumata" that could be better treated in group rather than individual therapy. I do not think here of a "corrective emotional experience" but of the possibilities of reliving in transference and of working through. Perhaps this will be one of the most interesting questions to which psychoanalytic group therapy will add some entirely new observations and data to psychoanalysis.

REFERENCE

Spanjaard, J. (1959), Transference neurosis and psychoanalytic group psychotherapy. *Internat. J. Group Psychother.*, 9:31-42.

7

Group Analysis and the Insights of the Analyst

JOSEPH WILDER

The present paper is based on experiences with group analysis used as an adjunct to individual analysis.

The groups studied were open groups; of no more than six patients; fairly homogeneous as to diagnoses, mostly anxiety, compulsion, and character neuroses; of both sexes; mostly middle and upper socioeconomic classes, age nineteen to forty-five. They consisted as a rule of patients with a history of long psychoanalysis, often with two or more successive analysts. In my analysis, and mostly also in previous analyses, they were at a stage of long-lasting resistance (stagnation). This was true for both psychoanalysis or analytic psychotherapy. The group sessions lasted one and a half hours. Rare "alternate" sessions (without the analyst) also were used. The group sessions took place once every week with some patients and once every two weeks with others. The individual sessions took place two to three times a week.

The introduction of such infrequent sessions of group analysis in addition to the otherwise unchanged individual analysis proved to be of great value in overcoming the resistant unproductive stage of the analytic process. In no instance was this process disturbed or damaged by the introduction of group sessions. It was obvious that

---

Dr. Wilder is Clinical Professor Emeritus, New York Medical College; former President, Association for the Advancement of Psychotherapy.

this result depended on the right preparation of the patient as well as on the tactics of the analyst and on the proper selection of cases.

Experience with group analysis has in general strongly confirmed the basic theses of individual psychoanalysis by offering new kinds of evidence. By placing the patient in action in a special social setting, both the analyst and the patient himself are offered directly observable evidences of his transference, projections, and fixations. His responses to a variety of interpretations of the same phenomena are shown, and a setting is created onto which not just the transference to one parental figure (the analyst) but to a group of figures (family) is easily projected. As the patient observes a variety of transferences to the analyst in other patients, the analysis of his own transference neurosis is facilitated. One reason group analysis is particularly advisable for patients who have been in individual analysis for a long time is the difficulty in the analysis and resolution of their transference neurosis.

In the group, the patient's distortions of other subjects' thoughts and emotions are often more clearly perceived by the other group members and sometimes by the subject himself — and not by the analyst alone. The analyst can quickly realize when the patient's responses to love, kindness, hostility, praise, submission, aggression, etc., vary from his descriptions in the private session. Analysis of the reasons for these discrepancies is fruitful.

On the other hand, individual analysis contains important elements not duplicated by group analysis and does not, in my opinion, change much by combination with group analysis. However, the addition of group sessions does permit the use of novel material in the individual session: the directly observable reactions of the patient to the other people, his acting out, and his dreams related to the group situation. It counteracts to an extent the deplorable stalemate of a "double life" observable in long-lasting treatments: progress in self-knowledge during the analytic sessions without any application of that knowledge outside the office. Furthermore, in the group both the analyst and the patient have a number of common experiences, which subtly influence their relationship and again supply novel material for the analysis.

This is not the place to discuss the fine points of the selection of patients for group analysis, of the proper timing for it, or the individual method of persuasion. One factor only should be stressed: we must avoid giving the patient the impression that he is being "dumped" into a group because the analyst has become tired of him or has lost hope in the success of individual analysis. On the other hand, the analyst must be pretty sure that these are not precisely his motives.

The chosen role of the analyst in the group was even less directive than in individual therapy. The differences were also characterized by a change of costume (a white jacket was worn in individual analysis only), of setting (cigarettes and candies on the table), and the presence of a tape recorded on many occasions. A new group that was "frozen" was often started by the analyst describing very frankly his own thoughts and emotions at the moment. It is not suggested here that this is a proper setting for other forms of group therapy or combined therapy.

The emerging phenomena of transference and countertransference, of projections, of overidentification, etc., were analyzed by the patient himself or by the other group members on the spot or became the subject of analysis in individual therapy. The emotions and situations that occurred in the group were not forced upon the patient in the individual sessions to the disadvantage of other material. Some patients rarely referred to them at all. However, even in these cases the influence of the group experiences was evident. It showed itself in shaken resistances, revised insights and infantile images, shifts of interest, and new reality testing. Sometimes the analyst referred to group experiences as a good illustration to what the patient was saying. The most important insights were those into the existence of positive and negative transferences.

It is clear that this method fills one great gap of individual analysis: the analyst is not at the mercy of the patient's version of his human interrelationships. He becomes an actual witness, free to formulate his own view of the events and compare it with that of the patient.

In my groups there is often another witness: the tape recorder.

This is used for therapeutic purposes in three ways: (1) A patient at his own or the analyst's suggestion listens to a whole group session once more in order to relive it and to check on his impressions of others or his own actual behavior. (2) The patient may catch up with a session he missed. (3) The analyst can supervise his own behavior and analyze it, if necessary.

"Group Dreams" as Evidence of Insights Into Transference to Groups

Occasionally a dream was analyzed by the group, followed by analysis of the reasons for different interpretations by different group members. The interpretations by these members, well versed in dream analysis, were often so patently wrong that the analyst had to intervene. At the same time, however, his alertness toward the relativity of his own interpretations was stimulated by his "fellow analysts." The dreams frequently dealt with group problems, especially in those patients who had problems with groups in life. A few examples may illustrate this.

In Anna's case three dreams showed successive stages of her groping with her problems. In her profession as a social worker she was considerably hampered by her complexes in speaking before groups of people. When she and the others noticed she had the same difficulty in group therapy, she recognized the similarity of these current feelings with those of childhood — daily experiences at the dinner table, which highlighted her entire situation at home. Her mother, a rejecting figure, engaged in lively conversations with her brother about personal matters while Anna would never open her mouth, convinced that no one could possibly be interested in what she had to say. In her first dream, after entering the group, she was seated during a banquet with a number of elderly ladies, while all her friends were at another table. When she tried to move over to their table she was stopped by a waiter who said that this table was reserved for important people only. In a later dream she was with a group of boys in the analyst's office. One boy cried and the analyst took him on his lap and kissed him. Anna was surprised and envious; she felt left out.

However, in the next sequence she was alone with the analyst, he took her on his lap, kissed her and she liked it very much. But then her mother appeared, angry and with a black face. In a subsequent dream she was again in the analyst's office. Here, the analyst attended to another patient while she was still there. She was slightly annoyed. Then, the analyst conducted an art class. There was a discussion on what is "subjective." She wanted to be helpful and suggested that four oil paintings should be given to those who have none. The analyst replied that Anna would get none because she already had a drawing. In reaction, Anna thought: "Despite the fact that this is just, I still feel cheated."

In capsule form our interpretations, given in this case in the individual sessions, were as follows: In the first dream she was forbidden to be on equal terms with people toward whom she felt friendly. In the second dream, the analyst could only love a boy, her brother, and the following oedipal wish fulfillment was punished by mother. In the third dream everybody got something (love) from the analyst; the fact that she got a little bit, too, did not meet her demands. Despite her frequent complaints about her mother, it was the love of her father which she missed more. The parents did not talk to each other for twenty years.

Sam was another patient who suffered from impotency and was struggling with tremendous sex taboos. He dreamed of a party at which a woman was telling a joke and groping for a word. He promptly supplied the word "shitless!" Everybody laughed gaily, but his brother and a few other people were slightly shocked. The next sequence of the dream was a flashback to the twelfth year of age and yielded an important withheld sex memory.

Ted was an extremely rigid personality whose neurotic system since his third year of age centered on repressing love in order to remain independent. He recalled a dream about a female figure made up of a swarm of bees, which was trying to pull him into her mouth in order to destroy him. This seemed like a perfect image of transference of a parental figure to entire groups.

It is well known that one of the most useful and frequent events in group analysis is the recognition of the patients' own projections and their confrontation with reality. Thus a forty-year-old man, who because of impotence as well as shyness had never had sexual intercourse and whose sex fantasies were all of the child-and-mother type, exclaimed after listening to the desperate complaints of an obsessive-compulsive pretty young lady who was in tears: "I cannot understand myself! There you are practically breaking down in front of me and yet I continue seeing you as I see women in general: superior, knowing all about sex and absolutely sure of themselves."

I had the opportunity to analyze many dreams of three group therapists. One, who felt quite secure as an analyst, had a "group dream" in which there was a suspicious emphasis that a friend, a senior analyst, had remnants of a castration complex while he, the dreamer, had none. The other two, who most of the time were thinking obsessively about their groups, never had a "group dream," although one dreamed often about single members of his group.

One of these, however, found himself in his dreams often in the middle of smaller and larger groups, always hostile and frightening. These groups did not consist of patients. This reflected his typical projections to people in real life as well as the nature of his negative, hostile, and defensive countertransference in the therapeutic group.

Group Therapy as a Tool to Sharpen the Insights of the Analyst

Besides the "supervision" of the analyst by the group members functioning as fellow analysts there are three ways in which the analyst can use the method described here for self-supervision: (1) the direct observation of the patients and of himself in the group; (2) the analysis of patients' experiences in the group during subsequent individual sessions; and (3) listening to the recordings made during the group sessions and individual sessions — soon after they were taken and again months or years later, when the final outcome of the therapy is known.

Certain mental attitudes are necessary in this self-supervision. We must break out frequent analytic inertia and become conscious of our mental predictions of each patient's reactions, which we are constantly making automatically and most subconsciously. It is bad indeed if we develop such a degree of inertia that we are not making any such predictions at all. In such cases we must force ourselves to make them consciously, so that we clearly formulate in our mind a hypothesis regarding the unconscious of each patient.

In group sessions there are sometimes moments when the analyst must frankly admit to himself that he is *surprised* by the patient's behavior or utterances. In such cases he has obviously made false predictions, otherwise there would be no surprise. In such situations we must fight any tendency to find easy and cheap excuses for these errors of judgment and must take them very seriously. They call for urgent self-analysis of the causes and motivations of the false predictions. At times these may prove almost trivial; at other times they may involve important insights, often concerning countertransference.

To give but one very superficially described example of such surprising behavior: A patient with compulsive homosexuality as his outstanding symptom agreed to join the group under the condition that he would not mention his homosexuality. Yet his first words to the group were: "My problem is that I am an homosexual." Although the analyst was well aware of the patient's ambivalences, he was nevertheless surprised. The patient, too, spontaneously expressed his surprise about this behavior during the subsequent individual sessions. This false mental prediction was the subject of analysis and self-analysis. The latter revealed that by his confession the patient was protesting against his guilt feeling. Originally this guilt feeling about homosexuality was so strong that it created an obstacle in the beginning of analysis. The analyst did a rather good job of reducing this guilt but in the further course of analysis unnecessarily continued minimizing it. This was motivated by subconscious overidentification with the patient, caused by the sexual guilt feelings that the analyst himself had retained from the time when he was the patient's age. Thus, the analyst subconsciously helped in repressing slightly these guilt feelings, which in the special social situation of the group broke out in the form of a protest: "I am a homosexual, so what?"

But the patient's reactions are not always so dramatically surprising. Much more often one can diagnose one's false predictions only if one asks oneself repeatedly: "Now, frankly, would you have predicted what has happened right now?" Or if one forces oneself to predict: "In this developing situation I predict that patient will react in the following way."

Sometimes it is interesting to observe a *patient's surprise* about another patient's behavior. Here it is the patient who has made the false prediction. Most often this is not difficult to analyze, especially where it is obvious that only one patient is surprised while the others are not. Here and there, however, when a patient expresses such a surprise, the analyst is forced to admit: "He is right, I should have been surprised, why was I not? What happened here?" Often this is nothing but an example of the analyst's inertia: he failed to make any predictions at all. In other cases self-analysis reveals: "I was not surprised because I had made a correct mental prediction; why then did I so readily accept the patient's suggestion that I should have been surprised." It often turns out that either the analyst never worked through the prediction or that he was overcritical of himself or had in his countertransference a submissive trait.

It is well known that the patient's general behavior in the group may prove to be quite different from the image the analyst has formed from talks with the patient alone. This calls for self-analysis as to why we were taken in by the patient's false reports and role playing and what conclusions we can draw from this for the analysis of transference as well as countertransference.

One of the most useful series of observations is the awareness of our own different attitudes toward different members of the group. This insight is sometimes brought out by direct criticism of a member who points out that the analyst favors or protects one member of the group or is being unfair to another. Certainly we shall first analyze the critic's motivations for seeing it that way and saying it at that particular moment. But we should not have a preconceived idea that the critic is wrong. It is sometimes too obvious that he is right and sometimes the other group members agree with him. The therapist's awareness of the actual existence in himself of the criticized attitudes may be aided by observation and analysis of similar attitudes in members of the group toward each other.

All this helps the analyst to recognize his ever-so-slight subconscious attitudes of protection, competition, sadism, masochism, or other sexual attitudes; also those of omnipotence, encouragement, breaking up of hostilities and of acting out. He can see himself better playing the role of a father, mother, teacher, or censor with the different patients in the group. Even where only slight traces of such attitudes are discovered, their analysis may lead to important insights concerning countertransference and thus help in advancing the analysis. The analyst may realize that he is too eager to achieve analytic success, to make scientific studies, or to use the material for teaching purposes. He may observe how such trends not only influence his group techniques but are also felt and often resisted by the patients. Thus I discovered — by listening to the tapings of group sessions — my tendency to use the word "interesting" too often, which betrayed a not-always-conscious attitude of learning or doing research.

What does the combined individual-group analysis do to the analysis of transference? In some cases it will change nothing: the analyst will be still experienced as the omnipotent father, understanding mother, etc. However, since the analyst's role playing in the group (conscious or unconscious) is flexible, different with various patients, this leads often in one or the other members of the group to an analytic insight into his own transference process. This is one of the reasons why not new cases but patients who had been treated individually for some time, patients in which the analysis of transference was neglected or strongly resisted, were chosen for my groups. The proper timing of the analysis of transference must be kept in mind.

We have mentioned that the analysis of countertransferences is helped by the group sessions. A deficient analysis of countertransference is, as we know, sometimes one of the causes of "stagnation" in individual analysis.

Patients criticize the analyst much more often in group sessions than in individual analysis. Even if the motivations for this criticism are obvious, like the need to deny in front of the group the dependence on the analyst, the criticisms may nevertheless be correct. One should not be too eager to accept or reject them. It is well known that patients sometimes reveal in the group things they are unwilling to reveal face to face. Thus one of my patients said in the group, all of a sudden: "Twice during my long analysis I showed the doctor love but he missed the boat." Such true statements should be investigated not only from the patient's but from the doctor's aspect too. Why did the patient not talk about it in individual sessions? How did he "show" love? Why did the analyst miss it?

Let us now say a few words about the second method of self-supervision: the use of experience of group analysis in the subsequent individual session. This situation presents a number of problems. The patient may be very eager to discuss his group experiences or he may not even mention them. He may also refuse to discuss them and resent the suggestion to do so. If he does not talk about them, it may indicate that there actually was not any emotional experience worth discussing in the entire group session. On the other hand, the opposite may be true: the experiences were too strong, there is marked resistance, occasionally even striking amnesia. The analyst has to decide on the proper procedure in every single instance. Another variety of the combined individual and group analysis is exemplified by the case of a patient who was assigned by his group therapist, a woman, to enter simultaneous individual therapy with me. This man, an overt homosexual, suffered from manic-depressive attacks and severe inferiority feelings. His resistances were particularly strong. Even with this combined therapy it took a long time until a noticeable partial improvement of anxiety and inferiority feelings could be seen. He had great difficulties in talking about himself directly. His favorite device was to talk to me about his experience in the last group session: "I was more aggressive, could not talk at all, was very angry at a certain patient." After a while he began to see that he displayed each time in the individual session with me attitudes identical with those he experienced in the group sessions. This accentuated the insight into his projections and was helpful in the analysis of his transference process (and the accompanying resistances) to both his group and myself.

Thus he told me a dream in which he saw his female group analyst speaking on the telephone. She was very persuasive; however, the patient was only a cool observer. The analysis of this dream deepened his insight into the resistances against both of his therapists — a transference in both cases of his ambivalent attitude toward his mother.

One of the most important sources of insight for the analyst in these after sessions is this: quite often something that appears as the most exciting, shocking, interesting experience to the analyst seems to make not the slightest impression on the patient.

On the other hand, the patient may appear in the subsequent session very excited about a new insight gained in the group, where the analyst sees only something that has been unearthed long ago and ventilated many times. Here again the situation is not simple: this "important insight" phenomenon may be just another product of resistance, an attempt to mislead the analyst. But it may just as well be genuine and in such case very important.

What does it mean? What is the difference between the reaction of the analyst and the patient to the same insight experience? The difference is not in the content of the experience but in the different degree of *importance* as seen by the analyst and the patient. For reasons calling for deeper analysis in both the patient and the analyst, a fact that appears as very important to the analyst is of minor importance to the patient and vice-versa. Similar things can be observed directly in the group session: a patient giving an account of his life history or his neurosis in the group may without hesitation claim a certain event as the crucial point of his life or his neurosis; however, the same event may not be presented as crucial in individual analysis or perhaps only in the first few sessions. Again the patient either covers up or reveals something in the group; but whatever it is, we are not dealing here with any new contents from the unconscious. It is only a shift in the emphasis, in the degree of importance — the unimportant is made crucial, the crucial unimportant. The content, however, has been either made conscious long ago or was never repressed at all.

This special mechanism of resistance was to me the most outstanding lesson derived from this special combined method in cases of particularly long-lasting analysis. Whether it applies to all patients or just to the modern intellectual patient, well trained in psychoanalytic thinking, I cannot yet tell with certainty. You will probably notice that it bears some resemblance to a normal mental mechanism: that of ignoring, diverting attention and not focusing on something unpleasant without repressing its content or correlations. This mechanism of not repressing the content but repressing or exaggerating the *importance* of certain conflicts in relation to the patient's self and his goals in life was the preferred defense mechanism in my long-treated patients.

The distinction between what is and is not important for us in our psychic life is, however, one of the highest functions of our superego. It is therefore easily vulnerable not only to repression but to disease, exhaustion, alcohol, drugs, etc. It is also easily distorted by the analyst's own prejudices, interests, and projections. This, in my limited group experience, was shown to be one of the most important causes of undue prolongation of analytic treatment. The awareness of this problem was perhaps the greatest benefit of the added group psychotherapy.

The defense mechanism of deemphasis or overemphasis is motivated by the same inner conflicts as repression. In the individual session patient's deemphasis may escape the attention of the analyst, or it may be innocently generated by the analyst. The overemphasis may be a maneuver to mislead the analyst, or it may originate in the analyst's bias. In the group the patient may use overemphasis for the same purpose of defense and misleading. In some cases, however, he liberates himself in the group from the submission to the analyst's deemphasizing bias (as in the case of the "confessing homosexual").

I shall not discuss in detail the use of recordings for self-supervision. We all know that our own voice sounds on recordings more like other people hear it and different from the way we hear it ourselves. This has physical reasons. I do not believe, however, that physical reasons alone are responsible, because it is often also the tempo, modulation, accent, etc., which may surprise us: our entire image of ourselves as a speaker has been in this case different from reality. If we listen carefully we may also notice the fine changes of that whole pattern as related to certain patients in the group or to certain topics. We notice that at times the analyst's behavior pattern is influenced by the group. I do not say it should not be, I only claim that the analyst should be conscious of it. We can observe and analyze our hesitations, our unintended directiveness, our avoidances. The separation of the disk or tape of the verbal communication from other communication systems (mimicking, gestures, psychosomatic effects) also permits interesting observations: sometimes one of these systems seems to function more immaturely than the others.

Thus, the combination of group analysis with individual analysis affords various opportunities for self-supervision. This in my experience is particularly useful in difficult cases, where individual analysis has continued over a long period without satisfactory and continued progress.

As to the future of group analysis in general and the combined forms, predictions should be made with caution. Right now a great variety of nonanalytic group therapies claim favorable results, rarely substantiated by reliable data. As long as we do not have figures comparing the quality of results (including long-term follow-up) and the duration of treatment (or rather the number of sessions) for the individual analysis as compared with group analysis and for the combined forms, we can base our judgment only on impressions.

8

Mental Health Groups: An Intensive, Low-cost Treatment Method

STEFAN DE SCHILL and DENISE LAHULLIER

THE NEED FOR A LOW-COST METHOD

Every increase in the effectiveness of therapy proportionately reduces the total treatment cost to the patient.

As the effectiveness of the procedure increases, the patient either will come for a shorter total treatment period or — if limited by his financial circumstances — he will be able to reduce his weekly expense by decreasing the number of sessions. This paper presents a new and intensive method of psychoanalytic therapy — mental health groups — which the writers have developed under the auspices of the American Mental Health Foundation over the last nineteen years. The name Mental Health Groups was chosen in order to distinguish this form of treatment from other using the group process and also to link this method to the name of the Foundation responsible for the creation of the procedure.

The Foundation, which was established in 1924 by eminent civic leaders and psychiatrists, has dedicated itself to research and the advancement of reforms in the field of mental health.

The Foundation views research into the functioning and

Dr. de Schill is Director of Research, American Mental Health Foundation; Vice President, International Institute for Mental Health Research, Zurich.

Denise LaHullier is Coordinator, International Studies, American Mental Health Foundation.

malfunctioning of the human mind as of paramount importance. Primary emphasis, therefore, has been placed upon such research and upon the testing and establishing of fundamental tenets of psychotherapeutic theory and technique. As an important part of its program, the Foundation has given great attention over the last twenty-three years to the development of better, and therefore less expensive, treatment methods. The urgent need for such methods was demonstrated by the Foundation's follow-up study, started in 1954 and conducted over a period of nine years. The study showed that only about one per cent of applicants for low-cost treatment were able to find adequate therapy.

Long-term research by the Foundation has pointed toward certain forms of intensive psychoanalytic group therapy as particularly suitable for many emotionally ill people. These methods utilize all the psychoanalytic fundamentals, such as transference and resistance analysis, free association, and dream analysis, and have additional unique features as well.

An outstanding factor in psychoanalytic group therapy is the multitude and variety of the interrelationships that take place. A person seeing the therapist only for private sessions reacts to a single individual on whom he projects his emotional patterns. In a group setting, however, the different male and female members evoke in the patient a *multitude* of diversified emotional reactions, resulting in a far clearer emergence of the person's emotional structure.

The group situation is more like the outer world we live in, as contrasted to the sheltered protection of the private session. For this reason any emotional conflict expressed and worked through in a group tends to be resolved in a more definite and permanent manner.

Nevertheless, in 1953 the foundation's survey of the literature on group therapy revealed that the majority of psychotherapists believed it was merely a less intensive form of treatment used for patients with milder emotional disturbances. Most therapists would recommend group therapy only for patients who had previously been in intensive individual treatment, and once in a group most patients would continue to receive regular weekly private sessions.

The Foundation's aim, therefore, was to develop a form of low-cost therapy, combining both individual and group sessions, that would show increased effectiveness, yet permit a substantial reduction in the number of individual sessions needed. The creation of such a treatment form would enable each patient — even those of limited means — to pay for his own intensive treatment without undue sacrifice. At the same time, the therapist trained in this procedure would not experience any reduction of income. Thus, such treatment would not require the financial support of a third party, private or governmental. Public and private funds can never suffice to take care of even a small portion of the vast numbers of emotionally ill persons.

The Development of Mental Health Groups

In view of the great need for an *effective, genuinely low-cost method of psychotherapy,* which, if successful, could be used by experienced psychotherapists everywhere, the writers began to experiment with the new method called Mental Health Groups. Patients were seen almost exclusively in group sessions and had only four to eight individual sessions per year. In this way patients who can pay only the equivalent of one individual session per week have been able for the first time to receive extensive and intensive psychotherapy. This is important in view of the fact that Foundation studies have shown that the majority of patients who have gone for only one individual session per week, even with a qualified therapist, are not able to make satisfactory progress in their treatment.

Seven such mental health groups have been conducted by the authors during the past nineteen years. In an effort to gain necessary material for comparison, evaluation, and validation of the techniques employed, four groups were led by one author and three groups by the other.

The method was originally presented in 1957 at the Second International Congress of Group Psychotherapy, in Zurich (de Schill, 1959). Progress studies of this treatment form were reported to the Sixth International Congress for Mental Health (Paris, 1961), to the Sixth International Congress of Psychotherapy (London, 1964), to the Twenty-Third Annual Conference of the American Group Psychotherapy Association (Philadelphia, 1965), to the Annual Meetings of the American Mental Health Foundation, and to other scientific meetings.

The present form of this new treatment method is the culmination of the work of many Foundation research efforts. Expanded knowledge of psychotherapeutic theory and techniques and the various forms of group therapy have been carefully tested and reorganized. Data collected over these years reveal that: (1) The increase in effectiveness with this form of treatment permits a drastic reduction in the frequency of individual sessions required. (2) Most patients can be placed in such groups at the beginning of treatment. (3) A great many emotional disturbances, even of a severe nature and previously considered not amenable to group psychotherapy, can now be treated in this setting. All of these factors contribute toward a substantial reduction in the cost of intensive and effective treatment.

The Setting of Mental Health Groups

Based on their experience with psychoanalytic group therapy, the writers carefully planned the composition of each Mental Health Group, placing emphasis on optimum heterogeneity.

As much as possible, each member selected for such groups had personality traits and structures different from those of the other group members. Patients with symptoms, forms, and degrees of emotional illness that were previously considered treatable only in individual psychotherapy were accepted in the Mental Health Groups. The only persons not admitted were those whose emotional problems might render group work impossible, e.g., psychotics who had no contact with reality, severe stutterers, feebleminded persons. To this list — as will be explained later — psychopaths have now been added.

The authors had a wider choice in their selection of patients than therapists in private practice ordinarily have. This is due to the fact that all patients applying to the Foundation for referral are first sent for a diagnostic interview with one of the psychiatrists especially assigned for this purpose. By studying these diagnostic reports the authors were able to select the more challenging and interesting cases for the mental health groups.

The age range of the group members was from twenty-two to fifty-five, with most members being between twenty-four and thirty-five. The number of persons in each group varied from seven to ten, with approximately as many men as women. Whenever a member left a group for any reason, he was replaced by a new patient, selected with care to maintain the proper balance of the group.

Usually psychoanalytic group therapy meetings last one and a half hours. The authors found that this limited time thwarts the withdrawn members, such as the silent and submissive. To avoid the submergence of these passive members, more time was allowed, thereby reducing considerably the competition for attention by the dominant and aggressive personalities who tended to monopolize the session. *The meeting time in Mental Health Groups began with a duration of two and a half hours per session and later was increased to approximately three hours per session.*

The occasional private sessions proved to be a helpful component in the mental health group method. Certain patients who were able to function in the group setting manifested anxiety when alone with the therapist. Others needed private sessions to reveal embarrassing material that they could not yet express in the group.

Each of the different situations — regular group sessions, alternate group sessions, and private sessions — provided diversified settings and often stimulated different conflict areas to be worked through by the patient. To these a fourth situation was advantageously added: the therapists suggested that the group members stay together for a while after sessions, perhaps over coffee at a nearby restaurant. In this social situation, additional aspects of each person's reactive and defensive patterns may become apparent.

Preparation of Patients Selected for Mental Health Groups

Mental Health Group members receive only two private sessions with the therapist before entering the group. The purpose of these sessions is to collect data, in addition to those obtained in the diagnostic psychiatric interview, in order to tentatively evaluate the psychodynamics and to help the patient overcome any fears and misapprehensions about joining the group.

Many persons initially object to going into therapy with others because of an inner dislike or fear of people, and they feel that in a group they would not be able to speak freely about their problems. Such resistance — in view of the limited number of individual sessions — is voiced even more frequently by patients to be placed in mental health groups.

In 1956 the Foundation published the "Introduction to Psychoanalytic Group Therapy." This text is directed to professionals and patients and describes the nature and purpose of psychotherapeutic groups. Having new patients read this publication often eases their initial anxiety about entering the group.

The new patient who experiences anxiety is helped to understand that his fears about entering a group are related to his problems and that it would, therefore, be more advantageous to work these through in the group rather than avoid them. By supplying the introductory booklet and by careful handling of anxieties and resistances, the initial period in the group proves to be of no particular difficulty for most patients. The rare exceptions are those patients who become overwhelmed with anxiety when exposed to emotion-arousing situations that occur through interaction within the group. Such persons need the protection of the therapist to temper their anxiety and may be instructed not to attend the alternate meetings at first.

Some therapists tell the group members initially that they must "help" each other, that they will have to behave in a "democratic" way, or that they must "relate in an adult manner" to each other. Such demands tend to inhibit the patient and may obscure the emergence of his individual behavior patterns.

In the Mental Health Groups the therapist emphasizes, as one basic fact in psychoanalysis, that *the success of the procedure is greatly dependent on the patient's efforts toward awareness and honesty in revealing and understanding of all his feelings and actions.* Although primarily for his own benefit, such efforts on his part automatically become a real contribution to group work, even when the expressed emotions may seem hostile, destructive, or embarrassing.

The Role and Work of the Therapist in Mental Health Groups

Difficulties Encountered in Mental Health Groups. The work with Mental Health Groups had to be conducted under rather difficult conditions, requiring great effort and perseverance on the part of the therapists.

The extended time period was made necessary by some of the following major difficulties:

The extreme limitation in the number of individual sessions meant that almost all of the therapeutic work had to be done in the group. This included the working through of difficult situations and problems, which previously were dealt with in individual sessions.

The handling of resistances — particularly in the early development of this method — became an almost insurmountable problem. The intensity of the patients' reactions was never encountered to such a degree in combined individual and group therapy. The anxiety-ridden patients experienced more anxiety than they would have otherwise, the withdrawn patients were more withdrawn, the hostile patients more hostile, and there was a far greater tendency for the patients to act out. Only with the development of more effective approaches were the writers able to overcome these prime obstacles.

Another factor increasing the difficulty in Mental Health Groups was the inclusion of a considerable number of severely disturbed patients who would customarily not be accepted for group therapy. Many of the patients were not as sophisticated and tended, therefore, to be more impulse-ridden than those usually seen in private practice.

In order to develop and maintain a feeling of participation and personal meaningfulness in the procedure, it was necessary for the therapist to relate to each patient during every session.

The writers came to the conclusion that it is essential to have as much knowledge of each patient's psychodynamics as if he were being treated in intensive individual therapy. To accomplish this, the therapists devoted much time outside the Mental Health Groups to careful rethinking of what happened during the session. Also, new patients were asked to write down all their dreams and phantasies so that they could be studied by the therapist, even though these might not be reported during the session.

Therapeutic Tools for Coping with Resistances in Mental Health Groups. The procedures used in Mental Health Groups are based upon theories and techniques tested and developed as part of the research program of the American Mental Health Foundation.

Traditionally psychoanalytic techniques are applied — that is, analysis of transference and the laying bare and working through of the various defense mechanisms and patterns. The therapists formulate tentative hypotheses concerning the unconscious forces and patterns active in each group member. These hypotheses are based entirely on the productions of each patient and not upon any rigid, dogmatic a priori position. As group work progresses, significant material that is detected in the patients' defenses and transferences, expression of feelings, free associations, dreams, phantasies, and behavior make possible continuous revisions of these hypotheses.

A major responsibility of the therapist is to focus on and clarify, at appropriate times, the direction of the efforts to be made by the patient. Mental Health Group members are channeled by the therapist toward meaningful exploration of the group interaction and understanding of underlying currents and mechanisms. The therapist constantly attempts to focus the group's attention on emotions and behavior as they arise, establishing their significance and function within the individual psyche by linking them with the near and distant past. (Direct interpretations, of course, are avoided as much as possible.) Thus the patient's childhood gradually becomes alive, and therapy is made an understandable, vital experience to the patient.

Such focusing diminishes the resistive digressions of the overintellectual, who tends to lose himself in theoretical speculations, and of the patient who engages in long-drawn-out recitals of his life history or recent happenings. It also minimizes repetitive acting out of transferences and multiple transference reactions, which does not result in any therapeutic exploration. Members are encouraged to express their reactions to any given group situation, which in turn serve as stimuli to the other patients. Therefore, at any given time a therapeutic situation exists for everyone, and the danger of merely having a series of individual sessions within the group setting is avoided.

The major difficulty in Mental Health Groups is coping with resistances. It is easier, in the Mental Health Group setting, for the patient to conceal or to act out his resistances and to frustrate the efforts of the analyst to work through the problem. The severity of this problem is in direct proportion to the degree of hostility prevalent in the group.

It has been found that resistances in Mental Health Groups are far more intense than in the usual combined treatment, and they frequently reveal themselves in manifestations that never appear in individual therapy. For instance, some group members tend to form seemingly "warm, positive relationships" that are, in effect, resistances to constructive therapy.

The handling of severe resistances in Mental Health Groups is always difficult since the therapist does not have recourse to frequent individual sessions. On rare occasions, it is advantageous to remove from the group a patient who constantly acts out his hostility or sadism and refuses to engage in any therapeutic effort. A number of these patients were psychopaths. Such discontinuance is likely to benefit the patient, since it might induce him to cooperate with his next therapist.

As a general rule, even intense resistances can be worked through in the group, frequently with the help of other group members. The methods used often go beyond what is customarily done in individual or group therapy. Experience in individual analysis and particularly in group psychoanalysis is increasingly forcing the abandonment of the concept that the analyst must be an impersonal constant and that interpretation is his only valid tool. It is becoming evident that the therapist must employ his own personality and experience.

Analysis of defense and of content, which many believe to be the only acceptable ways to work through resistances, are based chiefly on the reasoning that eventually the rational forces of the ego will help to overcome the irrational defense. The resolution of conflicts is supposedly brought about by the patient's understanding of the psychodynamics involved. Freud, however, said that the analyst must use all available means of suggestion to persuade the patient to give up his defenses. Going a step further, the writers are convinced that the therapist, guided by his knowledge and understanding, must use *all* possible techniques — of which suggestion is only one type — to bring about therapeutic progress. Whenever appropriate, the writers use the widest choice of instruments, whether or not they are interpretive steps. In Mental Health Group sessions, the therapist applies different procedures and rationales to the various group members.

Patients come to therapy primarily for relief of pain and gratification of emotional needs, but *not* for the kind of inner changes the therapist knows are necessary to accomplish lasting results. Therefore, when the analysis of defense and content are unsuccessful in working through a patient's resistance, the writers use the patient's own drives, neurotic motivations, and secondary gains for this purpose. Such techniques amount to an actual strategic handling of the patient and the group, a principle that influences analytic work in any case, as for instance in the use of the so-called "positive transference."

Some simple examples may serve as illustrations:

A female patient was on the verge of terminating therapy because of strong resistances. The patient had often spoken about her absent mother on whom she had been extremely dependent. Another group at the time included an older woman who manifested characteristics similar to those the patient attributed to her mother. The patient was placed in the group with the older woman and became sufficiently involved to remain in therapy until the resistance was worked through.

A patient who complained that his parents had been overprotective and doting was allowed as much freedom as possible by the therapist, who made only the most necessary comments in his direction. On the other hand, a patient who had experienced lack of paternal love in childhood was shown consideration and affection by the therapist. Any fears that such procedures interfere with the emergence of basic patterns are unfounded. The patient who was overprotected in childhood still complained that the therapist tried to control him, and the patient who was deprived of love accused the therapist of ignoring and neglecting him. These distortions in the transference relationship are far more readily observed by the other group members than by the patient himself, and they are used to work through the problem.

The analyst again and again applies pragmatic procedures in chess-like moves in order to subtly maneuver the group toward interaction producing the desired insights. He thus almost becomes a "subliminal" orchestrator, eliciting responses from one or more group members in order to stimulate insights in another member. The therapeutic process within the Mental Health Groups requires an appropriate balance of gratifying and frustrating the patient. At times, learning theory is applied in an attempt to give the patient rewarding experiences. By fostering and reinforcing properly timed ego-strengthening experiences within the transference relationships the therapist brings about positive emotional changes. In other situations frustrating a patient's needs or desires is useful and necessary. There are infinite possibilities to the application of such techniques, which require, however, most careful consideration by the therapist.

Even at best, the patient can acquire only partial cognizance of the processes involved. Conscious insight by the patient, while certainly sought, is usually far from complete and is but one of the factors bringing about personality change.

Patients are continuously encouraged to make certain specific efforts in the Mental Health Group treatment. They are urged to scrutinize their reactions to each situation in the group and to report *truthfully* their feelings toward the situation and toward group members who stimulate feelings within them. They are prompted to describe accurately to the group significant behavior as well as their phantasies and dreams. The therapist stresses that afterreactions to each group session are important and should be carefully remembered and brought up at the next meeting.

The group members are persuaded furthermore to seek out the "Why?" behind each feeling, behavior pattern, dream, or phantasy by establishing the connection with similar feelings and memories from childhood. They are made aware that childhood experiences are very important in analysis because they have influenced decisively the development of deeply ingrained emotional patterns. The patients are encouraged to relate all memories and associations, particularly those that are embarrassing. These may involve thoughts and feelings relating to the bodies of father, mother, siblings, or their own bodies and physical functions, such as bowel movements or early sexual behavior. Eventually a comprehensive picture of the patient's early childhood should emerge.

It is also explained that the patient's progress in treatment may be hampered, even completely thwarted, by his becoming superficial in therapy through avoidance of the requested efforts, by "acting out," by consciously presenting a false front to the group, or by engaging in actions within the group that are attempts to gratify himself yet conceal his real feelings. For instance, a patient may try discourage a new member from continuing in the group instead of expressing his hostility directly toward the therapist.

Patients are encouraged to translate insights, gradually gained, into real-life experience by applying them constructively, first in the group and then in their day-by-day battles against the old neurotic behavior patterns. For instance, patients who unconsciously have reacted to each interpersonal situation as fearful, helpless, and guilty children might then gradually assert themselves in a more appropriate manner.

No definite sequence of procedures or phases of progress are applicable to the group as a whole. Such techniques as "going around," whereby a patient expresses his feelings and phantasies toward each of the other group members,[1] dream interpretation, directiveness or nondirectiveness of the therapist, and others appear constantly in the group. Analytic as well as reeducative aspects of

[1]In mental health groups this technique has been modified in such a way that after the person who is "going around" has expressed his feelings to a member, this member relates the reactions stimulated within himself.

treatment are always present in the group process. Furthermore, a greater understanding of the therapeutic procedure is demanded from mental health group members so that the time might be used more advantageously.

The emotional reactions of the therapist are utilized as a helpful instrument for detection of the patient's various unconscious and semiconscious motivations, such as attempts to control or manipulate the therapist, make him angry, or humor him.

The therapist has to exercise considerable firmness with those patients who tend to waste valuable group time by monopolistic attitudes or long-winded speeches or by acting out their hostility and competitiveness. Such behavior is cut short by focusing on the underlying motivation of the patient. Careful attention must be given to asocial behavior and attitudes and their likely consequences to the patient.

In this connection, a reflection on the treatment of psychopaths by the Mental Health Group method is in order. As is to be expected, work with such persons has proved to be most troublesome and unpleasant, although quite interesting. Certainly, individuals with the most severe forms of psychopathy are not likely to come for treatment. However, there are many forms and types of psychopathic personalities, and eleven such cases have been treated over a longer period in these groups. In addition, a greater number of such patients dropped out after a short time in group therapy. Each one of the longer-term psychopathic patients made some progress in one or several areas, even though their true aim in coming to therapy was to become more successful in their psychopathy rather than to move in the opposite direction toward a truly desirable goal. Since they have never sufficiently developed a healthy, mature conscience (as contrasted to the superego of the neurotic) they — in a good number of cases — may appear as admirably fearless, free, and authoritative to the guilt-ridden, inhibited, and anxious neurotic group members. Persons who are not psychopaths themselves do not recognize that most psychopaths derive great pleasure from their asocial, destructive, and sadistic actions. Since it is the therapist's job to gradually elucidate the psychopathic, exploitative, destructive, and ultimately self-destructive patterns, the psychopathic patients will almost invariably, sooner or later, attempt to undermine the therapeutic group work and in direct or devious ways, or both, try to destroy the position of the therapist and to discredit him. This is particularly true when their attempts to exploit the therapist are thwarted by him. Over the years, quite a number of neurotic patients were induced by psychopaths to leave the groups or were otherwise damaged by them. As a consequence, the writers consider it preferable not to include psychopaths in mental health groups, even though such treatment, when properly conducted, is more effective for them than individual therapy alone.

The following enumeration of some prevalent psychopathic traits may help the therapist and the group members to identify such individuals with greater ease.[2] The psychopathic personality has not developed the mature conscience characteristic of a healthy and responsible individual. The psychopath does not feel guilty about his asocial and destructive actions, which stem from those specific psychological areas wherein his psychopathy has developed. This is in contrast to the psychological structure of the neurotic personality, whose infantile superego makes him feel far too guilty for actions as well as conscious and unconscious strivings that the conscience of a healthy individual finds acceptable. Traits listed may appear in varied combinations and degrees of intensity in any particular psychopathic personality.

The psychopath:

Lives for immediate gratification; schemes for further self-indulgence.

Is self-indulgent to the point of stupidity. (A former clinical term for the psychopath was "moral imbecile.")

Will engage without hesitation in such gratification regardless of how much suffering it may bring to others.

Will exploit others without hesitation when it seems advantageous to him and will rationalize such actions. (The guilt-ridden neurotic person easily falls victim to the psychopath.)

Finds meaning in the words "gratitude," "loyalty," and "duty" *only* if they refer to "obligations" of other persons to him.

Will always present a false front to cover those areas where his psychopathy is dominant. Often he is charming and appears to be sincere.

Will say anything in complete disregard of truth if it furthers his goals and creates a good image of himself. Many are quite well-spoken.

Is convinced — or at least very hopeful — that his psychopathic acts will go unpunished.

Will try to get sympathy when in trouble or endangered, but will return to his old patterns as soon as he feels safe.

Will ward off any criticism either by attacking those who might realize or reveal the truth about him or by various forms of seeming acquiescence.

Projects onto others his own psychopathy and selfishness.

Is almost incapable of changing, has a marked inability to learn from his mistakes and no desire to direct any effort toward socially constructive goals.

Makes himself far more vulnerable to destruction than most people without realizing it.

May well bring about his own eventual downfall due to his inner patterns and outward actions.

Many therapists nowadays speak of "gestalt of the group" and "group mind" as something above and beyond the individuals present in the group. They attempt to deal therapeutically with the group as a whole in a global approach.

The writers' contention, however, is that those trends in a particular group which give the appearance of a "group mind" are actually resistance. As the transferences are examined, the resistive motivations of each group member causing such conformity become apparent. Any neurotic submergence of the individual in the group must be analyzed and attacked by the therapist until it is resolved.

Psychoanalysts are quite capable of accurately describing the existing relationships in the basic group, namely, the family, without referring to terms such as "gestalt," "group mind," and others. The use of such terms is therefore both unnecessary and misleading.

The writers find that the patient's cooperation can counter some of the resistive and repressive forces that constantly tend to destroy the constructive aims of therapy. The following techniques would be unnecessary in individual analysis, where the patient is seen a number of times each week. However, they are helpful — to a limited extent — in the Mental Health Groups, since the patient sees the therapist only once weekly.

In an effort to prevent the patient's insights from slipping away, the therapist explains to him, at appropriate occasions and in the simplest possible terms, his particular neurotic patterns. The patient is encouraged to remember these formulations and, on occasions, to reinforce the insights by writing them down. For instance, an anxiety-ridden patient who unconsciously had to assume the role of his dictatorial, "lecturing" father was thus able to maintain the cognizance of this behavior pattern and therefore avoid some of its pitfalls.

In other instances, where a group member is approaching awareness of a certain problem area — for example, hidden hostility, fear of abandonment, a need to malign threatening figures — he is encouraged to search, even between sessions, for associations and feelings, particularly those stemming from childhood experiences. Patients are told that this remembrance of insights acquired and the focusing on problem areas must not become mere intellectual exercises but should involve real feelings. Such suggestions, which are merely at the conscious level, are most often followed only half-heartedly by the patients and are, most certainly, not equivalent in value to the traditional psychoanalytic techniques. However, these attempts diminish some of the confusion and distortion into which the neurotic patient regresses between sessions. He is given something to hold onto *outside* the therapeutic situation that may help him to deal more realistically with threatening environmental situations.

Initially, this technique was applied only with the patients of two groups in order to determine whether it would bring about noticeable therapeutic advantages. Results showed better integration and cohesiveness within these groups, and in less than a year, the technique was applied in all Mental Health Groups.

The therapist's communications with the patients are in simple, nontechnical language, always expressed on their level of understanding and referring to their own dynamics and their own imagery as evidenced in their dreams and phantasies.

As each patient is constantly made aware of his emotional reaction to each group situation, he gradually arrives at a better understanding of both outer reality and his own true feelings.

Just as it was the social world of the patient's childhood environment that originally gave rise to and became imbued with his fears, suffering, and emotional imprisonment, it is now the social experience of the therapy group that helps him to enlarge his awareness of reality and to gain greater emotional freedom and depth.

Dreams in Mental Health Groups. The actual presentation and analysis of dreams occupy a relatively small portion of the mental health group sessions. Yet, dreams are most important in this type of group work. After a patient tells his dreams, he is advised to speak about the feelings experienced in them as well as to relate any associations. The patient's understanding of his dream is aided by the associations, feelings, and interpretations of the other group members.

The therapist will utilize dreams to make the patient aware of the problem areas to which he must pay attention at each particular stage of his psychoanalysis. Constant parallels are made in the group between the defensive and neurotic behavior of a patient and his dreams. Furthermore, defenses and emotional reactions of the various patients are often compared, and similar, identical, or opposite patterns are pointed out. In this context, it is important to realize that the dreams of psychopaths often require a diametrically opposite interpretation to the dreams of neurotics. For instance, the same dream that would show progress by the neurotic may very well mean a status quo or even a hardening of his asocial tendencies by a psychopath.

Orthodox psychoanalysts who practice only individual analysis have expressed the fear that a premature interpretation of strongly repressed dream material by fellow group members would cause, in some instances, intolerable anxiety in a patient. The writers have not witnessed any such situation that could not be handled adequately. More often than not, it is sufficient simply to show no reaction to the correct but "dangerous" dream interpretation or, when appropriate, to probe its meaning for the "interpreting patient" rather than for the dreamer.

We know that at the beginning of therapy dream material is often quite repressed and strongly symbolized; e.g., patients may dream of animals, trucks, etc., which threaten them. As therapy progresses, dreams become clearer, and significant human images take the place. It has been noted that this process is often more accelerated in mental health groups than if the patient would only come for one individual session per week.

Because of the importance of dreams in analysis, and in view of the limited and severe conditions under which effective therapeutic service must be rendered in the Mental Health Groups, therapists who want to engage in this form of therapy must be skilled in the proper handling of dreams.

Transferences in Mental Health Groups. Transferences often take a different course in the Mental Health Groups, where there is far less individual contact with the analyst yet longer contact among group members. Even with the analyst's constant warm, positive attitude, more patients, particularly those of the same sex as the therapist, persists in projecting manifold negative feelings upon him. These hostile feelings are expressed in innumerable overt as well as covert forms. The so-called "positive transference" toward the therapist is less apt to develop to any intense degree, and, in many instances, it cannot be counted on as a prime tool in working through existing resistances. Transferences of the patient toward other members appear even more pronounced than in other forms of group therapy. Transference reactions such as withdrawal or acting out are more intense in this kind of group.

Freud has termed any therapeutic approach as psychoanalytic when it makes use of the transference. If this is the determinating factor, then analytic group work may be called the psychoanalytic therapy *par excellence.* The transferences of the group members toward each other and toward the therapist become the chief vehicle by which the emotional problems are worked through. Therefore, great attention has to be given to establish a group composition that allows emergence of a variety of significant transference relationships.

The transference relationships are allowed to develop and are elicited within the interaction during the group session. Focusing on the transference involvements, the therapist asks the patients to associate to the feelings presently experienced. Those associations are to recent as well as to childhood experiences, especially within the original family constellation. This procedure brings out the significance of the transference reaction, where it originated, how it has been reinforced, and the present need to maintain the defensive and resistive behavior patterns.

Free Associations. Associations in group therapy differ greatly from those in individual sessions. Often they are more emotionally charged because of the strong stimuli of group interaction. Such emotional responses may lead directly to the upsurge and revelation of repressed childhood material and traumas, often manifested in the dreams of the patients. This, of course, is far more therapeutically desirable than a more intellectual and sterile description of childhood history without affect.

There is frequently the danger that a patient may not verbalize his associations because much activity is occurring at the particular time. This can be used by his resistance and result in the loss of significant analytic material. Such an occurrence must not be taken lightly by the therapist, perhaps consoling himself with the hope that the lost affect will eventually become manifest again. In the Mental Health Groups, the therapists were most attentive in their efforts to prevent such a loss, which, in practice, is a difficult task. They attempted to observe the reactions of all group members and at the end of the session asked for unexpressed feelings. Of course, the longer sessions provide the Mental Health Group members with increased opportunity for self-expression.

Theoretical Considerations. The authors have been exposed to widely diversified experiences in psychotherapy and psychoanalysis, including different forms of group psychotherapy, which have increased significantly their understanding of the functioning of the human psyche. As has been stressed in the Foreword of this book, it is felt that group psychotherapy can make a most meaningful contribution to the improvement and refinement of psychoanalytic theory and technique. In this era, healthy examination and valuable discussion reevaluate the original dogmas and tenets of traditional psychoanalysis.

Freud was a genius in clinical observation, but he was forced to work as a pioneer in almost unexplored territory and his attempts at theory had to be largely speculative.

Even though Freud's structural theory represents an advance over his topographical theory, it still fails to present a workable and factual framework to sufficiently explain the interaction of psychological forces. Most certainly his many followers added notable corrections and improvements in later writings but, by and large, they were not able to free themselves to a desirable degree from what they had been taught. As with the adherents of other psychological schools, their observations are frequently limited by their concentrating on a somewhat restricted number of elements and thus ignoring and disregarding other essential factors necessary for an understanding of greater depth and scope. An even greater danger exists—particularly for overly intellectualized therapists—that they read into a patient's psyche concepts ingrained by their specific professional education which do not truly exist within the particular individual.

Group psychotherapists today have the benefit of some eighty years of psychoanalytic experimentation. They must, of necessity, have gained a thorough-going knowledge of the many psychic injuries that can afflict a patient in his early and subsequent years and of the many ways in which the human psyche reacts and defends itself against these traumas, anxieties, and conflicts; such as how the members within a family may attempt to exploit, seduce, manipulate, or destroy one another. As a rule, these psychological determinants will become more crystallized and visible in group psychotherapy than in individual psychoanalysis due to the presence of a variety of personalities of both sexes. The necessary regressions are fostered and can be far better understood as they reveal a variety of projections upon the other group members and the therapist *at the same time*. This phenomenon cannot occur in individual analysis as dramatically and with such clear-cut simultaneous separation of the different transferences. The distorted masks of each patient's early images are cast upon the other members and we view as many plays as there are patients in the group.

Thus group psychotherapy is singularly useful to the attentive and open-minded observer since he can test, enlarge and improve his psychoanalytic concepts and techniques by scrutinizing the interplay of the complex traumatic forces, specific to each individual, which brought about emotional disturbance. Careful and skillful psychoanalytic work in the group will unravel to a significant extent and in an impressive majority of cases, the child's world that operates within each patient and gradually remedy at least some of the damage.

The psychological forces and mechanisms as perceived by the authors will be presented in the form of "working hypotheses" in the next publication of the International Institute for Mental Health Research. These hypotheses have the advantage of providing a useful and verifiable base for further theoretical formulations, which, in turn, result in psychotherapeutic techniques more in accordance with psychological reality. The hypotheses also attempt to bring about fuller understanding of dreams in terms of their content, levels, the interplay of negative and constructive forces and their evaluation during treatment.

Finally, the authors would like to express a few words about the results in mental health groups. Although standards of evaluating results are usually highly subjective, some objectivity has been obtained in the present study through preparation of detailed comparison charts. In evaluating therapeutic progress, it must be remembered that many of the patients in these groups were clinically difficult cases such as severely damaged neurotics and ambulatory psychotics. Results in working through the patient's problems seemed very satisfactory for about one-third of the patients, satisfactory for about one-half, and somewhat less satisfactory for one-sixth even though they made progress in some areas. (Good results were also reported by the junior staff members who were trained in this method.) Progress was roughly proportionate to the effort made by the patient. An important task of the therapist, therefore, is to enable patients — even those with little motivation — to cooperate with the procedure.

The method of mental health groups proves convincingly that most ambulatory patients can be helped to a significant degree at minimal cost if they are willing to give the necessary cooperation.

It is the authors' conclusion that the intensive treatment done in such mental health groups can offer a most hopeful solution to the most pressing problem in the field of mental health: effective treatment at low cost.

REFERENCE

de Schill, S. (1959), *Mental Health Groups: An Effective Form of Low-Cost Psychoanalytic Therapy.* New York: American Mental Health Foundation.

9

A Combination of Psychodrama and Group Psychotherapy

SERGE LEBOVICI

It was from our experience in child psychoanalysis and our consequent interest in acting as a means of expression that we came to engage in the practice of psychodrama after World War II. In the course of psychotherapy sessions, it is a common occurrence for a child to play dramatic roles quite willingly. At that time we knew of Moreno's work only by hearsay, and thus we were obliged to improvise and make numerous experiments using diverse approaches, these early efforts being reflected in our first publications on this subject (Diatkine, Kestemberg, & Soccaras, 1950; Lebovici, Diatkine, & Kestemberg, 1952). We were concerned, moreover with the need to treat the greatest number of children with limited means. Hence we were interested in anything that seemed to be a technique for group psychotherapy.

Our method underwent rapid transformation. Extending psychodrama techniques to adults demonstrated to us that dramatic play, if customarily an infantile mode of activity, could fulfill an expressive and therapeutic function much greater in scope. In ad-

---

Dr. Lebovici is Professor of Psychiatry, University of Paris; Former Director, Psychoanalytic Institute of Paris; President, International Psychoanalytic Association.

Translated from the French by Joyce Diamanti.

dition, we recognized some of the ideas that had originally inspired Moreno and that had subsequently led him to formulate certain principles that are open to question. As psychoanalysts, we perceived in psychodramatic experiments a dynamic pattern that was familiar to us. Transference mechanisms were clearly manifest, and to a large extent they determined the behavior of the patients. This factor appeared to be ignored in Moreno's work; to us, it seemed important to focus attention on the specific modalities of transference occurring in psychodrama, since a precise understanding of these manifestations determines the handling of interpretations.

It was essential that this therapy be brought back to a generally acceptable psychopathological perspective: although the value of dramatic experimentation is indeed inescapable to anyone who may practice this method, the "theory of spontaneity" does not seem to us to give an accurate account of clinical reality. It is axiomatic that a specific experiment not be considered on the same plane as a general, and unsatisfactory, theory. Although greatly indebted to Moreno on a certain technical level, we have diverged from him completely on the theoretical plane. Our own experiments confirmed our psychoanalytic viewpoints, and thus psychodrama seemed to offer us the opportunity to conduct a psychoanalytic type of therapy in circumstances (age, personality structure) that usually contraindicate this type of psychotherapy in its classical form. Using this approach, we were able to study not only transference but at the same time the dramatic expression of defense mechanisms. Naturally, the general conduct of the treatment was modified.

As our method developed, another element proved to be important — group dynamics. In our first experiments with psychodrama we had been treating a group of children, and it was not until later that we dealt with adult groups. Gradually, we learned to see the group as a real entity, having effects that can be utilized therapeutically when properly understood but that are also apt to lead to harmful consequences if ignored or used imprudently. Furthermore, treatment of a group of children or adults cannot be likened to treatment of an individual by a group of psychotherapists. In the former case, each member of the group acts in his own interest, which gives a specific character to the dynamics of that group.

The complexity of the factors intervening in psychodramatic therapy (such as those just mentioned — dramatic play, transferential phenomena, individual dynamics of patients, or group dynamics) induced us to attempt a more precise and specific definition of this technique, which is particularly adapted to the personality of children and adolescents but is also applicable to adults whose personality does not permit sufficient emotional detachment. Our position is contrary to that of Moreno, who sees in psychodramatic experience a deeper reality than in life itself. This attempt to transcend human actuality on the psychodramatic stage defines, we believe, Moreno's philosophy as well as his methodology. He will not hold it against us for not following him in that realm. By no means, however, should this be taken to mean we are in accord with Slavson (1950) when he compares psychodramatic activity to perpetual acting out, which would imply a distortion of reality through the projection of images. Actual experience shows that this does not occur, even in schizophrenics.

If psychodrama always unfolds with a true-to-life reality, in each instance verifiable, we must not forget that it constitutes a wholly original and distinct experience; this is so whatever the structure of the psychodrama and whether it derives from what the patient perceives of the real world or from what he is capable of imagining in his daydreams. It is this uniqueness that gives properly handled psychodrama its maturational value.

Psychodrama as a Means of Expression

Psychodramatic Expression. From his earliest publications on psychodrama, Moreno has maintained that the value of acting is that it enables the patient in particular, and man in general, to recapture his spontaneity. Psychodrama, then, is thought of as a process of relearning what each of us has lost through the exigencies of group life. Thus, Moreno declares that the verbal era, symbolized by the psychoanalyst's couch, has been superseded: henceforth, psychotherapy, as carried out through psychodrama, will study man in action, achieving self-revelation and self-realization in a positive way. Our own findings differ.

The ability of disturbed patients to enter into psychodramatic action took us by surprise at first, so greatly did their spontaneity sometimes exceed that of reputedly healthy subjects. Yet it became apparent to us that their behavior was rigidly controlled by a series of factors among which we find the very same factors that govern what a patient says during psychoanalytic treatment.

In psychodrama, then, transference phenomena continue to play a major role in patient-therapist relations, and they determine the patients' relations among themselves. Action, like speech, is the result of impulses and what, in psychoanalytic terms, are called ego functions; therein lies its potential to be of great therapeutic value. There exist in this regard two misconceptions, one as erroneous as the other: the opinion of certain therapists who believe that it is a sign of imminent recovery when patients show acting ability thanks to a rediscovered spontaneity, and the opinion of many patients who think that playing a role is learning how to live.

If all the dynamics of human behavior are indeed manifest in dramatic expression, nevertheless our empirical findings would be robbed of their essence by a failure to see the specificity of this therapeutic method. It is true that the history of each individual unfolds through a developmental sequence in which gestural and imitative expressions constitute the matrix wherein verbalization is formed; but for all that, there is no justification for forgetting that it is a question of dialectical evolution in which the processes of cathexis and decathexis are not governed by some simple formula. Human groups have always found this mode of expression, the dramatic action that accompanies speech, to be an indispensable means of communication. Although it is not within everyone's power to say what he wishes in a way that his meaning is always understood, it is clear that movements and gestures, supplemented at times by a few basic words, are for one and all a reliable and effective means of expressing emotions.

All those who have had no experience with psychodrama might think that the fiction implicit in this mode of expression would be constraining, and they also might find a hint of derision in the word "play." Yet during our first experiences with adults (depressed and hypochondriac patients, little inclined to fun and games), we were struck from the outset by the total expressiveness with which they played their parts.

Without exception, they had been very suspicious when we first explained this method, and they, too, were amazed at the intensity of the emotional experience they underwent. We encountered this dramatic aptitude and gestural adaptability in a wide variety of patients — children, adolescents, adults, patients with neuroses or personality disorders — and in normal subjects as well. Further on, we shall discuss the case of psychotic patients.

Psychodramatic Communication. Psychodrama enables patients not at all predisposed to use dramatic language to express themselves with realistic intensity, much to their own surprise. It should be added that this mode of expression actually involves the entire group, not only those who contribute actively to the dramatic performance, but also all those who are present as the action unfolds and who make up the audience. Unwittingly, an individual imbues his actions with this special communicative value in proportion to the emotional reaction of other group members to his performance.

Having the usual alternatives of speech, gesture, or mime available, children and adults alike promptly find a supplementary means of communication in the added motor activity which comes so easily to them in a psychodramatic session. Psychodrama enables patients to assume a better distance, not only in the classical sense of object distance as used in clinical psychoanalysis, but also in the everyday meaning of the term: the patients move about, approaching or withdrawing from therapists and other group members, and these movements have a significance that is immediately perceived by everyone.

Relationship in Psychodrama. By virtue of the expressive opportunities psychodrama affords the participating patients, the importance of the emotional factors it brings out, the effects it has on the therapists and the audience — for all these reasons psychodrama is not simply a special means of expression on the verbal level; indeed, it enlists all the means of expression available to an individual in light of his situation within a group.

Experience shows that often from the very first psychodramatic sessions patients reveal — in a way that is no less striking to the therapists than to the patients themselves — certain aspects of their unconscious life. In an ordinary therapeutic dialogue, everything transpires in effect as if the subject, though capable of assuming a certain position vis-a-vis the doctor in whom he has placed his confidence, cannot make any departure whatever from that position. One frequently observes patients who make a frank and lucid presentation of their problems as they see them, and then, after a few interviews, can find nothing further to say — a concomitant of those very problems, limiting factors which circumscribe a patient's expressive capacity as well as his conceptual ability. A clinical session, like any psychotherapeutic treatment, takes place within the framework of a concrete doctor-patient relationship, and it progressively unfolds through dialogue: when a child plays and we understand his play, it is nonetheless true that he may often go on to reveal to us some radically new aspect of this play. Take the case of a five-year-old girl who constantly played at being a cat, explaining to us that she would like to be a cat because cats eat mice; she showed us her fantasy relationship to the mother image. Yet at the same time, perched on her mother's knee, she ardently declared that she would like to remain her baby forever and ever. Not only did she not say that a mother may eat her children, but, on the contrary, one could sum up what she wanted to say as follows: cats eat mice, but Mama can't eat me!

This aspect of negation has been well known since Freud, and one must always bear in mind the fundamental difference that exists between what a patient wants to say and what, precisely, he cannot say. It is not enough, however, to speak of the difference that may exist between what is made explicit and what remains implicit, between what is thought or imagined and what is actually experienced; further study is needed to determine how this gulf develops. We do know that it is formed by defense mechanisms, reaction formations, and, in particular, ego defenses.

Psychodrama brings us in direct contact with these reaction formations. The patient cannot fail to grasp their significance, although it is true that usually he does not accept their reality until well after the audience has become aware of them.

In this connection, we shall cite the case of Henri, an adolescent who, at the age of six, had been examined by several child psychiatrists. They had concurred in diagnosing his case as one of incipient psychosis. For several years the child underwent psychoanalytic therapy. We cannot retrace the course of treatment in detail here, but it proceeded along classical lines. The facets of Henri's oedipal identification with his father were examined at length through his fantasies about automobile races. The fact is that in his oedipal relations the father imago was bound to provoke both satisfaction and anxiety in Henri, for his father — an intelligent and attractive man, but weak alongside the mother — had actually been seriously injured in an automobile accident. The child's mother, the daughter of an Army officer who had died a hero's death in the First World War, continually identified herself with her father, imagining herself in her fantasies in the guise of a heroic amputee.

It was inevitable in this case, with such distinctive features, that the anxiety-provoking relationship with the mother, pregenital in nature, soon became the focus of treatment. The pattern of this relationship emerged visibly within the framework of the transferential relationship; the child would approach the analyst warily and with manifest guilt. During the same period, and this detail is not without importance, Henri had had an attack of ptomaine poisoning caused by a meal given to him by his teacher, a woman he idolized. In the wake of this illness, Henri was persuaded to accept certain interpretations concerning his fantasies about the dangers involved in oral incorporation of the mother object. Although this material was worked through interpretatively at great length, taking the most recent events just described as a point of departure, the fact is that the interpretations were given in symbolic terms that were attuned to Henri's psychopathological structure but were, after all, anachronistic.

During the latter phases of this psychoanalytic treatment, Henri's masochistic relationship with his mother became the object of systematic examination. The child, then in full latency, could still recall the sexual excitement that had unexpectedly come over him in the following circumstances: he had been irritating his mother by playing the fool, until suddenly she seized him by the wrists in anger. Despite the intensity of his interpersonal relations, both with his mother in real life and with the analyst in transference, an isolation phenomenon set in, which, it must be added, permitted Henri to resume a feasible *modus vivendi* with his mother and to make real progress in his behavior. A new gulf, however, was created between a certain elaboration of the mother imago and Henri's current conception of his real mother. This isolation was purposely respected by the analyst, for to have done otherwise would have plunged the child into regressive attitudes causing serious disturbances. A few weeks later Henri asked that the sessions be suspended. This desire to break off treatment, common in psychotic children, was agreed to. Subsequently, Henri did not revert to past behavioral problems, but he remained estranged, different from others, and his parents were concerned over his rather mediocre adjustment to school and his sudden and unexpected impulses. Moreover, he had a passive homosexual tendency, which caused him some unpleasant experiences and distressed his mother. This is why psychodramatic treatment was eventually undertaken.

In the very first session, a typical phenomenon occurred. Henri told us that his father had undergone major surgery and his mother wanted him to remain on vacation for another fortnight. He had then felt an irrepressible urge to return home; he had made one attempt to run off and in the end, against his mother's wishes, had returned home from where he had been asked to stay while his father was in the hospital. When we asked him how his mother had received him upon his arrival, he replied, "Very well." We suggested acting out this scene. The first time through he played his own role. The psychotherapist playing the part of the mother received him severely, scolding him for his disobedience. Henri played his own part with great naturalness and counterattacked convincingly. When questioned about what he thought of this performance, he maintained that that was not at all how it had really happened, insisting that his mother had greeted him warmly. So then we asked him to play the role of his mother. He depicted her as even more hostile than before, going on to say that his inopportune return would cause more work, an extra burden quite uncalled for in such trying circumstances. We pointed out to him that his portrayal only confirmed what had transpired in the preceding sequence. Henri seemed annoyed and said that we were, in fact, quite mistaken. So the same scene was begun again with the same assignment of roles: Henri, playing his mother, proceeded to explain that in spite of all the inconveniences caused by his return — extra work, added worries, one more mouth to feed — he was, after all, welcome. Thus, this adolescent wanted to tell us that his mother was really the best of mothers. He wanted to think so. For him to do that, all the interrelated elements had to be brought to a focus, a process which was, in fact, none other than working through his means of defense against the anxiety caused by his mother's behavior. Henri's psychosis manifested itself in this form of defense in particular.

This objectivation of defenses, with reference to their contemporaneous sources in the unconscious, is one of the specific advantages of psychodramatic therapy.

The session just described brings us directly to the question of the significance of role in psychodrama. This therapeutic method obliges a patient to identify himself through dramatic action, several times over and in different ways, with a wide variety of situations whose implications he does not fully comprehend on the verbal level.

The word "role" is usually associated with the theater arts: an actor plays a role, which he has memorized from a script. This usage is derived from the French term *roles,* designating the rolls on which dramatic parts, and acts of law as well, were formerly written. These different connotations of the word role brings us back to a matter that has already been discussed at length: the contrast that may exist between a patient's conception of himself (the role according to the script) and his live performance in a psychodramatic situation (the role he plays spontaneously).

Any study of role must take into account the work of modern microsociology. Moreno (1953) demonstrated the great importance of the concept of role taking. These first steps have led to some extremely interesting developments in light of which role should be defined as referring to the position taken by an individual within a given group. This position is determined partly by the personality structure of the individual, partly by the group's reaction to this structure, and lastly by the individual's reaction to the reaction of the group. Obviously, a given individual will have different roles in different groups, and great credit is due the microsociological method for studying how these aspects of personality vary as a function of diverse situations.

Comprehension Levels in Psychodrama. Thus, viewed from the perspective of microsociology it becomes clear that every individual can be studied and understood on four different levels: (1) the level of his personality structure as determined by recurring phenomena linked to his own life history and past experiences; (2) the roles he is capable of assuming because he happens to be in a group situation; (3) the organizational effects on his behavior that are determined by the pressures of the various groups he lives in, that is, the effects on individual structure that arise from group structure, which can in turn be seen to vary according to the leader's attitude and the character of the group as a whole (authoritarian, democratic, or anarchic); (4) the level of reciprocal interaction between these different individual and group structures, such as the reactions and counterreactions cited above.

Psychodrama and Role. In verbal therapy, one cannot forget that by definition patient and doctor are each confined to a very precise role: the patient comes seeking help; the doctor takes the attitude he feels is best suited to help his patient as much as possible—even perhaps remaining silent, as is often the case. But neither the one nor the other may step out of his role and, furthermore, *acting out* is recognized as an attempt on the part of the patient to do just that. In group psychotherapy using verbal methods, an analogous situation may be seen, that is, the doctor has a clearly defined role and the patient usually tries to get the doctor to depart from that role and at the same time attempts to break away from his own role. We know, however, that if the treatment is handled skillfully these attempts are vain, and in verbal group therapy, too, each participant is, in a way, a prisoner of his role.

In psychodramatic therapy the method is different, since right from the beginning we encourage patients to depart from their role through the fiction of drama. They are, moreover, quite surprised at first when we ask them to play persons other than themselves, especially since we agree to the performance of any type of situation. As a matter of fact, during the initial sessions patients exercise these options with moderation, and not without a certain embarrassment.

There are two aspects to consider in the results of this simulated reversal of role in psychodrama. The first lies in the fact that patients and therapists together enact situations which are totally different from those normally falling within the scope of the doctor-patient relationship. After some initial hesitance, patients think they can easily take advantage of this liberty to derive a great deal of satisfaction. Rather quickly, however, they meet with failure in this attempt to obtain the gratifications they desire, as we shall see in detail in the section devoted to transference.

In group psychodrama, the dramatic roles taken by an individual member of the group modify the permanent role of that patient with respect to the group. For this reason it is important to observe individual positions in relation to what is enacted on stage and also in relation to what actually happens within the group structure. Certain patients who play leader roles come to be regarded by the group as deviants. It is essential to watch for clues to such a development, for in a few sessions the deviant aspect of a patient's role usually becomes very marked, sometimes jeopardizing the group's cohesion.

The second aspect of role in psychodrama becomes apparent when we urge upon a patient a role that he would not have taken spontaneously. If a patient describes an incident involving someone close to him, we often ask him to take the part of the other person in order to reach a better understanding of the situation. We have already shown an example of this in the case of Henri, who was asked to play the part of his mother. For rather definite personal reasons, directly related to his identification problems, Henri clearly would never have taken this role spontaneously. Thus, we thrust him into a situation which was totally new to him, but he nevertheless adapted very quickly, playing a role that was to a large extent overdetermined. It was evident that in pretending to be his mother, he could portray her only as fear-provoking. Yet we had seen him introduce his mother to the audience as a good mother, one who corresponded, moreover, to the mother figure he would have liked to have. He was sincere, we maintain, in all his seemingly contradictory positions. We are of the opinion that this aspect of the mother imago could never have been experienced so directly without a long process of working through, without an extensive examination of resistances and defenses. This therapeutic shortcut — in Henri's case the rapid revelation of the mother imago, a portrayal quite contrary to what he wanted to show us — is surely one of the most advantageous aspects of the psychodramatic method; but at the same time it is one of the most difficult to achieve. It is particularly interesting to note that patients are unable to portray at will the role they want to play. Henri certainly wanted to play the role of a good mother; when we pointed out to him that his mother seemed singularly cold toward him in the previous scene, he wanted to do it over again and rectify that impression. But despite this conscious desire, he was unable to do so successfully.

With regard to what Freud called the economic aspect of neuroses and psychoses, the basic findings of miscrosociology show us that the role taken by an individual within a group determines in large measure the equilibrium between satisfaction and frustration that characterizes that individual. At the same time, the social aspect of individual behavior affects the very structure of personality, that is, it affects the individual even in an isolated context. We cannot, then, draw any hard-and-fast lines between these spheres, and we should never forget that even the most stable balance of impulses is continually being redetermined by the social milieu of an individual. It is equally true that a crucial component of skillfully handled psychotherapy is investigation of the disparity between an individual's character traits and the role he assumes in various groups.

Certain subjects show great flexibility in modifying their roles in conformance with the shifting balances between impulses and defense mechanisms, between satisfactions and frustrations. Such patients are susceptible to individual treatment, as in psychoanalysis. Others, however, show a marked difference between their roles and the character traits that come to light in private psychotherapeutic interviews. In our opinion, psychodramatic treatment is indicated for these patients because of the persistence of their ego defenses.

Psychodrama and Acting Out. In considering the therapeutic function of taking a role, one recalls Moreno's position that role playing offers great possibilities in the realm of therapy. We have already expressed our disagreement with this hypothesis. We do not, however, reduce psychodrama to acting out, since in that case it would amount to a deliberate effort on the part of the patient to violate therapeutic guidelines and obtain satisfactions he feels are denied him by his analyst. The fact is that psychodrama offers other advantages. To begin with, it is clear that in psychodrama the contribution of gesture and mime is significantly greater than in other methods, since these adjuncts to language are an integral part of this new means of expression. Furthermore, acting in a psychodrama also involves the use of speech. The language is direct and forthright, while in classical psychoanalysis the patient usually describes what he says and does, and hence the material is more assimilated and controlled. In psychodrama, certain gestures are also eventually assimilated, evolving into conventional forms whose true meaning must be determined. Sitting, walking about, pretending to eat may take on different implications due to the make-believe nature of the action, while other gestures will keep their normal social value.

The gestures and attitudes of the psychotherapists must also be taken into consideration. The very fact that the therapists participate is of great importance since their actions affect the value of the patient's gestures.

Psychodrama brings patients and therapists into a certain amount of physical contact. Some of these contacts are commonplace and at first glance would seem to pose no problem. When two persons pretend to meet, they shake hands, the accepted form of greeting in Western cultures. This social gesture might be considered as merely habitual. There are patients, however, even some who are only mildly disturbed, for whom this gesture is highly significant. Every psychoanalyst is familiar with patients who never shake hands either before or after sessions, while in a chance meeting these same patients perform this gesture easily and automatically. Hence we must weigh the significance behind the performance of even the most mundane type of physical contact.

Another problem arises from the apparent absence of any limits as to type of physical contact. Whereas certain types of contact occur routinely in public and are not out of place between doctor and patient, other types are debatable. Two possible lines of approach must be considered. On the one hand, certain gestures involving bodily contact — embraces, blows, etc. — are usually simulated. Some patients may make sport of such pantomime as a method of resistance. Many, however, find that a gesture is no easier to perform just because it is make-believe. All their fears intervene to prevent them from even imitating the gesture they want to make.

On the other hand, there exists a broad range of physical contacts which take on quite a different value when they occur between patients and psychotherapists. Often a therapist is induced to establish contact with a patient by putting a hand on his shoulder or taking his arm. The question here concerns gestures that are socially accepted and yet highly charged with affective significance. In many instances, certain patients derive real gratification from such contact. This satisfaction is counterbalanced, however, by the frustration arising from the fictitious nature of dramatic activity.

Generally speaking, it can indeed be said that while the action involved in psychodrama is never tantamount to acting in, it does quite often incur considerable difficulties in the performance of a succession of painful scenes, in spite of the annulment inherent in the make-believe quality of psychodramatic action.

This interweaving of denial of reality and intensely true-to-life experience that occurs in a dramatic performance is certainly one of the most distinctive characteristics of psychodrama.

It is for this reason that we do not believe this method can be used for individual reeducation. The truth of the matter is that playing out a situation one fears is not training oneself to be unafraid, contrary to what some patients may think. A man will not get a job more easily because he has gone through dialogues with a psychotherapist representing an employer; however, because a patient has been able to discover through psychodrama what his fantasized image of an employer represents in terms of displacement of his anxiety, he will be able to make progress toward recovery.

Psychodrama and Psychoanalysis

Being psychoanalysts, we have kept the dynamic perspectives taught us by analysis throughout all our psychotherapeutic activity. Furthermore, we have long since come to believe not only that there is no contradiction between the practice of psychodrama and the conduct of psychoanalytic treatment, but also that psychotherapy in terms of drama can be fully comprehended in all its aspects and implications only if one employs the theoretical concepts of psychoanalysis. This is why, in defining our techniques, we speak of psychoanalytic psychodrama and dramatic group psychoanalysis. Nevertheless, as we have stated before, we do not pretend that psychoanalysis makes it possible to understand all the processes at work in psychodrama. Consequently, psychoanalytic training — which to us seems so necessary, or at any rate highly desirable — is not alone sufficient to qualify psychotherapists to engage in psychodrama.

Transference in Psychodrama

Transference Toward the Director of the Psychodrama. This aspect of transference is similar to that observed in psychoanalysis, particularly in that the relations between patient and director are essentially verbal, albeit rather distinctive because of the manner in which psychodramatic treatment is conducted. The presence of a group of cotherapists, however, presents a rival image, which is inevitably reshaped by fantasies from the patient's past and integrated either into the privileged relationship with the mother object or into the triangular relationship characteristic of the Oedipus complex.

Transference on Auxiliary Psychotherapists. This aspect of transference is unique in psychodrama. It is manifested in a great many ways, depending, of course, on the individual case. For example, inhibited adolescents frequently refuse to choose who should take this or that important role in a dramatization. After numerous sessions, they often do not know the names of psychotherapists whom they nevertheless ask time and again to play the role of such or such an imago. The most remarkable aspect is that an auxiliary therapist is usually assigned the same specific role to play at each succeeding session. Obviously, this is a very special situation in that transference on auxiliary psychotherapists is determined not only by the attitude of the patient but also by the way in which the therapist responds. Transference on assistant therapists may also be a significant reflection of the prevailing situation within the therapeutic group. Following a clearly recognizable dynamic pattern, a patient may use transference on an assistant therapist as a defense against a more guilt-laden transference toward the director of the psychodrama, whether the thrust of the transference is positive or negative. In such cases, it may prove particularly difficult to distinguish between what is transference and what is defense against transference.

Transference Relative to the Group Situation. In groups, each patient seeks to gain the individual attention of the director or his cotherapists; in other words, the patient's transferential behavior tends to destroy the cohesion of the group as a whole. Numerous studies (Ezriel, 1951; Foulkes, 1957) have shown that one patient's transference on another patient is, as a rule, primarily a consequence of the group situation. It has the attributes of transferential displacement and resistance. A clear awareness of this situation would avoid many a debate about acting out in group psychotherapy. It would also make it possible to understand group equilibrium, which is manifested to the extent that a group is held together by a true common denominator expressing the fantasies shared by the group vis-à-vis more or less conscious impulses (Ezriel, 1951), a common denominator to which each group member reacts according to his individual makeup.

This reciprocal equilibrium plays a part in psychodrama as well as in verbal types of group psychotherapy. It is often during the assignment of roles among group members that its dynamic effects become strikingly clear. One must beware of making facile judgments: the reciprocal effects of transference should always be kept in mind when attempting to interpret the behavior of patients.

Resolving Transference Neurosis

One knows how difficult it is in any type of psychotherapy to resolve transference neurosis and avoid situations that become very long and drawn out. In psychodrama such situations are potentially even more detrimental than in psychoanalysis. The abreactive effects of psychodramatic therapy and the ostensibly more active collaboration of the therapist have some secondary advantages, but they are liable to perpetuate transference neurosis. The problem is all the more complex in that the countertransference of an entire group of therapists must be taken into account. As might be expected, this is one of the reasons why adequate interpretations aimed at both transference and countertransference are essential in psychodrama, as they are in any therapy that is analytic in nature.

Interpretation of Transference

In the course of analytic psychodrama, it is not only possible but necessary to offer interpretations. Those concerning transference show the patient how and why he inevitably recognizes past situations in the therapeutic situation, rediscovering events he has forgotten or buried in his unconscious. In the type of psychodrama Moreno advocates, such interpretations are not offered. He stresses the importance of the patient's actions *in situ,* his creativity, and hence holds that only his performance on the psychodramatic stage of past and present situations, real or fantasized, has any therapeutic value.

The fact is that the patient's actions obviously depend on what he wants to do or is asked to do, but they also depend on developments that may well be determined by transference on the therapist who directs the psychodrama, on the auxiliary psychotherapists, and on the other patients.

In certain cases, interpretations are greatly facilitated by the fact that the concept of role offers a solid footing on which to approach a dynamic understanding of transference. As we have already seen, psychodramatic technique often provides an opportunity to comprehend dynamic patterns with greater clarity than is possible with verbal methods. All the activity which is externalized in the distribution of roles — which roles patients may or may not choose to take themselves and, especially, which roles they assign to the psychotherapists — affords deep insights into transferential mechanisms, for role distribution is, in a way, clinical proof of transference phenomena. This method of understanding transference by examining roles — roles assumed, roles assigned — has time and again proved to be as applicable to individual psychoanalysis as it is to interpersonal relations. Transference is in part determined by the fact that the psychoanalyst is able to assume any and all roles his patient assigns him; he can be identified with any imago the patient projects on him, and his neutral attitude is pivotal to the dynamics that constitute transference.

Resistance and Psychodrama

Freud's basic law concerning the relationship between transference and resistance can be confirmed once again in psychodrama. If psychodrama is indeed a special means of expression, it is also inescapably true that for many patients it is a means of resistance. It represents, in effect, a compromise, which cannot be categorized as a compromise of either speech or action. In conformance with the rules of this therapeutic method, a psychodramatic performance will remain simulated and symbolic, and the activity on stage will remain within the confines of this framework. The fact is that this situation very often proves to be a source of resistance. When a patient treats a psychotherapist roughly, is overly familiar, or behaves insultingly, he is no doubt realizing, at least symbolically, one of his aggressive impulses, which in a man, for example, may be directed against the father image. What is undeniably distinctive in psychodrama is that the therapist who is the target of this aggressiveness acknowledges it and responds to it as if it were realized in actual fact. It is also true, however, that the patient knows that this situation is limited to the psychodramatic stage, and immediately afterwards he will again adopt the social conventions that normally govern a patient-doctor relationship. The pitfall is, then, that the patient may consider psychodrama the road to recovery, and he may shrink from any self-expression outside the therapeutic setting.

In psychodrama, it can be useful to examine defense mechanisms as described by Anna Freud (1936). For example, subjects with an obsessional personality are seen to avoid forbidden compulsions through a pattern of displacement, isolation, and annulment. Such patients suggest themes that are exceptionally aggressive, relying on the fictional format of psychodrama to ward off compulsions and fantasies they are not facing up to. As it happens — and this is what should be pointed out to them — at the last moment they often back down from playing a particular role or confronting a certain person. It is easy to see—and to make them see—the inefficacy of ever more elaborate defenses. In such cases, the conditions in psychodrama are relatively more favorable for therapy than those found in classical psychoanalysis, where problems arise from the fact that sometimes even a complete understanding of the motivations behind a patient's behavior remains highly intellectual, leaving the ego defenses intact.

Countertransference in Psychodrama

Countertransference proper, in the director of the psychodrama and in the auxiliary psychotherapists, should be examined with regard to its various implications. The director, to be sure, has a very special function in psychodrama. The patient, or group of patients, attempts to establish a privileged relationship with him and he must accept this transference without taking advantage of it or seeking refuge in psychodramatic technique to avoid giving verbal interpretations.

Similarly, the group of cotherapists must beware of countertransferential reactions that might better be termed transferential vis-à-vis the director. When a team is well synchronized, many a problem can be avoided by varying the functions of the therapists as the team goes from one patient or group of patients to another, so that each therapist in turn may serve in the capacity of director.

In attempting to define the ideal attitude of the psychodramatist as therapist, two points must be noted: Like any therapist, the psychodramatist should identify himself with the situations that come to light and consequently he should be able to maintain an open attitude, similar to the psychoanalyst's free-floating attention recommended by Freud; at the same time, the psychodramatist should take any role and accept any situation that the successive projections of the patients may call for. The exigencies of psychodramatic therapy are demanding and somewhat contradictory, requiring both presence and discreet effacement.

Psychotherapists may be acutely self-conscious due to their lack of experience or the difficult nature of certain cases. This can result in technical conduct detrimental to the patients, when therapists perform, no longer for their patients, but for their cotherapists, seeking their colleagues' approval. Briefly, the ideal attitude of auxiliary psychotherapists could be summed up as follows: On the technical level, they should be capable of playing the diverse roles demanded of them as convincingly as possible; at the same time, they should be able to afford the patients a basis of identification for the various imagos that may be encompassed in a single person, so the patients' fantasies and defense mechanisms can be brought to light.

In psychodrama, patients generally sense the underlying attitude of the therapists to a greater degree than in any other form of psychotherapy. The psychoanalyst is, after all, protected — or at any rate there is a chance he may seek protection — in his armchair, where his patient cannot see him. In any kind of group psychotherapy, however, the therapist is exposed to the patient's view (Grotjahn, 1953). In psychodrama, the situation is intensified by the fact that the therapist is not passive, immobile, and silent; he must make his presence felt by participating in the performance.

We must now turn our attention to the effects of the therapists' attitude on the progress of psychodramatic treatment. Fenichel (1945) has stated that a psychoanalyst should never play the role of his patient. It so happens that in psychodrama the therapist must take part, and we might define his position by saying: play he must, but without playing the game of the patient. The function of the psychotherapists is not fulfilled by merely performing the scenes the patients request. Although they should always respect the patients' wishes and the defenses activated by these wishes, the therapists' primary concern should be to confront the patients with their resistances. Here the art of the psychotherapist lies in creating veritable shortcuts through dramatic activity, thus proving his intuition and opening up fertile ground for therapeutic progress. In fact, it is the conduct of the auxiliary therapists that enables the director to fulfill his interpretative function. They are not limited to either playing whatever the patients wish or refusing to do so; different situations and different circumstances lead the psychotherapists to adapt their attitude to the demands of their patients and to introduce new behavior patterns through the shortcut of psychodrama.

The make-believe aspect of psychodrama also intervenes to determine the psychotherapists' conduct and thereby influence the evolution of the therapeutic process. There are, to be sure, situations that are easy to play, and their performance is not at all hindered by the therapeutic setting. For example, when a patient wants to reenact a game of tennis or some incident that takes place in a car, train, or plane, it is easily done despite the lack of props and scenery. On the other hand, as soon as one begins to deal with situations more deeply suffused with the fantasy life of patients — and this is often the case in group psychotherapy — problems concerning the attitude of the psychotherapists make it much more difficult to perform the proposed scenes. It is a fact that patients incorporate the most diverse behavior of psychotherapists into the portrayal of their fantasies. If one knows how importantly the imaginary representation of a scene from early experience, such as sexual relations between parents, figures in the fantasy life of the patients, one can understand that very often it is appropriate to introduce that theme, which involves guilt associated with sexual curiosity as well as frustration at being excluded from that privileged relationship. The transferential energy displaced onto psychotherapists is such that they need only appear to retire from the psychodramatic stage and stand side by side for patients to immediately incorporate this behavior into the context of their early experience; their reactions then express the effects of this fantasy on personality integration.

One can see that in our view psychodrama should go far beyond the confines of realism. The crux of the matter lies in making different patients actually live and relive emotional situations. From this standpoint, the physical aspects of a therapist are less important than his ability to directly influence the situation, not only by performing the proposed scenes realistically, but also by systematically refusing to follow paths of regression and resistance, and, ultimately, by maintaining the appropriate underlying attitude that makes it possible to reconstruct past experiences, to bring into play the fantasies and also the defense mechanisms that express the character structure of each of the patients.

Psychodrama and Regression

One might think that psychodrama would create almost insurmountable problems in regression. In fact, many psychotherapists who do not practice psychodrama or who criticize it categorically consider such acting to be regressive per se. They think of it as a strictly infantile activity, located on a very primitive level as compared with more highly developed verbal activity; consequently, in their opinion, all psychodrama falls within the realm of acting out and any psychodramatic activity is but resistance vis-a-vis verbal activity. We have shown that psychodrama is nothing of the sort and that acting is by no means a regressive mode of expression. It would become so only if the therapists' attitude were to encourage regression. It is not hard to imagine such a situation arising when therapists with little aptitude for psychodrama see in it merely action without meaning.

Psychodrama, like any psychoanalytic therapy, does, however, permit controlled regressions within the therapeutic setting and sanctions their examination and interpretation. The fact is that in many cases psychodramatic activity seems to enable patients to express their regressive desires and actions more easily and clearly. The more freely and fully these regressions are expressed, the better they are gratified. This perspective is necessary in order to understand a good many of the positive effects of all sorts of physical contact, which we have already discussed in terms of variations, limits, and significance.

Regression occurring in psychodrama may, however, also be a manifestation of resistance. Quite frequently, in fact, one observes that patients propose regressive activities in order to avoid, by virtue of the obstacles created by transference, other more mature types of interpersonal relations with the therapists. It is particularly striking to see how often patients, even adolescents and adults, suggest themes that entail eating together. They are thereby not only expressing their fantasized conception of the privileged relations between adults, they are also evading other, more anxiety-provoking contacts with the attending therapists. In view of this, it is interesting to note that maladapted transference on the part of certain therapists is also translated into activities that are regressive in nature.

With allowance made for those regressions that are expressed in any type of therapy, psychodrama included, it can be said that the psychodramatic method permits the therapist to treat regression as resistance and refuse to satisfy it, in the manner of the psychoanalyst who refuses to go along with regression as his patient would have him do. The truth of the matter is that acting is by no means inherently regressive and, as we observed in the first section, one cannot help but be impressed by the intensity with which patients enter into the make-believe of psychodrama. They participate in it without resorting to jest or mockery, which they would be bound to do if they thought of themselves as spectators at the theater or indulgent adults watching children play games that they themselves would not venture to join.

Notes on Techniques in Dramatic Group Psychoanalysis

We use the term dramatic group psychoanalysis to designate a specific type of group therapy in which the treatment of a group of patients usually entails the participation of a group of psychotherapists. Experience has led us to limit the number of participants to five or six patients, whatever their age, and two or three psychotherapists, both sexes being represented. One of the psychotherapists acts as director, getting the session under way, bringing the performance to a halt, and offering interpretations. In many of our experiments, these therapeutic functions were handled by a team of two psychotherapists, one male and one female.

The patients are first asked what they would like to act out. Children always enter into a psychodramatic session as if it were a real game. With older adolescents and adults, however, it takes longer to develop a theme of departure. The story that emerges should be general enough to concern everyone and yet remain sufficiently concrete so that none of its meaning is lost.

At times it is not easy for the patients to come up with a theme. In certain cases no one will say a word, while in others one particular patient will monopolize the floor at the beginning of every session, not without causing a most characteristic group reaction. In seizing the initiative, this individual evokes apparent complaisance on the part of the other patients; they are obviously uninterested in his proposals, and yet they profess complete agreement with what they have scarcely heard. This passive attitude is a typical manifestation of group resistance and may be viewed as acting in. It would be a mistake to follow the lead of the deviant patient on the pretext that he is making a contribution, for to do so would utterly destroy the group's cohesion. Rather, when such a phenomenon of group resistance is observed, the proper course is to regard that very resistance as the implicitly proposed theme and to suggest dramatizing it. Psychodramatic portrayal of group resistance usually provides very fertile material.

A striking example of group dynamics is found in the dramatic presentation of dreams. This approach may be particularly useful in the early stages of treatment.

Once the theme has been settled upon, each of the patients is asked to choose a role to his own liking, and then the group as a whole is asked to decide which roles the psychotherapists should take. In this distribution of roles, one can perceive different behavior patterns, which vary according to the age of the patients. Child therapy groups usually include a passively acknowledged leader; it is he who suggests the theme and his proposal is accepted with enthusiasm. Among adolescents, the group structure is more complex, the interaction is more highly organized. This is especially evident during the distribution of roles, when certain subjects may choose roles that others do not wish to allot to them. In particular, a patient may take a role that the others obviously intended to assign to a psychotherapist. This same phenomenon occurs among adults, and one can see in it an expression of the group situation and the specific transference developing therein.

When the casting has been completed, the play begins. It is then that the task of the psychotherapists becomes complex. They should serve as a catalyst to the session, while refraining from joining as one with the patients. The therapists' acting must be convincing, as we have already stated, if only so that acting may become the group's mode of expression. They must take careful note of all that happens and yet be most circumspect in their observation; any attitude that hints of a researcher in quest of material is strictly taboo. And all the while the psychotherapists must pay close attention to the group's cohesion, for during a session a group may develop a tendency to split up. Such a division must be considered significant material and should be handled accordingly.

We have cautioned against psychotherapists "playing the game" of their patients, as we say in psychodramatic parlance. Patients, however, may act as psychotherapists in order to give other patients gratification that has been denied. Such substitution has a special import and leads to reorganization of the group.

The psychotherapist directing the treatment is responsible for bringing the performance to a halt, and it is he who has the option of offering interpretations.

Certain attitudes taken by patients require an immediate reaction. The acting in peculiar to psychodrama can often be reduced by the response of the director, who may even go so far as to deliberately ignore the patient; thus, the patient drops out of the performance and his own behavior should bring awareness of the anxiety eliciting this particular mode of defense. Besides, the group itself stands in the way of a fellow patient taking an aloof attitude: each group member reacts so as to prevent any other member from breaking the conventions agreed upon by the group as a whole.

By and large, however, interpretations tend to reduce this kind of behavior. They are usually offered at the end of a session. The crux of this matter lies in observance of the following rule: never give an interpretation that does not apply to the group as a whole. In developing and performing the group drama, each individual has taken part in a way that can be fully explained only with reference to the behavior of the other group members. In those fairly frequent instances when one of the patients polarizes the group, it is appropriate to address that individual directly, clarifying his conduct to him and at the same time showing the others how and why they contributed to his behavior. We should point out here the dilemma involved in utilizing one's knowledge of a patient's past life. It would be absurd to pretend ignorance of such information inasmuch as patients are prone to bring up their life histories in an effort to capture the attention of the therapists and other group members. Therefore, while alluding to a patient's past, it is nonetheless essential to give strictly here-and-now interpretations. In psychodrama, recovery from infantile amnesia does not occur in the classical sense; rather, that process is replaced by working through fantasies shared in common by the group. Reference to the past often arises only tangentially through associations volunteered spontaneously by the patients.

As for the general course of psychodramatic treatment, the progress made by individual group members is very similar to that observed in classical psychoanalytic therapy. There are a certain number of special characteristics, however, that should be noted. In the artificially created social situation of psychodrama, the material is bound to focus on oedipal conflict, while fantasies of a pregenital nature prove to be much more difficult to explore.

One of the problems of group therapy lies in the fact that group members must usually show uniform progress. In psychodrama, however, where the fantasies presented in common are stripped down to basic essentials, it is possible to change the composition of a group if due consideration is given to the frustration reactions that may result from such modification. Contrary to the general rule adhered to in verbal groups, it is not necessary for all the patients in a psychodramatic group to improve at the same rate and be released at the same time. The departure of a patient who has recovered does not disrupt the group. The introduction of new patients, however, can be undertaken only in circumstances that have been very carefully reviewed with the aim of avoiding major reactions of rejection and exclusion.

These observations enable us to clarify the specific therapeutic applicability of group psychodrama. This method makes it possible to deal with the social reactions of individuals insofar as these reactions reflect object-related anxiety. The presentation of fantasies shared by the group in common, that is, the social elaboration of unconscious fantasies held by each member individually, serves a very useful purpose in the psychotherapeutic process.

The requisite research into case histories indicates that dramatic group psychotherapy has yielded beneficial results with respect to children, adolescents, and adults. It is not possible, however, to give a detailed analysis of those results here.

Beyond strictly therapeutic groups, psychodramatic techniques can also be applied to closed groups, or even to institutional or natural groups, particularly when treatment of the audience is contemplated.

The Psychotherapeutic Effect of Psychodrama on the Audience

Every psychodramatic performance has an effect upon the group — on the group of patients and on the group of doctors as well. In closed group psychotherapy it would be impossible to ignore the group dynamics that converge through the channel of mutual identification to a state of group cohesion. Elsewhere, however, psychodrama can have repercussions on the audience, that is, on the more or less structured group of seemingly passive spectators who are present as the play unfolds. This happens frequently in certain exploratory forms of psychodrama undertaken for diagnostic purposes or in certain types of group therapy practiced in institutions. In such cases, identification in the true sense of the word has clear and undeniable effects upon the audience. This phenomenon has its root source in the emotional participation of the spectators. Psychodrama can produce still more striking effects of identification than other types of group therapy, because it evokes problems that are common to the entire group. This is obvious in institutional groups, where individual problems are lived out in common, that is, they are experienced through the reactions, vicissitudes, frustrations, and satisfactions arising from the life in common.

At the risk of being cursory, we would like to distinguish two ways in which psychodrama affects the audience: (1) Certain spectators feel moved to enter into the dramatic action; whether a member of the audience participates actively obviously depends on his imitative response and his reaction to the particular scene being portrayed, but it is also related to his capacity to identify himself with the characters and the situation. Spectators take roles and refrain from doing so according to a dialectical contradiction, which expresses the symptomatic compromise of the moment. (2) The audience as a whole participates in psychodrama emotionally, and a performance may or may not be followed up with discussion.

This is why one can speak of the didactic effect of psychodrama, and it was with this in mind that we thought it useful to examine the techniques of role playing. As we have already stated, in no way does role playing constitute a learning procedure. However, self-expression through role is bound up with the difficulty one has in assuming a particular role, whether that difficulty is due to a real or fantasized situation; therefore, an individual's relationship to the imago of another, made explicit in role, emerges as the real focal point of role playing. One can understand one's own attitude vis-a-vis others only if one is able to identify oneself with others, whether through direct participation in the dramatic action or through indirect participation as a spectator. Every human situation perforce involves interpersonal relations, and learning to identify with others is a continuing necessity. Submission to others and identification with aggressors are but two sides of the same coin; they are both defensive attitudes, and everyone should recognize such behavior patterns in himself.

In this study we wished to place particular emphasis on the theoretical concepts and dynamic principles of psychodrama as it is conducted by psychoanalysts. Our discussion has focused primarily on techniques of group psychodrama; however, we often employ individual psychodrama for treatment of a single patient with the aid of a team of psychodramatists. In examining these various techniques, we have demonstrated their didactic value and, in addition, we have pointed out the advantageous emotional effects of psychodrama on the audience.

Throughout this study, the reader will have perceived that we feel, at least in certain cases, that psychodrama, a special means of expression, can be understood and handled in an adequate manner only by utilizing psychoanalytic concepts. To us it seems that psychoanalytic training is indispensable if the therapeutic process is to be fully comprehended and competently conducted.

One might well ask whether conversely the practice of psychodrama and group psychotherapy has enriched our clinical and theoretical conception of psychoanalysis. This could well be true beyond any doubt, for the scope of our activity has been enlarged to an extent not possible in classical psychoanalysis and we have thus been able to gain insights into the origins of psychosis.

To be more specific as to what we have learned from psychodrama, its extensive countertransferential effects put us on guard against the ways in which we may seek to manipulate our patients. There is no question that this prudence carries over into our psychoanalytic practice.

Finally, in community psychiatric services psychoanalysts are often called upon to contribute their expertise; their familiarity with group psychotherapy and experience in the sphere of psychodrama can be extremely useful in the task of teaching the professional or interprofessional groups assigned to them for training.

REFERENCES

Diatkine, R., Kestemberg, E., & Soccaras, F. (1950), Le transfert en psychotherápie collective. *L'Encephale*, 3:248-274.

Ezriel, H. (1951), The scientific testing of psycho-analytic findings and theory. *Brit. J. Med. Psychol.*, 24:30-34.

Fenichel, O. (1945), *The Psychoanalytic Theory of Neurosis*. New York: Norton.

Foulkes, H. (1957), Conférence au *II e Congrés International De Psychothérapie de Groupe*. Zurich.

Freud, A. (1936), *The Ego and the Mechanisms of Defense*. New York: International Universities Press, rev. ed., 1966.

Grotjahn, M. (1953), Some aspects of countertransference in analytic group psychotherapy. *Internat. J. Psycho-Anal.*, 25:95-101.

Lebovici, S., Diatkine, R. & Kestemberg, E. (1952), Application de la psychoanalyse a la psychoanalyse de groupe et à la psychothérapie dramatique en France. *Evolution Psychiatrique*, 3:397-412.

——— ——— ——— (1958). Bilan de dix ans de therapeutique par le psychodrame chez l'enfant et l'adolescent. *Psychiatr. Enfant.*,1:63-180.

Moreno, J. L. (1953), *Foundations of Sociometry*. Beacon, New York: Beacon House.

Slavson, S. R. (1950), *Analytic Group Psychotherapy with Children, Adolescents and Adults*. New York: Columbia University Press.

10

Analytic Group Psychotherapy with the Aged

JACK D. KRASNER

"What is to become of us?" This question is often heard from the young adult as well as older persons and frequently manifests the apprehension of growing old, the fear of aging, accompanied by the anticipation of the loss of vitality, mobility, and potency. This is a result of the very negative outlook for the elder person.

Modern science has improved living conditions so that longevity has been significantly increased. Octogenarians are increasing in number; living to the age of ninety is no longer unusual. Continued advances in biological sciences have resulted in the prolongation of life, and the day will soon arrive when reaching the age of 100 will be very common. Although frightening to some, this increase in age offers to individuals an opportunity for continued productivity and achievement. Contradictory feelings have arisen as to whether the increase in longevity is a blessing or a curse. Is humanity to be benefited from the experience of these elderly people or is the younger generation going to be saddled with the maintenance of useless human beings? The answer is yet to be determined and will be greatly influenced by what the biological, social, economic, and political scientists do to promote utilization of this potential wealth.

The American culture, not too differently from the European

Dr. Krasner is President, Group Psychotherapy Foundation; Associate Professor, Graduate Division of Pastoral Counselling, Iona College, New Rochelle, N.Y.

and the Asian, has developed with a pessimistic view for the older person. This competitive society has always fostered the idea that progress is restricted to the young. The elderly person, more and more, is being shelved because he is no longer productive to the family or to the company. There is a tendency for children to rebel against parents as being "old fogies." In the labor market and business world, professionals and other skilled workers usually have a forced retirement at the age of sixty-five. The spread of these attitudes has had tremendous influence in forcing older people to accept the role of pseudo-uselessness, sometimes even resulting in premature senility. Modification of society's destructive attitude toward the potential availability of the older person may be brought about by an overall educational and rehabilitative program. This program may include education and rehabilitation of the elderly person to function maximally and also make the general public aware of how to utilize the available potentialities. A program has already been initiated in the form of "Golden Age" clubs and several studies involving economic, social, medical, and psychological means of aiding the elderly. This beginning can be furthered by the leadership of those who have the courage and are willing to lend their energies to understanding the problems and values of this age group.

Psychotherapeutic Help

The increase in longevity has exposed many problem areas related to the mental health of the elderly. The major emotional problems of the older person appear to be a perpetuation of earlier conflicts. The exacerbation of these conflicts in the age group results from the decomposition of early defense mechanisms — reaction formation, compensation, etc. During this latter period of life, the process of aging brings on increasing feelings of dependency, as a result of cultural attitudes that tend to remove older persons from previous physical and mental activities. This restriction of activity very often provokes and reactivates early feelings of inadequacy. When unable to find ego support, the older person may either withdraw and become an isolate or seek physical ailments as a means of contact with others. The withdrawn older person frequently develops a lethargic condition manifesting symptoms that are also characteristic of senility. These symptoms, because of the person's age, are often misinterpreted as organic deterioration.

Interest in the psychological problems that afflict the aged has mounted. Many investigators have begun to report their findings with an emphasis on the origins of such disturbances and methods of aiding these previously neglected people (Busse, 1955; Ebaugh, 1956; Kopits, 1970; Wayne, 1955; Pfeiffer et al., 1968). The method of coping with these emotional problems has been limited essentially to environmental manipulation. Attempts have been made to help the older person to accept restricted activity and to guide him in limited pursuits (Fink et al., 1969). There are also reports of efforts to utilize psychotherapeutic techniques to aid this age group to resolve its emotional problems (Goldfarb, 1955). The psychotherapeutic approach has been tried in both individual (Gronewald, 1956) and group settings (Grotjahn, 1955). Most of these group efforts are socially oriented in an effort to make available participation in group activities, e.g., Golden Age clubs. The group therapy process has also been utilized in institutional settings (Kahn, Fisher, and Lieberman, 1969). However, scrutiny of the literature and verbal communications reveal that psychotherapy actually plays a small part in the total therapeutic endeavor. Linden (1953, 1955, 1956) has described various transferential relationships and their use in determining diagnosis and treatment progress. Goldfarb (1955) has recommended a course of treatment which closely resembles guidance and counseling. Rosen (in a group psychotherapy society panel discussion) has referred to the "Smith Remotivation Technique," which has been tried in Pennsylvania hospitals for the aged. The latter technique appears to be another form of group activity participation.

The writer has worked intensively with older people for over a decade in private practice, in an outpatient clinic of a general hospital and in an outpatient mental health center. In an effort to evaluate and determine more effective psychotherapeutic procedures and techniques, this age group has been seen in several different settings: individual psychotherapy, a mixed group which included young adults, a group limited to a minimum age of sixty, and combined individual and group psychotherapy. Psychotherapeutic experience with this age group has shown that transference problems that arise are time-consuming and difficult to work through. In individual psychotherapy, the initial transference is usually negative. Most often, the patient experiences the therapist as "child" upon whom he is forced to depend. When initially placed in a psychotherapy group with younger persons, most older patients assume a role of the parental figure and need to prove themselves a "good" parent. This rigid role thwarts the development of other transferential relationships as well as placing the older person in a defensive position. In these settings, the patient may be confronted with persons whom he experiences as trying to destroy him, i.e., deprive him of his rightful role in society. Any critical response is experienced as rejection and often results in hostile aggression and/or withdrawal. Grotjahn (1955) also has reported similar experiences. He theorizes that the neuroses of old age are defenses against castration anxiety, that advancing age tends to shatter the illusion of eternal youth. He also stresses the importance of having to work through the parent-patient relationship to the child-therapist. The writer has found that these phenomena and the intense, related negative effects are more readily worked through in a homogeneous group setting. Thus, although varying degrees of success have been attained in all settings, continued experience has shown that the psychotherapy of choice for these patients is to place the patient initially in a psychotherapy group homogeneous with respect to age.

A major psychotherapeutic force of the group process is to confront the patient with reality. A group limited in age range has the advantage that each person feels himself to be among his peers, rather than as a "good" or "bad" parental figure with the younger people in the group or as the inept parent leaning on the "child" in individual sessions. The acceptance of the older person by others permits the acceptance of his own needs as something other than weakness. He is afforded the opportunity to accept others and to relate with them interdependently. He is then in a better position to express his needs and to take from and give to others. This process results in the increase of ego strength, enabling the patient to better express his needs and seek satisfaction outside the therapeutic situation.

The multiple transference phenomena provided in the psychotherapeutic group setting allow more rapid uncovering and analysis of experienced overwhelming anxiety produced by repressed conflicts. The interaction among the members within the group elicits and more readily exhibits the manifestations of the characteristic defenses that have become life patterns with each individual. The author and Marks (1966) have reported their evaluation of the precipitating factors that result in patients' seeking psychotherapy at age sixty or older. This report reveals that each person had experienced a threat of separation or actual loss of an important figure. The real or phantasized threat of an object loss tended to reactivate an archaic threat experienced during the infantile oral phase of psychosexual development. The experienced or anticipated adverse life situation that created the threat varied widely, e.g., death of a parent, spouse, or lover; loss of a job; marriage of a child. Continued analysis of the symbolic meaning of the separating object revealed the presence of unconscious, intense oral dependency. There was an experience of intense anxiety related to feelings of anticipated annihilation, which would result from the loss of the source of nurture. The investigators found that the intensity of the anxiety appeared to be related to the degree of deterioration of previously developed mechanisms. During their lifetime, these older persons had developed patterns of living that tended to temper the anxiety-provoking threat of annihilation through separation. The defense pattern incorporated many different forms of behavior. Some persons attempted to gratify their dependency needs by developing an acquiescent, subservient role to nurturing figures; some projected their dependency needs onto the nurturing object, e.g., they would maintain a bond with the rationalization that the parental figure could not possibly exist without them. Others would identify with the succoring object, e.g., experiencing gratification by supplying, and sometimes, even forcing gratification of needs they had projected onto the child object. Still others attempted to cope with this threat by denial, and in so doing, assumed a role of complete independence. As these individuals respectively tend to reach and approach the later years of life, the prior effectiveness of their defense mechanisms tends to diminish, resulting in reactivation of the early threat, exacerbation of anxiety, and the appearance of related symptomatology.

It is the author's belief that personality reconstruction in the older person can be brought about through group psychotherapy, analytic in orientation and in a group specifically confined to this age range. This contention is strikingly in variance with a commonly held and certainly less optimistic view with which psychotherapy of these older persons has been regarded. Based upon years of experience with such a psychotherapeutic group, the author hopes to demonstrate a new and productive approach to the problem of the reconstructive psychotherapy of the elderly, heretofore regarded with undue pessimism.

In planning a reconstructive psychotherapy group, the therapist believed that psychoanalytic procedures should be utilized. From the beginning of the treatment, a nonauthoritarian approach was taken. There was no attempt to manipulate the environment or to place restrictions upon the patients' reactions in the group sessions. The therapist fostered an accepting, psychotherapeutic attitude towards the group members' needs and conflicts as an individual within the group constellation. The treatment plan and direction of therapy were as follows:

1. Establishment of psychotherapeutic relationships within the group setting by means of an accepting attitude by the therapist and transmission of this attitude to the group members.
2. Ego strengthening and support by offering understanding to present difficulties and focusing on the positive.
3. Activation of transference relationships and the relating of feelings and associations.
4. Focusing and analysis of resistances.
5. Focusing and analysis of acting out.
6. Surfacing, analyzing, and working through of early conflictual material by analysis and interpretation of dreams, transferential relationships.
7. The establishment and experiencing of new values and like

experiences within the group, which may be utilized in outside situations.

Prior to entering the group, each patient may be seen in individual sessions. The individual sessions are utilized to get acquainted and establish a therapeutic relationship with the elderly. The patients are encouraged to discuss the major problems that precipitated their seeking treatment; familial, social, and professional constellations and relationships; life patterns from early childhood to the present. Questions about psychotherapy and the group process may be explored in an enlightening, nonthreatening manner. This informal, empathic setting tends to foster a therapeutic relationship, and the patient may be motivated for psychoanalytic group psychotherapy. Although this motivational process is frequently accomplished in one session, it may be more propitious to see some patients in individual sessions over an extended period of time. After the patient has accepted group psychotherapy as the treatment of choice, he is assigned to and asked to attend group sessions. The psychotherapy groups of this age range, in which the writer has been therapist or supervisor, have always met for one and a half hours once a week. There have been no scheduled pre-, post- or alternate sessions, i.e., sessions where the therapist was not present. However, when occasions arise where the therapist is unable to attend a weekly session, the group is asked to meet without the leader. The occasional meetings of the group without the therapist do not disrupt the continuity of the therapeutic process. Actually, they may add another dimension — some patients may feel more free to express reactions, either positive or negative, which previously they have been unable to verbalize, or sometimes even experience, in the presence of the therapist.

The psychotherapeutic results of having persons over sixty in a psychoanalytic group setting are generally very good. This is especially true when the patients' initial group experience is in a homogeneous age group. In over a decade of experience, the writer has had only one complete failure, and this occurred in the first few years of work with this age group. Reevaluation of this therapeutic failure has revealed that the cause may be attributed to the therapist's lack of knowledge and understanding at that time and not to the patients' inability to benefit from the group psychotherapy. As a result of experimental zeal, the therapist prematurely put the patient in the group, rather than providing sufficient individual sessions to gain a more comprehensive understanding and establish a good therapeutic relationship. Many examples of the positive therapeutic effects may be illustrated. The writer will limit the illustrations to (1) the therapeutic progress of a male in his early sixties who has been in a group for two years and (2) the therapeutic progress of a group, including individual psychodynamics, group interaction, group psychodynamics, multiple transference, and psychotherapeutic change.

The Elderly in Group Psychotherapy

An Illustrative Case History. Carl is a white male in his early sixties who applied for therapy because of "depression, anxiety, shaking." He added: "I am disturbed by the fact that I want to return to my ex-wife and we broke up again. I lost my job, I get nervous and upset . . . At the age of fifty-two, I fell in love with a widow. She was forty with two grown sons. I was a bachelor for many years. She pressed the marriage. Suddenly, she backed away, and she met a man while she was away in Florida on a trip. I took it badly . . . We got together. I felt she was on the rebound from another man. She wanted again to marry . . . My wife left me for another man now." Patient was diagnosed as reactive depression with somatic symptomatology. He was seen individually for two sessions then placed in a psychotherapy group.

During the first several months of therapy, Carl's reaction in the group was primarily limited to expression of his irritability, nervousness, and inability to work. As the sessions continued, it became evident that a major secondary motivation for remaining in therapy was to be labeled "helpless." He applied to an insurance company for "total disability" benefits and requested that his therapist confirm this position. The therapist offered to submit the diagnostic evaluation, but refused to confirm Carl's hopeless prognosis.

Although he reacted with initial intense resentment, Carl experienced ego support from the therapist's optimistic prognostic evaluation. He began to explore job opportunities, accepted part-time positions, which, in the past, would have been considered below his deserved standards. He then sought out and encouraged a nephew to join him in partnership and took over a concession at a New York State resort community.

After the summer holidays, Carl informed the group that the partnership with his nephew had broken up on an unhappy note. He had asserted himself and had expressed his resentment toward the nephew's crude and exploitative behavior. When he discussed this experience with the group, he was able to see in the nephew traits of which he had not been conscious in the past.

Encouraged by the group, Carl got a job canvasing advertisements for a union magazine. He began developing more ego strength as a result of his newfound financial independence, and was able to cope effectively with an erratic supervisor.

While visiting his sister in a small town approximately fifty miles from New York during the summer, Carl had met and developed a close relationship with a widow, Mary, who was twenty years his junior. It was interesting to note that Mary also had two children, but younger than those of his ex-wife. During the fall, he made frequent visits to his sister, which enhanced his opportunity to further the relationship with Mary. He described to the group the satisfaction he derived from his sexual relationship with Mary and how he was becoming closely involved with her everyday life and her problems. In the group discussions, he expressed empathy with Mary and described the financial difficulty she had in supporting herself and two children on a relatively low income. The children had manifested emotional problems and the older boy had been placed in psychotherapy. Carl believed that Mary also had been drawn into therapy because of the son. In an effort to please Mary, and in so doing, become indispensable to her, Carl became more and more involved with the children. Although he had experienced initial feelings of irritation, he began to develop affection and fondness for them. He began to perceive that the children were lonely and did not experience or receive the affection they wanted from the mother. He also mentioned that the mother seemed cold and impatient and often considered the children a burden. While describing the "familial" relationship, Carl began to evaluate Mary's personality and her capacity for love.

As the therapy progressed, Carl began more and more to appraise his relationship with Mary in a more realistic fashion. He became increasingly aware of her unresolved dependency needs, immaturity, and emotional instability. When he spoke of his relationship with Mary, he described her attempts to dominate and demean him. Although he was beginning to see others' exploitative use of him, he continued to rationalize the abusive attitudes toward him. He ascribed Mary's behavior to her "nervousness, insecurity, and lack of experience in handling many converging problems she had to face." He said that she wanted security and marriage to a man who could support her and the children. He had told her of his inadequate financial situation and discussed the difference in their ages. When the group stressed that Carl was trapped in this relationship by his intense need for affection and acceptance, he initially defended himself by denial and reaction formation. In turn, the group persisted in an effort to aid Carl in developing his acute, realistic perception of Mary as a person; the working through and working out processes gradually continued and Carl became aware of his transferential reaction to Mary. "I treat her the way I used to treat my mother. I have a warm feeling for her. I want to make her comfortable, but I'm angry at her when she criticizes me." As a result of his understanding and increasing ego strength, Carl began to affect a more assertive role with Mary. On occasions when she attempted to dominate and demean him in the presence of friends, he would parry her attacks and "put her in her place." The change in his behavior resulted in anxiety-arousing situations, but there was no move on his part to separate from her. His need to be nurtured and sheltered by a mothering figure was still strong and the sexual relationship was too gratifying to abandon without replacement. During the group sessions, he continued his attempts to justify her ambivalence and unpredictable behavior towards him. "She likes me a great deal . . . needs to depend on me . . . she is very much under the influence of her mother and friends who keep talking about our differences in age . . . and how our relationship will never really work out because of my low income." He questioned what would happen in ten years when he would be over seventy and she would just be reaching fifty. In evaluating the situation, he once again was faced with an unavailable female. As the relationship persisted, Carl became very critical of her bad manners, vanity, materialistic approach to life and lack of decisiveness. He began to feel that her attraction to him was based on her need for sexual satisfaction. He was the only person who had ever gratified her sexual drives. During the interaction of the group, he became cognizant of the attributes that might contribute to a good relationship, i.e., his capacity for affection, kindness, and consideration and his sense of humor. The group members, particularly the women, emphasized that his behavior manifested a need to attach himself to "attractive, blond women," who would eventually reject him. At this time, the therapeutic direction for Carl was to build up self-esteem. The group utilized his relationship with Mary to illustrate his effectiveness, which, in turn, enhanced his feelings of masculinity.

Carl's ego strength continued to increase and he soon began to clash with Mary. He openly expressed his anger when she tried to conceal his age from her friends, would not disclose his occupation or income, objected to his interests in his family or became overly possessive. During the group sessions, he focused on evaluating the positives and negatives, as well as future outcome of their relationship. "Even if she decides to marry me on an impulse, I wouldn't do it." He became increasingly aware of the maternal role Mary symbolized for him, i.e., the ambivalent feelings he had towards his mother — strong dependency needs, coupled with intense anger at having to subjugate his own wishes in return for acceptance and affection. As a result of increased understanding and ego development, he began to wean himself from Mary. The separation was devoid of the anxiety and depression experienced as a result of parting from his wife. In the group sessions, he expressed empathy for Mary and manifested understanding for her needs. Although he continued to correspond with her, he persisted in declining her invitations to visit, even when she appealed to his affection for the children. Limiting his involvement with Mary, Carl initiated and participated in a number of social activities; he attended social gatherings for single people, meeting and dating and visiting several women whom he liked. He developed ability to relate to women with ease and enhanced as well as reinforced his ego strength. Carl's growth and development also became manifested in his occupational pursuits. In seeking advancement, he found a job opening with an urban renewal development project. He studied for and passed a qualifying examination and was immediately hired as a district manager at a relatively good salary with possibilities for advancement.

Reexamination of the analytic group process, i.e., working within the transference and multiple transference relationships, revealed the forces enabling Carl's psychotherapeutic progress.

After working through his initial anxiety related to his need for acceptance, Carl interacted with the group freely and spontaneously. He experienced the group in transference with his family; understanding and acceptance by the other members enabled Carl to disagree with them and to assert himself. These were reactions he could never allow himself to have in his own nuclear family. He expressed many positive feelings for one of the women (Gladys), whom he saw as his long-suffering mother. Another female group member (Betty) provoked intense, underlying resentment, which he had originally experienced from his silently demanding mother. He identified another female member, Ruth, as his helpless sister, who was unable to bring about changes. The fourth female, Alice, was symbolically experienced as his seductive, unavailable former wife, as well as his mother, whose affection he continually, but unsuccessfully, sought. The strongest multiple-transference relationship was to a male group member (Harry), in whom he saw his irascible, rejecting father, and at times, his younger brother, with whom he was an unsuccessful rival for his mother's affection. He anticipated, sometimes provoked, and always reacted to Harry's exploitative view of sexual relationships with women with intense hostility, reminiscent of the feelings for his father, who abused his mother.

The transference relationship to the therapist (female) was a strong, dependent attachment to "mother." Overt, emotional reactions were limited to positive feelings expressing extreme gratefulness "for all the help" given. Even when the therapist attempted to provoke and surface the negative feelings against which he was defending himself, Carl was unable to express any hostility. With the continuing development of ego strength, gradual, persistent stress was placed on his increased capacity to express feelings. After a period of a few months, he was finally able to chance disagreement with the therapist. An occasion arose when the therapist made a remark to the effect that Carl was trying to prove his love to Mary by becoming "a good uncle" to the children. He reacted with intense anger. Following the session, he wrote a letter full of apologies. At the next session, he again apologized. Apprehension of becoming independent of the nurturing mother figure had set in. He became frightened of losing the source of possible gratification for his dependency needs. Continued interaction within the transferential relationships provided an opportunity for Carl to see that the expression of anger did not destroy "mother" or even significantly modify their relationship.

Carl's outstanding attributes were manifested in his eagerness to explore his feelings, his receptivity to new ideas expressed in the group and his readiness to examine these. He worked through his mother relationship to Mary. He evinced his independence and his self-direction and became more aware and capable of expressing both positive and negative feelings. Above all, he demonstrated a developing, increased capacity for reality testing. As Carl spoke of it in the group, he felt that therapy helped him to overcome his depression and understand the unresolved mother conflicts involved in his relationship to his wife. Group therapy process enabled him to establish new and realistic relationships with women, while fostering the development of self-direction and productivity. At the time of writing, Carl expressed "a new feeling of freedom—there is a lifting of spirit, a sense of newfound joy in life."

Carl's psychotherapeutic progress is no exception. It is typical of the effects that can be obtained in a homogeneous, age-range psychotherapy group. The personality development and characterological changes illustrated, however, should not be taken as an indication that group psychotherapy, even in a homogeneous age group, is a panacea for all persons over sixty who suffer from emotional disturbances. A patient's entering into a group does not automatically establish a psychotherapeutic relationship between him and the therapist. It is most important, actually essential, that the patient understand the psychotherapeutic *contract* between himself and the therapist. This contract includes the patient's investment of time, energy, and agreed-upon monetary fees (the author has found that the payment of monetary fees is not *always* an essential for psychotherapeutic progress). In exchange for the therapist's knowledge, effort, and time to aid the patient in bringing about beneficial changes, resulting in a more constructive and fulfilling life, the contract also includes the patient's willingness to attend the group therapy sessions throughout the course of treatment. Although it is not essential to explain every aspect of the group therapy process, it is both good therapy and advantageous for the therapist to clarify and reassure the patient regarding some of his possible reactions during the initial phase of group therapy. As occurs in all age ranges, the older person may experience discomfort and feel that "I don't fit in with this group of people." Upon entering the group, he should be made aware that there are individual differences and that some people take several sessions before "fitting in" with the other group members. It is also essential that the patient understand the importance of his reactions to other members in the group. It is a good procedure on the part of the therapist to be available and let his availability be known, so that the patient may seek him out if unable to verbalize intense, anxiety-provoking reactions in the group situation. If the therapeutic contract is not clarified and accepted by the patient, it is very likely that a lack of early adaptation or adjustment to the group therapy process will result in the patient's flight. The therapeutic effects may also vary, depending upon the individual patient's needs, desires and aspirations. Some patients enter into therapy with the exclusive, limited goal of reducing their anxiety, which is manifested by "nervousness" or "depression."

There are some who seek to work out familial conflicts with spouse or children; a few, even though past sixty, experience frustration and seek to bring about personality changes leading to more optimal utilization of their potential and satisfactory fulfillment of constructive aspirations. The therapeutic progress of each patient will depend to a greater or lesser degree upon his respective goals, preparation for group psychotherapy, and acceptance of the psychotherapeutic contract.

Profile of a Therapy Group. Perhaps the best illustration of the possible effects of group psychotherapy with both positive and negative manifestations with older people is to review such a group from its inception and over a period of years. This particular group, homogeneous in relationship to age range, was initiated in 1956 and introduced a gerontological program in a community mental health center. The patients involved were referred by physicians, relatives, social agencies, and other sources who had learned of this new psychotherapeutic program. The only qualifications or restrictions were age (patient must be at least in mid-fifties) and that the patient was willing to accept group psychotherapy as the treatment modality. The group was initiated and has continued up to the time of writing as an ongoing, open group (patient members entering or leaving or completing their therapy at any time). Some time after its inception, the group became part of a training program. The author, the first therapist, was with the group for about three years. The group has since had several therapists, each, with one exception, remaining with the group for one or more years. The author has continued to maintain contact with the group, usually in a supervisory capacity. At the time of writing, all of the initial members of the group, again with one exception, have terminated therapy. One of the original members has remained in the group over nine years. Although this may appear to be a long period of time, the patient, Jack, has continued to make significant progress, which has warranted the time and effort spent.

The patients to be discussed will include the eight initial members who entered the group during the first few months of its formation. These patients were all voluntary and had been referred by physician, friend, relative, or social agency. They were representative of a cross-section of the middle socioeconomic population. The vocational areas represented included: college professor, bookkeeper, engineer, nurse, business woman, window cleaner. All group members were, or had been, active in some business or profession. As previously mentioned, selection of patients for the group was limited only by age and the patient's acceptance of group therapy as a means of help. The initial age range was from mid-fifties to the mid-sixties. Also, each of these patients had been referred for psychological tests and complete physical examinations before entering the group.

The group began with four members — Bill, Jack, Mabel, and Hilda.

Bill was in his early sixties, unemployed and twice divorced. Very little information could be obtained about the estrangement of his first marriage. The second marriage was arranged for him (very probably by a marriage broker) and he accepted with the idea that he would be taken care of by this woman. The second marriage terminated when the wife could no longer accept his complete dependency upon her. He had formerly owned a window-cleaning business, but was unable to continue on his own or to seek other employment after losing some of his customers. Past episodes of depression had been treated with electroconvulsive therapy. He was referred for treatment by his son, who felt that the father might become more active through psychotherapy. Psychological tests results revealed characteristics of senility with a diagnosis of organic psychosis and a prognosis of "he will soon be helpless enough to need the supervision of a home for the aged."

Jack, an engineer employed by a municipal government, had been a childless widower who remarried in his mid-fifties. This second marriage occurred after his physician had informed him that his acute abdominal reactions would be helped by "seeking the aid of a psychiatrist or marry this woman." The marriage was marked by continual strife and at the time he sought treatment, Jack had separated from his second wife. The clinical diagnostic impression during the initial interview was "anxiety reaction in a passive-aggressive personality." The psychological test results, however, "suggested the presence of a paranoid, schizoid disorder . . . the quality and level of intellectual and emotional impairment are also suggestive of the possibility of some organic disorder, if not lesional, then perhaps on a vascular basis."

Mabel, a housewife in her late fifties, also worked with her husband in a manufacturing business. She had two sons, one in his mid-twenties, the other in his late thirties. Her older son had been divorced twice and was, at the beginning of her group treatment, engaged to be married for the third time. Mabel had undergone one year's psychotherapy approximately twenty years prior to her being seen for group therapy. As a young mother, she had become frightened when handling knives. The thought of hurting her children had become so intense that she sought treatment. The present reasons for seeking psychotherapy were complaints of vaginal stirrings associated with sexual anxiety and guilt when in the presence of a male, regardless of age, color, or race. The clinical diagnosis was "anxiety state and a passive-aggressive personality." The psychological test results were interpreted as "borderline schizophrenia on the brink of a psychotic outbreak," with a "bad" prognosis.

Hilda was in her mid-sixties and was employed as a senior bookkeeper for a labor organization. She had been divorced for over twenty years and had one living child, a thirty-three-year old daughter. Her married life had been fraught with conflict, finally ending in separation from the husband, whom she characterized as a psychopath. Approximately twenty years ago, a son, age ten, was killed by a fall from an apartment building window. She had had intermittent psychotherapy sessions since 1944 at a psychosomatic clinic in a general hospital. She applied for treatment at this time because of asthmatic attacks and also because she felt withdrawn and was unable to effect close relationships with people. She anticipated retiring from work soon and hoped, with retirement, to be able to enjoy this period of life. She was having intense conflicts and overt battles with her daughter, who she felt was self-destructive. A clinical overview led to a diagnosis of "passive-aggressive personality, psychophysiological reaction (asthma)." Her reactions on the psychological tests suggested "borderline schizophrenia with paranoid trends."

Bill left the group after a few sessions. Agnes, Joan and Henry joined the group soon afterwards. Lila joined the group a few months later.

Joan was a housewife in her mid-fifties. She was reared in a home with many children. The mother became ill during Joan's early youth, leaving the responsibility of rearing the brothers and sisters to her. She felt overwhelmed with the burden and felt an obligation to assume the mother role and was never able to satisfy any childhood feelings or desires. The constant and continual feelings of having to "give" while never experiencing "receiving" resulted in intense resentment. She had a son in his early thirties who had become engaged and who was planning to marry in the near future. She experienced the son as the only possession that was hers alone, and his marriage represented complete loss and anticipated desolation. This loss resulted in depression and suicide attempts. Psychological tests evaluated her as follows: "At present, patient appears to be at a precarious balance, where she seeks support in order to retain contact with reality, but which she finds difficulty to accept."

Agnes was a married, childless woman in her mid-fifties, who had continued her profession as a registered nurse. She was the younger of two female siblings born in Russia. The parents appear to have favored the older sister, leaving her to fend more or less for herself. As a teenager, Agnes was sent to the U.S. to live with relatives. She studied nursing, became interested and active in what might be considered avant-garde activities and lived what she described a "bohemian" life. She lived with her husband for some time before getting married. She had no desire to be married but felt forced into matrimony by her husband, who threatened to commit suicide if she did not marry him. She had been diagnosed as "passive-aggressive personality" and received intermittent psychotherapy from 1948 to 1953, either in mental health clinics or privately. She sought treatment at this time because she was unable to concentrate on her work, "feelings of depression . . . feelings of inferiority," and a panic reaction that she associated with an inability to relate to, or gain sexual satisfaction, with her husband. A Rorschach examination administered in 1948 revealed "although paranoid tendencies are strong, there is still sufficient contact with reality to mitigate against a psychotic withdrawal. The present trend in the intellectual activity is on an obsessive level apparently. Anxiety, at times, may amount to panic, but generally, it is fairly well controlled by neurotic defense mechanisms."

Henry was a married man in his mid-fifties who had two married daughters. His history revealed a lifelong pattern of functioning in a very compliant manner. He felt that through compliance, his dependency needs might be satisfied. His marriage was centered on his wife, who not only dominated the family, but also appeared to have been the driving force in his business. His only feelings of "adequacy" were experienced in the relationship to his children during their youth. When the children married and began to assume their own individuality and independence, Henry felt that he no longer had any control or power. His only feelings of ego strength appeared to be derived from the children's dependency upon and acquiescence to him. He had been a retail merchant but had been forced to sell his business because of anxiety reactions when dealing with women customers. He felt coerced by any aggressive action, which resulted in feelings of overwhelming panic. The initial psychiatric interview revealed a diagnosis of "involutional syndrome with depressive state." Prognosis was noted as "guarded" and his acceptance for treatment was questionable, dependent upon his acceptance for this age group. Although he had had no previous psychotherapy, he had received two series of electroconvulsive shock treatments in 1954 and 1955. Following the last series of five E.C.T., he suffered memory impairment. He had applied for treatment because of depression since 1954 and his inability to deal with women. Psychological testing results revealed "presence of a picture of severe depression where involutional features and/or repressed sexual problems play important roles. The presence of additional symptomatology is indicated. Patient appears greatly in need of supportive treatment at the present time, as well as assurance and help in re-repressing the disturbing sexual material."

Lila was a spinster in her sixtieth year of life and was working as a college professor. The clinical diagnosis on the initial psychiatric interview was "reactive depression (involutional personality), passive-aggressive personality." Although she had previously applied to two agencies for treatment, she had been refused because of age. She presently applied for treatment because of experienced problems with creativity and an inability to effect a marriage with a man she had been seeing for twenty years. She described having wanted to get married all her adult life. However, she always felt unable to satisfy this desire because of obligations to an aged father. Upon the father's death two years prior to her seeking treatment, she experienced herself in a state of "complete loss." She felt herself to be completely alone and was unable to effect a marriage.

Reevaluation of the sessions showed the group therapy process to be consistent and continuous. The course of treatment for each of the patients who joined the group, however, varied. With regard to the initial attitudes, as well as reactions to the group and progress, reactions varied from intense enthusiasm to hopelessness. The group therapy process was very similar to heterogeneous groups of adults in a younger age range. The first session was initiated by silence, each one looking around and waiting for someone else to start. The therapist remained silent, allowing the patients to take the initiative. After a few minutes, introductions began, and the members of the group questioned each other and told their reasons for coming to treatment.

Hilda was the only person who had had any prior knowledge of group psychotherapy and had applied specifically for this treatment modality. Her information had come from lectures on mental health, which she attended regularly. She told the group her early feelings of rejection, which she attributed to feelings of inferiority and inadequacy. She described her inability to ask for anything, feeling that this would only demonstrate inadequacies and, in turn, result in rejection. During the time she lived with her husband, she constantly needed to "give" him and was never able to ask for anything for herself. The severity of her inability to allow herself to depend upon anyone was manifested in her inability to ask the husband to work and support her and the children. As she continued to describe her lifelong pattern of relationship, she attributed her major problem to constant and persistent feelings of anticipated rejection and an inability to relate to people on an informal, personal basis. She felt and hoped that the group situation would offer an opportunity to learn and overcome the reasons for her withdrawal from personal and emotional involvements. She entered the group with great enthusiasm and in the first session assumed the role of assistant therapist. She was most helpful to everyone. In a very forceful manner, she clarified questions about the value and techniques of psychotherapy; she offered support and advice to those with intense anxiety; she probed and questioned; and she presented problems in relationship to childhood experiences. The group members' reactions to her became very ambivalent — those in need of answers looked to her as a fountain of knowledge yet resented her authoritarian manner.

Hilda continually supplied and fed others, but could ask no direct help for herself. To ask for help directly would be to admit dependency needs, which to her meant weakness and, in turn, would expose her to rejection. The resulting frustration of not being able to ask for or accept help from others provoked and brought about an exacerbation of an existing asthmatic condition. Since she was unable to accept help from family or friends during the anticipated course of treatment, her physician was forced to hospitalize her for special medication. When she returned to the group, the therapist focused on her problem of denying "dependency needs." When asked to associate to this reaction pattern, Hilda spoke of a lifetime, repetitive pattern which reinforced childhood experiences that "proved" she could depend on no one but herself. Persisting in her efforts to work through this conflict, she experienced no further acute attacks, and the diminution of her rigid "self-sufficiency" was slow, but continuous. After several months of apprehensive caution that other group members would not accept her as a person, she finally expressed the desire for some social contact among the members following the group sessions. Expression of this need and desire precipitated the recognition and working through of her self-sufficiency as a reaction formation to dependency needs. The other group members began to accept and relate to her as a peer rather than as the "voice of authority."

Hilda's relationships with persons outside the group, as reported, manifested growth toward emotional maturity. The relationship with her adult child became that of mother and daughter, with each being able to accept her respective role. During the summer, Hilda, for the first time, was able to take and enjoy a holiday. She took a cruise to the Pacific and upon her return, reported having been able to socialize and develop friendships among the other passengers. At work her relationship with co-workers became increasingly satisfying and the fear of approaching retirement disappeared.

Mabel's initial reaction to entering group therapy was extremely ambivalent. She expressed reluctance as well as doubts about her ability to discuss her sexual anxiety with "strangers." She also feared that instead of getting help, her "vaginal stirrings" would be provoked by the men in the group. At the same time, she expressed a great desire to please the therapist by accepting "what you feel is best for me." During the pregroup individual sessions, her overt reactions and nonverbal communication suggested feelings that she could evade discussions of her conflicts and by some magical means passively resolve her problems. This hypothesis tended to be proven valid when Mabel entered the group. Her problems and conflicts became unknown to her. She described herself as a successful business woman who although "not more intelligent" was much stronger and more effective than her husband. Childhood experiences were described in a manner which implied emotional deprivation and unwarranted demands, e.g., mother's entrusting the entire household activities to her. When anyone probed as to her problems, she would respond, "If I knew them, they wouldn't bother me and I wouldn't have to be here." During her early experiences in the group, Mabel continued to deny any personal needs and assumed the role of the "good mother" who continually supported and encouraged others to reveal their problems. After a relatively short time, members of the group began to dispute her facade of being a devoted and "perfect wife and mother." This confrontation by the group provoked intense anxiety, resulting in a modification of her "good mother" role in the group. Her rigid hold on "having no problems" disappeared, she began to ask help from other members, as well as to interact on an emotional level with them. She developed a strong, transferential sibling relationship with Agnes and reported that while talking with Agnes, she felt they were like "two little girls who were exchanging confidences." She experienced intense antagonism toward Jack's passive-aggressive behavior and identified him with her "weak husband." Jack's impotence reinforced the transferential relationship with him. She spoke of occasional sexual relationships with her own husband and insisted that the infrequency was because she did not want to "tire him out." As the course of therapy continued, Mabel's concept of the therapist as the sole agent for help began to wane and she was able to rely upon and relate to other members of the group. Although somewhat sporadic, she was persistent and questioning of the other patients' exclusive dependency upon the therapist, insisting that other members could also offer help and insight. Her relationships and reactions within the group precipitated associations of early childhood experiences of her mother's complete domination over all the children, which appeared to have continued to the present time. Although having taken care of the younger male siblings during childhood, she could not recall having seen a naked male until she got married. All men in her life, starting with the father and including siblings and her husband, took on the image of weakness and ineffectiveness. She described the promiscuity of her thrice-divorced son, whose behavior became clear to her as an acting out of her own unconscious sexual drives and fantasies. Focusing on the fixation of her psychosexual development, Mabel began to work through her intense dependency needs on the mother. Her dreams began to manifest her conflicts and her associations pointed up the dependency needs in conflict with intense rivalry and hostility to mother's authoritarian role in the patient's home. As she continued to work through her infantile role with the mother, Mabel's relationship with her husband and children took on a more mature and realistic role. The resulting progress of Mabel's persistent therapeutic efforts was manifested in two significant incidents that occurred approximately twenty-four and thirty months respectively, after she entered the group. One evening Mabel came to the session with a feeling of exhilaration and excitement. Although speaking infrequently, her occasional reactions were vibrant and effective. She then told of a dream and during the associations to the dream, reported that during the past week, she had experienced sexual orgasm on two occasions. This was the first time in her life, after forty years of marriage to the same man, that she had experienced a sexual orgasm. Several months later, during a group session, Mabel manifested anxiety and was unable to attend to the group interaction. When questioned, she reported that her mother was in the hospital and she was quite concerned about her health and was to visit her after the group session. At the next meeting, Mabel told of visiting the hospital after the previous session and of being informed that her mother had just died. She reported and manifested grief at her mother's death, but said she had no undue depression or overreaction of anxiety. She then described having taken mother's death as a natural course of life, which she would not have been able to do only a few months before.

Jack's initial position in the group was one of contradiction. He described his life situation as a picture of perfect adjustment. However, when other members of the group received any emotional support, he reacted with intense resentment. Inquiries about why he was in the group provoked an antagonistic response to the effect that his story had already been reported to several people on an individual basis. He said that repeating it in the group was unnecessary. He was "not a believer in confession" and would not reveal the traumatic experiences in his life unless the therapist convinced him this would be of value to him. During the first two months, his efforts, other than those used to deny all personal problems, were directed towards proposing jobs for Bill and giving advice to the other members in a rather condescending manner. Attempts to provoke Bill resulted in negative reactions from the other group members. Upon confrontation, he denied any hostility, insisting that he was merely trying to be helpful. He would then use the negative reactions for withdrawing, saying that he did not have to talk and remaining silent for long periods of time. When the therapist and other members of the group focused upon this passivity, Jack denied its use as a means of drawing attention to himself. At the same time, he denied any desire for help for himself. His continued hostility and aggressive "help" were used by Bill to justify withdrawal from the group. When he experienced the feeling that he "drove" Bill out of the family, Jack reacted with guilt feelings and remorse. However, with the addition of new members, he again became hostile toward both Joan and Henry for their means of controlling others through their passive behavior.

Persistent focusing on his resistance precipitated Jack's discussion of his difficulties with his second wife. He elaborated on the gastrointestinal reactions when his sexual adequacy was questioned or doubted, e.g., his dancing being unfavorably compared to his stepson's, followed by his wife's leaving him to dance with her son. He said that his wife told him he had no "fatherly feelings" towards her twenty-eight-year old son. As Jack began to reveal himself, the other group members' reactions to him became positive. As he attained awareness, discussion of anticipated threats from the "female" relieved some of his anxiety. Jack began to date a widow whom he had silently admired for a number of years. After a few more months, he initiated and carried through annulment proceedings against his second wife. Following the annulment, the relationship with the widow became quite "romantic" and after several months of dating, resulted in an engagement. During the early dating with his "new love," Jack had a dream in which he had flown a kite. He associated the sudden lifting of the kite to experiencing sexual excitement and temporary erections. This dream and his associations of related experiences brought Jack's first hope that group psychotherapy could offer him help with his sexual problems.

Jack's rigidity began to diminish and he became aware of and to express competitive feelings towards the therapist. He associated these feelings with early childhood reactions to his father. As the group continued to focus on his passivity and its meaning, he remembered and described more frequent dreams and he associated them to his past. During his association to one dream, he suddenly remarked, "I have never thought of this before, but it suddenly occurs to me, that in about our tenth year of marriage, I was told my (first) wife could never have a child, and right after this, right in the middle of intercourse, I suddenly had the feeling of 'what's the use!'" The anticipated failure to achieve had resulted in feelings of "what's the use" and the adoption of a passive role. As a result of subsequent dreams and associations, it became more clear that Jack had found and used passivity as a nonincriminating means of expressing his hostile aggression.

His entire demeanor continued to change. He no longer restricted his reactions to objective or intellectual retorts. He began to allow his imagination to function more freely and interacted with others on an effective emotional level. His behavior and its significance became more meaningful through interaction, dreams and associations. The pattern of passivity and its utilization as a means of aggressive control became evident and were focused on by the group. Jack was then able to scrutinize and attain more meaningful understanding of his behavior. With a lessening of apprehension and self-guardedness, he became more free in describing the relationship with his new fiancee. His newfound "open" attitude brought about awareness and allowed him to recognize that he had once again developed a relationship of acquiescing subservience, which was provoking intense resentment toward the female. He associated his behavior in this involvement with earlier frustrating efforts to please and win his mother by attempting to gratify her every wish and expectation. He broke his engagement and began to seek and date other women.

Jack developed increased ego strength through his positive relationship in the group, complemented and reinforced by his expanding social relationships outside. He worked through his apprehensive feelings of anticipated isolation and was able to retire from his job with little anxiety. Following this action, he was able, for the first time, to leave the New York area and spend the winter in Florida. In the spring, he returned to the group with continued efforts towards working through his unresolved conflicts with the mother and related, hostile, aggressive, competitive feelings toward father and brother. It was also significant to note that during this time, he was able, on intermittent occasions, to attain and maintain erections, and, on occasion, attempted, with some relative success, to have sexual intercourse with some of the women he dated.

Bill was experienced by the other group members as "the helpless child of the family." He was brought to the first session by his son. He usually sat in a dazed manner, appearing to be completely unaware of what was going on around him. His usual reaction to questioning was silence. On occasion, he spontaneously mumbled something to the effect that he had nothing to say or did not know what to say. These reactions were usually sudden and unexpected and had the effect of attracting attention and stopping whatever activity was going on at the time. The women adopted maternal roles, offering complete sympathy and support and encouraged him to talk about his problems. Somewhat incoherently, he described his first and second marriages and separations, blaming his business for all his difficulties. He had lived in the New York area for a number of years but pleaded an inability to get from one place to another. Later, he contradicted this by saying that he was able to travel but did not know where he wanted to go. He described being isolated in his room and unable to get out, unless his son came for him. With the group's encouragement, he continued to discuss and clarify the reality of his situation. He revealed his ability to get about and the existence of people with whom he might socialize. His "inability" was a defense mechanism developed as a means of manipulating others to gratify his intense dependency needs. As the group became more aware of his restricted existence, they encouraged him to take a part-time job and, in so doing, experience some feeling of independence from his son. The women encouraged by cajoling and seducing. Jack pressured with an air of condescension. The other patients' lack of acceptance of Bill's passive role created a threatening feeling of losing the dependency relationship with his son, finally resulting in withdrawal from the group. The therapist's initial lack of comprehensive understanding of Bill's passive defense mechanism may also have aided his withdrawal.

Joan, as a result of attempts to act out her suicidal ideas, replaced Bill as the focus for emergency action. However, the therapist's experience with Bill enabled him to cope with the situation more effectively, preventing an initial panic reaction by any of the group members or by Joan. The therapist's intervention had a positive effect. Instead of badgering her with ideas that her suicidal attempts were "bad" or "foolish," the group interacted emotionally, as well as analytically, and developed multiple transference relationships. Hilda and Henry identified with her; Agnes related to her as to "sister." (Agnes blamed herself for her sister's successful suicide.) Mabel adopted a supporting, maternal role; Jack assumed an objective, helpful role, which manifested his resentment toward the utilization of passive-aggressive behavior. The experiencing of emotional support from the group enabled Joan to interact and relate associative material. With the therapist's focusing, the group helped Joan understand the use of her suicidal attempts as a method of preventing her son's marriage. The suicidal attempts ceased and her behavior in, as well as outside, the group sessions changed. Joan's sadness slowly was replaced by smiles, and she began to describe increased activity in household and social relationships. During the group's summer holiday (the therapist was also on vacation), Joan began seeing an individual therapist near her home. She was able to establish a positive therapeutic relationship with the new therapist and decided to remain with him when the group reconvened in the fall.

Agnes entered the group with feelings of total helplessness and expressed an inability to relate to any member of the group. She eagerly told of incidents that contributed to existing feelings of "depression." She attempted to monopolize the group by revealing a lifetime of frustration and sadness. She disclosed early rivalry relationships with an older sister. As Agnes was "prettier," and the "brighter" of the two, the mother became overprotective of the sister. She also described experiences of intense feelings of rejection when sent from her homeland (Russia) to the U.S., thus separating her from the family. In an attempt to defend herself from the continuous experience of being thwarted and rejected in any dependency relationship, Agnes developed a role of "pseudo-independence." Her efforts to attain this "independence" had taken two directions: attaining a job that would keep her financially secure, and at the same time rebelling against the mores and conventions of society (parents) and following what she termed a "Bohemian" life.

In the group, she continued to attract attention by describing anxiety-provoking incidents but was unable to reveal or discuss her sexual problems with her husband or her intense guilt resulting from the sister's suicide. Joan's suicidal attempts provoked her already intense anxiety, resulting in an inability to interact for the first few weeks. Joan provided an object for a sister-transference, and Agnes' major concern became the prevention of Joan's death. As Joan began to improve, Agnes' anxiety diminished and she was able to relate to other members of the group. Although initially professing an inability to relate to others on a conversational level, the increased interaction of the group members resulted in Agnes' allowing herself to respond more openly. During the interaction with the group members, she began to discuss her need to be independent. She recalled early parental conflicts and mother's cry that financial dependency on the father was the only bond that kept the marriage together. The intense rivalry with sister during childhood was discussed, and the group aided her in bringing out and recognizing the meaning of her guilt over the sister's suicide. Her interactions in the group brought out that although she shared her bed over the years, Agnes' need to be independent postponed marriage for ten years. The marriage took place only after her husband threatened to commit suicide if she continued to refuse. The effectiveness of her denial of dependency on the husband completely deteriorated when she was confronted with the threat of losing him. Agnes made efforts to participate in the group, yet her conflicts regarding dependency needs continued to thwart any free interaction within the group session.

Agnes' therapeutic progress in the group was very slow. Her demeanor was characteristic of a help-rejecting complainer. Her behavior in the group was usually that of a petulant, demanding child who sought and insisted upon the exclusive attention of mother (therapist). The multiple transference relationships with the other group members were to siblings and manifested continuous and intense rivalry. Reactions manifesting experiences of gratification occurred only when she was able to monopolize the therapist's attention. When attention was paid to someone else, she experienced feelings of rejection and often reacted with intense hostility. These reactions were often accompanied by accusations of receiving no help from either the therapist or other group members and threatening to reject by leaving the group. Encouraged by the therapist, the other group members began to focus the transferential relationships manifested by Agnes' reactions. Gaining awareness and some understanding of her experiences with the mother, Agnes was able to develop tolerance for frustration. The group's reaction to her anxiety, rather than to her hostile reactions, precipitated a modification of her relationship in the group and permitted the development of a "childhood friendship relationship" with Mabel.

Although feelings of sibling rivalry with the group persisted, Agnes continued to experience acceptance by other group members. She began to discuss and describe her relationship with her husband, and said he had made every possible effort to satisfy her. His efforts, however, always appeared to be in vain. Sexually, he was experienced as inadequate and she had not been loath to let him know her feelings. Intellectually, he was considered to be her inferior and she insisted upon comparing him negatively with her "intellectual" friends. His only attribute, as she described it, was his physical strength as a young man. His occupation required lifting heavy objects and he had been able to lift well over 100 hundred pounds with little effort. With chronological aging, his physical strength had waned somewhat, resulting in his image becoming even more demeaned to her. Continuing to deny her dependency, she claimed that the relationship continued only because of recurrent illnesses during the last several years (a coronary condition) and that he was very dependent upon her. With the aid of the group, Agnes was able to see the similarity between the relationship with her husband and the relationship with her sister and that her own dependency needs and her inability to accept these, resulted in the development of relationships in which she could experience others as depending upon her. However, threatened loss of the other person provoked the underlying anxiety related to her own denied dependency needs. The awareness and partial understanding of her relationship with others, coupled with the support gained through the acceptance by the other group members, was most important for Agnes. A few months later, the husband had a coronary attack, resulting in his death. Although the trauma resulted in a negative depression, it was of relatively short duration and was not, as she anticipated, completely incapacitating.

Henry entered the group with an air of oppression, making his presence known by expressing the complete inability to function vocationally or socially. He continually sought out the therapist, pleading to be told what to do. When he received no prescription from the therapist, he turned to the group and asked continually for an evaluation of his problems and progress. He overtly identified with the helplessness of Joan and was successful in provoking the group's anxiety relating to their own dependency needs. Reacting to their own respective anxieties, several group members took various defensive measures. Hilda encouraged him to look at childhood experiences and made some superficial suggestions with regard to vocational opportunities. Jack became extremely hostile to Henry. He suggested demeaning jobs that Henry might accept "in order to keep him occupied." Mabel attempted to take him under her wing, as if he were a small, helpless child. She encouraged and supported, advised him as to job opportunities, and tried to protect him from Jack's hostility.

Initially, Henry sought out and wallowed in the attention extended by the women in the group. He reacted to Jack's hostility by sulking and expressing feelings of complete defeat. Also, in a passive, dependent manner, he looked to the therapist for support, expressing his need for protection from Jack. He continued to accept, and verbalized appreciation for, the attention and concern shown to him by other group members and continued to function in a self-defeating manner. Focusing on the relationship with the therapist, the latent meaning of his reactions became more significant. Although he overtly sought help, his repeated failures manifested an attempt to degrade and deny the effectiveness and adequacy of the father figure. When the group inquired about his activities, Henry was always ready to describe his inability to follow through and succeed in any endeavor. He described his frustration in marriage and his inability to ever experience sexual satisfaction. His wife dominated his actions, had always made the final decisions regarding any activity inside or outside the home. When the children came, he began to experience some feeling of worth — at least the children were dependent upon him and thus he was able to assume a temporary position of "power." As the children matured and began to assume independent roles, Henry's feeling of "power" started to dissipate. When the children married and had families of their own, Henry's defense mechanism against his own dependency needs began to deteriorate, resulting in an anticipation of overwhelming anxiety. As the group focused on and explored Henry's passivity, he was ready to grasp any source of relief. However, when an area of possible success was explored, he manifested intense irritation and began to withdraw. One day, Jack asked him how much money he had in the bank and he reacted with intense anxiety and abrupt hostility, saying, "I came here to get help with my problems — not to show my bankbooks!" Upon further inquiry, it was learned that Henry had been able to accumulate a relatively large sum of money but feared that if this became known, he would be asked to give and lose his dependency role in the community.

Following Henry's "exposure" that he could succeed, the group began to focus on his passivity as a block toward developing a dominant, assertive role. His interactions with Jack began to change. Overt passivity was replaced by aggressive outbursts. He began to retaliate to Jack's demanding remarks and thus lost his role of "baby" in the group.

Although intense dependency needs continued to be manifested in his behavior and dreams, Henry started to show initiative and active aggressiveness. After several years of unemployment, he obtained and successfully held a job for five months. He experienced success on the job and left only because the employer needed to cut expenses.

Henry's acceptance and the support he experienced in the group, reinforced by successful activity in his environment, resulted in the development of increased ego strength, which permitted him to become a more active participant in the group, as well as outside activities. He began to assume a more dominant role in his marriage and was rewarded with experiences of satisfaction rather than a repetition of former frustrations.

Lila came to the group with a great deal of eagerness and anxiety. She anticipated obtaining a great deal of "learning" from others' experiences but was very apprehensive about the acceptance of her problems by the other group members. She entered the group after an integrated, therapeutic working relationship had developed among the members. The multiple transference interactions at this time were of a positive nature, and Lila's reaction to the experienced "openness" and "friendliness" of the group resulted in her feeling "completely at ease."

During her second session, she was able to freely express her positive feelings toward all the group members, as well as negative reactions to specific behavior. She also expressed the feeling that she could relate her problems with little apprehension and felt that the other group members would offer her help. A resume of her life history was then related. She described childhood and adult experiences and conflicts. Her description of childhood experiences emphasized the need and attempt to comply with mother's ideals and demands. Her only reservation was in disclosing that she was a college professor. Her desire to give and reach out to the group members resulted in Lila's immediate inclusion within the group circle. After several more sessions, she began to express her specific needs for help from the group. The overt expression of needs and desires reinforced the group's positive reactions. The therapist focused on this interaction and encouraged other members to express their wants overtly and more specifically.

Lila continued her active participation within the psychotherapeutic group process. Typically, as in any analytic psychotherapy group, the presence of other patient members afforded Lila an opportunity to develop multiple transference relationships. Interactions revealed the persistent overprotectiveness of a mother to an only child and the effective resolution of early dependency needs. Although she had been able to achieve educational and professional success, Lila had never experienced herself as an adequate individual who could effectively function in an interpersonal relationship. She sought out heterosexual relationships, but protected herself from any permanent involvement by holding onto the home situation. When her mother died, she used the need to care for an aging father as a defense against becoming involved in a marital relationship. With the death of the father and the loss of her dependency object, she reacted with intense anxiety and began to withdraw. As she worked within the multiple transferential relationships, Lila was able to work through her intense dependency needs and began to develop mutually satisfying relationships outside the group situation. After eighteen months in the group, she developed a relationship with a man. She felt that this relationship was mutually satisfying, and her relationship with colleagues became more meaningful. She also experienced a sense of achievement in her work. Soon after this, she left the group, expressing the feeling that she had obtained the goal for which she had entered the group. The other group members, although reluctant to have her leave, agreed that she could continue to grow and mature on her own. Her need to feed others as a defense against her own dependency needs had been resolved, and she was now in a position to establish interdependent, mutually satisfying relationships.

Reflections on the Therapeutic Group Process

An analysis of the psychotherapeutic group process reveals that in the initial therapist-centered stage, the therapist was able to offer support and to present a figure with whom the patients could identify. Taking cues from the therapist, patients initially imitated him and then spontaneously began to interact with one another. As this process continued, the group's intellectual facade began to crumble. Although they were not consciously aware of this, the effects of emotional involvements became manifest in the patients' interactions. Thus, the therapist was offered appropriate opportunity to intervene by focusing on individual, as well as group, resistances.

The understanding of each patient's psychodynamics was relatively slow in coming. Following Bill's departure and the arrival of Henry, Joan, and Agnes, the therapist became more aware of the meaning of each individual's behavior. With the passing of time, it became evident that each patient in his own way was acting out lifelong, neurotic reaction patterns. The therapist neither condoned nor rejected; he accepted each member's right to his own feeling and desires. Consequently, rigidity began to diminish, resulting in the patients' ability to accept themselves, as well as others in the group.

Thus, the group members were able to relate to each other with more intimacy; they explored more intimate details of their lives and offered emotional, rather than intellectual, support to each other.

A wide variety of defense mechanisms were manifested, but the most predominant and persistent defenses were passivity, denial (of dependency needs), emotional detachment, and depression. After careful study, it was also noted that the most frequent precipitating factor that brought the patient into therapy was the actual or anticipated loss of the dependency figure. Once the patients began to interact with each other, the therapist began to focus on the meaning and effectiveness of the defense mechanisms. As a result of working through Joan's suicidal attempt, the group members, for the first time, recognized and understood how behavior might result from unconscious needs and drives. They also became cognizant of the process by which these unconscious forces might be made conscious. They continued to perceive and utilize cues from the therapist and, although offering ego support, began to probe and analyze their own as well as others' interactions and dreams. This procedure allowed for and reinforced the continuing development of ego strength, which, in turn, constituted the psychotherapeutic group process. The initial classroom atmosphere of the group sessions dissipated and the therapist became an object for transference relationships rather than a teacher. Emotional interaction became more spontaneous and multiple transferences were manifested in the patients' interrelationships.

Analysis of the various patients' multiple transference reactions revealed an acting out of neurotic patterns as an attempt to cope with unresolved dependency needs. Hilda's efforts at extreme self-sufficiency, i.e., offering, but never asking for or accepting anything from anyone, was symptomatic of a reaction formation. Although her life was filled with activity and responsibilities, she had never experienced any feelings of personal closeness or emotional satisfaction. Mabel unsuccessfully sought to deny her dependency needs on the powerful mother figure by constantly placing herself as "the mistress of the house." She expressed no desires or thoughts for herself, yet felt completely frustrated that her efforts were not properly or graciously accepted and utilized by others, especially her husband and sons. The early anxiety and fears of hurting her children with a knife were associated with incestuous guilt, distorted into feelings of power held over these young humans. When the eldest son, after two previous marriages, was contemplating a third marriage, her strong sexual drives were reactivated. On an unconscious level, she experienced the son's behavior as a reflection of her own "controlled" sexual needs, which she anticipated might erupt in uncontrolled, promiscuous behavior. These sexual needs became manifest in her "sexual stirrings" when in the presence of any male, regardless of age or species (e.g., young children, animals). Agnes chose a career and an early life of "Bohemianism" to display to the world and to constantly reaffirm to herself her independence. However, when the rejected suitor threatened suicide, she married him in order not to lose this object of dependency. Jack, although constantly and emphatically denying any needs, continuously utilized passive-aggressive means of manipulating others into doing things for him. Henry's oppressed feelings of complete inadequacy at the time he sought treatment were precipitated by the loss of his children's dependency upon him. These children were the only ones over whom he had any power and provided suitable objects for reaction formation. The intense anxiety reactions of the other members of the group might also be attributed to a similar deterioration or failure of previous defense mechanisms.

The most frequent feeling expressed by the patients was depression. Why a depressive reaction? An exploration of earlier life patterns reveals that the depression had always been present. Further observation shows that although each patient may have been involved in various activities (to a lesser or greater degree), there is no evidence that any of these people had experienced any emotional satisfaction on a lasting basis. It appears that these individuals never realized satisfaction or resolved their oral dependency. None of these patients appears to have realized his strong dependency drives or to have been aware of the inappropriate, frustrating means taken to gratify these needs. A review of the history reveals that initial childhood dependency (with or without outside encouragement) fostered the illusion that the parent was a source of unlimited gratification. One may further find that the frustration of these needs during the childhood years tended to be experienced as rejection by the all-powerful figure, rather than as limitations of the parent. The child, unable to develop self-initiative to explore potential sources and in turn to gain experienced of satisfaction, reinforced and perpetuated the distortion that the parental figure was the only possible source of gratification. As the need for continued dependency intensified, and in an effort to regain or retain the gratification, the child adopted various defense mechanisms. In some instances, further frustration led to resentment and in turn, in an effort to provide self-gratification, may have resulted in the introjection of the all-powerful figure. Failures in this new role appear to have resulted in inwardly directed resentment and hostility to the introjected parental figure. Thus, the individual experiences a loss of self-confidence, a demeaned self-image and a rejection of self. Often the older person, as is seen in adolescents with similar character structure, behaves in a self-defeating fashion, manifested in what the author has termed "defeat by default." The anticipation of failure and the threat of frustration result in an avoidance of initiative. The apperception of dependency, as experienced by these persons, was a sign of weakness — something that an "adult" should not have. This weakness, symbolized by dependency, was thus rejected, and the individual anticipated that it would be rejected by others. These dependency needs had to be repressed by means of reaction formation or other defense mechanisms. One may also note that some persons attempted to maintain the dependency relationship by establishing a role reversal, i.e., the dependent individual attempted to affect a nurturing role with a "sick" or "aging" parent, a sibling, an ineffective spouse, or others.

As the aging process continues, the reduction of physical activity resulting from biological changes, the modification of familiar and social relationships, as well as cultural attitudes towards the aged tend to force reality upon the older person. Those who have attempted to deny their dependency needs by developing a role-reversal relationship begin to lose the nurturing through death (as happened when Jack's wife died) or anticipate the loss of object relationship with the nurturing figure (as exemplified by Joan, when her son was to be married). This object loss, actual or anticipated, tends to provoke the latent feelings of abandonment and annihilation, which, in turn result in overwhelming anxiety or a panic reaction. In other instances, the older person can no longer conceal intense dependency needs by excess physical activity and therefore begins to reexperience the effects of the early, weak ego development. The depression and accompanying tendency toward withdrawal, manifested by impotence and decreased professional and social activities, become another defensive move to encapsulate and protect the brittle ego structure from experienced outside destructive forces. The older person no longer is able, with any effectiveness, to confront the threat, which he experiences as coming from the outside, and must seek and develop new methods for self-preservation. Stripped of the temporary effectiveness of previous defense mechanisms, his only recourse is to retreat within a shell of apathy. The intense resentment and hostile aggression resulting from the feelings of abandonment are directed toward the introjected parental figure.

The major therapeutic forces and advantages of the psychotherapy group process are the multiple transferential relationships and interactions and the patients' confrontations with reality factors. The additional advantages of the limitation of the group constellation with respect to age range for the older person is that each individual is able to experience himself as being among peers. The acceptance by others enables the individual to accept his conflicts as a manifestation of unresolved early needs, rather than as a manifestation of weakness. Also, he is able to develop an ability to accept others and to relate to them interdependently. He learns more appropriate means of expressing his needs to "take," as well as to "give" help to others. This giving, taking, and sharing bring about development of increased ego strength and the experiencing of himself as an individual. The ego boundaries become more flexible and his mobility becomes less restricted, resulting in a modification of the self-image. The awareness of himself as an entity in the reconstructive psychotherapy group appears to be a completely new experience for the older person. With the gaining of ego strength and the modification of his self-image, the patient is thus able to express his needs appropriately, and he seeks satisfaction outside the therapeutic constellation. This latter situation may be exemplified by Henry's change from complete compliance and submission to a position where he was able to attend a fraternal organization meeting and, for the first time, demand his rights as a member.

Group therapy is not and should not be considered as a panacea for treating all psychological problems of older people. Although group psychotherapy has proven to be most effective with this age group, limitations exist and have been demonstrated in the group described. One definite therapeutic failure was Bill. The question arises as to whether Bill failed to benefit from group psychotherapy because of faulty selection, because of the other patients' emotional reaction to him, or because, prognostically, he was a very poor psychotherapeutic candidate. It is the author's opinion that the first two and possibly the third factor may have been involved. The therapist permitted, and in so doing perhaps inadvertently condoned, the group's demand that Bill relinquish his dependency upon his son. The therapist also did nothing to prevent the son from withdrawing Bill from treatment. (No follow-up was done to encourage Bill to return to the group or to be seen individually.) It is also possible that Bill's lack of participation in any outside activity may have created a feeling of being different from the others and thus an isolate in the group. If so, it may be advisable that such patients (isolated in society) be placed in Golden Age clubs, "social rehabilitation groups," day centers for the aged, or other activity groups. Participating with others in daily activities may aid the socially isolated individual to experience feelings of acceptance, encouragement, and recognition for his efforts. With this continued activity, he may begin to experience satisfaction in achieving, eliminating, or at least diminishing the feeling of complete uselessness and frustration.

The psychoanalytic treatment of the older person by group psychotherapy has provided ample evidence that this method, with rare exception, can effect reconstructive psychological changes. The degree of change tends to vary, and one must note that experiences with this age group, as compared with younger adults, reveal that the degree of psychotherapeutic progress is not exclusively dependent upon age. Individuals initiating group psychotherapy in the middle and late sixties and continuing in psychotherapy until their seventies have shown personality changes manifesting successful reconstruction. On the other hand, there is the rare exception who terminates therapy with no observable change (e.g., Bill). Also, there are some individuals who show varying degrees of change, vacillating from a state of effective functioning to one of almost being inept, and who appear to need psychotherapy on a more or less lifetime basis. It is suspected that individuals typifying this latter group have undergone traumatic experiences of affect starvation and deprivation during their early development (very likely the first year). The faulty initial ego formation has become *fixed* and is receptive to little modification or permanent change. These persons, young or old, very likely will always function on an orally dependent level, requiring continued nurturing object relationships and ego support to enable them to function on any effective level. Their oral dependent needs cannot be satiated, and the loss of nurturing object relationships is experienced as an overwhelming threat to a very brittle ego structure. Agnes, in the aforementioned group, may typify the affect-starved and deprived individual. For as long as she could remember, the mother favored the older sister, continually depriving and rejecting Agnes. One may suspect that the affect deprivation existed from birth, resulting in a distortion during the initial development of the ego. Although she experienced occasional aid and support during her course of psychotherapy, there appeared to be no persisting positive effect. When her dependency needs and demands were gratified, she felt "pacified" and was able to function in a relatively effective manner. However, she had a low tolerance level for frustration, and when her demands were not immediately met, she would react with intense hostility and threats. Also, she left treatment on several occasions when she felt "good." The loss of needed ego support obtained from the psychotherapeutic experience would result in a deterioration of functioning, forcing her return to psychotherapy.

Summary

Recapitulating, a decade of experience with older people has revealed significant evidence of the efficacy of psychoanalytically oriented treatment of this age group by group psychotherapy. An effective psychotherapeutic relationship can be established in a relatively short time. Limiting the age range of this group during the initial treatment tends to avoid destructive, transferential relationships fostered by the presence of younger ("child") persons. The older person does not have to defend himself as a "parental figure" but is allowed to relate to peers. Such a constellation offers members of the group additional identification with one another and facilitates awareness of individual, as well as mutual, reactions in multiple transference relationships. Initial reactions by isolated individuals are supplanted by emotional interactions with others, resulting in the formation of a psychotherapeutic process within a functioning group. These changes initiated by imitation of the therapist soon develop spontaneously. Manifestations of ego strengthening and reconstructive psychotherapy may be observed in overt behavior, in transference interactions, as well as in dreams described and associated to by the patients. The major psychotherapeutic forces in group psychotherapy are the opportunity for development of multiple transferences and the confrontation of the patients with reality factors. The interactions within the group psychotherapy process tend to activate the production of awareness of the dynamics of the respective disturbances in the individual members of the group. The awareness and the working through within the multiple transference relationships allow for healthful modification of long-standing attitudes and modes of reaction. Most emotional problems of the older person appear to be a perpetuation of early conflicts. The exacerbation of these conflicts tends to result from the decomposition of earlier defense mechanisms, such as reaction formation and compensation. The results of the group psychotherapy experiences with older people present significant evidence of the value of this technique in preventing mental illness as well as in aiding individuals with emotional and psychological problems.

REFERENCES

Busse, E. W. (1955), Treatment of the non-hospitalized, emotionally disturbed person. *Geriatrics,* 11:173-179.

Ebaugh, F. G. (1956), Age introduces stress into family. *Geriatrics,* 11:146-150.

Fink, R., Shapiro, S., Goldenson, S. et al. (1969), The filter-down process to psychotherapy in a group practice medical care program. *Amer. Public Health*, 59:245-257.

Goldfarb, A. I. (1955), Psychotherapy with aged persons; patterns of adjustment in a home for the aged. *Ment. Hyg.*, 39:609-621.

Gronewald, T. W. (1956), Involutional psychotic reactions. *J. Lancet*, 76:8-10.

Grotjahn, M. (1955), Analytic psychotherapy with the elderly. *Psychoan. Rev.*, 42:419-427.

Kahn, E., Fisher, C., and Liebermann, L. (1969), Dream recall in the normal aged. *J. Amer. Geriat. Soc.*, 17:1121-1126.

Kopits, I. (1970), Observations on 750 geropsychiatric patients. *J. Amer. Geriat. Soc.*, 18:353-364.

Krasner, J. D. and Marks, M. (1966), The psychoanalytic treatment of the elder person via group psychotherapy. II. Anxiety reaction precipitated by threat of separation or object loss. Presented at the annual conferences of the American Group Psychotherapy Association, Philadelphia, Pa.

Linden, M.E. (1953), Group psychotherapy with institutionalized senile women. Study in gerontologic human relations. *Internat. J. Group Psychother.*, 3:159-170.

——— (1955), Transference in gerontologic group psychotherapy. *Internat. J. Group Psychother.*, 5:61-80.

——— (1956), Geriatrics. In: *The Fields of Group Psychotherapy*, ed. S.R. Slavson. New York: International Universities Press, pp. 129-152.

Pfeiffer, E., Vervoerdt, A., and Wang, H. S. (1968), Sexual behavior in aged men and women. I. Observation on 254 community volunteers. *Arch. Gen. Psychiat.*, 19:753-758.

Stern, K., Smith, J. M. and Frank, M. (1953), Mechanisms of transference and counter-transference in psychotherapeutic and social work with the aged. *J. Geront.*, 8:328-332.

Wayne, G. J. (1955), Modified psychoanalytic therapy in senescence. *Psychoan. Rev.*, 42:419-427.

Name Index

Subject Index